OPERATIONAL
AND
INFORMATION MANAGEMENT

OPERATIONAL
AND
INFORMATION MANAGEMENT

Editor
Samson Lobo

DPH

DISCOVERY PUBLISHING HOUSE
INDIA

Published by:

DISCOVERY PUBLISHING HOUSE
4383/4B, Ansari Road, Darya Ganj
New Delhi-110 002 (India)
Phone : +91-11-23279245, 43596065, 23253475
E-mail : discoverybooksindia@gmail.com
discoverypublishinghouse@gmail.com
namitwasan9@gmail.com
web : www.discoverypublishinggroup.com

First Published: **2023**

ISBN: 978-81-19205-11-0

Operational and Information Management

Printed at:
Infinity Imaging Systems
Delhi

PREFACE

In today's business environment, the role of information in supporting processes in firms' operations has become increasingly important. Information management has become a crucial component for effective process management, which is necessary for creating long-term competitive advantage. Process management involves improving the efficiency, effectiveness, and flexibility of production, as well as the quality of the final product. However, the potential for improvement is often limited without the coordination and support of external parties along the supply chain.

Effective supply chain management requires the integration of inter-firm processes, which we refer to as external process management (EPM). When combined with effective internal process management (IPM), firms can achieve a supply chain characterized by timely deliveries and increased flexibility in responding to changes in market demands. This enhances operational performance and enables firms to achieve their objectives.

Information management plays a crucial role in effective process management. It involves the availability and management of timely and relevant information, which is essential for achieving efficient and effective processes. Modern information technology allows firms to capture a large amount of internal and external information, making internal information management (IIM) and external information management (EIM) more important than ever before. Business intelligence systems are increasingly important for firms to analyze internal and external processes, enabling them to make data-driven decisions. Effective IIM and EIM enable firms to manage their internal and external processes more efficiently and effectively. Internal information management involves the collection, storage, and analysis of data from within the firm, while external information management involves the collection, storage, and analysis of data from external sources. Both types of information management are necessary for effective process management. Effective information management allows firms to identify opportunities for process improvement and to implement changes more efficiently. It also enables firms to monitor their processes and to respond quickly to changes in the market environment. By improving their processes, firms can achieve long-term competitive advantage and enhance their operational performance.

This book focuses on how managing information can help improve business processes and make them more efficient. The book also discusses how this can lead to better performance in day-to-day operations. It provides helpful tips and tools for creating and implementing effective enterprise information systems. The contributors of the book are experts in fields like supply chain management, revenue management, and e-commerce, and they use their knowledge of information technology and consumer research to provide valuable insights.

This book is designed to help managers, business users, and students as well. It uses real-life examples to demonstrate various concepts and ideas, so that the readers can understand them better. Whether you're a professional in the business world or a student trying to learn about business, this book will provide you with practical insights that you can apply in your own work or studies.

Editor

CONTENTS

1

Performance Management Systems

Trade-off between Implementation and Strategy Development

Roman A. Lewandowski Ph.D. & Giuseppe T. Cirella Ph.D., D.Sc.

Institute of Management and Quality Science, Faculty of Economics, University of Warmia and Mazury in Olsztyn, Olsztyn, Poland
Faculty of Economics, University of Gdansk, 81-824, Sopot, Poland

Abstract

The aim of this study is to understand how performance management systems (PMS) affect the strategy development process. The research examines PMS implementation and evaluates how the implementation of PMS links measures with rewards, i.e., financial and non-financial, to influence strategy formation. This qualitative study is based on 74 semi-structured face-to-face in-depth interviews with board members, mid-level managers, and other employees in nine organizations. Theory-building is comprised of the transcribed and analyzed interviews using MAXQDA 12 software. Theory-testing, i.e., a verificatory stage, consisted of analyzing previously identified phenomena. Results suggest that PMS affects strategy development processes by influencing both employee relational and calculative trust in their superiors. It also indicates a direct behavioral effect on employee knowledge sharing and manager trust in their subordinates. As a result, this may determine the extent to which managers exploit shared knowledge while formulating a strategy. The research demonstrates there is a trade-off between PMS implementation and strategy development. A gap in the literature is filled by integrating relational and calculative trust with PMS implementation and showing how such changes in trust mediate knowledge sharing behavior and strategy development.

Keywords: *Balanced scorecard · Strategy process · Trust · Theory-building · Theory-testing · Knowledge sharing · Qualitative method*

1 Introduction

Performance management systems (PMS) have achieved immense popularity in academic and business communities. PMS generally can be defined as a set of management control mechanisms with the overall purpose of facilitating the delivery of organizational goals by influencing people's behavior and performance (Broadbent and Laughlin 2009; Ferreira and Otley 2009) by embracing five fundamental elements: (1) a planning phase which includes the goals that reflect organizational expectation and delineate performance; (2) a measurement comprising of the metrics used to operationalize performance; (3) a review referring to the evaluation and feedback of performance information; (4) a performance-related reward system, and (5) a "refreshing" phase (Franco-Santos and Otley 2018). "Refreshing" of PMS is a crucial element since the environment and the organization itself changes over time and, thus, a constant re-evaluation of the existing performance measures as well as PMS as a whole must be rendered (Schleicher et al. 2018). PMS is an important tool in operations and strategic management since it allows for the integration of sets of metrics, namely, quantitative and qualitative data. Such data is used to quantify strategic objectives both on the operational and business level, so as to make it possible for decision making to better formulate (and adapt) a business model of efficiency and effectiveness of an organization's actions (Glas et al. 2018). Additionally, it must be flexible to adapt to strategic changes that otherwise may affect performance and overall success.

From the literature, the most prominent PMS appears to be the balanced scorecard (BSC) (Bryant et al. 2004; de Waal and Kourtit 2013) which became a standard for other PMS dating to the early 2000s (e.g., Rampersad (2003)). Speckbacher et al. (2003) announced that 44% of companies worldwide claim to be using BSC, and more recent studies prove this popularity (Tapinos et al. 2011). A detailed analysis of PMS implementation indicated, however, that many organizations started its implementation but only a few of them implemented it fully, i.e., linking strategic and operations objectives with financial and nonfinancial measures as well as combining these measures with rewards (Albertsen and Lueg 2014; Speckbacher et al. 2003). This linkage seems to be a central aspect of every PMS' full development (Glas et al. 2018; Lee and Yang 2011) as a strategic management system, capable of translating strategy into action (Kaplan and Norton 2006; Malmi and Brown 2008). Decades of research has shown that there is no agreement among researchers of whether PMS improves or deteriorates organizational performance (Bonner and Sprinkle 2002; Bourne et al. 2007; Laitinen 2003; Liedtka et al. 2008; Nørreklit 2000, 2003; Nørreklit et al. 2012; de Waal and Kourtit 2013). Extant studies have indicated a number of PMS weaknesses (Butler et al. 1997; Laitinen 2003; Levy et al. 2017; Liedtka et al. 2008; Nørreklit 2000, 2003; Nørreklit et al. 2012) and negative unintended consequences such as information manipulation (Kalgin 2014; Li 2015), selective attention (Kerpershoek et al. 2014), myopia, gaming, illusion of control (Franco-Santos and Otley 2018), as well as increased tendency towards being in a rigid state, constraining responsiveness, and resisting change (Mannion and Braithwaite 2012). However, they have not pointed out that its primary purpose of supporting strategy implementation may negatively affect strategy formation. Thus, confirmation of PMS influence on strategy formation and explanation of mechanism changes would be an essential contribution to the existing theory on operations strategy process.

There is a significant number of publications concerning PMS, but only a few of them investigated its full implementation, e.g., where measures were linked with rewards (Albertsen and Lueg 2014) and those regarding strategy development in a processual model (Tapinos et al. 2011) work is an exceptional example that examines the impact of

BSC on six elements of the strategy process—quantitatively and internationally. Their research confirmed BSC is an effective tool for strategy implementation and rejected the idea of its influence on strategy development. However, their lack of statistically significant evidence may have originated from a number of research limitations, i.e., by not considering different levels of BSC implementation (Lee and Yang 2011; Speckbacher et al. 2003) such as the link between measures and rewards. These limitations can considerably alter results since only a small portion of organizations link measures and rewards in their BSC (Albertsen and Lueg 2014; Speckbacher et al. 2003). Even assuming that Tapinos et al.'s (2011) quantitative investigation was suitable for examining the statistical correlation between users and non-users of BSC—i.e., regarding their overall view of BSC impact on the strategy process—it was unable to reveal sophisticated mechanisms underpinning strategy formation. At length, there is an important scientific gap in the literature on how the implementation of PMS links measures with rewards to influence strategy formation. Similarly, from the literature concerning operations or other types of functional strategy formation, there are no studies referring to the influence of PMS on strategy formation. Moreover, evidence that PMS may affect strategy development is perceptible, since strategy implementation is not a one-direction process but an ongoing flow in which development and implementation are intertwined. This engagement is central to how it affects trust and the trade-off relationship between strategy development and strategy implementation. Several studies investigated this relationship (Deluga 1995; Earley 1986; Mayer and Davis 1999; Mayer and Gavin 2005; Podsakoff et al. 1990; Rich 1997; Zaheer et al. 1998), but very few investigated the interplay between trust and PMS—and the few that did, did not sufficiently explained the relationship (Chenhall and Langfield-Smith 2003; Yang and Holzer 2006). There are no studies which investigate in what way the implementation of PMS affects trust, what types of trust, and how the changes of trust mediate knowledge sharing behavior and, hence, strategy development. This paper addresses these questions as complementary issues to the examination on PMS linkages.

2 Materials and methods

2.1 Framework and definitions

2.1.1 Strategy process and strategy formation

The strategy process can be defined "as a more or less formalized, periodic process that provides a structured approach to strategy formulation, strategy implementation, and control" (Wolf and Floyd 2013). This definition, when applied to strategy formulation supporting organizations, specifies three primary stages, including: (1) principal problems, (2) set objectives (i.e., by analyzing and evaluating alternatives), and (3) selection of the strategy for implementation (Mintzberg et al. 1998). The first stage requires information from the organization and their environment to detect strategic opportunities needed to narrow down any suitable alternative. The second stage focuses on the implementation of the chosen alternative by translating strategy into action (Johnson et al. 2008; Kaplan and Norton 1996). The last stage is the control to what extent the chosen strategy is achieved. Figure 1 depicts a model of strategy process adapted from Dyson (2000), Tapinos et al. (2011), and Kaplan and Norton (1996, 2006). It illustrates not only the business level strategy but also the functional strategies such as operations, supply chain, and marketing strategy. As such, an organization is capable of developing effective strategies when any of the elements in the model are in place and working effectively (Dyson 2000) as well as when the functional strategies are aligned with the business level strategy (Adamides 2015).

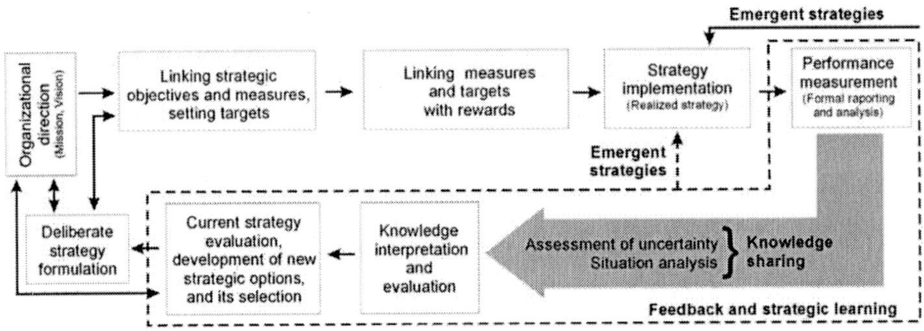

Fig. 1 *Strategy process after the implementation of a performance management system, adapted Dyson (2000), Tapinos et al. (2011), and Kaplan and Norton (1996, 2006)*

Deliberate strategy formulation, both business level and functional, refers to the rational, formal, and centralized top-down process performed by top managers. It is driven by a situation analysis comprised of identifying an organization's (or function's) principal problems as well as monitoring and anticipating its internal and external environment. It is important, that the functional strategies are developed within the guidelines of the overall business strategy (Kim et al. 2014; Kremer 2019). The effectiveness of a situation analysis depends on the source of information and transfer of knowledge to back the monitoring of broad market trends—inclusive of technologies and policies—as well as internal capabilities. Thus, the central element of the model is feedback and strategic learning, which can be regarded as both feedback and feedforward control. Feedback control is focused on monitoring whether determined plans and objectives are achieved. The feedforward approach is future-oriented. It utilizes accessible information from performance measurement and employees observing and experiencing internal and external uncertainties that may affect previous assumptions based on the selected strategy. Through feedback and strategic learning, knowledge is interpreted and evaluated by employees and forwarded up the organizational hierarchy (Bol 2011; Ittner et al. 2003). Based on this structure, managers evaluate the current strategy, develop new strategic options, and select, according to their knowledge, the most effective. In the process of strategy development, the most critical factor is the quality of knowledge managers acquire from their subordinates and other sources (Mintzberg 1994).

The next element of the adopted model links the strategic objectives with measures by formulating performance targets. This is the fundamental element that improves strategy understanding and allows for its realization (i.e., the activities supporting its implementation) (Kaplan and Norton 1996; Kim et al. 2014; Kremer 2019). Linking measures and targets with rewards strengthen employee willingness to achieve these targets by involving them at a personal level. Objectives, measures, targets, and rewards are fundamental parameters of every PMS. The actual set of decisions are not only the results of purposeful planning (i.e., a deliberate strategy) but also are affected by any emergent strategies (Mintzberg and Waters 1985). Emergent strategies are autonomous strategic decisions or actions taken by employees located deep inside the organization as a response to immediate changes in their task environment or as a reaction to perceived opportunity (Burgelman 1996; Mintzberg 1978; Mintzberg and Waters 1985). Employee autonomous strategic actions can also be linked to the feedback and learning process since they acquire knowledge from their day-to-day activities specific to the organization's ecosystem as well as on certain specificities on how performance (i.e., optimization) can be rendered (Kremer 2019). Through the immersion of the feedback and strategic learning process employees are not only sharing but also gaining knowledge which could drive individual actions "off the management radar" and be entirely different than those recommended by top managers. In relation to Fig. 1, deliberate strategies are the result of managers interpreting the knowledge from the feedback and strategic learning process. Emergent strategies are initiatives taken by employees, partially based on the same feedback and strategic learning process, however entirely different and independent from those of top managers, i.e., marked by a dotted arrow. Strategies emerging without connection with the organizational feedback and strategic learning process are marked by a solid arrow.

Both types of strategy development processes indicate the critical role of middle managers and other low-level employees (Andersen and Hallin 2017; Burgelman 1983; Jarzabkowski and Balogun 2009; Kremer 2019; Spee and Jarzabkowski 2011). Recent strategic research emphasizes "compromises, interactions, and negotiations that take place over the planning process [and] social and political interactions over strategy making" (Jarzabkowski and Balogun 2009). Thus, the important issue is how the roles and responsibilities of middle- and low-level actors emanate in organizations and how this influences knowledge sharing and strategy development? Wooldridge et al. (2008) underline that "what makes middle managers unique is their access to top management coupled with their knowledge of operations." Hence, they are an essential nexus of delivering knowledge about markets, competitors, and new technologies—gathered by themselves or acquired from their subordinates. Other research has demonstrated that middle managers involved in strategy development activities also improve organizational performance (Wooldridge and Floyd 1990) and strategic planning (Schaefer and Guenther 2016), two factors that compliment strategy formation experimentation.

2.1.2 Knowledge and trust

Knowledge can be defined as information integrated with personal experience, i.e., a subjective vision of reality located in a particular field of activity; in other words, a subjective interpretation of reality dependent on individual actors' values, interests, experience, and view of the truth. Foucault (2019) claimed that there are several truths but different ways one can express the same truth (White and Jacques 1995; Willcocks 2004). This means that each person can possess their own version of the truth, and that version of the truth may depend on individual interests. As there is no "one truth" and knowledge is "a subjective vision," organizational actors may perceive and interpret reality in a divergent manner possibly more congruent with their interests. Further, they may exploit knowledge and subjectivity of the truth to influence others by sharing knowledge in such a way that supports their interests (Westley and Mintzberg 1989) and thus affect strategic learning. In this environment, trust in organizational members appears to be a vital factor. Ko et al. (2005) claim that trust facilitates knowledge transfer, i.e., defined as an exchange of knowledge between a source and a recipient, in a way that knowledge can be applied. Trust makes people more willing to share genuine information (Holste and Fields 2010; McKnight and Chervany 2006; Sankowska 2013), even sensitive information, which can be used against them (Dirks 2006; Gargiulo and Ertug 2006; Szulanski 1996). The willingness to share genuine information results from trust properties, as trust leads to the optimistic acceptance of vulnerable situations in which the trustor (i.e., trusting party) believes the trustee (i.e., to-be-trusted party) will care for the trustor's best interests, irrespective of the ability to monitor or control the trustee (Hall et al. 2001). The above conceptualization of trust draws attention to the trustor's willingness to engage in risk-taking behavior. For example, employees may share knowledge which is vital for an organization but affects their interests mostly in situations when they trust that managers will ensure their interests in the future. The extent to which the trustor will be willing to accept vulnerability to other people depends on the perception of a particular person's trustworthiness. Overall, the decision of whether to adopt or share knowledge is based on trust (Renzl 2008).

Rousseau et al. (1998) claim that managers can promote two types of trust: calculative and relational. When subordinates develop calculative trust in their managers, they believe that their actions complying with manager requirements will benefit them in calculable ways (Williamson 1993) and every fulfilled obligation concerning reward for performance strengthens this type of trust. Subordinates who maintain relational trust believe that their managers will consider their interests irrespective of their ability to control these managers (Rousseau et al. 1998; Sitkin and Roth 1993). In order to have trust in managers, employees need to believe not only that superiors will hold their words (i.e., are persons of integrity), but also have the ability and willingness to take care of their interests.

In organizations, it is not only important to have employee trust in managers but also manager trust in their subordinates, since it may determine the extent to which managers use the knowledge shared by their employees. However, how can managers recognize who transfers genuine knowledge and who is providing a distorted view based on their own interests? Dirks and Ferrin (2002) claim that beyond the previous experience with employees, managers might evaluate their level of trust in subordinates based on the source and degree of conflict with them. They may also judge the misalignment of task preferences or goals, or incompatibility of values between themselves and their subordinates as well as evaluate the risk of employee opportunism (Williamson 1993). Trustworthiness may also be assessed by the estimation of the level of motivation to lie, i.e., if subordinates have something to gain by lying (Hovland et al. 1953 in Mayer et al. (1995)). When measures are linked to rewards, there are always some underlying interests. Thus, it is essential to investigate how patterns of trust relations and knowledge sharing behavior affected by PMS implementation influence strategy development.

2.2 Research methods

While it is understood how PMS influence strategy implementation, it is not understood how the linkage of strategic objectives with financial and non-financial measures and measures with rewards affect strategy development. To deepen the understanding of strategy development process under PMS, the research was designed as a type of "naturalistic inquiry" in which inductive reasoning was used to obtain insights (Lincoln and Guba 1985). During the field study, interview data were gathered from top managers and some key employees, including middle managers, directly involved with the organizational PMS as well as from relevant archival documents accessible in each organization. Hence, part of the dataset is perceptual in nature and may reflect informant and author bias (i.e., something not easily observable). The study, however, is designed in a way which should diminish the effects of this bias via the division of a two-stage process: (1) theory-building and theory-testing and (2) multiple-case study design in each stage. According to a number of studies, multiple cases typically leads to a more robust, generalizable, and testable theory than single-case research. It, among others, allows comparisons between cases to clarify whether an emergent phenomenon is unique for one case or is present in all of them (Eisenhardt and Graebner 2007; Tsang 2014; Yin 2014). In this replication, logic cases are treated as a series of experiments, each serving to confirm or disconfirm inferences (Eisenhardt and Graebner 2007). Multiple cases also deliver more empirical evidence supporting emergent findings.

The clear division between theory-building and theory-testing stages could be perceived as artificial, and one might consider that just analyzing more cases together would be more appropriate for congruency with the analytic cycle of moving from an inductive to more deductive attitude as the interpretations crystallized (Miles et al. 2014). In this research, however, the split is justified by the construction of distinct research samples and different manners of data analysis. For the theorybuilding stage, the selected organizations utilized were ones that fully implemented PMS and then abandoned it after a few years. It was assumed that organizations which abandoned the PMS must have noticed some critical problems with the concept. In such cases, "hard" evidence was sought—reasons which convinced organizations to abandon further exploitation of PMS. While in the theory-testing stage, the selected entities were organizations that currently use PMS, with the assumption that strategy development issues should also exist but were not visible. Thus, studying such cases, small signs of phenomena revealed in the first stage were sought. Combining organizations that abandoned the PMS and those which were actively using them at the time of the research brought together retrospective and real-time data. Retrospective accounts allowed the research to delve into organizations that experienced time after PMS abandonment and were able to see from a distance some changes in phenomena, while real-time data improved in-depth understanding of how events evolve over time. This, according to Eisenhardt and Graebner (2007), should mitigate bias concerning retrospective sensemaking. If retrospective bias were an issue, significant differences in accounts in these two groups of cases should appear, however, it did not.

2.2.1 Sampling

The research sample in the theory-building stage consists of three organizations that abandoned BSC and one that discontinued another PMS. In this study, BSC and the other PMS are considered the same (Kaplan and Norton 2006; Malmi and Brown 2008), i.e., regardless of how an organization named it, since linked objectives with financial and non-financial measures are associated with rewards. The research started from one case (i.e., "Konsta") that was accidentally discovered by the first author during other similar research which sparked the idea of connecting PMS utilization and strategy development.

Through consulting companies, seven additional organizations were found in Poland from different sectors which abandoned their PMS, five of them (i.e., “Konsta”, “Office”, “Hospital”, “Construction”, and “Center”) agreed to participate in the research. For the theory-testing stage, two organizations were selected that actively use BSC (i.e., “Bureau” and “Furniture 1”) and two firms that exploit the other PMS (i.e., “Furniture 2” and “Center”) (Table 1). During the research it appeared that organizations hesitate to reveal information about their internal problems with PMS. To motivate informants to provide accurate data, confidentiality and anonymity for all organizations in both stages were agreed on and promised (Miller et al. 1997).

Table 1 Research sample characteristics

Area of activity	Employment	Ownership	Nickname	PMS type and its status	Interview date
Construction of production lines for the industry	480	Private	Konsta	BSC, abandoned	September 2015 – November 2016
Network of offices selling financial products	450	Private	Office	BSC, abandoned	
Children hospital	320	Public	Hospital	BSC, abandoned	
Construction company	350	Private	Construction	Other PMS, abandoned	
Local government	250	Public	Bureau	BSC, active	
Production of furniture	520	Private	Furniture 1	BSC, active	June 2016 – January 2017
Production of furniture	640	Private	Furniture 2	Other PMS, active	
Research center	80	Private	Center	BSC, abandoned	February 2022 – March 2022
Financial enterprise	750	Private	Financial	Other PMS, active	

2.2.2 Data collection

In the theory-building stage, 41 semi-structured face-to-face in-depth interviews were conducted from September 2015 to November 2016 and from February 2022 to March 2022, while in the theory-testing stage 33 informants were interviewed from June 2016 to January 2017 and from February 2022 to March 2022. All 74 interviews were recorded and later transcribed, and analyzed using MAXQDA 12 software—i.e., software that is specifically designed for qualitative analysis. Apart from the chief executive officers (CEOs) or board members, typical case studies regarding BSC also include mid-level managers and some key employees since, according to the literature (Albertsen and Lueg 2014), they may play an important role in strategy formation processes. Additionally, multiple informants mitigate subject bias (Miller et al. 1997) and lead to a thicker, more elaborated model (Schwenk 1985). In every case, the first interview was conducted with the CEO, who was also asked to indicate the most experienced staff with PMS. In two cases, the CEO, chief financial officer, and some key informants who had implemented BSC changed their place of work, but they were interviewed anyway. Taking informants from different levels (i.e., superiors and subordinates) allowed for comparative interviews and some ancillary questions relating to the same events. This was important since informants had to recall facts from the past.

The duration of each interview ranged from 30 to 115 min and began with open-ended questions about the reasons for PMS implementation, possible resignation or its continuation, as well as the time before the PMS implementation and after the eventual abandonment. To avoid responses that could lead informants to specific answers, direct questions regarding strategy development were not asked. It was preferred to gather data more freely to allow the informants' natural, undirected narration.

2.2.3 Theory-building stage

In the theory-building stage, cases were used as a base to inductively recognize phenomena and patterns of relationships—firstly within one case and then across all five cases (Eisenhardt and Graebner 2007). Interviews and relevant sections from archive materials were transcribed as well as grouped around repeated statements and related subjects, creating qualitative unit types (Graneheim and Lundman 2004). Then, to facilitate the understanding of the unit types and relationships contained in the dataset, they were condensed to a certain degree, i.e., the reduction of the text while still maintaining the same meaning. This consisted mainly of removing redundant statements. Table 2 presents an example of how the process was performed. Next, the condensed unit types were carefully reviewed with frequent reference to the original transcripts. At this point, the analysis was, to some extent, latent. Condensed unit types were interpreted using what already was known about the subject and the context within which the data was gathered to create themes (Downe-Wamboldt 1992). While developing themes, it was obvious that there was no single correct meaning but only the most probable from a particular perspective. Once all themes were established, their meaning were triangulated with archival materials (Yin 2014). The themes are defined as an expression of the observed and latent (i.e., subjective) content of the dataset.

When the procedure to develop themes was initiated, similar unit types were collated and new meanings appended in subsequent cases. This cyclical procedure codified all the cases to create the condensed unit types. In a few instances, some informants were also called back to clarify meanings. All coherent unit types were condensed and summed up into themes and justificatory narratives. Only the unit types which were replicated, in some way, in all cases remained. When all themes were identified, the research became more systematical and iterative between the themes and relevant literature to develop appropriate codes and phenomena. Next, the research concentrated on searching through

Table 2 Example of condensation and categorization procedure

Unit type	Condensed unit type	Themes and justificatory narratives	Codes and phenomena
• "Office": Measurement of the market share is not credible. […] Units challenged selected measures. They claimed that in different parts of the country there were different levels of affluence, population density, and even propensity to buy insurance. • "Konsta": For the department of production preparation, the board introduced a measured "number of innovations", […] anything new they introduced, even an insignificant amendment in the product construction, sometimes perhaps even unnecessary, […] their measure grows, […] sales department had to sign a contract, and it is not that simple. […] Some [employees] were distressed […] • "Hospital": Patient satisfaction [measure] is unfair. In the rehabilitation ward, patients [children] stay for a few weeks, […] personnel have time to get to know them, to establish a deeper relationship, children also have time to adapt. […] In our ward [pediatrics] patients arrive stressed, stay only a few days, there is no possibility to establish a deep relationship with them. They have no time to get to know the staff. […] In my opinion, wards cannot be compared.	Measurement of the market share is not credible. […] anything new introduced, even an insignificant amendment, […] their measure grows Patient satisfaction [measure] is unfair. […] wards cannot be compared.	Employees questioned the choice of measures because it did not provide equal opportunities for all and made people feel unfairly treated.	Sense of injustice

literature without any preconceptions or established theory using keywords from condensed unit types and themes. When some threads were found (i.e., areas of research), the literature was further refined to those more relevant to knowledge sharing, communication, strategy process, and trust. In this procedure, nine phenomena were identified which were coded as follows: the subjectivity of PMS parameters, perception of personal interests, sense of injustice, trust in managers, enhancement of calculative trust, unfulfilled expectations, psychological contract, pressure on the board, and manager trust in subordinates.

2.2.4 Theory-testing stage

Data analysis in the theory-testing stage was different. While during the theory-building stage, the search concentrated on objective evidence, here the focus went to less apparent signs of previously identified phenomena. Replication logic also determined how informants were interviewed in this verificatory stage. After asking similar questions as in the first stage, the research openly referred to the phenomena from the emergent theory. In this stage, two phenomena identified in the previous stage were not confirmed: unfulfilled expectations and psychological contract. The other seven phenomena were present in all four cases, although with a few informants it was confirmed only after direct questions. Since the interpretation of the dataset always involved multiple meanings and the researchers' interpretation and personal history, a draft report (i.e., before translation) was consulted with the CEO of each organization. In the draft report, the words "manager", "superior", "executive", and "CEO" were assigned to top managers and board members including city mayor, while "employee" and "subordinate" were assigned to lower rank managers.

3 Results and discussion

Seven categories were identified as possibly being associated with strategy development processes in organizations using PMS: (1) subjectivity of PMS parameters, (2) perception of personal interests, (3) sense of injustice, (4) trust in managers, (5) enhancement of calculative trust, (6) pressure on the board, and (7) manager trust in subordinates.

3.1 Subjectivity of PMS parameters: Identification of the cause-and-effect relationships, selection of measures of intangible assets, and determination of their optimal value

The study revealed that at the beginning of BSC implementation organizations were able to reach a consensus concerning measures of tangible assets quite quickly. However, to establish measures of intangible assets linked to valued organizational outcomes, their reference values and cause-and-effect relationships were much more challenging. According to the interviewees, non-financial measures proposed by the consultants, and also mentioned in the literature (Ivanov and Avasilcăi 2014), were problematic to quantify and difficult to interlink correlatively with the organizational outcome. Respondents also indicated a lack of objectivity concerning both reasons for the selection of measures and the assessment of their optimal value. These obstacles weakened the effectiveness of the boards' social accounts. For example, the CEO of "Konsta" noted:

There is no problem with the development of measures relating to production processes, quality, or sales, but that we have done it without BSC. [...] I was convinced to use BSC with the promise that it would allow the measurement of our intangible assets and protect our growth in the future. [...] But when it came to its implementation, it turned out that the consultants did not have much to offer.

Malina and Selto (2001) suggest critical conditions that measure optimal value should be "accurate, objective, and verifiable. Otherwise, measures will not reflect performance and may be manipulated, or managers could in good faith achieve good measured performance but cause the organization harm." In practice these conditions are rarely met. The chief financial officer of "Office" described it in this way:

In our network we tried a lot of non-financial indicators and most of them created problems. When we adopted sales growth, [...] they [employees] questioned it as unfair. They argued that offices which were effective earlier, already had a large share of their market, and had smaller growth opportunities than those which were initially lazier. [...] The absolute market share—as a measure—was also criticized because in large cities where there were lots of competing agencies, our share was only a few percent, but in smaller towns we were sometimes the only ones.

Hence, even in an organization that has a homogeneous network of offices, the choice of measures may favor some locations over another. Management can establish different levels of indicators for individual offices, but the problem of optimal value for each office remains. Managers also indicated, that rarely they were able to identify cause-and-effect relationships before the implementation of new objectives and measures, thus they had to test them in practice, which led to their frequent changes. Other researchers also raised similar problems, claiming comparable results lead to an imperfect BSC structure (Chenhall and Langfield-Smith 2007; Laitinen 2003; Nørreklit 2000, 2003; Nørreklit et al. 2012).

3.2 Perception of personal interests, sense of injustice, and trust in managers

In all of the surveyed organizations, the same pattern was repeated to a greater or lesser extent. All changes to BSC parameters, especially those related to rewards affected the interest structure in the organization. For some employees this was also perceived as displeasing or as an incumbrance to their position. As such, managers tried to explain the reason for their decisions, but as was mentioned earlier, many goals and measures were determined arbitrarily and they encountered difficulties in terms of their rational justification to make them. People who felt that they might lose would develop a sense of injustice and consequently suspect others, who in their opinion gained. This led to conflicts within the board. An employee from "Office" complained, "when superiors do not clearly explain reasons for new goals or measures, and we see that others gain […] For us this means that they [the board] give in under the pressure from the stronger [stakeholders] […] How can we trust them then?" When employees had problems in achieving desired results and boards had not reacted upon their claims they often felt unfairly treated and were losing relational trust in their executives (Dirks 2006; Robinson and Rousseau 1994). Managers also felt that subordinates lose trust in them; for instance, the CEO of "Konsta" said, "one change in the reward system is not a problem. After sometime people got used to new conditions, even if they were not convinced at the beginning, but frequent not well justified changes eventually undermine trust." Before BSC implementation, board members were prepared for BSC reviews and changes. However, most of them admitted they did not envision that changes would be so frequent and in practice produced a number of negative consequences.

Executives emphasized that in many cases subordinates had complained that the changes of BSC were breaking their agreement with the company, although the modifications concerning rewards were within the legal framework of their formal employment agreements. The CEO of "Furniture 1" said:

After the implementation [of BSC] it turned out that certain measures in general cannot be achieved [...] and that staff did not question their changes. [...] The problem has been with measures in which employees successfully achieved. Change of these measures, mostly induced resistance and resentment, even though employees were informed that it was necessary—since in practice it appeared that they [these measures] did not support an [organizational] outcome. [...] I have to say that each change, especially when related to items associated with the rewards, the concept often undermined trust in us.

For each new objective, measure, or related reward adopted by employees, i.e., a kind of two-sided commitment can be said that it is not solely about remuneration. Additional notes included respect and the feeling that people are taken seriously. When employees devoted themselves to the realization of a goal, they expected that it would be important for the organization and that their contribution was to be appreciated. Frequent changes of objectives undermined this belief.

The team leader from "Konsta" stated, "when the board had set a goal, they expected us to engage in it wholeheartedly, [...] people often devoted their private time. [...] We expected that our work would be respected. [...] When it occurred that the goal was changed after a short time we felt disrespected." The research demonstrated that in organizations where the changes of BSC parameters were frequent (e.g., "Konsta") and strategic goals ambiguous (e.g., "Hospital"), levels of conflicts with employees and their feeling of injustice were more intensive. In situations where goals were imposed by law or other forces independent from the organizations (e.g., regional government), or they were easy to explain (e.g., via effective social accounts), interviewees less intensively reported their feeling of injustice. A clerk from a local government mentioned, "sometimes the changes are incomprehensible to us, [...] but what to do [...] its politics! [...] Our boss must somehow be involved in this." This comment paralleled a number of individuals who were also working in regional and local government positions.

3.3 Enhancement of calculative trust and pressure on the board

Experienced managers learnt that frequent changes of BSC parameters connected with incentives may harm employee trust in them. They noted, however, especially at the beginning of BSC implementation, that effective performance measurement and related rewards schemes would substitute the loss of relational trust. A manager from "Office" said:

At the beginning of the implementation [BSC], I believed that employees do not need to have trust in us. It will be sufficient that they will efficiently carry out their tasks, achieve measures, and this should allow us to accomplish our objectives. [...] And, indeed at the beginning, staff are heavily involved in achieving agreed targets. [...] However, after a few changes of measures, I had the impression that they began to use different tactics, for example, they were approaching near optimum level, but did not cross it, although I think, they could.

In a broader sense, managers using BSC have built calculative trust which supports or substitutes relational trust. This is similarly noted by Fadlallah et al. (2018) and Spreitzer and Mishra (1999).

Trust based on financial incentives, invoked employee engagement mainly in these activities which brought them tangible benefits. Employees had known that measures were more or less arbitrarily determined by the board therefore they were trying to influence this process. They could do it by manipulating information they delivered to their superiors or by directly exerting pressure on them. Consequently, employees often were more focused on building pressure on the board to change BSC parameters, than overcoming external obstacles and stepping up efforts to achieve targets. The CEO of "Furniture 1" said, "I had the impression that sometimes employees were putting more energy in convincing us that a measure or goal is unachievable, than it would cost them to achieve it." Rewards, as such, produced employee engagement mainly in these activities, which brought them benefits.

3.4 Manager trust in subordinates

Manager conflicts with employees in terms of objectives, measures, and rewards made executives suspicious of subordinates' actions. Superiors realized that the interpretation of reality, communicated by the staff, might be misshaped by their interests. A few interviewed managers suggested that before BSC implementation, i.e., when the incentive schemes were based either on the aggregated financial indicators or on overall company performance, there was greater congruence between the organization and employee objectives—even though this relationship was much less intensive. However, after the assignment of specific measures, employee interests were more closely aligned to the measures than to organizational outcomes no matter how the market situation changed. This awareness (i.e., sometimes only faint suspicion) made the managers become more mistrustful to knowledge provided by employees, especially the one that could have an impact on the selection of BSC parameters. Generally, interviewees indicated that BSC may change the flow of information. The CEO of "Office" stated:

After linking measures to bonuses [...] in conversations [with the staff], I always had at the back of my head questions like: "what can they lose or gain by giving me this information?" and "what is being marginalized, or even ignored, and what is being overexposed?" [...] After the implementation [of BSC] we have become more distrustful of each other.

In the same tone, the hospital director admitted, "employees not only openly questioned some measures, but I am convinced that they also manipulate shared information to gain better rewards." Hence, managers reaffirmed a potential awareness of mistrustful of employee knowledge and understood that the implementation of a BSC changes the flow of knowledge in an organization.

3.5 Strategy formation process after PMS implementation

The study indicates that the strategy development process is affected by PMS implementation, mostly through its influence on knowledge sharing behavior in an organization (Fig. 2). Each change within a set of PMS parameters may lead to a situation in which some people perceive that they are losing more or gaining less than others and develop a sense of injustice (i.e., moving closer towards victimhood). Frequent changes to some PMS parameters may lead to ongoing alteration of the organization's structure (i.e., in terms of employee interest) and increase likelihood some employees may feel that their position worsens. In this situation, "victims" may struggle to assert their rights and may try to press the board to produce another modification of PMS to favor them. The influence can be explicit or implicit or both.

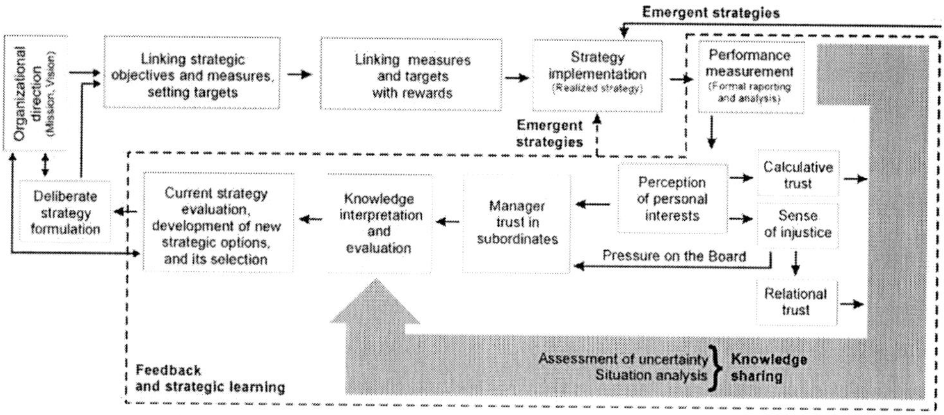

Fig. 2 *Strategy process after PMS implementation comprising of the identified phenomena*

Explicit influence may be exerted by the open questioning of PMS parameters. Managers may reject victimhood claims or accept them and make appropriate modifications to the parameters. When they reject these claims, the "victims" might have a proof that the board has violated their interests, which may reduce employee relational trust in managers (Rousseau et al. 1998; Sitkin and Roth 1993). However, when superiors manage to convince employees that the changes were justified, the trust may be saved or even increased (Lines et al. 2005; Tucker et al. 2013). Acceptance of such claims in conjunction with amendments to PMS parameters does not automatically save trust, especially if repealing any previous decision caused a certain level of harm. According to interviewees, retreat may also reduce trust in managers since it proves that adopted parameters of PMS were arbitrary and showed that exerting pressure on managers is effective. Annulment of the decision might confirm managers susceptibility to backstage forces from interest groups or individuals competing within the organization. Moreover, another change of PMS may also lead to a violation of interests in the organization's structure and claims via subsequent groups. Employees, however, may exert an implicit impact on management decisions by manipulating knowledge they share by way of the feedback and strategic learning process. As a result, they do not necessarily need to lie, they need only selectively share knowledge.

Decreased level of relational trust in managers has been shown to mean that employees do not strive to achieve assigned objectives. As long as rewards exceed incurred efforts, however, employee trust within the organization has been shown to fulfil its obligations and achieve its goals (Long and Sitkin 2006). Long and Sitkin's (2006) research is analogous with this study and confirms that a strategy formation process after PMS implementation can encourage open questioning of superiors' decisions—revealing: interest incongruence, lead to the emergence of conflicts, and raise manager suspicion (i.e., rejecting employee claims by which subordinates may undertake opportunistic action). At length, this consciousness contributes to the decline of manager trust in their subordinates. Hence, from the above analysis, it could be inferred that the implementation of PMS may affect knowledge sharing behavior as well as the whole feedback and strategic learning process (Fig. 2), which influence strategy formation.

3.6 Knowledge sharing

To gain a competitive advantage, the strategy development process (i.e., including functional strategies such as operations strategy) must be based on recent knowledge, encompassing the broadest group of stakeholders (Jarzabkowski and Balogun 2009; Mintzberg 1994; Schaefer and Guenther 2016; Spee and Jarzabkowski 2011), and functional strategies that should be developed within the guidelines of the overall business strategy (Kremer 2019). People are willing to share their knowledge, even unfavorable to their interests, when they trust each other (Dirks 2006; McKnight and Chervany 2006). Thus, the level of trust determines the knowledge sharing behavior. For this study, two types of trust in managers have been identified: relational and calculative. The level of relational trust may determine the genuineness of the knowledge (i.e., the tendency to share knowledge, including unfavorable knowledge against one's actual interest) (Krishnan et al. 2016; Lado et al. 2008). Calculative trust may also motivate people to share knowledge, but mainly if it is favorable (Claro and Claro 2008; Poppo et al. 2016; Williamson 1993). To affect knowledge, it is sufficient that organizational actors, sometimes even unconsciously, interpret their environment (i.e., surrounding reality) in the context of their interests. They do not have to lie, as stated by Foucault (2019), since an understanding and interpretation of the same truth by different people, and even by the same people in a different situation, can be different (Willcocks 2004). In addition, knowledge transfer, which stands in contrast with manager assumptions, may affect the assessment of such an employee by inhibiting the realization of organizational strategy. Therefore, the transfer of knowledge maybe incompatible with current parameters of PMS and requires a high level of relational trust in superiors that have nonconformist behavior so not to adversely affect the subordinate.

Taking into account different levels of relational and calculative trust in managers, distortions of knowledge might be predicted (Fig. 3). There may be four possibilities. In the case of the low-level relational trust, employees are not willing to share genuine knowledge because they might be afraid that this may lead to organizational change violating the status quo. It may also bring the risk of deterioration of their situation by way of employees not trusting superiors to take care of them. Low-level calculative trust would imply employees do not believe that managers will reward their effort. Acquisition of valuable knowledge about an organization and its environment as well as sharing knowledge requires intentional exertion. Thus, in a situation where there are low-levels of both relational and calculative trust employees might not share their knowledge. In the case of a low-level relational trust and high-level calculative trust, knowledge might be distorted by a structure of interest in the organization. Employees would have the motivation to exhibit this knowledge which would be beneficial to them and, due to the weak relational trust, there would be a diminishing level of trust, i.e., even though it would be genuine. In a situation of a high-level of relational trust and low-level of calculative trust in managers, knowledge might be the most "genuine" due to employees not being afraid of imposing their particular narrative. They would be neither lured by incentive nor discouraged by fear of losing their interests.

An ambiguous situation occurs when there are simultaneously high-levels of relational and calculative trust. Both types of trust motivate people to share knowledge, but it is problematic to predict the extent to which transferred knowledge may be affected by personal interests. In this environment, employees may take two types of actions concerning knowledge sharing. Having a high-level of relational trust, they can openly share their knowledge, believing that the possible change would not worsen their situation, i.e., because managers would look after their interests. But, having a high level of calculative trust they may also succumb to "short-term temptations to grab the golden opportunity or cut corners" (Six and Sorge 2008) and try to gain more by sharing knowledge in a way favorable to their actual interests. It is likely, however, that different people could behave differently and, consequently, knowledge could be mixed. In this situation, however, a discussion between employees could arise that would reveal several arguments which would help managers recognize which knowledge is genuine. It is essential to notice that in none of the four instances, knowledge is purely genuine or distorted, it is always a matter of probability and proportions.

		Calculative trust	
		Low	High
Relational trust	Low	Lack of knowledge sharing	Distorted
	High	Genuine	Genuine and distorted

Fig. 3 *Impact of relational and calculative trust on knowledge sharing behaviour*

3.7 Use of shared knowledge

Employees who possess unique knowledge might gain considerable power in an organization. In the case of data or information, manipulation may be verified and forgery discovered. However, knowledge defined as a personal interpretation of reality, in the light of individual experience, by its very nature cannot be easily verified. Thus, even if shared knowledge is firmly focused on securing employee interests, the discovery of the distortion is challenging. For instance, suppose the board performed an action based on employee knowledge. After some time, it might be known that this action has not brought expected results, however, to prove employee intentional manipulation is highly unlikely. Undoubtedly, if in the next few situations poor outcomes repeat, managers may lose trust in their employee capability, but they would not be certain whether the failure was due to intentional manipulation or lack of competence. In a turbulent environment, it is likely there would be even no possibility to verify whether taking different actions would be more effective. This means that managers having virtually no objective grounds, enabling them to verify received knowledge and only relying on trust in employees, may determine the extent to which they would benefit from acquired knowledge (Long and Sitkin 2006; Spreitzer and Mishra 1999). Taking into account the four configurations of relational and calculative trust in managers and the level of manager trust in employees benefits from shared knowledge can be predicted.

Organizations may achieve the greatest benefits from shared knowledge when two conditions are met simultaneously, i.e., when the knowledge is genuine and superiors trust their employees. This may encourage managers to apply, in practice, the acquired knowledge and exploit opportunities by making quick and bold strategic decisions based on actual and comprehensive knowledge. From Table 3 it appears that this would happen in two cases—when there is a high-level of relational trust and low-level of calculative trust and when there are high-levels of both types of trust. However, the second situation is ambiguous since it is more complicated to predict to what extent the knowledge is distorted. Moreover, managers might not be inclined to formulate a strategy based on subordinate knowledge if they do not trust in their employees' willingness to reveal knowledge impartially and honestly. In this case, they would wait for a confirmation of the genuineness of the knowledge through their observations or other sources, or they would select strategic options inconsistently—pending actual trends—even though shared knowledge was available and genuine. Irrespective, the decision would force delay or error, which could significantly reduce the chance of formulating an effective strategy and opportunities may be lost.

Table 3 Usage of shared knowledge depending on employee trust in managers and manager trust in employees

Relational trust	**Calculative trust**	**Manager trust in employees**	
		High	**Low**
High	Low	Exploited opportunities	Lost opportunities
Low	High	Naivety	Justified skepticism
Low	Low	N/A	N/A
High	High	Exploited opportunities or naivety	Lost opportunities or justified skepticism

If employees present a low-level of relational trust and a high-level of calculative trust in managers (Fig. 3), shared knowledge might be significantly affected by personal interests. When managers overlook the game of interests and naively trust in the knowledge, the organization may be exposed to adopt an unsuccessful strategy. In contrast, when managers have low trust in the knowledge, then the skeptical approach is justified. Although this prevents an organization from errors, due to knowledge distortion, it also dooms it to drift or search "blindly" for an effective strategy. Low-levels of relational and calculative trust offer no incentives to employees, thus sharing of knowledge is likely weak, and managers may not be able to use it, regardless of the trust bestowed on their subordinates. When employees possess high-levels of both relational and calculative trust in managers, then the knowledge sharing behavior may be mixed. In this situation, managers have to evaluate which part of knowledge is genuine.

4 Conclusions

The qualitative study reported mechanisms through which PMS may influence the strategy development process both on the functional and operational level as well as on the business level. It shows that employee relational and calculative trust in superiors influence knowledge sharing behaviors while manager trust in their subordinates determines the usage of this knowledge. From the study, it appears that calculative trust may support strategy implementation since it increases the motivation for the achievement of PMS targets and, correspondingly, organizational objectives. Development of an effective strategy is supported rather by relational trust, which facilitates genuine knowledge sharing. This means that organizations should try to maintain, at the same time, high-levels of both types of trust: relational by enhancing strategy development and calculative by supporting strategy implementation. Notwithstanding, this is difficult to achieve.

After implementation, during which managers were able to agree with the majority of employees, a set of PMS parameters, both relational and calculative trust in managers may rise. Since employees at the same time can observe their requirements were included in the set of PMS parameters and they are rewarded, in relation to their achievements, successful implementation can be considered. However, this state is difficult to maintain in the long run because, sooner or later, either PMS parameters need revision (i.e., since they may effectively not support the implementation of the current strategy) or the current strategy needs amendment and, consequently, also will the PMS parameters. As such, in all of the studied organizations, changes in PMS parameters lowered relational trust in managers. From the research, it appeared that high-levels of relational and calculative trust could be maintained in organizations which do not undertake numerous PMS changes or such changes are based on objective premises understandable for all actors. It is challenging to fulfill each of the above requirements in a turbulent environment where organizations, in order to win, must introduce a strategy before its foundations would be apparent for all employees, also for competitors. Therefore, both types of trust may be maintained when there is a low frequency of PMS changes resulting either from the fact that an organization operates in a stable environment, or managers deliberately delay changes.

Intentional avoidance of changes of strategies in organizations that have implemented PMS may have its sources of origins also in other areas. Subordinates, for instance, who are aware that superiors' trust in them depends on their compliance with superiors' priorities (i.e., manager priorities emanating from the selection of objectives and measures which they link to rewards) may be more prone to share knowledge that is more compatible with the current PMS parameters than with reality. In this way, subordinates support positive evaluation about current strategy, even though it is ineffective, instead of challenging it. Superiors, on the other hand, may feel a sense of comfort being convinced of employee trust in them. Hence, having at the same time access to genuine and distorted knowledge, because of high-levels of both types of trust, managers may select the part of the knowledge which is more compliant with the present status quo. Maintaining the status quo allows managers to avoid the change of PMS parameters that may threat trust in them. All these forces may create an environment in which new ideas are not shared openly by subordinates and are not accepted eagerly by superiors, thus, focalizing an organization towards a stable fantasy instead of responding to an evolving reality (Mintzberg 1978; Mintzberg and Waters 1985; Westley and Mintzberg 1989). The same mechanisms may also restrain employee willingness to involve themselves in activities that can lead to emergent strategies and manager openness to adapt it. Thus, postponing of organizational change both by limiting the formulation of deliberate strategies and hampering adoption of emergent initiatives may lead to the stiffening of an organization.

Overall, the study contributes to the existing theory about strategy process by revealing mechanisms through which PMS affect strategy development. It shows that there is a trade-off between strategy development and implementation. This trade-off relationship may be responsible for the inconclusive results of the research concerning PMS influence on organizational performance (Bonner and Sprinkle 2002; Bourne et al. 2007; de Waal and Kourtit 2013). Organizations strongly linking employee rewards with present organizational objectives reinforce strategy execution but, at the same time, are affecting knowledge sharing behavior and weakening organizational ability to develop effective strategies. This trade-off might also be a cause which discourages managers from the implementation of PMS as strategic management systems and forces organizational leaders to abandon PMS even though significant resources were devoted to its adoption. Moreover, there are several practical implications for when organizations may be looking for more genuine knowledge to form new strategies or review their current one, i.e., this is often related to when managers implement relational trust-building policy at the organizational level. Such policy should focus on "(1) creating a culture in which positive relational signals are the desired way to interact ([e.g.,] a relationship oriented culture); (2) facilitating ([i.e.,] unambiguous) relational signaling; (3) socializing newcomers; and (4) managing and matching competencies" (Six and Sorge 2008, p. 881). At the same time, an organization should consider diminishing the tie between rewards and current strategy but in such a way that it preserves employee perception while maintaining a mutual, two-way positive rapport.

Moreover, this research showcases the importance of trustworthiness of a manager via their ability, benevolence, and integrity (Mayer et al. 1995) as well as the regular delivery of social accounts and signaling interest in the well-being of employees. Managers trying to implement a strategy by strongly interlinking measures with reward systems or endeavoring to achieve short-term objectives by "cutting corners" and succumb to the temptation of taking advantage of employees, have to be aware that this may destroy relational trust, hence strategy formation capability in the future. Superiors should be conscious of their employees' trust in them while absorbing knowledge from employees as well as their trust in employees when using the knowledge for evaluation or formulation of a strategy. This awareness may also allow them to recognize distorted and genuine knowledge and improve their strategy formulation ability. At large, a vital contribution of the study is the suggestion that there is a trade-off relationship between strategy formation and implementation. This means that managers have to choose which activity they are going to support "more" in a specific period in terms of the organizational life cycle, since both processes cannot be supported at the same strength. In all, this study opens the new field of research linking performance management and strategy development with trust.

References

Adamides ED (2015) Linking operations strategy to the corporate strategy process: A practice perspective. Bus Process Manag J 21(2):267–287

Albertsen OA, Lueg R (2014) The balanced scorecard's missing link to compensation: A literature review and an agenda for future research. J Acc Organ Chang 10(4):431–465

Andersen TJ, Hallin CA (2017) Democratizing the Multinational Corporation (MNC): Interaction Between Intent at Headquarters and Autonomous Subsidiary Initiatives. *Responsive Glob. Organ.* Emerald Studies in Global Strategic Responsiveness. Emerald Publishing Limited, Bingley, pp 71–86

Bol JC (2011) The Determinants and Performance Effects of Managers' Performance Evaluation Biases. Acc Rev 86(5):1549–1575

Bonner SE, Sprinkle GB (2002) The effects of monetary incentives on effort and task performance: theories, evidence, and a framework for research. Acc Organ Soc 27(4–5):303–345

Bourne M, Melnyk S, Faull N (2007) The impact of performance measurement on performance.Int. J. Oper. Prod. Manag.27(8)

Broadbent J, Laughlin R (2009) Performance management systems: A conceptual model. Manag Acc Res 20(4):283–295

Bryant L, Jones DA, Widener SK (2004) Managing Value Creation within the Firm: An Examination of Multiple Performance Measures. J Manag Account Res 16(1):107–131

Burgelman RA (1983) A process model of internal corporate venturing in the diversified major firm.Adm. Sci. Q.:223–244

Burgelman RA (1996) A Process model of strategic business exit: Implications for an evolutionary perspective on strategy. Strateg Manag J 17(S1):193–214

Butler A, Letza SR, Neale B (1997) Linking the balanced scorecard to strategy. Long Range Plann 30(2):153–242

Chenhall RH, Langfield-Smith K (2003) Performance measurement and reward systems, trust, and strategic change. J Manag Account Res 15(1):117–143

Chenhall RH, Langfield-Smith K (2007) Multiple Perspectives of Performance Measures. Eur Manag J 25(4):266–282

Claro DP, Claro PBO (2008) Managing trust relationships: calculative, affective, belief and performance. BAR - Brazilian Adm Rev 5(4):289–303

Deluga RJ (1995) The relation between trust in the supervisor and subordinate organizational citizenship behavior. Mil Psychol 7(1):1

Dirks KT (2006) Three fundamental questions regarding trust in leaders. Bachmann R, Zaheer A, eds. *Handb. Trust Res.* (Edward Elgar Publishing, Cheltenham), 15–28

Dirks KT, Ferrin DL (2002) Trust in leadership: Meta-analytic findings and implications for research and practice. J Appl Psychol 87(4):611–628

Downe-Wamboldt B (1992) Content analysis: Method, applications, and issues. Health Care Women Int 13(3):313–321

Dyson RG (2000) Strategy, performance and operational research. J Oper Res Soc 51(1):5–11

Earley PC (1986) Trust, perceived importance of praise and criticism, and work performance: An examination of feedback in the United States and England. J Manage 12(4):457–473

Eisenhardt KM, Graebner ME (2007) Theory building from cases: opportunities and challenges. Acad Manag J 50(1):25–32

Fadlallah R, El-Jardali F, Hemadi N, Morsi RZ, Abou Samra CA, Ahmad A, Arif K, Hishi L, Honein-Abouhaidar G, Akl EA (2018) Barriers and facilitators to implementation, uptake and sustainability of community-based health insurance schemes in low- and middle-income countries: A systematic review. Int J Equity Health 17(1):13

Ferreira A, Otley D (2009) The design and use of performance management systems: An extended framework for analysis. Manag Acc Res 20(4):263–282

Foucault PM (2019) Discourse and Truth and Parresia, 1st edn. University of Chicago Press, Chicago

Franco-Santos M, Otley D (2018) Reviewing and Theorizing the Unintended Consequences of Performance Management Systems. Int J Manag Rev 20(3):696–730

Gargiulo M, Ertug G (2006) The dark side of trust. Bachmann R, Zaheer A, eds. *Handb. Trust Res.* (Edward Elgar Publishing, Cheltenham), 165–186

Glas AH, Henne FU, Essig M (2018) Missing performance management and measurement aspects in performance-based contracting: A systematic process-based literature analysis of an astonishing research gap. Int J Oper Prod Manag 38(11):2062–2095

Graneheim UH, Lundman B (2004) Qualitative content analysis in nursing research: concepts, procedures and measures to achieve trustworthiness. Nurse Educ Today 24(2):105–112

Hall MA, Dugan E, Zheng B, Mishra AK (2001) Trust in Physicians and Medical Institutions: What Is It, Can It Be Measured, and Does It Matter? Milbank Q 79(4):613–639

Holste JS, Fields D (2010) Trust and tacit knowledge sharing and use. J Knowl Manag 14(1):128–140

Hovland CI, Janis IL, Kelley HH (1953) Communication and persuasion: Psychological studies of opinion change. Yale University Press, New Haven

Ittner CD, Larcker DF, Meyer MW (2003) Subjectivity and the Weighting of Performance Measures: Evidence from a Balanced Scorecard. Acc Rev 78(3):725–758

Ivanov CI, Avasilcăi S (2014) Measuring the Performance of Innovation Processes: A Balanced Scorecard Perspective. Procedia-Social Behav Sci 109:1190–1193

Jarzabkowski P, Balogun J (2009) The Practice and Process of Delivering Integration through Strategic Planning. J Manag Stud 46(8):1255–1288

Johnson G, Scholes K, Whittington R (2008) Exploring corporate strategy: Text and cases, 8th edn. Pearson Education, Essex

Kalgin A (2014) Implementation of Performance Management in Regional Government in Russia: Evidence of Data Manipulation. Public Manag Rev 18(1):110–138

Kaplan RS, Norton DP (1996) The balanced scorecard: translating strategy into action. Harvard Business Press, Chicago

Kaplan RS, Norton DP (2006) Alignment: Using the balanced scorecard to create corporate synergies. Harvard Business Press, Chicago

Kerpershoek E, Groenleer M, de Bruijn H (2014) Unintended responses to performance management in dutch hospital care: Bringing together the managerial and professional perspectives. Public Manag Rev 18(3):417–436

Kim YH, Sting FJ, Loch CH (2014) Top-down, bottom-up, or both? Toward an integrative perspective on operations strategy formation. J Oper Manag 32(7–8):462–474

Kremer K (2019) Operations strategy: Literature review and case study of IKEA. *Proc. FEB Zagreb Int. Odyssey Conf. Econ. Bus.* 1:606–616

Krishnan R, Geyskens I, Steenkamp JBEM (2016) The effectiveness of contractual and trust-based governance in strategic alliances under behavioral and environmental uncertainty. Strateg Manag J 37(12):2521–2542

Lado AA, Dant RR, Tekleab AG (2008) Trust-opportunism paradox, relationalism, and performance in interfirm relationships: Evidence from the retail industry. Strateg Manag J 29(4):401–423

Laitinen EK (2003) Future-based management accounting: a new approach with survey evidence. Crit Perspect Account 14(3):293–323

Lee CL, Yang HJ (2011) Organization structure, competition and performance measurement systems and their joint effects on performance. Manag Acc Res 22(2):84–104

Levy PE, Tseng ST, Rosen CC, Lueke SB (2017) Performance management: A marriage between practice and science - Just say "I do." *Res. Pers. Hum. Resour. Manag.* (Emerald Group Publishing Ltd.), 155–213

Li J (2015) The paradox of performance regimes: Strategic responses to target regimes in Chinese local government. Public Adm 93(4):1152–1167

Liedtka SL, Church BK, Ray MR (2008) Performance Variability, Ambiguity Intolerance, and Balanced Scorecard-Based Performance Assessments. Behav Res Account 20(2):73–88

Lincoln YS, Guba EG (1985) Naturalistic inquiry. Sage Publications, London

Lines R, Selart M, Espedal B, Johansen ST (2005) The production of trust during organizational change. J Chang Manag 5(2):221–245

Long CP, Sitkin SB (2006) Trust in the balance: How managers integrate trust-building and task control. Bachmann R, Zaheer A, eds. *Handb. Trust Res.* (Edward Elgar Publishing, London), 87–106

Malina MA, Selto FH (2001) Communicating and Controlling Strategy: An Empirical Study of the Effectiveness of the Balanced Scorecard. SSRN Electron. J

Malmi T, Brown DA (2008) Management control systems as a package—Opportunities, challenges and research directions. Manag Acc Res 19(4):287–300

Mannion R, Braithwaite J (2012) Unintended consequences of performance measurement in healthcare: 20 salutary lessons from the English National Health Service. Intern Med J 42(5):569–574

Mayer RC, Davis JH (1999) The effect of the performance appraisal system on trust for management: A field quasi-experiment. J Appl Psychol 84(1):123

Mayer RC, Davis JH, Schoorman FD (1995) An integrative model of organizational trust. Acad Manag Rev 20(3):709–734

Mayer RC, Gavin MB (2005) Trust in management and performance: Who minds the shop while the employees watch the boss? Acad Manag J 48(5):874–888

McKnight DH, Chervany NL (2006) Reflections on an initial trust-building model. Bachmann R, Zaheer A, eds. *Handb. Trust Res.* (Edward Elgar Publishing, Cheltenham), 29–51

Miles MB, Huberman AM, Saldaña J (2014) Qualitative Data Analysis: A Methods Sourcebook, 3rd edn. Sage, Los Angeles

Miller CC, Cardinal LB, Glick WH (1997) Retrospective reports in organizational research: A reexamination of recent evidence. Acad Manag J 40(1):189–204

Mintzberg H (1978) Patterns in strategy formation. Manage Sci 24(9):934–948

Mintzberg H (1994) The fall and rise of strategic planning. Harv Bus Rev 72(1):107–114

Mintzberg H, Ahlstrand B, Lampel J (1998) Strategy Safari: A Guided Tour Through The Wilds of Strategic Management. Free Press, New York

Mintzberg H, Waters JA (1985) Of strategies, deliberate and emergent. Strateg Manag J 6(3):257–272

Nørreklit H (2000) The balance on the balanced scorecard a critical analysis of some of its assumptions. Manag Acc Res 11(1):65–88

Nørreklit H (2003) The Balanced Scorecard: what is the score? A rhetorical analysis of the Balanced Scorecard. Acc Organ Soc 28(6):591–619

Nørreklit H, Nørreklit L, Mitchell F, Bjørnenak T (2012) The rise of the balanced scorecard! Relevance regained? J Acc Organ Chang 8(4):490–510

Podsakoff PM, MacKenzie SB, Moorman RH, Fetter R (1990) Transformational leader behaviors and their effects on followers' trust in leader, satisfaction, and organizational citizenship behaviors. Leadersh Q 1(2):107–142

Poppo L, Zhou KZ, Li JJ (2016) When can you trust "trust"? Calculative trust, relational trust, and supplier performance. Strateg Manag J 37(4):724–741

Rampersad H (2003) Total Performance Scorecard. Redefining Management to Achieve Performance with Integrity. Routledge, New York

Renzl B (2008) Trust in management and knowledge sharing: The mediating effects of fear and knowledge documentation. Omega 36(2):206–220

Rich GA (1997) The sales manager as a role model: Effects on trust, job satisfaction, and performance of salespeople. J Acad Mark Sci 25(4):319–328

Robinson SL, Rousseau DM (1994) Violating the psychological contract: Not the exception but the norm. J Organ Behav 15(3):245–259

Rousseau DM, Sitkin SB, Burt RS, Camerer C (1998) Not so different after all: a cross-discipline view of trust. Acad Manag Rev 23(3):393–404

Sankowska A (2013) Relationships between organizational trust, knowledge transfer, knowledge creation, and firm's innovativeness. Learn Organ 20(1):85–100

Schaefer T, Guenther T (2016) Exploring strategic planning outcomes: the influential role of top versus middle management participation. J Manag Control 27(2–3):205–249

Schleicher DJ, Baumann HM, Sullivan DW, Levy PE, Hargrove DC, Barros-Rivera BA (2018) Putting the System Into Performance Management Systems: A Review and Agenda for Performance Management Research. J Manage 44(6):2209–2245

Schwenk CR (1985) The Use of Participant Recollection in the Modeling of Organizational Decision Process. Acad Manag Rev 10(3):496–503

Sitkin SB, Roth NL (1993) Explaining the Limited Effectiveness of Legalistic "Remedies" for Trust/Distrust. Organ Sci 4(3):367–392

Six F, Sorge A (2008) Creating a High-Trust Organization: An Exploration into Organizational Policies that Stimulate Interpersonal Trust Building. J Manag Stud 45(5):857–884

Speckbacher G, Bischof J, Pfeiffer T (2003) A descriptive analysis on the implementation of Balanced Scorecards in German-speaking countries. Manag Acc Res 14(4):361–388

Spee AP, Jarzabkowski P (2011) Strategic planning as communicative process. Organ Stud 32(9):1217–1245

Spreitzer GM, Mishra AK (1999) Giving Up Control without Losing Control: Trust and its Substitutes' Effects on Managers' Involving Employees in Decision Making. Gr Organ Manag 24(2):155–187

Szulanski G (1996) Exploring internal stickiness: Impediments to the transfer of best practice within the firm. Strateg Manag J 17(S2):27–43

Tapinos E, Dyson RG, Meadows M (2011) Does the Balanced Scorecard make a difference to the strategy development process? J Oper Res Soc 62(5):888–899

Tsang EWK (2014) Generalizing from Research Findings: The Merits of Case Studies. Int J Manag Rev 16(4):369–383

Tucker DA, Yeow P, Viki GT (2013) Communicating During Organizational Change Using Social Accounts: The Importance of Ideological Accounts. Manag Commun Q 27(2):184–209

de Waal A, Kourtit K (2013) Performance measurement and management in practice: Advantages, disadvantages and reasons for use. Int J Product Perform Manag 62(5):446–473

Westley F, Mintzberg H (1989) Visionary leadership and strategic management. Strateg Manag J 10(S1):17–32

White RF, Jacques R (1995) Operationalizing the postmodernity construct for efficient organizational change management. J Organ Chang Manag 8(2):45–71

Willcocks L (2004) Foucault, power/knowledge and information systems: reconstructing the present. Wiley, Chichester

Williamson OE (1993) Calculativeness, trust, and economic organization. J Law Econ 36(1):453–486

Wolf C, Floyd SW (2013) Strategic Planning Research: Toward a Theory-Driven Agenda. J Manage 43(6):1754–1788

Wooldridge B, Floyd SW (1990) The strategy process, middle management involvement, and organizational performance. Strateg Manag J 11(3):231–241

Wooldridge B, Schmid T, Floyd SW (2008) The Middle Management Perspective on Strategy Process: Contributions, Synthesis, and Future Research. J Manage 34(6):1190–1221

Yang K, Holzer M (2006) The performance–trust link: Implications for performance measurement. Public Adm Rev 66(1):114–126

Yin RK (2014) Case study research: Design and methods, 5th edn. Sage, Thousand Oaks, CA

Zaheer A, McEvily B, Perrone V (1998) Does trust matter? Exploring the effects of interorganizational and interpersonal trust on performance. Organ Sci 9(2):141–159

2

Lean Service

A Contingency Perspective

Sophie Fenner, Torbjørn Netland

Department of Management, Technology, and Economics, ETH Zurich, Weinbergstrasse 56/58, Zurich, Switzerland

Abstract

Many firms launch consolidated lean initiatives across all their service units, but because services differ, mandated lean practices may have a poor fit with the receiving unit. Whereas plenty of research has investigated the fit of lean implementation at the service industry level, this is the first to delineate how standard lean service practices fit different service types. Taking a contingency theory perspective, we study a leading European utility company comprising distinct service types. Using purposeful sampling, we interview 36 employees from 15 different teams representing three different service types – professional services, service factories and service shops – and 11 employees from the headquarters who are supporting these units in their lean transformation journeys. We also collect secondary data, including lean programme documentation and audit data. We find that one size does not fit all for lean service; there are important nuances to the relevance of standard lean service practices across different service types. Ten propositions are put forward suggesting how standard lean practices need to be adapted to fit the context of different service types. The findings reject the idea that all service units can progress along the same trajectory in lean service programmes. This paper informs managers how lean service programmes can be tailored to increase the fit with different service types.

Keywords: *Lean service · Operational excellence · Change management · Contingency theory · Service types*

1 Introduction

To improve productivity, many service companies have taken inspiration from 'lean production'. Consequently, a growing number of service companies have launched lean initiatives (Allway and Corbett 2002; Netland and Powell 2016; Liker and Ross 2017; Fenner et al. 2022). This research is motivated by the real-world observation that many global service firms run consolidated corporate lean programmes across all their service units. Such programmes are unlikely to have the same fit for different types of service processes (Ansari et al. 2010; Netland and Aspelund 2014). We challenge the implicit assumption in many studies of universality of lean practices in service settings. We do so by exploring how employees in different service types perceive the relevance of standard lean service practices for their job contexts and how they respond to the mandate of adopting them. Hence, our research question is, 'How do standard lean service practices fit different service types?'.

There is general agreement in the lean production literature that lean practices, when properly used, improve operational performance in manufacturing firms (Shah and Ward 2003; Dal Pont et al. 2008; Onofrei and Prester 2019). However, the effectiveness of lean practices in the service industry is more contested. On the one hand, many articles have suggested that lean improves performance in various service industries: examples include financial services (Holweg et al. 2018), information services (Staats et al. 2011), education (Alves et al. 2016), hospitality services (Rauch et al. 2020), call centres (Piercy and Rich 2009), public services (Bateman et al. 2018) and healthcare (Meredith et al. 2011). On the other hand, other empirical studies have shown that lean does not deliver its promise in service industries. For example, Poksinska et al. (2017) found that healthcare institutions that apply lean practices do not have more satisfied patients than those that do not focus on lean; Holweg et al. (2018) and Secchi and Camuffo (2019) reported failed lean transformations in the banking sector; and Radnor (2010) and McCann et al. (2015) found that public service organisations that adopt lean production did not realise the expected benefits. Clearly, there is mixed evidence of the effectiveness of 'lean service'.

Rather than trying to understand how lean differs across service industries (banking, healthcare, telecom, education, etc.) or fits a particular service industry (cf. Langabeer et al. 2009; McDermott and Venditti 2015; Vanichchinchai 2021), we focus on different service types. This paper explores the fit between service types and standard lean service practices. Service companies comprise many different types of service operations (Johnston and Clark 2008). Consider the example of education services where tasks are as different as student enrolment, classroom teaching, facility management, examination and grading. Or in restaurants where service tasks include booking and table placement, order taking, cooking, serving, cleaning, billing etc. Furthermore, also manufacturing firms comprise various service operations, such as purchasing, maintenance, accounting, internal audits, sales, marketing and after-sales services. The key idea of this paper is that – because service operations differ in terms of customer contact, routine variability and technology usage, among other dimensions (e.g. Thomas 1978; Silvestro et al. 1992; Ponsignon et al. 2011) – the applicability of lean practices is likely to be more associated with the service type than with the service industry.

For this research we studied a multinational utility company that comprises many different types of services but deploys a consolidated corporate lean programme across all units. We conduct qualitative embedded case study research, which means studying different subunits within the same organisation and comparing them to identify common and conflicting patterns. The sample included four professional service teams, five service shop teams and six service factory teams. We conducted in total 47 interviews: 36 interviews with team members who adopted lean and 11 interviews with senior managers who oversee the lean programme. The interview data were analysed using a structured qualitative analysis. The findings are summarised in ten propositions that seek to explain what conditions reduce or increase the fit between standard lean practices and service-type settings.

This paper contributes a process-based perspective on lean services to the literature. It supports the idea that many standard lean service practices are applicable across various service types but emphasises that some require more adaptation to the context. We find that practice adaptation is more crucial for managerial lean practices than for technical lean practices and in a service context characterised by higher employee skills and discretion, less routine work, and in field and front office work. Overall, our research findings challenge the rationality of generalising lean to a whole industry, as in 'lean healthcare', 'lean education','lean governments' or 'lean utility'. For practitioners, the findings can help companies overcome the challenge of context–practice fit, which is a critical success factor in corporate programmes. Managers can use this paper's insights to tailor the lean programme expectations and actions to different service units within their firms.

2. Theoretical background

Over the past three decades, lean production practices have been introduced to many industries (Netland and Powell 2016; Cusumano et al. 2021). The industries classified as services have not been an exception, showing a growing interest in 'lean service' (Bowen and Youngdahl 1998; Allway and Corbett 2002; LaGanga 2011; Leite and Vieira 2015; Gupta et al. 2016; Hadid et al. 2016; Liker and Ross 2017; Seddon 2019; Fenner et al. 2022). In the next subsections, we first review the literature on lean service and summarise standard lean service practices; secondly, we discuss differences among service types; and thirdly, we derive the research gap concerning the fit between service types and standard lean service practices.

2.1 Lean service

Danese et al. (2018) reported that only 11% of the lean literature investigates the service sector—of which half concentrates on healthcare. This is not much considering the service industries' contribution to GDP in most countries. For example, according to World Bank 2020 data, the service sector contributes an average of 65.6% to the GDP in the European Union, 54.5% in China and 80.1% in the USA. Despite its importance, it is repeatedly noted that the service sector has been lagging behind the manufacturing sector in terms of productivity (Allway and Corbett 2002; Liker and Ross 2017; Seddon 2019). We take this as a motivation to study lean services.

Several authors have conceptualised lean in service industries and specified how it differs from lean production (e.g. Bowen and Youngdahl 1998; Allway and Corbett 2002; Leite and Vieira 2015; Liker and Ross 2017). Although there is no general agreement on which specific practices constitute lean services, a review of the literature by Gupta et al. (2016) reveals a set of practices that are commonly included in lean services listed in Table 4 in Appendix A. These practices can be separated into three systems based on what they aim to transform (Found and Bicheno 2016):

- The operation system
- The management system
- The culture system

A lean operations system is characterised by the efficient use of resources, which makes service production flow without disturbances. Practices that are commonly used to achieve this include process mapping, process standardisation, pull production, waste reduction, process capability (e.g., simplification, error prevention, built-in quality), workload balancing and workplace organisation (e.g., '5S') (Gupta et al. 2016).

A lean management system refers to the managerial practices needed to establish and support a lean operations system. Frequently mentioned examples of such practices in the lean service literature are visualisation ('visual management'), supporting organisational infrastructure (e.g., 'lean teams', 'champions'), performance management (e.g., 'daily huddle meetings', 'visual performance boards'), hands-on management (e.g., 'gemba walks', 'early triage' in hospitals) and training and skill management (e.g., 'multiskilling') (ibid.).

Lastly, a lean culture system is the foundation for sustained lean transformation (Liker and Ross 2017). Common practices that foster a lean culture include continuous improvement practices (e.g., 'kaizen events', 'rapid improvement events' and 'plan-do-check-act'), customer orientation (e.g., 'voice of the customer' and 'value for the customer') and employee involvement (Gupta et al. 2016).

Because manufacturing and services differ, it is likely that lean practices should also differ in these two contexts. Whereas manufacturing delivers material products, services are activities that produce immediate, intangible and nonstorable products. However, considering the practices mentioned above, it is not apparent how lean services differ from lean production. Except for 'early triage' (a lean practice in hospitals), all the mentioned practices are also common in manufacturing. It seems that lean service deviates from lean production in what is absent. In addition to the lean 'service' practices listed above, production companies tend to include a range of lean practices directly related to making physical products in factories. For example, practices related to total productivity maintenance, total quality management, takt time, supplier integration and supply chain, and inventory management are more prominent in production settings (e.g. Shah and Ward 2003; Netland 2013; Leite and Vieira 2015).

2.2 Service types

The service industries are highly heterogeneous (Johnston and Clark 2008; Victorino et al. 2018). Running a fast-food restaurant is entirely different from running a prison, utility company, hospital, university or consultancy. Even within a service firm, there are numerous different types of services. For example, there are fundamental differences in the job context of those who work in the internal audit department, human resources department or sales department. Hence, rather than looking at lean service at the firm level or across different service industries, we follow the advice of Shostack (1987), Wemmerlöv (1990) and Safizadeh et al. (2003), who suggest studying services at the process level.

Several operations management authors have suggested service process typologies (Chase 1978; Schmenner 1986; Wemmerlöv 1990; Silvestro et al. 1992; Ponsignon et al. 2011). As evidenced by Cook et al. (1999) comprehensive review of service typologies, there is considerable overlap between the typologies suggested in the literature. Typologies usually separate three or four types of services according to different service process characteristics. We adopt the typology proposed by Ponsignon et al. (2011) in their paper 'Service delivery system design: Characteristics and contingencies'.

The service typology of Ponsignon et al. (2011) represents a meaningful classification of service process types. Ponsignon et al. (2011) draw on previous service classifications to propose three service process types: 'professional service', 'service shop' and 'service factory'.1 The typology has much in common with the classifications of Silvestro et al. (1992) and Kellogg and Nie (1995). However, unlike the many typologies that use their process typologies to categorise firms in service industries, Ponsignon et al. (2011) categorise service units within a firm. They sort services into three archetypes based on the role of people, the role of technology and equipment and the role of location and layout in the service process (Ponsignon et al. 2011). Each of the three 'roles' covers two dimensions, resulting in six dimensions of the service delivery mechanisms: level of skills and degree of employee discretion, degree of routineness and (potential) degree of automation and location and front-office versus back-office configuration. Figure 1 illustrates the dimensions of the typology and the resulting three service process types.

Professional services tend to require specialised skills, provide a high level of discretion for the employee, be customised with a low automation potential and be delivered close to the customer in the field front office. On the opposite side of the spectrum, service factories require less specialised skills, provide a low level of discretion for the employee, follow standardised processes, have a high potential for automation and are delivered distantly to the customer in the back office. The service shop is characterised as something between professional services and a service factory. The typology is a stylised model that does not perfectly match all service processes. For example, there are also back-office jobs that require specialised expertise.

Other frameworks include 'mass service' as a fourth process type. Considering the characteristics of 'mass service', it is essentially a 'service factory' (cf. Schmenner 1986; Wemmerlöv 1990).

2.3 Fit between practices and service type

A lean transformation aims to instil a set of carefully selected lean practices throughout an organisation. Because service firms span a variety of internal and external environments, contingency theory is a useful theoretical perspective for studying lean practices (Donaldson 2001; Sousa and Voss 2008). According to Danese et al. (2018), contingency theory is the most frequently used theory in the lean literature (for examples, see Peng et al. 2011; Netland 2016).

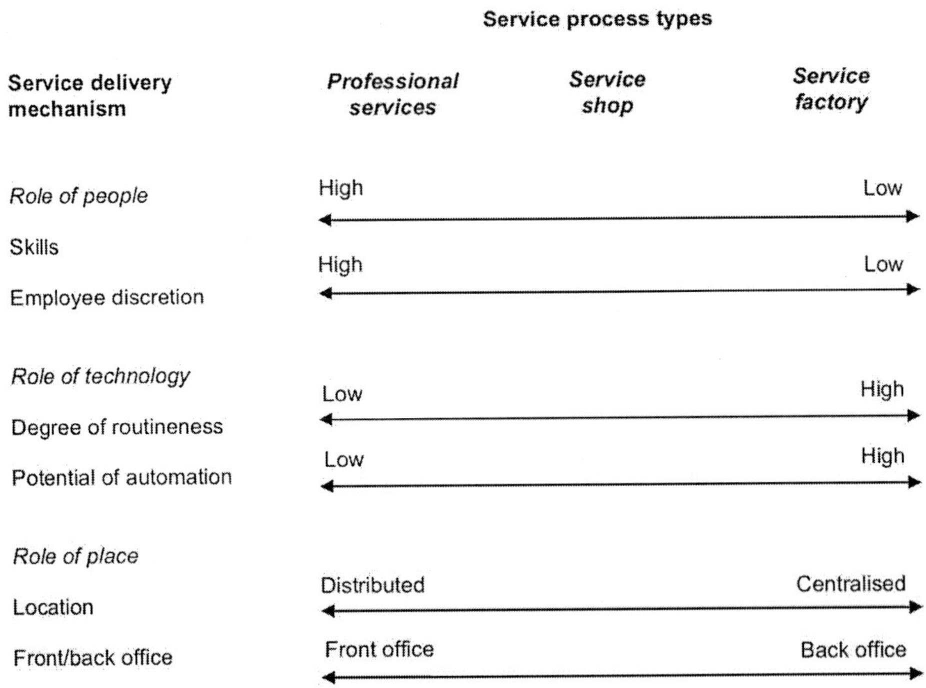

Fig. 1 *A typology of service processes (based on Ponsignon et al. 2011)*

Central to contingency theory is the concept of 'fit' (Drazin and Van de Ven 1985; Donaldson 1987, 2001; Sousa and Voss 2008). The concept of fit has also been discussed thoroughly in the strategy literature – explicitly or indirectly taking a contingency theory perspective (see Drazin and Van de Ven 1985; Donaldson 1987; Ansari et al. 2010; Volberda et al. 2012). Contingency theory suggests that organisations seek to achieve fit (or congruence) between their practices and their internal and external institutional environments. Hence, according to this theory, not all lean service practices should fit similarly well across different service types.

According to contingency theory, units that experience a high degree of fit between their environment and a specific lean service practice are expected to adopt the practice, whereas units that experience a low degree of fit are likely to reject or adapt the practice (Ansari et al. 2010). Here, adoption refers to an implementation of the practice that comes close to the original template, and adaptation 'refers to the process by which an adopter strives to create a better fit between an external practice [by adjusting it] and the adopter's particular needs to increase its "zone of acceptance" during implementation' (Ansari et al. 2010, p. 71). It is worth noting that fit is not a binary variable but a continuous one. It is dynamic, multidimensional and dependent on the perceptions of humans (Ansari et al. 2010).

Against this theoretical background, we set out to conduct an explorative study into the fit of standard lean service practices across different service types.

3. Research method

To investigate our research question, we chose a qualitative embedded case study research design (Voss et al. 2002; Yin 2013). An embedded case design investigates several sub-units within the same case firm (Scholz and Tietje 2002). The phenomenon we study occurs in a context-rich environment with complex social structures. In this setting, case studies are recommended (DeHoratius and Rabinovich 2011). Case studies allow the exploration and formulation of propositions in order to generate new theoretical insight (Yin 2013).

We decided to conduct this research in one company to hold many contextual variables constant. We needed a firm that spans a range of service types and has deployed the same corporate lean programme across all units for a few years. We were lucky to team up with a leading European energy supplier, which we call 'Energy Co.', in the autumn of 2016. Energy Co. is a leading international company in its industry. We worked with Energy Co. until 2019. At the time of our research, it employed over 40,000 people, served over 30 million customers and had an annual revenue of approximately 40 billion euros. The company focuses on renewables, energy networks and energy-related customer solutions.

3.1 Energy Co.'s corporate lean programme

Facing increased competition and cost pressures, Energy Co. embarked on a corporate lean programme in 2014. Energy Co. selected and tailored commonly known lean practices into a programme aligned with its company culture and characteristics. The programme consisted of nine sets of lean practices clustered into three 'blocks': operating processes, management systems and mindset and behaviour. The blocks consist of nine sets of lean practices, which are summarised and exemplified in Table 1. The practices pursued by Energy Co. overlap considerably with the standard lean service practices reported in the literature (see Section 2.1). The practices were intended to fit all units and teams of Energy Co. To track the status and incentivise the implementation of the lean programme, Energy Co. conducts regular lean maturity assessments on a team level. A maturity assessment consists of interviews with team members, observations of meetings and work areas, discussions and a feedback session. This results in a score of the team's performance in each of the nine sets of practices. Two assessors spend one or two days onsite conducting an assessment. The unit receive an aggregated score ranging from 0 to 100%. The scores are represented as 1 to 3 'stars', with a cut-off value > 25% for 1 star, > 50% for 2 stars and > 75% for 3 stars. In 2018, Energy Co. received external certification for its lean programme and won a prestigious international award for its efforts, indicating that the lean programme is a serious effort.

3.2 Data collection

We applied a purposeful group characteristics sampling strategy (Patton 2014, p. 267). According to Patton (2014), purposeful group characteristic sampling chooses cases that meet specific criteria to highlight relevant patterns within groups. In this study, we looked for teams representing the three service types of Ponsignon et al. (2011): professional service, service shop and service factory.

Table 1 The three blocks and nine sets of practices of Energy Co.'s lean programme, with descriptions and examples

Blocks	Set of practices	Description	Three examples of practices
Operating processes	1. Standard working environment	Establish a defined state for the working environment that is maintained and that triggers problem solving in case of deviations	i. Standard work instructions ii. Team standards iii. 5S checklists and rules
	2. Process optimisation	Identify customer value and maintain processes that efficiently deliver this value	i. 'Voice of the customer' ii. Process mapping iii. Waste reduction
	3. Resource planning	Provide a clear overview of the resources needed to meet customer demand and reduce waste, variability and overburden	i. Visibility of workload ii. Workload balancing iii. Ensuring equipment availability
Management system	4. Capability building	Ensure workers' skills related to operational tasks and improvement of work	i. Lean coaching ii. Skill assessment (e.g. skill matrices) iii. On-the-job coaching
	5. Performance management	Create transparency in team performance to trigger problem solving on performance deviations and establish a systematic approach for root-cause problem solving	i. Visual team performance boards and daily dialogues ii. Goal deployment ('hoshin kanri') iii. Root cause problem-

Blocks	Set of practices	Description	Three examples of practices
			solving practices
	6. Organisation	The set of practices related to 'Organisation' aimed to ensure the necessary organisational support for a lean transformation	i. Corporate and local change agents and lean teams ii. Lean programme governance iii. Establishing a vision and goals for the transformation
Mindset & behaviour	7. Understanding & commitment	Promote the idea of continuously improving the service provided to the customer	i. Communicatin g the purpose ii. Linking firm objectives with the transformation iii. Empowering and engaging all employees
	8. Continuous improvement mindset	Establish an organisational culture of continuous improvement	i. Feedback culture ii. Standards as a basis for improvement iii. Running experiments
	9. Leadership	Foster lean leadership behaviours that drive and sustain the lean programme implementation	i. 'Go-and-see' ('gemba walks') ii. Coaching team members iii. Leader standard work

To avoid an undesirable selection bias, the teams should not have been recently established or reorganised and should have more than a year's experience with the lean programme. We also wanted diversity in each of the service types. We sampled teams from three different countries: Germany, the United Kingdom and Romania. Energy Co. mandated that all teams implement the Energy Co. lean program around the same year (from 2014 onwards), which reduces concerns about bias due to prior differences in experience with lean services. In total, we examined 15 teams. Table 2 reports an analysis of the teams according to the six service supply mechanisms discussed in Ponsignon et al. (2011) and shown in Fig. 1. The analysis is based on observations from interviews during field visits and discussions with Energy Co. The sample included four professional service teams, five service shop teams and six service factory teams.

We interviewed 36 employees directly supporting or leading the lean transformation projects in the teams (e.g. department manager, team leader, lean coach or lean auditor) at different locations in Energy Co. To understand the extent of local adoption or adaptation from the perspective of headquarters, we also interviewed 11 senior managers who were responsible for the entire lean programme at Energy Co. Figure 2 shows an overview of all interviews conducted at Energy Co. and Table 5 in Appendix B provides details of the interviewee profiles and the interview locations and durations.

Table 2 The 15 Energy Co. teams were ranked and sorted according to the service typology of Ponsignon et al. (2011)

	Role of people		**Role of technology**		**Role of place**		**Resulting service type**
Team	**Skills required**	**Employee discretion**	**Degree of routineness**	**Potential of automation**	**Location**	**FO-BO configurations**	
Field services power grid distribution DE	High	High	Medium	Low	Field	Front office	Profession al services
Field services network distribution RO	High	High	Medium	Low	Field	Front office	Profession al services
Field services metering UK	High	High	Medium	Low	Field	Front office	Profession al services
Field services metering support UK	Medium	Medium	Medium	Low	Field	Front office	Profession al services
Power grid new connections planning UK	High	Medium	Medium	Low	Centralised	Back office	Service shop
Back-office complaint management RO	Medium	Medium	Medium	Low	Centralised	Back office	Service shop
Power grid	High	Medium	Medium	Medium	Centralised	Back office	Service

	Role of people		Role of technology		Role of place		Resulting service type
Team	**Skills required**	**Employee discretion**	**Degree of routineness**	**Potential of automation**	**Location**	**FO-BO configurations**	
calculation DE							shop
Power grid operational support RO	Medium	Medium	Medium	Medium	Centralised	Back office	Service shop
Compliance support for field services UK	Medium	Medium	Medium	Low	Centralised	Back office	Service shop
Customer care centre DE	Low	Low	High	Medium–High	Centralised	Front office	Service factory
Customer care centre 1 RO	Low	Low	High	Medium–High	Centralised	Front office	Service factory
Customer care centre 2 RO	Low	Low	High	Medium–High	Centralised	Front office	Service factory
Customer care centre UK	Low	Low	High	Medium–High	Centralised	Front office	Service factory
Workforce planning DE	Low	Low	High	High	Centralised	Back office	Service factory
Billing department UK	Low	Low	High	High	Centralised	Back office	Service factory

*Call centres are classified as front office operations because they have direct customer contact, even when limited to voice, chats and/or email

More than half of the interviews were conducted face-to-face during onsite visits and the rest were conducted through online telecom conferences (cf. Appendix B). The interviews were semi-structured, allowing for the 'reconstruction of the interviewee's subjective view (Flick 2014, p. 207) about lean services. We used two interview guides: one for the teams based in Energy Co.'s subsidiaries (Appendix C) and one for the lean programme management team at headquarters (Appendix D). Both guides were pretested on employees at Energy Co. and carefully reviewed after the pre-test. Small adjustments were made as we progressed with the interviews and learned which questions triggered the most valuable information. The interviews ranged from 30 to 60 min in length and were conducted in German, English and Romanian. The German and Romanian interview guides were translated and back-translated to English by native-speaking staff in the research organisation. With the interviewees' consent, we tape-recorded all interviews and offered them the opportunity to review the transcripts. We transcribed all interviews in full, resulting in about 700 pages of raw text. To increase internal validity, interviewees were invited to review their recorded statements.

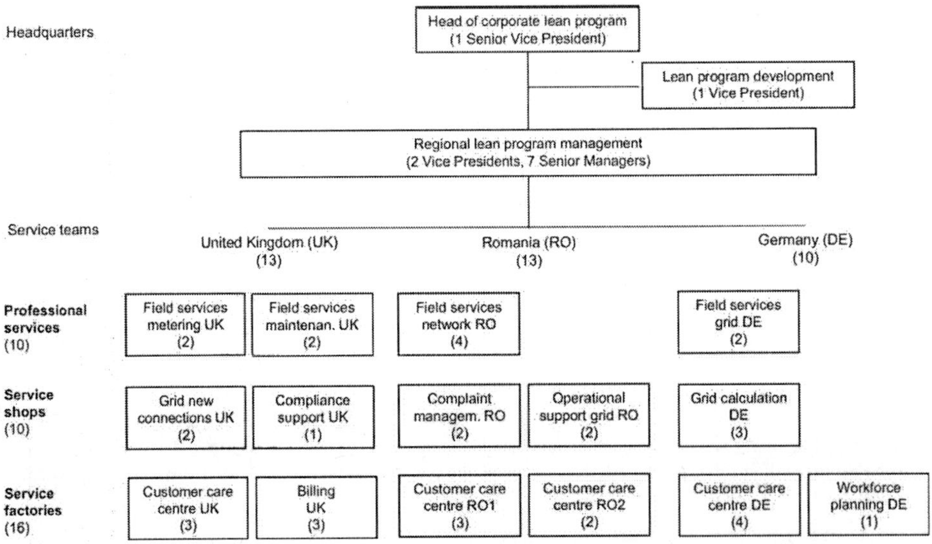

***Fig. 2** Interviews in Energy Co. (number of interviewees in parentheses)*

We also collected a range of secondary data, including audit scorecard data and performance board data for the teams we interviewed. In addition, we attended two full-day lean maturity assessments and a three-day lean conference at Energy Co. and took field notes from numerous informal discussions. Shadowing the lean assessments and reviewing programme documentation allowed us to gain in-depth knowledge about Energy Co.'s lean programme and its application across different service types. We also collected data about the activities of the teams and the headquarters unit. All secondary data were stored and indexed in the research database.

3.3 Data analysis

For the data analysis, we followed the general three-phase process of Miles et al. (2014). In the first phase, we sorted and coded the data. In the second phase, we searched for patterns within and across cases. In the third phase, we sought to explain the emerging propositions. As is typical in qualitative research, our approach was iterative (Eisenhardt 1989).

In the first phase, we created a data inventory with transcribed interviews with team-level employees, company scorecard data (lean assessment scores) and observations and notes from team-level visits. We used Atlas.ti software to structure, codify and map emerging associations. Following Saldaña (2015), we chose descriptive coding. We first descriptively coded the text according to the three defined service types (professional service, service shop and service factory) and the three lean programme blocks of Energy Co. (operating processes, management system and mindset & behaviour).

We coded quotes reflecting either fit or incompatibility between Energy Co.'s lean practices and the team. These quotes typically referred to different reactions, emotions, actions and experiences associated with the fit of the lean practices to the interviewees' working context. Practices that were positively perceived and reportedly implemented in line with corporate standards indicated fit and were coded as 'adoption'. Practices that were negatively perceived and reported to be rejected, changed, or only superficially implemented indicated a low level of fit and were coded as 'adaptation'. Practices that were not mentioned or mentioned without evoking any particularly positive or negative feelings, were not considered. In a subsequent step, we searched the interviews conducted with interviewees from headquarters for comments that would support or oppose the team-level findings. We uncovered only a few occurrences of discrepancy and decided to remove the affected quotes from further analysis.

Second, we searched for patterns in the data (Miles et al. 2014). We iteratively developed propositions (or 'hypotheses' in the language of Eisenhardt), which we sought to explain with the data and literature (Eisenhardt 1989; Yin 2013). During the data analysis process, different propositions emerged and were subsequently either discarded or refined. We triangulated between the two-level interview data, quantitative assessment scores and observation in Energy Co., and – as a result of this process – kept the propositions that could be backed with convincing evidence and that we found interesting in terms of practical and theoretical contributions.

Finally, we challenged the emerging propositions by looking for discrepancies or competing arguments and findings in the literature and through discussions with Energy Co. We also used post hoc discussions with Energy Co. to understand the underlying mechanisms in the suggested propositions.

4. Findings

By triangulating the quantitative and qualitative data, we sought patterns in lean service practice adoption and adaptation among the service types. Sorted by service type, Table 3 summarises the lean assessment scores of all teams at the end of the data collection. Sorted by the set of lean practices, Table 6 panels A, B and C in Appendix E illustrate the coding of exemplary quotes and their sorting into 'adoption' or 'adaptation'. As explained in the methods section, we focused our analysis on practices that evoked clear responses—negative or positive. This reduced the number of lean practices explored in the analysis. The practices included are 'standard working environment' and 'process optimisation' from the operational lean practices set, 'performance management' from the managerial lean practices set and 'leadership' from the cultural lean practices set.

We structure the within-case narratives by service type: professional service, service shop and service factory. For each service type, we briefly introduce the teams and draw on the quantitative and qualitative material to present their perspectives on the fit of operational, managerial and cultural lean service practices.

4.1 Professional services and fit with lean service practices

All the professional services we include are field services (cf. Silvestro et al. 1992). The four teams included one team doing technical field services of a power grid in Germany, one team working in network distribution in Romania, one team installing meters and another team maintaining them in the UK. All these teams employ educated electricians with a large degree of autonomy in their work tasks. They are used to being alone for long periods and have limited interactions with their peers. Overall, we found that the employees performing professional services felt that the lean service practices of Energy Co. did not cater to their specific contexts and needed to be adapted to fit.

Table 3 Team-level lean assessment scores by summer 2019 (percentage points)

Team	Type	Operation System	Management System	Culture System	Team average lean score
Field services power grid DE	Professional services	62.2	40.6	56.6	53.1
Field services network distribution RO	Professional services	97.7	100.0	85.0	94.2
Field services metering UK	Professional services	89.0	52.0	90.0	77.0
Field services metering support UK	Professional services	n/a	n/a	n/a	n/a
Average	*Professional services*	*83.0*	*64.2*	*77.2*	*74.8*
Power grid new connections planning UK	Service shop	91.0	88.0	89.0	89.3
Back-office complaint management RO	Service shop	100.0	100.0	97.4	99.1
Power grid calculation DE	Service shop	79.3	59.4	80.4	73.0
Power grid operational support RO	Service shop	n/a	n/a	n/a	n/a
Compliance support for field services UK	Service shop	97.3	78.0	75.5	83.6
Average	*Service shops*	*91.9*	*81.4*	*85.6*	*86.3*
Customer care centre DE	Service factory	90.9	76.7	90.8	86.1
Customer care centre 1 RO	Service factory	100.0	96.9	92.0	96.3
Customer care centre 2 RO	Service factory	100.0	96.9	99.4	98.8
Customer care centre UK	Service factory	98.0	81.0	100.0	93.0

Team	Type	Operation System	Management System	Culture System	Team average lean score
Workforce planning DE	Service factory	95.8	73.3	81.7	83.6
Billing department UK	Service factory	85.7	78.0	82.5	82.1
Average	*Service factories*	*95.1*	*83.8*	*91.1*	*90.0*

As shown in Table 3, the lean maturity assessment scores are diverse in this group,[Footnote2] ranging from '1 star' (53.1%) to '3 stars' (94.2%), averaging 74.8%. Across all sets of lean practices, professional services scores were, on average, the lowest in Energy Co. As can be calculated from Table 3, professional services scored an average of 83% for operational lean practices, 64% for managerial lean practices and 77% for cultural lean practices. The exception is the Romanian field service team, which stands out due to its superior performance on the managerial lean practice set (100%). We learned that the manager in this Romanian team was fully devoted to the lean programme and received sustained support from senior managers in Romania.

The qualitative evidence explains the relatively higher levels of adaptation of lean service practices in professional services. Our data suggest that employees in this service type see themselves as experts and enjoy more freedom in how they conduct their work than do back-office employees. A team leader in the UK reported, 'Field technicians are quite different [from office workers]. A seasoned person who has been out in the field spends days walking around in storms, blizzards and everything'. Generally, this autonomy makes field service technicians question and challenge any new practices coming from the office environment.

However, this evidence does not suggest that lean practices do not apply to professional services; rather, they must be implemented with greater caution and adapted to the context. The Romanian team provides evidence that professional service teams can achieve high levels of lean implementation. For example, one team leader on another professional service team in the UK gave a powerful testament in favour of the lean programme: 'I am a massive fan of it [the lean programme]; [it is] the best thing that could have happened to me. Lean really put my interest back into work'. Other interviewees reported that there were clear benefits to having a standardised work environment, even in highly variable work environments. For example, one UK-based interviewee from a field services team explained that common process documentation 'brought everyone to a [common] standard', which improved the team's know-how and performance. Other interviewees reported that the introduction of workplace organisation principles (e.g., '5S') in the service cars helped them 'become more organised'.

All field service teams, except the Romanian team, struggled mainly with managerial lean service practices. For example, field service teams struggled to implement the daily 'performance dialogues'[Footnote3] that were mandated by the programme. As one team leader in a UK team lamented, 'It takes me up to four hours to update the board every week'. We also heard accounts of negative experiences with lean training sessions from many of the field service teams. Apparently, it was hard to get all the teams together (due to the geographically spread activity of field services), and the standard training had a poor fit with professional services. 'Long-term projects were not considered, and the applied examples were not relevant to field services', according to team leaders from Germany and the UK.

Managerial lean practices appear as more difficult to implement and sustain in field services and it is also a challenge to build a common lean culture among field services colleagues. For example, the lean leadership practice of 'go and see' is experienced as impractical in field services. A lean manager in the UK reported, 'We sort of fail [the lean programme], as we cannot fit four go-and-sees into our day jobs as expected'. When people work autonomously and remotely with limited network or office access, it can be harder to create a shared lean culture. It can, however, be argued that it is precisely under such conditions—when managers have limited possibilities to control and follow up—that a shared lean culture is most important for good performance.

We also noticed that there were benefits to the lean programme that the field staff were surprised to experience but that the headquarters staff had expected. The joint programme lowered the organisational walls that had prevailed in their relationships with back-office operations and headquarters. The lean programme helped forge a bond between field workers and office staff. Imposed meetings (for example, the mandatory and daily 'performance dialogues') improved transparency, team interaction and empowered people to solve inter-departmental problems.

4.2 Service shops and fit with lean service practices.

Our sample of service shop teams consisted of five teams: a planning team for new power grid connections and a field compliance team in the UK, a complaint management team and an operational support team for grid field services in Romania and a grid calculation team in Germany. These teams work in centralised back-office functions and handle work tasks with a medium level of variation and complexity.

As can be seen in Table 3, the lean maturity assessment scores range from '2 stars' (73.0%) to '3 stars' (99.1%). The average scores for operational practices were 92%, for managerial practices 81%, for cultural practices 86%, and overall, 86.3% (note that the Romanian operations team did not receive a lean maturity assessment at the end of the data collection). The scores and our interviews indicate that lean practices have a reasonable fit with service shop teams. A team leader in Germany suggested that the lean programme 'applies to four of five of the processes in our context, while the remaining processes (typically large, long-term projects) require other methods and tools'.

As in all service types, we noticed resistance to work standards. One team member grumbled, 'I am back office, so why does it matter what my desk looks like?' Another said, 'We lost our family atmosphere [after the introduction of standards]'. However, the thorough creation of user guides improved the teams' clarity regarding the main work streams and promoted a uniform work style. The teams reported that they were more aligned. The team leader in the Romanian field service operational support team reported, 'Lean standardises our responses and provides a clear working procedure for the different customer requests'. Other teams reported positive bottom-line effects. For example, one team in the UK reported that the lead time for a difficult process was reduced by three months.

Service shop teams were generally receptive to managerial lean practices. Several interviewees reported that team communication had improved due to the introduction of daily performance dialogues. 'Meetings without a detailed agenda don't take place here anymore', said the team leader in the German grid calculation team. Visualising performance metrics accelerated the daily performance review and helped track work progress during staff absences. Sometimes the lean practice was adapted to fit the context of the teams. For example, one of the German teams was located in several cities and struggled to conduct daily performance dialogues. Rather than a physical meeting in front of a whiteboard, the team implemented a digital board that was accessible online and updated during daily conference calls. A challenge for all service shop teams was to select meaningful key performance indicators to track and follow up on. Several teams reported that they found the standard metrics irrelevant for order fulfilment. As for professional services, the interviewees reported that the lean training lacked a relevant business context for them.

Service shop teams mentioned that the prescribed leadership and coaching practices were generally difficult to implement and sustain. In particular, team leaders found more substantial hands-on leadership involvement to contradict the team's desired work autonomy and employee empowerment. At the same time, team members in the UK asked 'for a bit more motivation' and felt that they lacked 'lean buy-in from top management'. A grid planning team in the UK complained that information on efficiency savings from lean programme implementation was not shared.

4.3 Service factories and fit with lean service practices

Four of six of the service factory teams in our sample are customer care centres (two in Romania, one in Germany and one in the UK). These teams are commonly known as call centres. Modern call centres focusing on productivity have been equated with factories in several reports (e.g. Frenkel and Donoghue 1996; Gilmore 2001; Hudson 2011). They seek to operate based on strict standards and are subject to continuous performance measurement. The work tasks of 'call agents' include customer care, complaint management, error handling and customer retention initiatives. Our sample of service factories also includes a workforce planning team in Germany that supports the staffing of a call centre and a UK billing team that performs routine billing of electricity and gas usage.

Service factories report the highest implementation rates of the corporate lean programme (cf. Table 3). This is true for lean operational practices (an average score of 95%), lean managerial practices (84%) and lean cultural practices (91%). Our qualitative data suggest that the service factory teams adopted almost all lean operational practices and achieved high scores on managerial and cultural practices by adapting them slightly to their specific contexts.

Regarding operational practices, all call centre teams report that these practices are already part of their DNA. One team leader in Germany stated, '5S and working standards are clearly our strengths... we were already on a good standard... we are actually super at this. We are very well-organised people'. Another manager in one of the call centres explained, 'We adopted the lean standardised work practices quickly, as we have always operated according to standards'. Creating additional process documentation and user guides provided the call centre teams with increased transparency, improved resource management and faster customer response times. 'Customer guides are more [of] a consistent approach... everybody is doing the same thing when dealing with the customer', according to a team leader in a call centre in the UK. The implementation of lean operational practices showed tangible results. For example, the UK-based billing team reported, 'We had 66,000 exceptions... we completely reviewed our process, developed a customer guide, put timings behind to actually give us targets. In a matter of six months, we were down to 5,000 [quality exceptions]'.

The managerial lean practices are also at a high level but require a higher level of adaptation. In particular, performance measurement practices evoked negative responses. 'Some of that is difficult because we don't have the measures (…) sometimes, what worked for one area doesn't work for another one—but you have to go with it', reported a team leader in a call centre in the UK. A lean leader shared the following sentiment: 'Team managers here didn't really understand what metrics to track on their boards'. Call agents welcome team initiatives as an alternative to their usually isolated jobs because they provide a 'platform for everyone's voice to be heard', as a team leader put it. Transparency of performance metrics and skills matrices enables smoother cross-team communication. We noticed that the daily performance dialogues did not always follow the corporate blueprint. For example, the reporting frequency requested by the lean programme did not align with the availability of metrics (daily meetings discussing week-old metrics are not very efficient).

Cultural lean practices also show high implementation levels, with a certain degree of adaptation. A general problem for teams working in the front office is the availability of quickly solving problems, as prescribed by the lean programme. For example, a team leader in the UK explained, 'If we know we have a problem, we can't walk out there right now and grab eight people and go, right, let's problem solve, because then the customers would be waiting'. In addition, the long incubation time for process improvement conflicts with the service factory's usual fast-paced work. We also noticed that Energy Co.'s increased focus on performance management in teams fuelled the teams' competition and comparability, which does not necessarily align well with a lean culture where problems should be surfaced and problem-solving experiments should prevail. Rather, the result in Energy Co.'s service factories was greater individual performance pressure and increased conflict between call agents' effectiveness and efficiency when answering call queries. As one agent in a team in the UK stated, 'It felt at times as if we were working against each other, although we were simply taking care of the business'.

5. Discussion

According to one of the team leaders at Energy Co., 'Lean application requires a lot of empathy... they [corporate] cannot preach the same standards to different types of businesses'. While this makes intuitive sense (cf. Ansari et al. 2010, 2014; Netland and Aspelund 2014), it is of little help to those who teach and support lean across different service types. Exactly how should the programme and practices allow unit-level adaptation? By comparing the within-case findings and drawing on the literature on practice adoption, we develop propositions regarding the fit between standard lean service practices and different service-type contexts.

A first observation is that all teams had reached some level of lean implementation, and none had actively opposed the lean programme. All teams we interviewed mentioned the general benefits of the lean programme, spanning from an improved collaboration climate and a more organised workplace to concrete performance improvement. Hence, we lend support to the branch of the lean service literature that suggests that lean *can* be implemented in a wide variety of service processes (e.g. Piercy and Rich 2009; Gupta et al. 2016; Liker and Ross 2017; Seddon 2019).

However, we find convincing evidence that several lean practices must be adapted in content or implementation to better fit different service contexts (e.g. Allway and Corbett 2002; Netland and Powell 2016; Tay et al. 2017; Seddon 2019; Rauch et al. 2020). This is as expected, according to contingency theory (Donaldson 1987; Sousa and Voss 2008; Lawrence and Lorsch 2015). At the highest abstraction level, we notice that lean practices have a particularly good fit with the service factory and the lowest fit for professional services. Service shops are somewhere in between professional services and service factories. Energy Co.'s Vice President for Lean Programme Development acknowledged this need: 'We expect them to customise and tailor the lean practices to fit their context'. Confirmed by our findings, this is a useful advice, but it doesn't tell when and how. We now turn to the specific propositions developed in this reseach.

5.1 Propositions for operational lean service practices

The set of operational lean service practices demonstrated the highest lean maturity score (91.3%) across all service types and was consistently the highest scoring set of practices within each service type. The scores and case narratives suggest that they have the best fit for service factories compared to service shops and professional services. Building on the service delivery mechanisms listed in the service typology of Ponsignon et al. (2011), we put forward the following three propositions:

Proposition 1a

> The higher the employees' skills and discretion needed in a service process, the lesser the fit of operational lean service practices.

Proposition 1b

> The higher the degree of routine work and potential automation of a service process, the better the fit of operational lean service practices.

Proposition 1c

> Centralised service processes have a better fit with operational lean service practices than field services.

To our surprise, we noticed that lean operational practices did not necessarily have a better fit with back-office operations than with front-office operations. A common argument is that back-office processes are shielded from the variability introduced by customer interaction and hence can run more like a factory (Safizadeh et al. 2003; Ponsignon et al. 2011). We could not find support for this argument. On the contrary, the back-office operations in our study seem to reject standards. 'They claim it hinders their creativity', explained a senior manager in the corporate lean department. We also found that front office operations, such as call centres, had a high degree of adoption and implementation of process optimisation and standardisation. Perhaps because front office services are subject to more significant variation introduced by customer interaction (Chase 1978; Shostack 1987; Johnston and Clark 2008), they benefit from practices that aim to reduce and control this variation (Shah et al. 2008). Standards are 'a basis for managing uniformity and quality' (Shostack 1982). Using a script-based, standard approach also controls customers' expectations and standardises service consumption. A senior manager at headquarters confirmed this finding: 'Call centres, for example, are more receptive to standards as they are very much process-driven'. Therefore, we propose the following:

Proposition 1d

> Operational lean service practices are effective in repetitive front-office operations because they reduce variations in customer interaction processes.

An investigation of contingencies motivates a further proposition. Operational lean practices seem to be adopted more when the service is delivered by a team of agents dependent on each other. When an autonomous individual service agent delivers the service, there is more room for individual variation than when the service is delivered by a team that must be coordinated. To provide an everyday example, in a restaurant, it is more important that the team that serves the table is 'lean' than the barista who serves coffee at the bar. Thus, we propose the following:

Proposition 1e

> Operational lean service practices fit less when employees have higher work discretion.

5.2 Propositions for managerial lean service practices

Managerial lean service practices generally have a lower implementation rate than operational and cultural lean service practices. The managerial practices discussed in this research relate to performance management. We found that managerial lean service practices seem most effective in services that are centralised, measurable and do not require specialised skills – that is, service factories and service shops. In these settings, managers can understand service delivery and tend to have more management tasks. In professional services, in contrast, the service operator tends to be given greater autonomy and the ability to 'self-manage'. Especially in field services where service agents often work distantly from their managers, managerial lean practices fit less.

Proposition 2a

> The higher the employees' skills and discretion in a service process, the lesser the fit of managerial lean service practices.

It follows that a higher degree of adaptation of managerial lean practices is needed in professional services. We observed professional service teams that tried to establish online meetings, 'gemba walks', and performance reviews. However, these initiatives were hard to sustain for two reasons. First, in professional front-office services, service delivery always takes priority over internal meetings. Second, geographically distributed service delivery involves a host of technical problems, such as, for example, lack of internet connection (in some cases, even lack of telephone signal), no suitable workspace for meetings (often the service car) and scheduling problems. Some of the interviewed field service teams mentioned that the best they could do was telephone meetings in a car park on a bimonthly basis. With no access to the performance board and only a fraction of team members having sufficient telephone reception, it is clear that these performance review meetings are not very practical for professional field services. This discord leads to the deviation of communication style, level of discretion, format, frequency and communication channel of managerial lean service practices. We propose:

Proposition 2b

> Managerial lean service practices fit less in distributed field services than in services delivered from a centralised office.

5.3 Propositions for cultural lean service practices

Lean practices aiming to build a culture of continuous improvement are more ambiguous than practices aiming to change operations and management systems. It is not easy for managers to know exactly what, for example, 'coaching' and 'empowerment' mean. Since these practices can take different forms, they generally fit all service types. With an overall lean maturity assessment score of 86.2%, cultural lean practices appear to fit any service setting.

However, a deeper look at the qualitative data reveals that creating a culture of continuous improvement is immensely difficult for all service types. For example, all teams struggle to institutionalise the leadership behaviours needed for effective problem-solving sessions (see also Tortorella et al. 2019; Vanichchinchai 2021) – but seemingly for different reasons. Because service factories are under high-performance pressure, there is little time for structured problem solving with root cause elimination. A lean coach in a German call centre observed, 'They [the call centre] solve the problem, but do not see the need to record the solution and learnings'. In professional services, it is hard to get operators or teams together due to distributed fieldwork. In addition, autonomous service agents experience a reduced need for a coordinated and uniform lean culture. In service shops, we observed that leaders and employees often avoided problem-solving sessions because they did not see a need to improve. In back-office teams, we observed that team members were reluctant to give up autonomy and power related to tacit knowledge.

Proposition 3a

> The higher the employees' skills and discretion in a service process, the lesser the fit of cultural lean service practices.

Proposition 3b

> The lower the degree of routine work and potential of automation of a service process, the lesser the fit of cultural lean service practices.

Whether or not the service is delivered in the field or in an office seemed to play a particular role for cultural lean service practices. When professional services are delivered in the field, the culture-building leadership practice of 'go and see' ('gemba walks') is perceived as impractical. One team member in a field service unit shared the following sentiment: 'It is a bit tongue-in-cheek because I totally get the value of the go and see, but it takes three to four hours every time, and the set plan is to do a go and see three times a week'. We propose:

Proposition 3c

> Cultural lean service practices fit better with centralised service processes than distributed (field) services.

6. Conclusions

We investigated the fit between lean service practices and three different service types: professional services, service shops and service factories. We concluded that standard lean service practices do not have the same fit across different service types and require different levels of adaptation. We summarised our findings as ten propositions.

6.1 Contributions to research

The results contribute new insights to the growing literature on lean services (e.g. Leite and Vieira 2015; Gupta et al. 2016; Hadid et al. 2016; Liker and Ross 2017; Seddon 2019; Rauch et al. 2020; Fenner et al. 2022). Instead of researching lean services at the industry level, which most studies do, we contribute a *process-based perspective* on lean services. In particular, this research demonstrates that studying a general lean service perspective across many different service types is an inaccurate simplification. Even when studying lean services in one industry or company, researchers must pay attention to the important nuances introduced by different service types. Overall, our findings draw into question the validity of concepts that generalise lean to an industry, such as 'lean healthcare', 'lean education', 'lean policing', 'lean utility' and so on.

Based on the service process typology by Ponsignon et al. (2011) and the concept of fit, we elaborate on how standard lean service practices must be adapted to three different service-type contexts: professional services, service shops and service factories. The propositions suggest how underlying mechanisms affect the fit level across these service types. We offer these propositions as promising avenues for future research on lean services.

6.2 Contributions to practice

Managers in service companies, as well as in manufacturing and governmental institutions, can use the findings to inform the lean journeys of their service units. We find that lean practices can be implemented effectively in a range of service types, but that the practices must be adapted to fit the service context. In particular, managerial lean practices require a higher level of adaptation in all service types.

More adaptation of lean is required when the service context is characterised by the following: higher employee skills and discretion, lower levels of routineness and potential for automation when the service occurs in the field and the front office. Conversely, standard lean service practices tend to be adopted when lower skills and discretion are needed in the service delivery process, when the routineness and potential of automation are higher and when the service takes place centrally in the back office. Hence, lean service practices have a higher fit with service factories than with professional services. Managers can use this insight to create different action plans and set different expectations for different service units.

We submit that a higher level of adaptation in some contexts should not discourage the implementation of lean in these service types. Because it is more 'difficult' to implement lean in these settings, it can provide a potent source of competitive advantage. For example, we found that front-office services that introduce standards reduce process variation in customer contact, which increases process cycle times and improves communication and coordination in service delivery teams.

6.3 Limitations and future research

This paper has the usual limitations of qualitative case-based research. We cannot claim general validity of the suggested propositions; therefore, we offer them only for future scrutiny and testing. Furthermore, we cannot rule out the possibility that some of the results were driven by contextual variables other than service type. Team size, managerial commitment, history and network integration are examples of other variables that affect lean adoption. Moreover, national and micro-organisational cultures can affect the implementation and fit of lean practices. We mitigate these limitations by conducting a deep case study in a single firm, which arguably keeps many confounding variables nearly constant: all units had the same lean programme, comparable senior management commitment and resource distribution, and were subject to the same industry dynamics. We encourage future research to use cross-sectional data or multiple case studies to investigate how contingencies affect lean implementation in different service processes.

Another limitation relates to the choice of service typology. The literature offers no commonly accepted typology, and no typology perfectly caters to all different service contexts. By sticking to the convention in the literature – specifically, building on the service typology of professional services, service shops and service factories (Ponsignon et al. 2011) – instead of describing the specificities of the service teams we study, we trade internal validity against greater external validity.

Relatedly, as we were working with one company, we were restricted to its available service types. For example, all our professional service teams were working in the field. These field services employ staff with higher seniority and experience than other service types. Moreover, they were organised into separate units with more autonomy from headquarters. It is possible that an office-based professional services service (e.g. specialised software development or consulting) with a younger staff would have led us to other propositions regarding professional services. Future research could draw on quantitative methods to explore such questions.

Notes

1. Other frameworks include 'mass service' as a fourth process type. Considering the characteristics of 'mass service', it is essentially a 'service factory' (cf. Schmenner 1986; Wemmerlöv 1990).

2. For professional services, one team had not received a lean score, but our discussions with managers in this team and the headquarters indicate that the scores would be similar to the other team from the UK.

3. Daily performance dialogues are short daily meetings that increase awareness of the current status and eventual problems that must be solved. They are also known as 'huddles', 'shop-floor meetings', or 'daily layered accountability' in the lean literature.

Acknowledgements

The authors thank Energy Co and its employees in Germany, Romania, and the UK for their cooperation during this project. We acknowledge financial support from Energy Co covering travel expenses for interviews.

Appendices

Appendix A: Common lean service practices

Table 4 Analysis and categorisation of Gupta et al.'s (2016) summary of lean practices across 32 peer-reviewed lean service articles

Lean service practice	Other terms used	Mentions*	Ops	Mngm	Cult
Process mapping	Value stream mapping; Process-based view	23	x	7	8
Continuous improvement practices	Kaizen / Rapid Improvement Events; Problem solving (e.g. PDCA; A3)	19	9	10	x
Process standardisation	Standardisation	17	x	11	12
Pull production	Flow; Just in time; Cellular	14	x	13	14

Lean service practice	Other terms used	Mentions*	Ops	Mngm	Cult
	production; Layout; Single-piece flow				
Customer orientation	Voice of the customer; Value (for the customer)	11	15	16	x
Visualisation	Visual management	8	17	x	18
Employees involvement	Employees empowerment; Employees engagement; Respect for workers	8	19	20	x
Waste reduction	Waste; Elimination of non-value-add	7	x	21	22
Process capability	Process simplification; Poka yoke (error prevention); Quality control	7	x	23	24
Workload balancing	'Jidoka'; Line balancing; 'Takt time'; Resource planning	6	x	25	26
Training and skill management	Training; Shared learning; Cross-skilling; Employee development	6	27	x	28
Workplace organisation	'5S', '6S'	5	x	29	30
Performance management	Communication; Daily meetings; Visual control board	5	31	x	32
Hands-on management	'Go to gemba'; Early triage (hospitals)	4	33	x	34
Supporting organisation structure	Team	3	35	x	36

Ops Operations system, *Mngm* Management system, *Cult* Culture system
* Only items mentioned three or more times are included

Appendix B: Interviewee profiles

Table 5 Interviewee profiles and interview details

No.	Interviewee	No of years in this role	Location	Service type	Duration (min)	Interview location
1	Team leader power grid	14	Germany	Professional services	24	Online

No.	Interviewee	No of years in this role	Location	Service type	Duration (min)	Interview location
2	Lean coach power grids	2	Germany	Professional services	45	Online
3	Team leader network distribution field services	22	Romania	Professional services	31	Onsite
4	Team member network distribution field services	12	Romania	Professional services	28	Onsite
5	Team member network distribution field services	28	Romania	Professional services	31	Onsite
6	Lean coach	3	Romania	Professional services	42	Online
7	Section manager B2B field services	1	England	Professional services	34	Onsite
8	Team member metering	7	England	Professional services	53	Onsite
9	Team leader metering	14	England	Professional services	38	Onsite
10	Lean coach field operations	3	England	Professional services	44	Online
11	Team leader new connections	18	England	Service shop	49	Online
12	Lean coach for corporate sales	2	England	Service shop	56	Onsite
13	Director field operations support services	1	England	Service shop	39	Online
14	Team leader power grid analysis and calculations	12	Germany	Service shop	68	Online
15	Team member power grid analysis and calculation	27	Germany	Service shop	56	Online
16	Lean coach grid and technical support services	2	Germany	Service shop	52	Online
17	Team leader special technical operational services	3	Romania	Service shop	28	Onsite
18	Team member	20	Romania	Service shop	29	Onsite
19	Team leader	32	Romania	Service shop	36	Onsite

No.	Interviewee	No of years in this role	Location	Service type	Duration (min)	Interview location
20	Team member special technical operational services	10	Romania	Service shop	25	Onsite
21	Team leader call centre	5	Germany	Service factory	49	Online
22	Lean coach	2	Germany	Service factory	46	Online
23	Lean coach	3	Germany	Service factory	53	Online
24	Lean coach	2	Germany	Service factory	48	Online
25	Team leader call centre	10	Romania	Service factory	30	Onsite
26	Call agent call centre	2	Romania	Service factory	28	Onsite
27	Senior lean coach	4	Romania	Service factory	66	Online
28	Team leader	20	Romania	Service factory	40	Online
29	Call agent call centre	1	Romania	Service factory	29	Onsite
30	Section manager call centre	30	England	Service factory	31	Onsite
31	Team manager call centre	10	England	Service factory	38	Onsite
32	Lean coach customer care	1	England	Service factory	59	Onsite
33	Team leader call centre	4	Germany	Service factory	35	Online
34	Section manager residential billing	10	England	Service factory	39	Onsite
35	Team member billing	14	England	Service factory	46	Onsite
36	Lean coach	1	England	Service factory	61	Onsite
37	Senior VP Lean (HQ)	6	Germany	N/A	36	Onsite
38	VP Lean Delivery Manager	6	Germany	N/A	33	Onsite

No.	Interviewee	No of years in this role	Location	Service type	Duration (min)	Interview location
	(HQ)					
39	VP Lean Delivery Manager (HQ)	3	Germany	N/A	47	Onsite
40	VP Lean Development Manager (HQ)	4	Germany	N/A	42	Online
41	Corporate Lean Manager (HQ)	3	Germany	N/A	46	Onsite
42	Corporate Lean Manager (HQ)	2	Germany	N/A	41	Onsite
43	Corporate Senior Lean Manager (HQ)	3	Germany	N/A	62	Onsite
44	Corporate Senior Lean Manager (HQ)	7	Germany	N/A	73	Onsite
45	Corporate Lean Manager (HQ)	1	Germany	N/A	52	Online
46	Corporate Senior Lean Manager (HQ)	4	Germany	N/A	19	Onsite
47	Corporate Senior Lean Manager (HQ)	3	Germany	N/A	16	Onsite

Appendix C: Interview guide for the team-level

Interviewee data

1. Name and contact information
2. Background, education, career
3. Position, role and experience in case company

Questions

General understanding of Energy Co.'s Lean Programme (ELP) in unit

1. What is ELP, as you understand it?
2. Please describe the implications of ELP in your unit.
3. What does ELP not cover?
4. Has your work changed since the implementation of the ELP programme? If yes, how?
5. Have you had something similar before ELP?

Competitive advantage and fit

6. What do you see as the pros and cons of ELP?

7. Where do you see the benefit of ELP on the corporate level and on the individual level? How does ELP contribute to a competitive advantage for your unit?

8. What did you achieve/not achieve by means of ELP?

9. Which ELP principles and tools do you find useful to apply to your type of business?

10. Which ELP principles and tools do you not find applicable to your type of business?

Implementation

11. Is ELP part of your daily business routine? If not, please explain.

12. How do you get others enthusiastic about ELP?

13. Which outcome do you expect from ELP?

Measurement and assessment

14. How do you measure and assess ELP guidelines and principles?

15. Which ELP guidelines and principles do you find harder to measure? Which are easier?

16. Which ELP areas do you/your team perform best? Which do you perform worst?

17. Are you satisfied with the ELP audit results of your team?

Acceptance

18. Do you find it easy to adapt to the ELP culture and guidelines? Please specify.

19. Do you experience any ELP resistance? Please quantify.

20. How do you mitigate the resistance?

Closure

21. [Additional questions relating to earlier quotes or findings]

22. [Any further comments]

Appendix D: Interview guide for the headquarters

Interviewee data

- Name and contact information
- Background, education, career

- Position, role and experience in case company

Questions

1. How do the local units in your area of responsibility adopt lean practices?
2. Do the locally applied practices differ from the intended practices? If yes, why and how do they differ?
3. How do you ensure sufficient local support and engagement?
4. Which lean practices are well adopted in your area of responsibility?
5. Which lean practices are not well adopted in your area of responsibility?
6. How could lean be improved in your area of responsibility?
7. What is the local commitment level for lean: low, medium or high?

Closure

8. [Additional questions relating to earlier quotes or findings]
9. [Any further comments]

Appendix E: Qualitative data reduction analysis (examples)

Table 6 Qualitative analysis: adoption and adaptation of lean service practices across different service types

Panel A. Operational lean service practices			
Exemplary quotes	**Service type**	**Practice**	**Response**
'Working standards and process documentation has put everybody on a standard... prior to that, we failed.'	Professional services	Standard working environment	High fit ➜ Adoption
'If we did 5S at my colleagues' desks, then we would interfere quite heavily with their individual privacy.'	Professional services	Standard working environment	Low fit ➜ Adaptation
'It is the endless process maps which are thrown at your face. I just don't know why we are doing that... they oppress us with this.'	Professional services	Process optimisation	Low fit ➜ Adaptation
'Lean standardises our responses and provides a clear working procedure for the different customer requests.'	Service shop	Standard working environment	High fit ➜ Adoption
'We have got, within that area, very, very experienced people. When you suddenly gave them a guide that said, 'You must follow these	Service shop	Process optimisation	Low fit ➜ Adaptation

Panel A. Operational lean service practices			
Exemplary quotes	**Service type**	**Practice**	**Response**
steps'. It was almost like, 'Who do you think you are? I know better. I have done this for 20 years.''			
'5S and working standards are clearly our strengths... we were already on a good standard... we are actually super at this. We are very well-organised people'	Service factory	Standard working environment	High fit ➔ Adoption
'Customer guides are more a consistent approach... everybody is doing the same thing when dealing with the customer.'	Service factory	Process optimisation	High fit ➔ Adoption
'We achieved more structure in our team and could discuss certain topics a lot easier as we had everything documented. It was hard work at first but worthwhile as it shortened our processing and communication times significantly... everyone got involved. An increased motivation followed instantly.'	Service factory	Process optimisation	High fit ➔ Adoption
Panel B. Managerial lean service practices			
Exemplary quotes	**Service type**	**Practice**	**Response**
'It is the technology in certain cases that don't support even a virtual performance dialogue.'	Professional services	Performance management	Low fit ➔ Adaptation
'The fact that it goes across the board gives you transferable skills you can take into lots of other areas. There are so many benefits. It is that we are all working in the same way.'	Service shop	Performance management	High fit ➔ Adoption
'Some of that is difficult because we don't have the measures... It's just the MI we have available... Sometimes what worked for an area doesn't work for another one, but you have to go with it.'	Service factory	Performance management	Low fit ➔ Adaptation
'If we know we've got a problem, we can't walk out there right now and grab eight people and go straight to problem-solving because then the customers would be waiting.'	Service factory	Performance management	Low fit ➔ Adaptation
'They are not measuring the right KPIs. They are not making their problems visible in order to problem solve them.'	Service factory	Performance management	Low fit ➔ Adaptation

Panel C. Cultural lean service practices			
Exemplary quotes	**Service type**	**Practice**	**Response**
'How often they should be seeing their team... It is probably up to 50% of their time spent doing go-and-sees.'	Professional services	Leadership	Low fit → Adaptation
'I as a manager see no need for leadership involvement in problem-solving sessions... it simply does not suit our way of working... my colleagues are very independent.'	Service factory	Leadership	Low fit → Adaptation
'The lean programme does not affect leadership and motivation of employees... we have no influence on the leadership style managers apply.'	Service shop	Leadership	Low fit → Adaptation
'The biggest weakness across our team is leadership... it is hard to measure qualitatively.'	Professional services	Leadership	Low fit → Adaptation

References

Allway M, Corbett S (2002) Shifting to lean service: Stealing a page from manufacturers' playbooks. J Organ Excell 21(2):45–54

Alves AC, Flumerfelt S, Kahlen F-J (2016) Lean education: An overview of current issues. Springer

Ansari S, Reinecke J, Spaan A (2014) How are practices made to vary? Managing practice adaptation in a multinational corporation. Organ Stud 35(9):1313–1341

Ansari SM, Fiss PC, Zajac EJ (2010) Made to fit: How practices vary as they diffuse. Academy Management Review 35(1):67–91

Bateman N, Radnor Z, Glennon R (2018) The landscape of Lean across public services. Taylor & Francis, pp. 1–4

Bowen DE, Youngdahl WE (1998) "Lean" service: in defense of a production-line approach. Int J Serv Ind Manag 9(3):207–225

Chase RB (1978) Where does the customer fit in a service operation? Harv Bus Rev 56(6):137–142

Cook DP, Goh CH, Chung CH (1999) Service typologies: a state of the art survey. Prod Oper Manag 8(3):318–338

Cusumano MA, Holweg M, Howell J, Netland T, Shah R, Shook J, Ward P, Womack J (2021) Commentaries on "The Lenses of Lean." J Oper Manag 67(5):627–639

Dal Pont G, Furlan A, Vinelli A (2008) Interrelationships among lean bundles and their effects on operational performance. Oper Manag Res 1(2):150–158

Danese P, Manfè V, Romano P (2018) A systematic literature review on recent lean research: State-of-the-art and future directions. Int J Manag Rev 20(2):579–605

DeHoratius N, Rabinovich E (2011) Field research in operations and supply chain management. J Oper Manag 29(5):371–375

Donaldson L (1987) Strategy and structural adjustment to regain fit and performance: in defence of contingency theory. J Manag Stud 24(1):1–24

Donaldson L (2001) The contingency theory of organizations. Sage, Thousand Oaks, Calif

Drazin R, Van de Ven AH (1985) Alternative forms of fit in contingency theory. Adm Sci Q 30(4):514–539

Eisenhardt KM (1989) Building theories from case study research. Acad Manag Rev 14(4):532–550

Fenner SV, Arellano MC, von Dzengelevski O, Netland TH (2022) Effect of lean implementation on team psychological safety and learning. International Journal of Operations & Production Management, Vol. ahead-of-print, No. ahead-of-print

Flick U (2014) An introduction to qualitative research. SAGE Publications

Found P, Bicheno J (2016) Lean production. In: Netland TH, Powell DJ (eds) The Routledge Companion to Lean Management. Routledge, New York, pp 23–33

Frenkel S, Donoghue L (1996) Call centres and service excellence: Design and management challenges to support a service excellence strategy: A knowledge worker case study. Cent Corp Chang Aust Grad School Manag

Gilmore A (2001) Call centre management: is service quality a priority? Manag Serv Qual Int J 11(3):153–159

Gupta S, Sharma M, Sunder M, V. (2016) Lean services: a systematic review. Int J Product Perform Manag 65(8):1025–1056

Hadid W, Mansouri SA, Gallear D (2016) Is lean service promising? A socio-technical perspective. Int J Oper Prod Manag 36(6):618–642

Holweg M, Staats BR, Upton DM (2018) Making process improvements stick. Harvard Business Review, No. November-December, pp. 16–18

Hudson A (2011) Are call centres the factories of the 21st Century? BBC, bbc.com

Johnston R, Clark G (2008) Service operations management: Improving service delivery. Pearson Education

Kellogg DL, Nie W (1995) A framework for strategic service management. J Oper Manag 13(4):323–337

LaGanga LR (2011) Lean service operations: Reflections and new directions for capacity expansion in outpatient clinics. J Oper Manag 29(5):422–433

Langabeer JR, DelliFraine JL, Heineke J, Abbass I (2009) Implementation of Lean and Six Sigma quality initiatives in hospitals: A goal theoretic perspective. Oper Manag Res 2(1):13–27

Lawrence P, Lorsch J (2015) Contingency theory of organizations—differentiation and integration. Organizational Behavior 2. Routledge, pp. 244–270

Leite HDR, Vieira GE (2015) Lean philosophy and its applications in the service industry: a review of the current knowledge. Production 25(3):529–541

Liker JK, Ross K (2017) The Toyota way to service excellence: lean transformation in service organizations. McGraw-Hill Education, New York

McCann L, Hassard JS, Granter E, Hyde PJ (2015) Casting the lean spell: The promotion, dilution and erosion of lean management in the NHS. Hum Relat 68(10):1557–1577

McDermott CM, Venditti FJ (2015) Implementing lean in knowledge work: Implications from a study of the hospital discharge planning process. Oper Manag Res 8(3):118–130

Meredith JO, Grove AL, Walley P, Young F, Macintyre MB (2011) Are we operating effectively? A lean analysis of operating theatre changeovers. Oper Manag Res 4(3):89

Miles MB, Huberman AM, Saldana J (2014) Qualitative data analysis: a method sourcebook. Sage Publications, USA, CA, p 91320

Netland T (2013) Exploring the phenomenon of company-specific production systems: One-best-way or own-best-way? Int J Prod Res 51(4):1084–1097

Netland TH (2016) Critical success factors for implementing lean production: the effect of contingencies. Int J Prod Res 54(8):2433–2448

Netland TH, Aspelund A (2014) Multi-plant improvement programmes: A literature review and research agenda. Int J Oper Prod Manag 34(3):390–418

Netland TH, Powell DJ (2016) The Routledge companion to lean management. Taylor & Francis, New York

Onofrei G, Prester J (2019) The relationship between investments in lean practices and operational performance. Int J Oper Prod Manag 39(3):406–428

Patton MQ (2014) Qualitative research & evaluation methods, 4th edn. SAGE Publications, USA

Peng DX, Schroeder RG, Shah R (2011) Competitive priorities, plant improvement and innovation capabilities, and operational performance. Int J Oper Prod Manag 31(5):484–510

Piercy N, Rich N (2009) Lean transformation in the pure service environment: the case of the call service centre. Int J Oper Prod Manag 29(1):54–76

Poksinska BB, Fialkowska-Filipek M, Engström J (2017) Does Lean healthcare improve patient satisfaction? A mixed-method investigation into primary care. BMJ Qual Saf 26(2):95–103

Ponsignon F, Smart PA, Maull RS (2011) Service delivery system design: characteristics and contingencies. Int J Oper Prod Manag 31(3):324–349

Radnor Z (2010) Transferring lean into government. J Manuf Technol Manag 21(3):411–428

Rauch E, Matt DT, Linder C (2020) Lean management in hospitality: methods, applications and future directions. Int J Serv Oper Manag 36(3):303–326

Safizadeh MH, Field JM, Ritzman LP (2003) An empirical analysis of financial services processes with a front-office or back-office orientation. J Oper Manag 21(5):557–576

Saldaña J (2015) The coding manual for qualitative researchers. SAGE Publications, London, UK

Schmenner RW (1986) How can service businesses survive and prosper. Sloan Manag Rev 27(3):21–32

Scholz RW, Tietje O (2002) Embedded case study methods: Integrating quantitative and qualitative knowledge. Sage

Secchi R, Camuffo A (2019) Lean implementation failures: the role of organizational ambidexterity. Int J Prod Econ 210:145–154

Seddon J (2019) Freedom from command and control: Rethinking management for lean service. Product Press

Shah R, Goldstein SM, Unger BT, Henry TD (2008) Explaining anomalous high performance in a health care supply chain. Decis Sci 39(4):759–789

Shah R, Ward PT (2003) Lean manufacturing: context, practice bundles, and performance. J Oper Manag 21(2):129–149

Shostack GL (1982) How to design a service. Eur J Mark 16(1):49–63

Shostack GL (1987) Service positioning through structural change. J Mark 34–43

Silvestro R, Fitzgerald L, Johnston R, Voss C (1992) Towards a classification of service processes. Int J Serv Ind Manag 3(3):62–75

Sousa R, Voss CA (2008) Contingency research in operations management practices. J Oper Manag 26(6):697–713

Staats BR, Brunner DJ, Upton DM (2011) Lean principles, learning, and knowledge work: Evidence from a software services provider. J Oper Manag 29(5):376–390

Tay HL, Singh PJ, Bhakoo V, Al-Balushi S (2017) Contextual factors: assessing their influence on flow or resource efficiency orientations in healthcare lean projects. Oper Manag Res 10(3):118–136

Thomas DR (1978) Strategy is different in service businesses. Harv Bus Rev 56(4):158–165

Tortorella G, van Dun DH, de Almeida AG (2019) Leadership behaviors during lean healthcare implementation: a review and longitudinal study. J Manuf Technol Manag

Vanichchinchai A (2021) Assessing lean satisfaction and its enablers: a care provider perspective. Oper Manag Res 14(1):95–106

Victorino L, Field JM, Buell RW, Dixon MJ, Meyer Goldstein S, Menor LJ, Pullman ME, Roth AV, Secchi E, Zhang JJ (2018) Service operations: what have we learned? J Serv Manag 29(1):39–54

Volberda HW, van der Weerdt N, Verwaal E, Stienstra M, Verdu AJ (2012) Contingency fit, institutional fit, and firm performance: A metafit approach to organization–environment relationships. Organ Sci 23(4):1040–1054

Voss C, Tsikriktsis N, Frohlich M (2002) Case research in operations management. Int J Oper Prod Manag 22(2):195–219

Wemmerlöv U (1990) A taxonomy for service processes and its implications for system design. Int J Serv Ind Manag 1(3):20–40

Yin RK (2013) Case study research: Design and methods, 5th edn. SAGE Publications, California, USA

3

Big Data Analytics Applications in Information Management Driving Operational Efficiencies and Decision-Making

Mapping the Field of Knowledge with Bibliometric Analysis Using R

Konstantina Ragazou[1, 2], Ioannis Passas[3], Alexandros Garefalakis[3], Emilios Galariotis[4] and Constantin Zopounidis[5]

[1]*Department of Accounting and Finance, University of Western Macedonia, GR50100 Kozani, Greece*
[2]*Department of Business Administration, Neapolis University Pafos, Pafos 8042, Cyprus*
[3]*Department of Business Administration and Tourism, Hellenic Mediterranean University, GR71410 Heraklion, Greece*
[4]*Department of Finance, Audencia Business School, 44300 Nantes, France*
[5]*The Financial Engineering Laboratory, Technical University of Crete, GR73100 Chania, Greece*

Abstract

Organizations may examine both past and present data with the aid of information management, giving them access to all the knowledge they need to make sound strategic choices. For the majority of contemporary enterprises, using data to make relevant, valid, and timely choices has become a must for success. The volume and format of data have changed significantly over the past few years as a result of the development of new technologies and applications, but there are also impressive possibilities for their analysis and processing. This study offers a bibliometric analysis of 650 publications written by 1977 academics on the use of information management and big data analytics. The Bibliometrix function in the R package and VOSviewer program were used to obtain the bibliographic data from the Scopus database and to analyze it. Based on citation analysis criteria, the top research journals, authors, and organizations were identified. The cooperation network at the author level reveals the connections between academics throughout the world, and Multiple Correspondence Analysis (MCA) identifies the research holes in the area. The recommendations for further study are influenced by the findings.

Keywords: *agile management; business model; data analytics; decision-making; efficiency; information management; operational performance; SMEs*

1. Introduction

The corporate climate might be characterized as sumptuous in terms of novel prospects and chances, as well as challenges brought on by the recent COVID-19 crisis. The modernization of administrative procedures and the enhancement of decision-making processes have been essential for businesses to properly address these new issues [1,2,3]. Thorough insights into the environment, the business, and the timely implementation of crucial information are prerequisites for making better judgments; however, many academics throughout the world concur that one of an organization's most significant assets is information. The aforementioned explains why information management (IM) has lately been the focus of attention in the corporate sector [4,5].

Information management (IM) is a strategy used by organizations to maximize the efficiency with which they plan, gather, organize, use, control, store, distribute, and dispose of their information. It also ensures that the information's value is recognized and fully used [6]. Additionally, IM allows a company to learn, assess circumstances and events, forecast trends and upcoming occurrences, and innovate [7]. The gathered data is converted into knowledge that the administrative team uses to take suitable actions, enabling the development and successful completion of business objectives. Systems used by IM are specialized data systems that offer reliable information. The data used to create the information is qualitative and aggregated, and it is analyzed using software. The capabilities of these systems, which enable speedier information access, simpler system querying and report creation, enhanced data analysis, and improved data quality, are responsible for the improvement in information quality [7].

The services that may be offered that are connected to information management are changing as a result of advances in software and modern technology. Since improper data organization will undoubtedly result in higher costs and inadequate business alignment, the overall architecture and organizing principles are more crucial. In the last several years, there has been a great increase in the use of big data and analytical technologies as firms have brought more data under management and done more with that data through analytical discovery. Big data is a phrase typically used to describe data sets that are too big to be efficiently acquired, managed, and handled by widely used software solutions. A new class of technologies and techniques to address it have emerged as a result of the sheer bulk of the data, complexity of analysis, and economic necessity to produce value from it [8,9,10]. Descriptive, predictive, and prescriptive analytical techniques, as well as data-mining technologies, have become well-known in business analytics along with advancements in data creation and administration. As a result, the variety of applications used by enterprises to handle their information positively enhances operational effectiveness and productivity [11].

Business operations at several levels, including supply chain management, risk management, product management, and financial controls, can be facilitated by IM and big data. When applied to the supply chain, for instance, IM and big data techniques can offer data on inventory levels and costs difficulties at various points throughout the chain. Customer satisfaction is assured, and the proper administration of revenues and costs is carried out [12]. Moreover, all the actions that organizations make entail some level of risk, therefore IM can offer the tools that allow for a better assessment of these risks by analyzing past data and developing customer "risk profiles" against which to analyze potential new clients. According to the logic of product management, one of the main goals of businesses in the product manufacturing industry is to cut production times so that their products can keep up with consumer demand. Profits quickly grow as a result of doing this. At this stage, IM and big data provide precise and prompt feedback on the degree of the product-related decisions' success. Financial controls are also crucial for a corporation, to summarize [13]. In order to increase profit margins and decrease expenses, IM and big data might be used. The quantity of items, customers, and geographical regions that are lucrative for the firm are identified using extensive information about every aspect of corporate operations. All things considered, the aforementioned benefits of IM may guarantee firms a simple boost in their productivity and operational effectiveness.

Nevertheless, none of the academics, scholars, or practitioners have applied a bibliometric analysis in the context of the investigation of the relationship between big data analytics and management phenomena, specifically information management and the decision-making process. Only the contribution of big data analytics to the transition of businesses to big data analytics and firm resources, capabilities, and performance has been briefly discussed in the scientific article, entitled "A bibliometric analysis of research on big data analytics for business and management" by Ardito et al. The above research paper was one of the first attempts to comprehend the research streams which, over time, have paved the way to the intersection between big data analytics and management fields [14]. Therefore, the goal of this study was to demonstrate, for the first time through bibliometric analysis, how the incorporation of big data analytics has changed the academic field of information management in the digital era. Simply, this study aims to illustrate how information management has changed as a result of the incorporation of big data analytics and to demonstrate how these two concepts—information management and big data analytics—help businesses become more operationally efficient and improve their decision-making processes [4]. The investigation of information management and big data analytics as a self-sufficient research topic and the presentation of the key journals, organizations, and authors in the field under study were conducted using a six-step methodological approach that is based on bibliometric analysis. The results of the bibliometric analysis aid in mapping the theoretical underpinnings of the subject area and suggest potential directions for future study. Additionally, bibliometric analysis demonstrated the global network of author collaboration while outlining and examining the research clusters that have evolved in the field under study. Additionally, as was already noted, the last phase involved integrating the results and moving forward with suggestions for additional research. As previously noted, 650 articles' worth of bibliographic information were taken from the Scopus database from the years 2013 to 2022 and examined using the Bibliometrix function in the R package and the VOSviewer program.

The rest of this study is organized as follows. The review of the literature is presented in Section 2. The materials and methods used are described in Section 3. The bibliometric analysis and results are presented in Section 4, and the discussion of the results, a list of restrictions, suggestions for further study, and a conclusion are all presented in Section 5.

2. Big Data Analytics and Information Management for Operational Effectiveness and Decision-Making

We are currently living in cutting-edge information ecosystems built on big data. Organizations are searching for ways to efficiently collect and analyze information to provide valuable information for better information management. Information is key in computer science, management, accounting, and decision sciences. Information can refer to "any news that is transferred from one system to another or describing what happened or did not happen or used as a tool for the investigation of a phenomenon or a set of phenomena" [15,16]. Creating information begins with collecting facts and primary data. Subsequently, these data are processed and analyzed appropriately and used in decision-making and problem-solving [15]. A dynamic business model used by companies in the last decade for information management, especially in the accounting field, is that of the Accounting Information System (AIS) [17]. The AIS, like all information systems, registers, collects, stores, and processes data of accounting interest to provide information to the executives of businesses and proceed to a rational decision-making process. The complex information from a quantity and value invoice that indicates an accounting event is transformed by the AIS into information and knowledge that will be processed and reproduced to spread messages that can ensure the viability of the business [18]. The functions of AIS are: (i) the transformation of data into information such as the classification, calculation, grouping, and comparison of data in order to provide appropriate and valuable information to the executives of the company, as well as third parties who are interested in it, (ii) the promotion and reliability of necessary controls in order to protect the company's assets from risks and external threats, and (iii) the accuracy and control of information [19].

Moreover, Enterprise Resource Planning (ERP) systems are integrated information systems that aim to support all business activities [20]. These systems integrate all the important activities of the business as well as all the processes in a central control system, providing an overall picture of the operation of the business. In the 1970s, we saw the emergence of Material Requirement Planning (MRP) systems based on the concept of planning production. In the following decade, MRP systems which included other functions such as production and distribution were developed. The integration they incorporated made them particularly attractive to other functions and thus gradually spread their influence into finance, human resources, and project management. MRP II, therefore, gradually evolved into ERP systems [21,22]. The utility and power of ERP systems lie beyond the functional limits of MRP II. Today ERP systems play an important role in supporting business activities as they automate business operations and unify business processes through a common database. The flow of an ERP system consists of functional programs (functional modules), allowing the company to install only those it deems necessary. An ERP system provides the ability to support and organize information related to the following business activities: (i) finance and accounting, (ii) management, (iii) human resources, (iv) production planning, (v) workflow management, (vi) inventory and materials management, and (vii) purchasing management [23].

The Paris Industrial Exhibition in 1801 is where the history of information management can be found. Punch cards were invented there by Joseph Marie Charles Jacquard. These cards, which were used in weaving machines to create detailed patterns in cloth, were comparable to the punch cards used by computers for most of the 20th century. The origins of management information systems might be disputed, even though the history of IM can be broken down into five distinct periods (Figure 1).

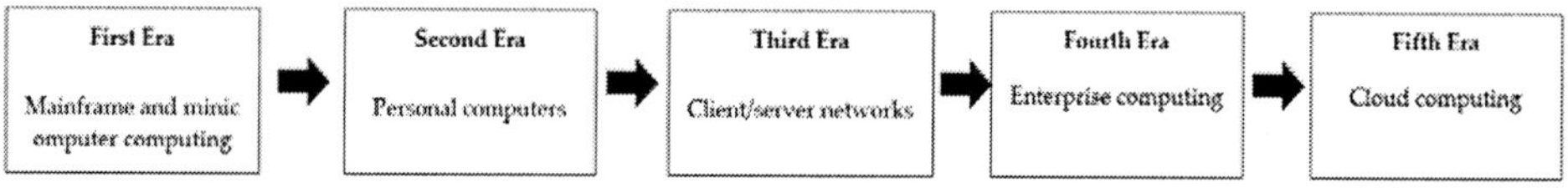

Figure 1. *Timeline of information management.*

However, recent studies have received a lot of traction to help businesses navigate the numerous organizational and technological opportunities and difficulties that come with using big data analytics (BDA) and information management (Figure 2). BDA, often described as a firm's capacity to handle, process, and analyze big data, is becoming a popular topic among academics and in information management. The benefits of BDA within organizations are being highlighted in a rapidly growing body of literature. For instance, Hagel (2015) demonstrated how BDA is rapidly becoming an important part of decision-making processes in many types of enterprises, as a part of a new proactive and forward-looking attitude [24]. The value that may be derived from data, though, partly depends on the effectiveness of the many procedures used to gather and analyze the data. Numerous participants from various disciplines, as well as various procedures and techniques, are frequently needed for this [25,26]. Managers must coordinate the organizational culture and competencies already in place throughout the whole organization in order to fully benefit from big data. The primary difficulty in utilizing big data, according to Barton and Court (2012), is ensuring that all employees can trust and comprehend it [27]. They served as an example of how front-line workers in the retail sector were hesitant to embrace big data because they either did not rely on a big-data-based model or were unable to comprehend how it worked. Shah et al. (2012), for instance, stated that business analytics knowledge is still restricted to the "expert" level and has not yet been shared throughout organizations [28]. Although, in order to maximize the benefits of using big data, it is imperative that all levels of employees are knowledgeable about big data, which can be achieved through training. Without the ability of staff members at all levels to comprehend and use data in their decision-making, the return on investment in big data will not materialize.

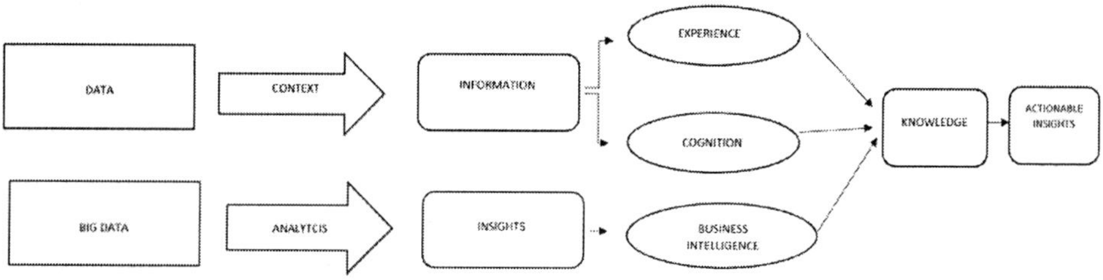

Figure 2. *The convergence of information management and big data analytics.*

Consequently, the new decision-making process brought about by big data analysis results in a shift in how choices are made and by whom. It made sense to delegate the task to well-positioned individuals up until this point, without taking into account the information provided by big data, because these individuals typically base their decisions on patterns and relationships they have noticed, as well as experience they have gained through their careers. The decision-maker and the so-called highest-paid person's opinions will lose value as a result of the shift brought on by big data because of its analytical knowledge [29]. In essence, managers may focus on more successful interventions in areas where gut instinct and intuition have previously reigned rather than facts and rigor. By developing the habit of asking, "What do the data say?" executive managers may make decisions based on big data. Despite this, some researchers believe that just two in three corporate executives have confidence in the data they use to make choices. Therefore, "if information is not of adequate quality by the time it has been merged with other data and information, a spurious correlation might result in the company making an inaccurate interpretation of a business opportunity" [25,30].

Moreover, according to Yiu (2012), BDA enables more inventive methods to organize, learn, and develop as well as better data-driven decision-making. This leads to better management of various company operations, such as CRM, operational risks, and production efficiency, which improves performance. Information management (IM) and resource-based view (RBV) research from the past have demonstrated that an organization's capacity to process information has a favorable impact on company performance, such as improved profitability or return on investment [31]. Organizational capacities may comprise practices and skills for converting knowledge inputs into more valuable outputs. The capacity of an organization to gather, prepare, and analyze massive data might therefore make a difference, especially if the organization makes these procedures challenging to mimic due to quirks or route dependence effects. Businesses should integrate and utilize a variety of firm-level resources and competencies in order to gain a competitive edge. Big data is not enough in this scenario to develop BDA skills [32]. Therefore, in order to develop these superior, uncommon, and difficult-to-imitate capabilities, a complex interrelationship between various financial, human, physical, and organizational resources is necessary. This leads to better performances, such as improved customer retention or return on investment, as well as an increase in sales growth and profitability.

Finally, information management may be set up and managed to improve the performance of the organization through efficient action. The three recognized primary IM processes are information gathering, conversion, and application. Information conversion refers to making the gathered information valuable for the organization by arranging it or turning it into explicit information. Information acquisition is the procedure utilized to produce new knowledge from the received data [33]. Accordingly, IM encompasses the company's procedures for gathering new information, transforming it into a form that can be used and easily accessed, and using this information throughout the organization to affect firm performance. In order to increase customer happiness, market share, and financial success, businesses can use information management (IM) techniques to efficiently collect, store, and transmit information [34].

3. Materials and Methods

As it enables them to manage huge amounts of data and provide a high level of research impact, bibliometric analysis is a widely accepted study approach among academics and researchers throughout the world. Using a set of criteria to examine and classify the articles, this approach seeks to categorize the published materials in a study field [35]. With regard to the current study, we based our analysis on Bibliometrix, which provides all the resources necessary to carry out a comprehensive bibliometric analysis in accordance with the Science Mapping Workflow. Its reputation is founded on a number of attributes, such as the creation, availability, and use of a large number of bibliometric tools included in the R package, a computer language used for statistical computation and graphics. The R package and its software-based bibliometric application, Biblioshiny, were both utilized. Acquiring the data from the Scopus bibliographic database was the initial stage in the R process. The data was then uploaded into R studio, which is the R environment that aids in performing the analysis on the study topic and exporting dynamic graphics [35,36,37].

3.1. Bibliometric Analysis Method

The research issue for the current study was addressed using a six-step bibliometric methodological approach (Figure 3). The information gathered through a thorough literature study is referred to as Step 1. Step 2 is divided into two sections: the first (2a) focuses on a thorough evaluation of the field through bibliometric citation analysis, and the second (2b) presents a network analysis to identify the research trends of the publications of the most influential journals, research works, institutions, and authors, with the goal of highlighting the network of collaboration between scholars around the world. Content analysis is demonstrated in Step 3, while bibliographic coupling analysis is presented in Step 4. Moreover, cluster analysis is illustrated in Step 5 and combines MCA and factorial analysis. Finally, the results and potential future study areas are presented and discussed in Step 6.

In order to: (i) test Lotka's law; (ii) illustrate an overview of the research trends; (iii) find the most pertinent journals and articles, as well as the most influential authors globally; (iv) illustrate the thematic map; and (v) develop the collaboration world map, various bibliometric citation analysis measures were applied after retrieving the bibliographic data of 650 articles from the Scopus database [38]. Authors' frequency of publishing in the scientific literature is described by Lotka's law. Its main premise is that, while a sizable portion of authors only create one article, very few authors are very productive in any given topic area. According to Lotka's law, the number of authors who publish x number of articles is approximately $1/x^b$ of those who publish only one article [39,40]. Thus, a high b value highlights a higher degree of concentration of authors, and a low value indicates the absence of a specific group of authors in a particular scientific discipline. The general formula of Lotka's law is the following:

$$x^n * y = c \tag{1}$$

where c: a constant term,

y: relative frequency of authors with frequency x number of articles,

n: illustrates an exponent that is a constant for a given set of data,

x: indicates the number of the published articles.

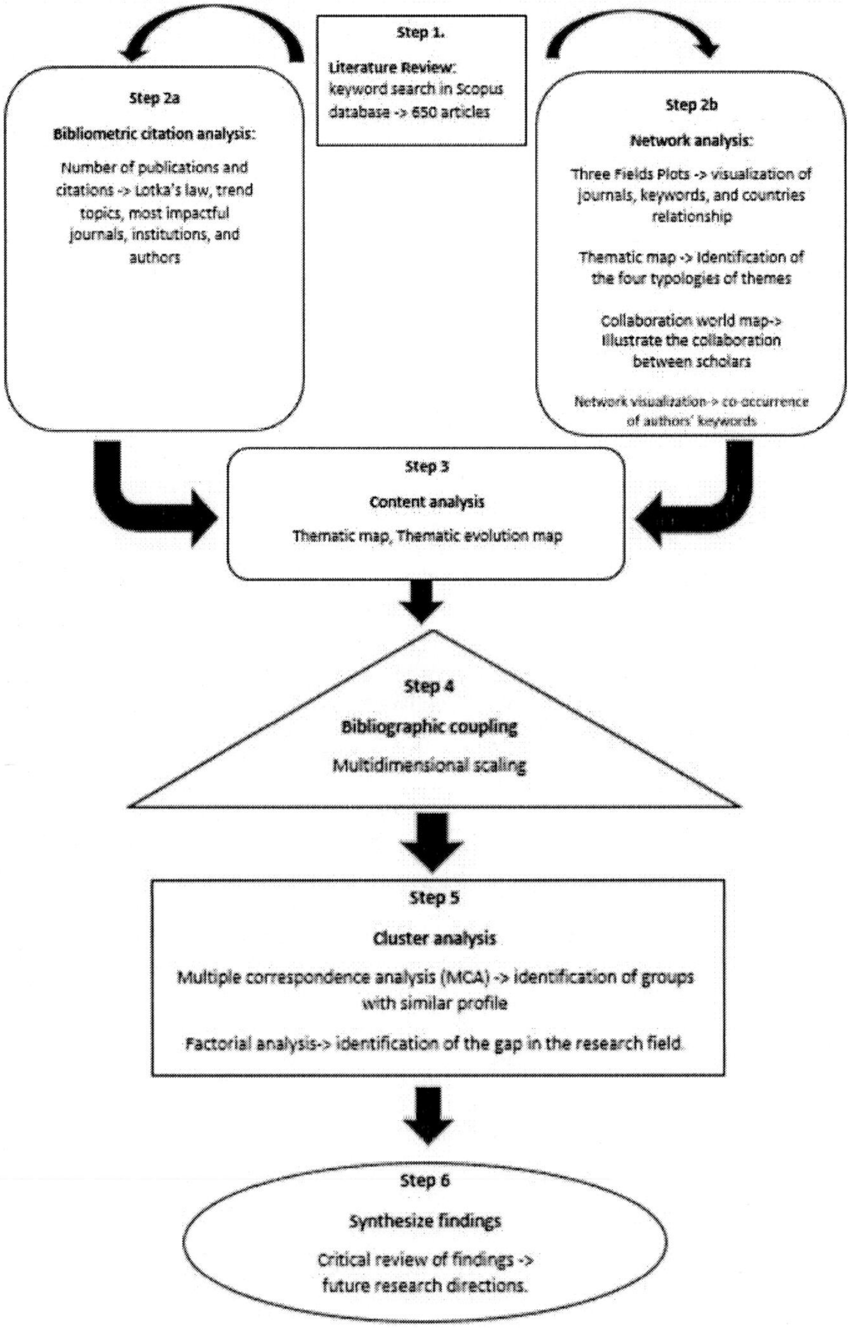

Figure 3. *Methodological workflow for bibliometric analysis.*

In addition to Lotka's law, a three-fields-plot based on a Sankey diagram has been developed and helped to illustrate the relationships between journals, keywords, and nations. Additionally, the underpinning research cluster was investigated, and a map of current research trends was created using the bibliographic coupling technique. The method of Multiple Correspondence Analysis (MCA), the major objective of which was to examine the bibliographic data and combine it into a collection of components, was finally implemented. Using this technique, authors may emphasize the research gap in a particular scientific field and summarize the bibliographic data.

3.2. Data Extraction

The well-known database Scopus served as the basis for this study's data collection for the bibliometric analysis. Elsevier established the Scopus database in 2004. It serves as a multidisciplinary repository for reports. It is one of the biggest "peer-reviewed" databases in the world, including more than 24,000 active academic journal titles on a variety of subjects with a high level of research interest, including life, social, and health sciences. More than 230,000 book titles and more than 10,000,000 conference papers are also included in Scopus [37,41]. Scopus has the fewest "inconsistencies" in content verification and quality compared to other academic-research databases (like Google Scholar or Web of Science). Accurate information is available through Web of Science and Google Scholar; however, they include double copies of certain citations, even triple copies in some situations. As a result, the same information can appear in a large number of reports, which results in erroneous statistics. Additionally, Scopus offers its customers access to online bibliometric analysis tools for their publications, including the h-index calculation and statistical analysis tools like frequency charts of publications over time and more.

While the key-word search is shown and thoroughly explained in Table 1, the bibliographic data were retrieved from Scopus in May 2022. In Step 10, a final keyword with four parts emerged. Big-data-analytics-related articles are contained in the first portion ("big data analytics" OR "big data" OR "data analytics"). The second portion ("information management") discusses big data analytics' important role in revolutionizing the information management industry. The third part of the formula ("operational performance" OR "operational productivity" OR "efficiency" OR "productivity") demonstrates the contribution of the transformation of information management with the use of big data analytics to the enhancement of operational performance. The fourth and final element of the Boolean function, "decision-making process", highlights the close connection between operational effectiveness, contemporary information management based on big data analytics, and the decision-making process. Thus, 650 papers were still available after research purification for evaluation and bibliometric analysis. Only articles were included in the chosen papers, hence all other document types have been disregarded (i.e., conference paper, review, book, book chapter, editorial). Additionally, only publications from the years 2013 to 2022 were chosen for the analysis. The following information was combined with the data from the bibliometric search: (i) the title of the paper, (ii) the date of publication, (iii) the main author details (name/s and affiliation/s), (iv) the title of the article, (v) the authors' keywords, (vi) the abstract, and (vii) the number of citations. The data was analyzed and presented using R Studio's Biblioshiny packages and VOSviewer [36,42]. Both tools provided graphs and maps, such as thematic maps, country cooperation maps, and network visualizations, that demonstrate the research scenario and the dynamics of the new model of information management, which improves the operational effectiveness of enterprises all over the world.

Table 1. Keyword search process in Scopus database.

Step	Keyword Search	Articles
1	"big data" AND "information management"	8902
2	"data analytics" AND "information management"	1865
3	"big data analytics" AND "information management"	802
4	"operational performance" AND "information management"	149
5	(("big data analytics" OR "big data" OR "data analytics") AND "information management" "operational performance")	901
6	(("big data analytics" OR "big data" OR "data analytics") AND "information management" AND ("operational performance" OR "operational productivity"))	902
7	(("big data analytics" OR "big data" OR "data analytics") AND "information management" AND ("operational performance" OR "operational productivity" OR "efficiency"))	1354
8	(("big data analytics" OR "big data" OR "data analytics") AND "information management" AND ("operational performance" OR "operational productivity" OR "efficiency" OR "productivity"))	1454
9	(("big data analytics" OR "big data" OR "data analytics") AND "information management" AND ("operational performance" OR "operational productivity" OR "efficiency" OR "productivity") AND "decision making")	3210
10	(("big data analytics" OR "big data" OR "data analytics") AND "information management" AND ("operational performance" OR "operational productivity" OR "efficiency" OR "productivity") AND ("decision making process") (LIMIT-TO (DOCTYPE, "ar"))	650

4. Results

This research aims to review the transformation of information management through big data analytics, which helps businesses improve their operational efficiency and decision-making processes globally. The reviewed sample includes 650 related studies that were published in the period 2013–2022. These documents were written by 1977 authors, with an average of 4.027 citations per document. Most of the authors (96.6% of the total sum) are part of multi-authored studies (1910 authors), while only 3.4% are single-authored studies (67 authors).

4.1. Information Management and Big Data Analytics: A Discrete Research Domain

Authors' scientific productivity (Table 2), calculated based on the theorem of Lotka's Law in information management and big data analytics research, shows that 1801 authors have produced only one scientific paper in the studied field. However, findings present that those two authors have contributed to a maximum of six published articles. Thus, information management and big data analytics and their contribution to the operational efficiency of businesses can be characterized as discrete research domains but with a high degree of authorship concentration.

Table 2. Author productivity through Lotka's Law.

Documents Written	N. of Authors	Proportion of Authors
1	1801	0.911
2	140	0.071
3	22	0.011
4	10	0.005
5	2	0.001
6	2	0.001

4.2. Annual Publication and Timespan Trend

Figure 2 shows the number of studies in the subject of big data analytics and information management that have been published, along with how these studies have helped firms operate more effectively and make better decisions. Prior to 2017, there was very little research growth, but after 2018, publications began to rise. To be more precise, 51 articles were produced over the first four years of study (2013–2016), which is much less than the 602 publications produced during the previous five years (2017–2022). The most publications were made in the year 2021, but 2022 appears to have a high record of publications as well, as evidenced by the findings in Figure 4, which indicate that in the first half of 2022, the number of publications was nearly equal to that of the prior year. This indicates that there is a persistent increase in interest in IM and big data analytics research. Additionally, Figure 2 depicts the impact of publications that have been published through the number of citations (TCPY and TCPA) in the research area each year. The overall citation per year is shown in the first measure, while the total citation per article is shown in the second. Results from both measures indicate that there are not many citations for publications that were published recently, which is predicated on time, as new research takes time to sink in and have an influence on the academic community.

4.3. Most Influential Journals, Institutions, Authors, and Documents

For the period of 2013 to 2022, Table 3 lists the journals that have published the most papers on big data analytics and information management that have a positive impact on operational effectiveness and corporate decision-making. The corpus of knowledge on information management and big data analytics has been significantly impacted by "Sustainability," which is in the frontier journal with the most papers published in the study subject (68) throughout the research timespan 2013–2022. The journal "Benchmarking" came in third with 50 articles, while the "International Journal of Production Economics" came in second with 56 published papers. There were 42 articles in the "Production Planning and Control" journal. The list of the top five research-related journals was completed by the "International Journal of Supply Chain Management". Additionally, Scopus, Sci-mago, and ABS list have indexed a large number of the most widely read journals in information management and big data analytics.

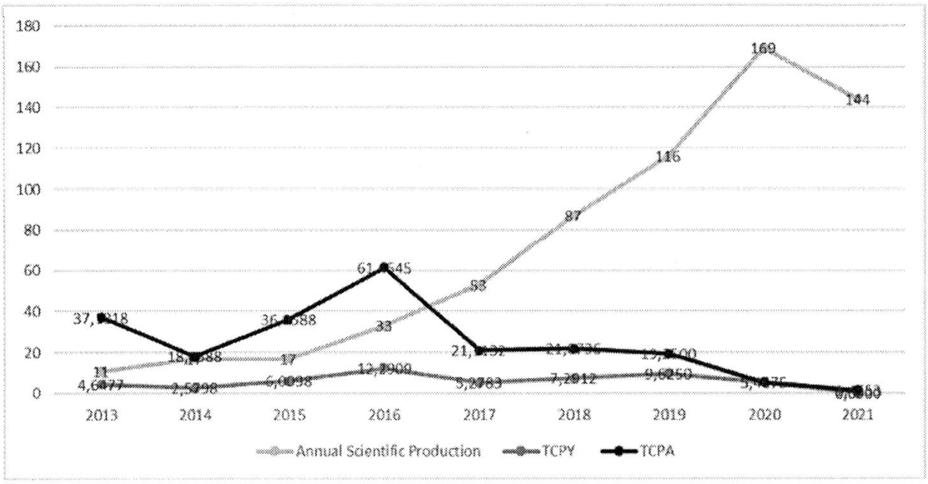

Figure 4. Annual research growth (TCPY: total citation per year, TCPA: total citation per article).

Table 3. Most relevant resources in the research field.

Sources	Subject Area	Number of Articles	h-Index	Ranking by ABS List	Ranking by Scimago List
Sustainability (Switzerland)	Management, Monitoring, Policy and Law	68	109		Q1
International Journal of Production Economics	Decision Sciences	56	197	3 ***	Q1
Benchmarking	Business and International Management	50	66	1 *	Q1

Production Planning and Control	Decision Sciences	42	85	3 ***	Q1
International Journal of Supply Chain Management	Decision Sciences	41	20		
International Journal of Production Research	Decision Sciences	37	153	3 ***	Q1
International Journal of Operations and Production Management	Decision Sciences	36	146	4 ****	Q1
Journal of Enterprise Information Management	Decision Sciences	35	67	2 **	Q1
International Journal of Logistics Management	Business and International Management	33	80	1 *	Q1
Supply Chain Management	Business and International Management	33	125	3 ***	Q1
Business Process Management Journal	Business and International Management	29	87	2 **	Q1
International Journal of Information Management	Decision Sciences	28	132	2 **	Q1
TQM Journal	Business and International Management	26	72	1 *	Q2
Industrial Management and Data Systems	Decision Sciences	25	109	2 **	Q1
Journal of Cleaner Production	Strategy and Management	24	232	2 **	Q1

Uncertain Supply Chain Management	Decision Sciences	19	19		Q2
International Journal of Productivity and Performance Management	Business and International Management	18	67	1 *	Q2
Technological Forecasting and Social Change	Business and International Management	18	134	3 ***	Q1
Journal of Operations Management	Business and International Management	17	199	4 ****	Q1
International Journal of Logistics Research and Applications	Decision Sciences	15	38	1 *	Q2

* This symbol is referred to those scientific papers that are published by Journals that are indexed by the Academic Journal Guide and produced by the Chartered Association of Business Schools (CABS). The journals are given a star rating from 1 * to 4 * (the highest).

Table 4 lists the most significant companies that disseminate research on information management and big data analytics to help enterprises operate more effectively and make better decisions. The top five universities, which account for the majority of research-related publications, have offices in various locations. The Politecnico Di Milano in Milan, Italy, is the institution that has published the most (20 papers) in the subject of research. The Hong Kong Polytechnic University is in third place with eighteen published papers, followed by the Najran University in fourth place with thirteen articles, and the Universiti Kebangsaan Malaysia in fifth place with five publications. The Universiti Kebangsaan Malaysia ranks in second place overall (eleven articles). The fact that technical colleges make up the majority of the institutions illustrates the significant impact that new technologies, such as big data analytics, have made to information management.

Examination of the most prominent writers can help shape the research domain after the bibliometric analysis [42]. Table 5 illustrates the authors with the highest impact in the research community of the studied field, while the metric of the articles fractionalized of the individual authors has been integrated and presents the fraction of their co-authored publications. According to Table 5, Dwivedi Yk is recognized as the most related author in the research domain, and Akter S. is ranked in second position in the list of the most

Table 4. Most relevant institutions.

Affiliations	Articles
Politecnico Di Milano	20
Universiti Kebangsaan Malaysia	20
The Hong Kong Polytechnic University	18
Najran University	13
Lut University	11
Norwegian University of Science and Technology	11
University of Minho	11
Universiti Teknikal Malaysia Melaka	10
Universiti Teknologi Malaysia	10
University of Malaya	10
Notreported	9
Rmit University	9
Spiru Haret University	9
Swansea University	9
University of Ljubljana	9
University of Lorraine	9
Cefet/Rj: Federal Center for Technological Education of Rio De Janeiro	8
Chang'an University	8
Dalian University of Technology	8
De Montfort University	8

relevant authors of the studied field. Figure 5 represents the authors' collaboration network. Each node highlights an author, and the edges indicate the co-authorship relation between them [43]. The blue cluster can be characterized as the most impactful and essential collaboration network between authors. The purple cluster consists of four authors' networks, while the red, orange, and brown clusters consist of three authors' networks. Moreover, the green cluster indicates the weakest collaboration network, as it consists only of two authors' networks. It is noteworthy that neither of the clusters are linked, so there is enough space for improving the overall author collaboration within the information management and big data analytics field.

Finally, the most influential academic papers in the fields of big data analytics and information management are presented in Table 6. The table below contains published scientific publications that were based on both qualitative and quantitative analyses. Additionally, some of them have investigated how big data analytics can help businesses perform better, as described in the paper "Big data analytics and firm performance:

Findings from a mixed-method approach", which draws on complexity theory to look into the resource configurations and environmental variables that contribute to performance gains from big data analytics investments. However, neither paper has discussed how big data analytics might help manage information or enhance the decision-making process.

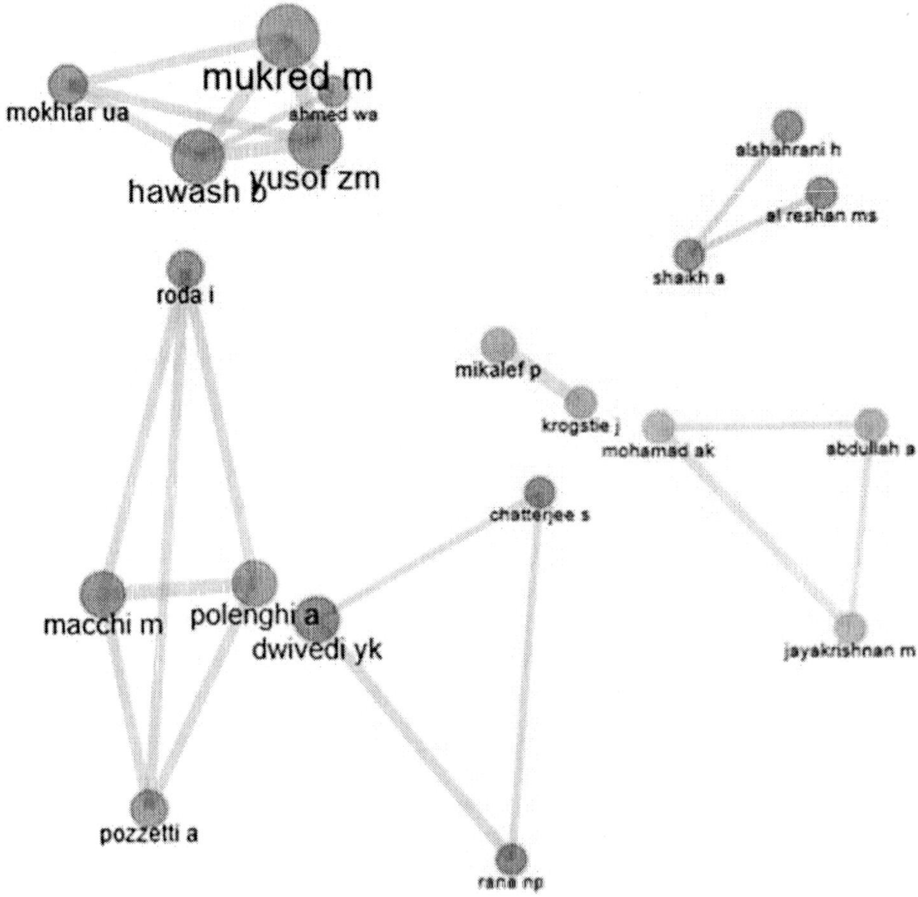

Figure 5. *Author collaboration network.*

4.4. Network, Content, Bibliographic Coupling, and Cluster Analysis

Visualizing the linkage between authors, countries, and research topics can offer interesting insights into the scientific community [43,64]. Thus, Figure 4 presents the innovative three-field plot, which presents the interchange among the most related authors (left), countries (middle), and keywords (right) within the research domain of information management and big data analytics. Results show that American, British, and

Indian scholars mostly author studies on big data analytics. However, emerging technologies such as artificial intelligence (AI) and machine learning (ML) seem to be integrated into the information management search domain. Figure 6 presents Italian and Chinese scholars with the most publications in AI and ML. Generally, the USA, UK, and India have excellence in big data analytics, Italy in ML, and China in AI.

Table 5. Most impactful authors.

Authors	Articles	Articles Fractionalized
Dwivedi Yk	6	1.62
Akter S	5	1.37
Mikalef P	5	1.25
Gunasekaran A	4	1.2
Hawash B	4	0.78
Krogstie J	4	1
Kumar A	4	1.2
Macchi M	4	1.08
Polenghi A	4	1.08
Teixeira L	4	1.5
Wang H	4	1.05
Yusof Zm	4	0.78
Zhang Z	4	1.33
Ali S	3	0.83
Chatterjee S	3	0.83
Foropon C	3	0.92
Gupta S	3	0.75
Ismail Z-A	3	3
Jayakrishnan M	3	0.83

Moreover, Figure 7 presents the geographical collaboration of the authors in the research domain of information management and big data analytics [37]. The visualization of this scientific collaboration was actualized using the tool Bibliometrix, denoted as Biblioshiny. This geographical collaboration analysis aims to highlight the social structure of the research community in the studied field. The nodes in the graph represent the authors, while links represent their co-authorship. The map shows that the USA is the origin of most of the scientific collaborations in the field. The most robust scientific channel is between USA—China and USA—India. Additionally, American scholars have developed a strong scientific collaboration with the Europeans. Specifically, the British and Italians are linked with the Americans, as well as with the Indian and Chinese scholars in the subject area of information management and big data analytics with a

Table 6. Most impactful scientific articles in the field of big data analytics and information management.

Paper	Total Citations	TC per Year	Normalized TC
Critical analysis of Big Data challenges and analytical methods [44]	931	133	7.1261
Big data analytics in E-commerce: a systematic review and agenda for future research [45]	347	43,375	4.6344
The Internet-of-Things: Review and research directions [46]	305	43,571	2.3345
Assessing business value of Big Data Analytics in European firms [47]	228	32,571	1.7452
Exploring the relationship between big data analytics capability and competitive performance: The mediating roles of dynamic and operational capabilities [48]	224	56	7.4692
Agri-food 4.0: A survey of the supply chains and technologies for the future agriculture [49]	213	53,25	7.1024
A unified foundation for business analytics [50]	210	21	1.7872
Big Data Analytics Capabilities and Innovation: The Mediating Role of Dynamic Capabilities and Moderating Effect of the Environment [51]	207	41,4	5.6573
Big data analytics and firm performance: Findings from a mixed-method approach [52]	203	40,6	5.5479
The Effect of Big Data and Analytics on Firm Performance: An Econometric Analysis Considering Industry Characteristics [53]	177	29,5	4.1788
Roles of artificial intelligence in construction engineering and management: A critical review and future trends [54]	172	57,333	14.5858
Identification of critical success factors, risks and opportunities of Industry 4.0 in SMEs [55]	167	41,75	5.5686
Industrial information integration—A literature review 2006–2015 [56]	161	20,125	2.1503
Operational research from Taylorism to Terabytes: A research agenda for the analytics age [57]	158	17,556	3.1349
Getting value from Business Intelligence systems: A review and research agenda [58]	157	22,429	1.2017
A framework for Big Data driven product lifecycle management [59]	156	22,286	1.1941

The impact of big data analytics on firms' high value business performance [60]	143	23,833	3.3761
Leveraging Customer Involvement for Fueling Innovation: The Role of Relational and Analytical Information Processing Capabilities [61]	142	20,286	1.0869
Consumers' Decision-Making Process on Social Commerce Platforms: Online Trust, Perceived Risk, and Purchase Intentions [62]	139	34,75	4.6349
Understanding the determinants of big data analytics (BDA) adoption in logistics and supply chain management: An empirical investigation [63]	139	23,167	3.2816

view on the contribution of operational performance and decision-making process. Furthermore, the collaboration map between the scholars confirms the findings of the three-fields plot and bibliographic coupling based on countries (Figure 8).

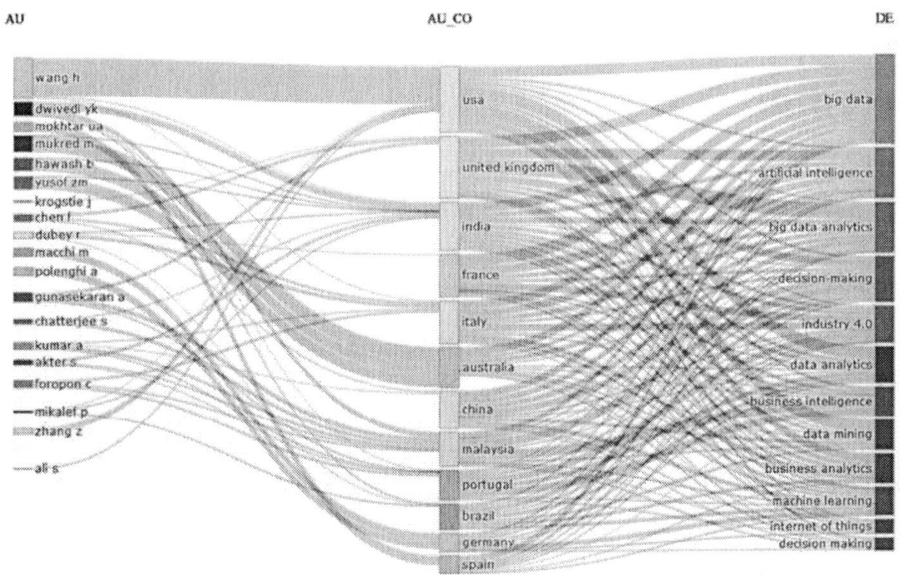

Figure 6. *Three-Fields Plot.*

Keyword analysis, which is a component of network analysis, is a useful technique that offers insightful information. The goal of a keyword analysis is to draw attention to the distinction and important trends within a study topic. Based on the co-occurrence of the writers' keywords, Figure 9 shows a network visualization. The VOSviewer program was employed to show the co-occurrence of the writers' key terms. VOSviewer is software that aids in the development of a bibliometric network and the display of the data inside it. Each circle in the graph represents an instance. The greater the co-occurrence of writers' terms, the larger the circle size [36,65]. The circles of a similar color signify a cluster of keywords, and the lines connecting the circles illustrate a connection between the keywords. 120 keywords in total were chosen, and five clusters were created, each with a unique color. The blue cluster draws attention to the close connection between information management and decision-making. The significance of big data in the field of information management research is shown by the cluster in green.

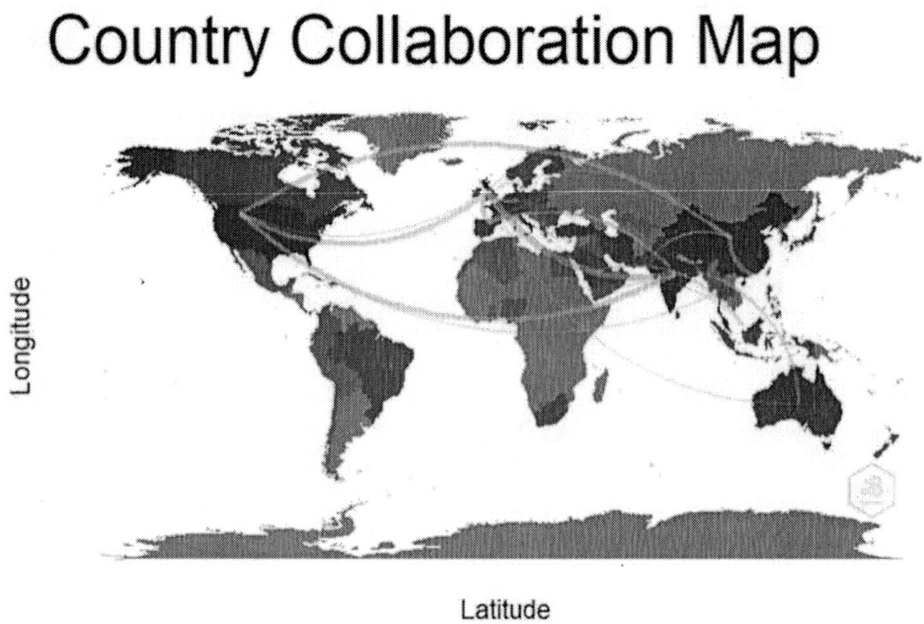

Figure 7. *Country collaboration map.*

In contrast, the yellow and red clusters draw attention to the new trends in the information management field, which are the Internet of Things and artificial intelligence, respectively. Additionally, the purple cluster emphasizes how closely information management and the decision-making process are related to the Knowledge-Based System (KBS). KBS is a type of artificial intelligence that aims to synthesize the expertise of human experts to aid in decision-making. The fact that these systems depend on human CEOs gives them the name "expert systems".

Although big data analytics has a strong linkage to information management and improvement, the operational research and decision-making of an organization and bibliometric analysis of the studied field indicate new research paths in the domain [66,67]. Figure 8, which presents the thematic map of authors' keywords, describes the above. This figure illustrates the research themes obtained from the conceptual structure of the documents included in the Bibliometrix analysis. The map is divided into four

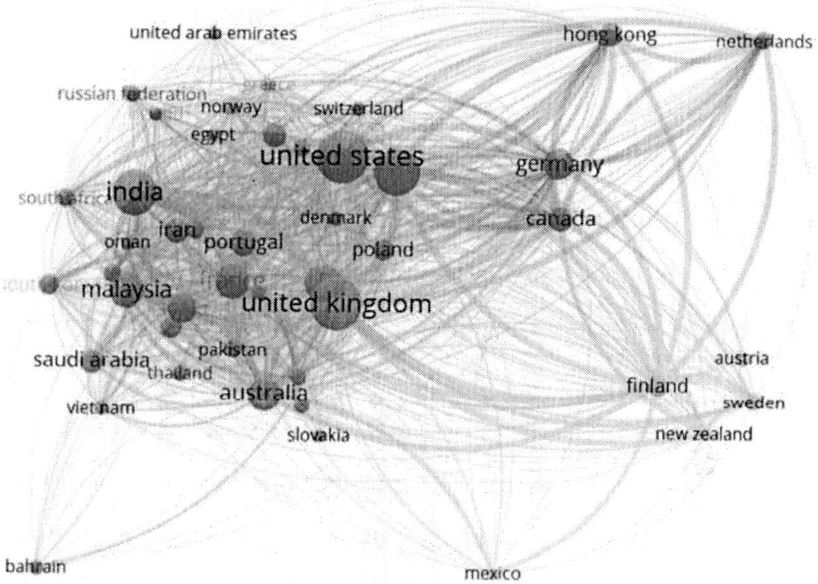

Figure 8. *Bibliographic coupling based on documents.*

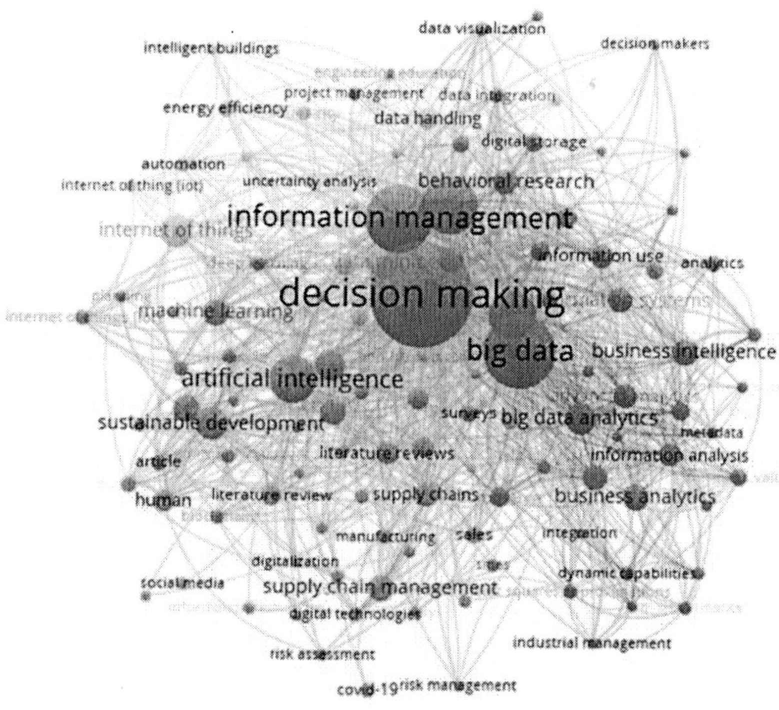

Figure 9. *Network visualization—co-occurrence of author keywords.*

quadrants,and each quadrant represents a different research theme regarding the studied research topic. In addition, the clusters' sizes highlight the proportion of the number of keywords. The thematic map uses two dimensions: density and centrality. The dimension of density illustrates the degree of the development of each theme, as measured by the internal linkages between the authors' keywords. The second dimension, the centrality, stipulates the relevance of each theme, as measured by the external linkages between the authors' keywords. Furthermore, the map presents four themes: (i) the motor themes, shown in the quadrant in the upper-right position and characterized by both high density and centrality, are the themes that are most developed in the literature, (ii) the basic themes, shown in the quadrant in the lower-right position and defined by high centrality but low density, are the themes that are not yet well developed, (iii) the niche themes, shown in the quadrant that is positioned in the upper-left of the map and characterized by high density and low centrality, are the themes that are well developed and very specialized but are marginal in the overall studied field, and (iv) the emerging themes, which are positioned in the bottom-left of the map and are characterized by low centrality and density [68].

The basic themes of the thematic map presented in Figure 10 indicate emerging technologies like big data analytics and artificial intelligence, which play a crucial role in the decision-making process of companies. However, uncertain factors, such as the COVID-19 pandemic, have enhanced the role of big data analytics. The COVID-19 pandemic has obliged many businesses to transform their operational systems by crossing to a new environment dominated by different procedures and rules. Moreover, the contribution of big data analytics in the management of e-business complaints is noteworthy, which helps an organization improve its operational efficiency and productivity. Consumer complaint behavior and management have been studied in different forms in the literature, but e-complaint business management has not been thoroughly studied. Following the role of the e-complaint and its importance for businesses, it is crucial to highlight the relationship between e-complaints, which are based on big data analytics, and SMEs. Gaining insights into client behavior that would not be attainable using conventional data analysis techniques is one of the main advantages of big data. Large data sets can be swiftly analyzed using big data technology, allowing for the discovery of trends and patterns that smaller data sets would not be able to reveal. SMEs may then utilize this knowledge to enhance their goods and services and better serve their clients. SMEs may also leverage big data to improve marketing campaigns, better target consumers, and provide customized customer experiences. The above can also be confirmed by the thematic map, as the e-complaint factor is dominated by the other niche themes.

Furthermore, to fully examine the research problem, we proceeded with the content analysis by developing a number of maps based on the usage of keywords plus terms. Based on the principles of Bibliometrix, keywords plus terms are categorized in the metadata that can help to perform content analysis [69]. Keywords plus are generated automatically by the index keywords from the names of the referenced articles. In addition, keywords plus terms should be applied more than once and are sorted from multi-word phrases to single terms [69,70]. Additionally, these words enhance the retrieval of titles or keywords that are typically used. For the purpose of the current

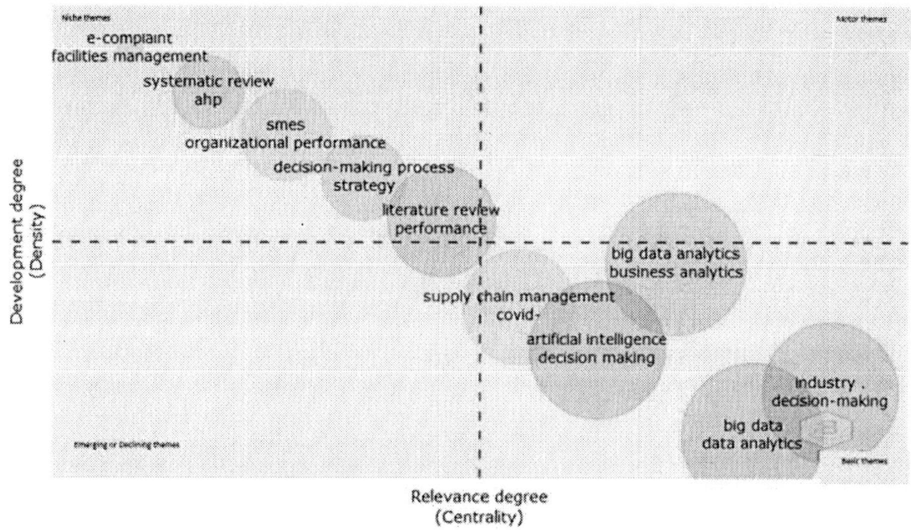

Figure 10. *Thematic map based on authors' keywords.*

research thematic map, the thematic evolution and research trends maps have been developed based on the above word type. Figure 11 presents the thematic map based on keywords plus terms. As described above, the thematic map consisted of four quadrants with each of them illustrating a different theme (niche, emerging, motor, and basic themes). Figure 11 highlights predictive analytics, as a branch of analytics that can contribute to information management. Predictive analytics uses real-time and historical data mining, among other methods, to forecast events and assist corporations and other organizations in decision-making processes [71]. Even though predictive analytics are crucial, it was discovered that bibliographies combining predictive analytics and information management are rare. By linking predictive analytics and information management, businesses can achieve not only the ability to manipulate data for analysis, but also the ability to learn to communicate their analysis and results to decision-makers, become leaders in using data, and facilitate the decision-making process. Furthermore, emerging themes illustrate that the neural network is an important factor for information management. The neural network is a technique used in artificial intelligence which instructs computers to analyze data in a manner modeled after the human brain [72,73]. Deep learning is a type of machine learning that employs linked nodes or neurons in a layered structure that resembles the human brain.

Moreover, the research field of multi-criteria decision-making (MCDM) is of particular relevance to big data analytics and information management. Figure 12 presents the thematic evolution map based on keywords plus terms and illustrates the importance of big data analytics and information management in the multi-criteria decision-making process. Complex information management is a critical component of modern decision-making. Nowadays real-world situations require a variety of data sets, some exact or objective and others unclear or subjective. To simulate complicated commercial or engineering processes, a variety of statistical and non-statistical decision-making strategies have been offered in the literature. Multiple-criteria decision-making (MCDM) procedures are among those that have recently gained enormous popularity and widespread use and can be facilitated by the contribution of big data analytics and information management.

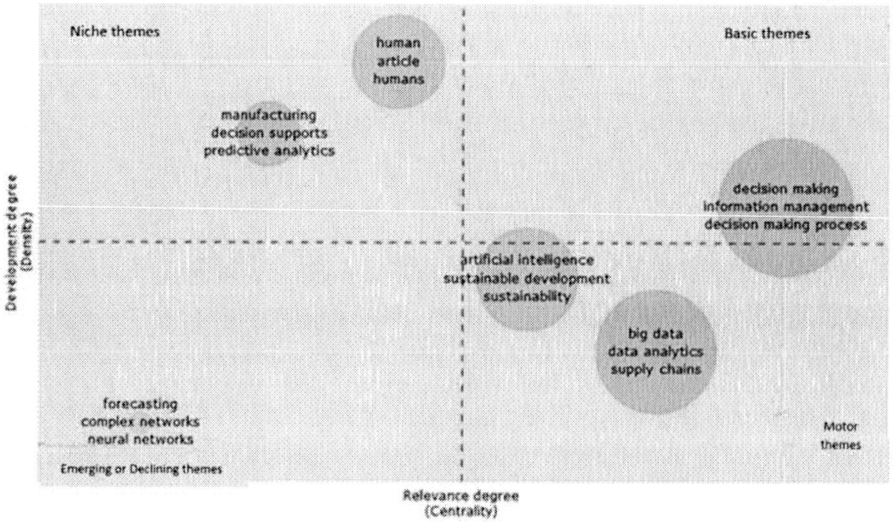

Figure 11. *Thematic map based on keywords plus terms.*

Instead, scholars have noticed the importance of big data analytics in the domain of information management, which leads to operational efficiency and decision-making process; there is limited research on the contribution of other emerging technologies such as artificial intelligence [74]. Additionally, academics have not yet looked at the contribution of developing technologies to achieving a lasting competitive advantage. Along these lines, this bibliometric research emphasizes how important the aforementioned phrases are in incorporating new emerging technologies into enterprises' information management systems. The Internet of Things, blockchain, and other technologies, when combined with big data analytics, may provide an agile decision-making process and a long-lasting competitive advantage, according to a factorial study using the Multiple Correspondence Analysis (MCA) approach (Figure 13) [75]. In terms of the MCA method, this is a grid that combines co-word analysis (Document Word) with the keywords mapped out on a two-dimensional map. According to the following dimensions: (i) the frequency of each keyword and (ii) the joint reference of the keywords in each recovered document, the MCA approach categorizes the keywords of the original retrieved articles. The results of the MCA approach are interpreted in terms of the locations of the points and the distribution of those points along each dimension. Therefore, the closer the terms are depicted on the Conceptual Structure Map, the more similar they are in their distribution.

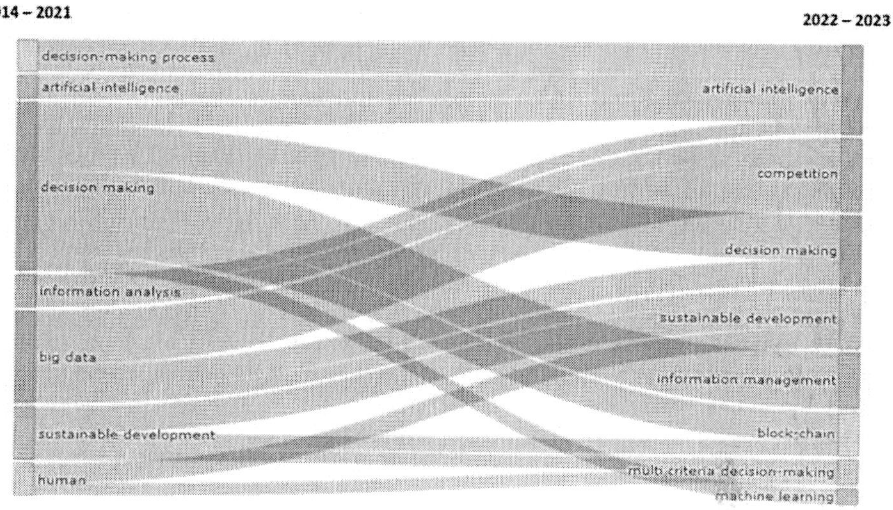

Figure 12. *Thematic evolution map based on keywords plus terms.*

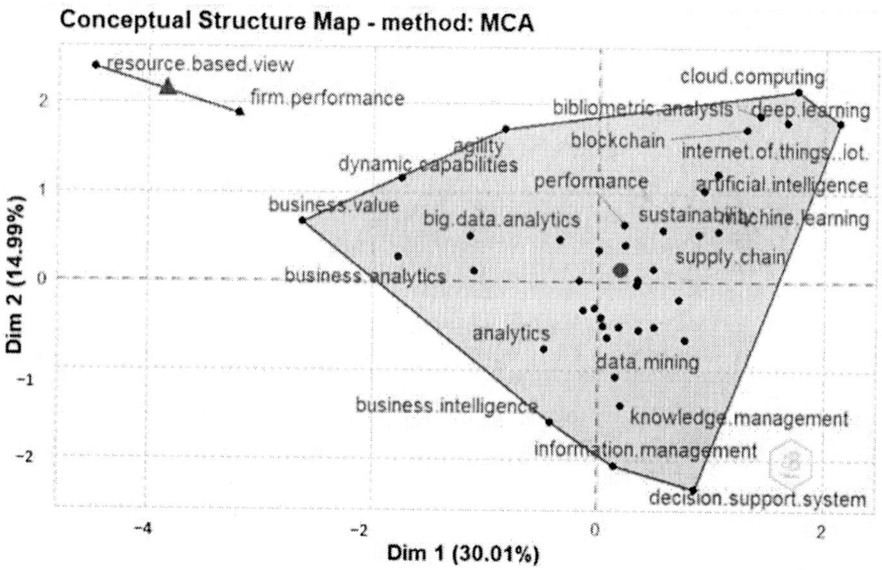

Figure 13. *Factorial analysis based on the MCA method.*

The cluster in red color highlights the strong connection between emerging technologies (cloud computing, deep learning, Internet of Things, blockchain, and artificial intelligence) and information management. Both can contribute to the facilitation of the decision-making process of businesses and help them achieve sustainable competitive advantage, increase their value, and adopt agile management practices. The above can be achieved in many ways. Tracking employees' efficiency and productivity can be integrated into the multiple advantages that the combination of information management and emerging technologies can offer. Adopting both can help businesses guide the human resource department to hire someone new or find ways to boost the existing workforce's confidence and make them more proactive and productive within the company. Moreover, the integration of technology and information management systems can contribute to the detection of illegal practices in the workforce, such as fraud, money laundering, corruption, and bribery. However, businesses should concentrate their efforts on two key areas where agility may make a significant impact, rather than trying to be "more agile." Access to networks comes first. Prior to COVID-19, a sufficient number of employees were connecting to the network using their own devices. This has become the norm now. Researchers have found that fraudsters are targeting home gadgets more than ever before in an effort to break into corporate networks. All businesses that have a substantial number of remote employees ought to make this one of their top priorities. IT teams can simply implement the proper network controls with the aid of a more adaptable cybersecurity architecture, which can also guarantee that such controls are continuously and automatically updated even in the face of never-before-seen threats. If used properly, it may assist in establishing a foundation where employees can securely log in from any place using any device, giving IT staff peace of mind.

On the other side, the blue cluster illustrates the resource-based view as a fundamental managerial framework applied to determine the strategic resources an organization can exploit to accomplish a sustainable competitive advantage. Furthermore, the resource-based view theory provides a valuable way for academics and researchers of the studied field to consider how Information System Management can be related to the strategy and performance of a business. In addition, this theory provides direction on how to differentiate among various types of information systems, such as emerging technologies and information systems, and how to study their separate influences on performance.

5. Discussion and Conclusions

Information is the new "oil". This statement is frequently used by experts to convey the significance of digital information to the corporate sector [76]. However, 'water', the resource we all rely on for our existence and well-being, is a better metaphor for the crucial function of data. In the modern economy, everyone has access to data, but, as with water, this depends on their capacity to access it, comprehend how it flows, and accept the source's reliability. Water becomes polluted and worthless if it is not handled properly. People suffer when water access is restricted, therefore data breaches, misuse, and access management are significant concerns. The same is true for how data is now organized [77,78].

Organizations in the modern business world, which is defined by its digitization, are required to handle a massive volume of data from many data sources in a timely, effective, and qualitative manner [79]. Any business information system, including those used by customers, production, warehouses, sales, suppliers, website users, or even social media platforms, may be used to gather this information [13]. Executives and analyst specialists should have a productive approach to organize and evaluate the millions of transactions that come from various databases each month. Businesses may now use specialized information systems thanks to new technologies, which also make it simpler to write reports, perform complex data analysis, and obtain information more quickly [80]. A significant part in the processing of a huge volume of data is played by information management. Information management techniques are a collection of technologies and analytical methods that are intended to analyze the available data and extract meaningful information from it in order to help corporate decision-making processes. A company may also learn, perceive circumstances and occurrences, forecast trends and future events, plan, and develop thanks to information management [81,82]. The collected data is transformed into knowledge that management may utilize to take the proper actions that will result in the definition and accomplishment of company objectives.

Information management relates to all enterprises and has an impact on all organizational activities. Information management systems, namely, have an impact on a company's personnel as well as its clients or suppliers. However, efficient user usage of information management systems is the only way for them to benefit the company [74,83]. Performance of organizations is not impacted by just having greater access to data; rather, the difference is in how they handle the data. However, a variety of approaches based on cutting-edge technology, from big data analytics to artificial intelligence, have greatly enhanced the overall process of data while also enhancing the accuracy of customer-specific data [84]. Consequently, this might provide companies with the assurance that the data they have access to will be pertinent to their clients' needs. The aforementioned can serve as a roadmap for businesses to help them make better operational decisions.

The findings of the bibliometric analysis indicated the crucial role of big data analytics in the transformation of the research domain of information management. Integrating such emerging technologies in the field of information management can offer organizations a couple of benefits, such as collecting data regarding their customers, like demographic and psychographic data, which are related to their preferences, purchasing habits, and the amount they consume. Especially, for the SMEs big data may be used by them to enhance their operations. Businesses may utilize big data, for instance, to streamline operations, spot inefficiencies or waste, and enhance decision-making. Big data may also assist SMEs in having a better understanding of their target markets and clientele. The competitiveness of SMEs may then be increased by using this knowledge to make more educated business decisions. Big data offers small and medium-sized businesses a wide range of chances to enhance their operations and more successfully compete in the modern market. Although big data technologies may initially appear intimidating, SMEs may rapidly pick them up and put them to great use.

It is noteworthy that the current study's findings emphasize the role of predictive analytics, as a branch of analytics that can contribute to information management and big data analytics. Predictive analytics uses real-time and historical data mining, among other methods, to forecast events and assist corporations and other organizations in decision-making processes. Even though predictive analytics are crucial, it was discovered that bibliographies which combine predictive analytics and information management are rare. By linking predictive analytics and information management, businesses can achieve not only the ability to manipulate data for analysis, but also the ability to learn to communicate their analysis and results to decision-makers, become leaders in using data, and facilitate the decision-making process. Furthermore, the results of the current analysis demonstrate that big data analytics play a role in capturing client concerns through e-complaint. By managing, processing, and providing data analyses of the complaint, the service e-complaint automates the manual procedure and offers transparency [85]. Additionally, the ability of online complaints adds to: (i) improving customer satisfaction, (ii) enhancing customer communication, (iii) improving policies and processes, and (iv) improving company image [86]. The above information may also help firms stand out from the competition, giving them a competitive advantage and empowering them to make business decisions that will optimize their earnings. To sustain a company's competitive edge, however, and to significantly increase an organization's operational efficiency, big data analytics must be integrated into the systems of information management [87]. The investigation of technological developments in the online complaint procedure, as well as their contribution to the assurance of transparency and the prevention of any fraud occurrence, might be suggested as a topic for future research based on the current findings.

Nevertheless, the past two years (since the COVID-19 pandemic started) can be characterized as years of building information management [6]. To promote future economic growth, businesses are continuously attempting to regain some of their prior normalcy and to increase their operational effectiveness. Thus, in addition to big data analytics, the results of the current bibliometric analysis demonstrate that the technological advancements of artificial intelligence, machine learning, Block-chain, and the Internet of Things are significant tools and can assist executives in making rational decisions [81,88]. Artificial intelligence is likely going to be utilized more by businesses in the future since it provides applications in many business fields that aim to provide employees and management with the best judgments. One illustration is the use of artificial intelligence in the field of supply chain management [9,89]. Information management is necessary for a variety of jobs in this industry so that choices may be made quickly. One of the most crucial aspects of supply chain management (SCM) is supply chain planning (SCP), which addresses the scheduling of production, demand, and sales.

Managers must be able to monitor and access all data in order to make choices since supply chains change quickly and business demands are always changing [12]. Hence, a company has to have trustworthy tools available to it in order to create successful plans and make wise judgments. Supply chain decision-makers may dramatically improve their selections by utilizing AI. A large number of data sets are analyzed by AI algorithms, and the results are then presented to management automatically. Additionally, as AI programs examine previous data and offer pre-made recommendations, firms may effectively estimate the demand for their items. One of a company's most important tasks is demand forecasting since a deficit in one area may lower sales and increase turnover. Nevertheless, flaws can negatively impact how customers perceive a company [90]. AI offers useful algorithms that forecast trends. In spite of this, artificial intelligence (AI) can forecast demand patterns based on a variety of factors, including weather, seasonality, holidays, real-time sales and any restrictions that the business may impose. Therefore, future studies should examine how big data analytics and artificial intelligence work together to enhance operational research and decision-making processes. [91].

Further, Figure 14 offers a number of interesting ideas for subsequent investigation. Information technology, according to a sizable proportion of researchers in the scientific field of decision-making, may help businesses be more agile in their decision-making processes. Additionally, agility enables firms to react quickly to shifting market situations while facilitating internal and external communication. As the real time to notice and respond to attacks increases, so do the frequency and intensity of the cyberattack

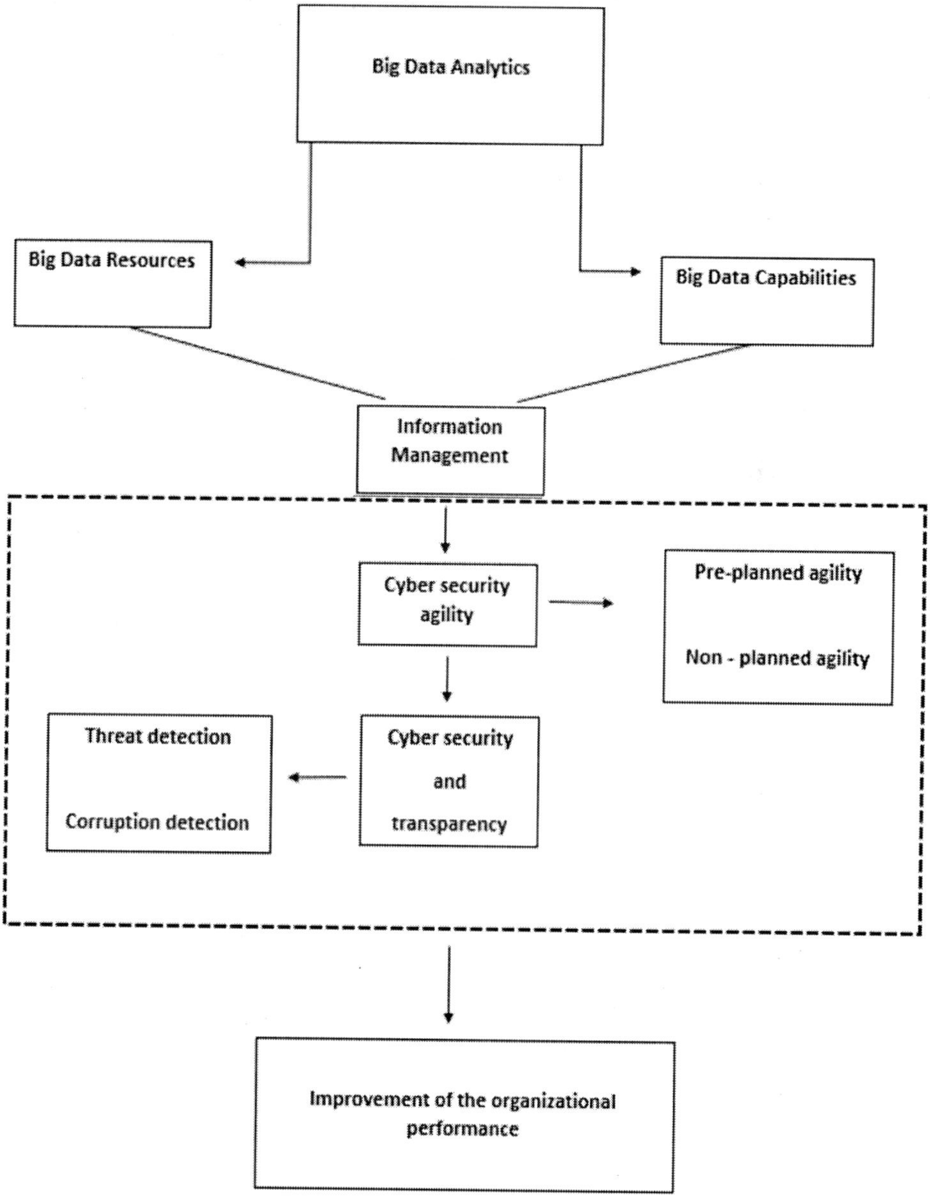

Figure 14. *Proposed business model.*

phenomena. Businesses must create IT solutions that might enhance cyber response skills, such as cyber agility, in order to handle the aforementioned concerns. The fact that cyberattacks happen instantly and have equally instantaneous and destructive impacts makes this element vital. Therefore, a suggestion for future study may be to look at how companies' agility in cyberspace affects the effective security and safeguarding of their essential information. Additionally, no matter the size of the business, the rising frequency of cyberattacks increases the complexity of cyber security. Businesses have direct access to various data sources and regularly evaluate a vast amount of data. However, they are unable to adequately evaluate, utilise, and assure the security of this data. Because it allows for fast analysis and storage, which increases the danger of leakage, traditional data storage and analysis methodologies have been found to be ineffective by organizations. In order to enhance the technologies related to cyber security, it is required to adopt a new method of storing and analyzing the data. Businesses can immediately and affordably handle and analyze a large volume of data with the aid of big data analytics. Big data analytics enhances the diagnostic and automated data analysis required to produce insights and respond to difficult security problems by using analytical techniques including data/text mining, machine learning, and pattern matching. In general, massive data analysis methods provide a substantial contribution to stopping harmful conduct. Therefore, in future study, the analysis of big data analytics' contribution to better cybersecurity might be expanded upon.

Finally, we may note at least three theoretical contributions to this work. In this paper, we outline another advantage of enhancing IM skills and orientation, which adds to the body of IM research. By dynamically selecting and managing critical knowledge that is both internal and external to the company, these abilities may optimize the benefits of BDA on firm performance while lowering the risks associated with big data management. The proposed business model's ability to strike a balance between cyber security agility and digital transformation might serve as the second theoretical contribution. To maintain balance, one must be aware of the possibility of an attack and use integrated network security policy management to lessen the likelihood of a compromise. Recognizing the advantages and disadvantages of digital transformation initiatives is one aspect of this. The third theoretical contribution refers to the importance of the three significant capabilities, and the beneficial links between them are addressed in this study, which may add to the body of knowledge on dynamic capabilities. Prior research supporting the idea that information management, big data analytics, agility, and business performance are positively correlated may be used to supplement this.

Author Contributions

Conceptualization, K.R., I.P. and A.G.; Data curation, K.R., I.P. and A.G.; Formal analysis, K.R.; Investigation, K.R., A.G. and E.G.; Methodology, K.R. and A.G.; Project Administration, K.R., A.G. and I.P.; Resources, K.R. and A.G.; Software, E.G.; Supervision, C.Z.; Validation, C.Z. and A.G.; Writing—original draft, K.R., I.P., A.G., E.G. and C.Z. All authors have read and agreed to the published version of the manuscript.

References

Tang, J.; Zhang, S.X.; Lin, S. To reopen or not to reopen? How entrepreneurial alertness influences small business reopening after the COVID-19 lockdown. *J. Bus. Ventur. Insights* 2021, *16*, e00275.

Nebolsina, E. The impact of the Covid-19 pandemic on the business interruption insurance demand in the United States. *Heliyon* 2021, *7*, e08357.

Zarghami, S.A. A reflection on the impact of the COVID-19 pandemic on Australian businesses: Toward a taxonomy of vulnerabilities. *Int. J. Disaster Risk Reduct.* 2021, *64*, 102496.

Kettinger, W.J.; Ryoo, S.Y.; Marchand, D.A. We're engaged! Following the path to a successful information management capability. *J. Strat. Inf. Syst.* 2021, *30*, 101681.

Huang, P.Y.; Niu, B.; Pan, S.L. Platform-based customer agility: An integrated framework of information management structure, capability, and culture. *Int. J. Inf. Manag.* 2021, *59*, 102346.

Manandhar, R.; Siebeneck, L.K. Information management and the return-entry process: Examining information needs, sources, and strategies after Superstorm Sandy. *Int. J. Disaster Risk Reduct.* 2021, *53*, 102015.

Sharma, A.; Rana, N.P.; Nunkoo, R. Fifty years of information management research: A conceptual structure analysis using structural topic modeling. *Int. J. Inf. Manag.* 2021, *58*, 102316.

Omar, Y.M.; Minoufekr, M.; Plapper, P. Business analytics in manufacturing: Current trends, challenges and pathway to market leadership. *Oper. Res. Perspect.* 2019, *6*, 100127.

Donaldson, D.A. Digital from farm to fork: Infrastructures of quality and control in food supply chains. *J. Rural. Stud.* 2021, *91*, 228–235.

Óskarsdóttir, M.; Bravo, C.; Sarraute, C.; Vanthienen, J.; Baesens, B. The value of big data for credit scoring: Enhancing financial inclusion using mobile phone data and social network analytics. *Appl. Soft Comput. J.* 2019, *74*, 26–39.

Doumpos, M.; Zopounidis, C.; Gounopoulos, D.; Platanakis, E.; Zhang, W. Operational research and artificial intelligence methods in banking. *Eur. J. Oper. Res.* 2023, *306*, 1–16.

Koot, M.; Mes MR, K.; Iacob, M.E. A systematic literature review of supply chain decision making supported by the Internet of Things and Big Data Analytics. *Comput. Ind. Eng.* 2021, *154*, 107076.

Nespeca, V.; Comes, T.; Meesters, K.; Brazier, F. Towards coordinated self-organization: An actor-centered framework for the design of disaster management information systems. *Int. J. Disaster Risk Reduct.* 2020, *51*, 101887.

Ardito, L.; Scuotto, V.; Del Giudice, M.; Petruzzelli, A.M. A bibliometric analysis of research on Big Data analytics for business and management. *Manag. Decis.* 2019, *57*, 1993–2009.

Ding, Y.; Wu, Z.; Tan, Z.; Jiang, X. Research and application of security baseline in business information system. *Procedia Comput. Sci.* 2021, *183*, 630–635.

Jiang, X.; Ding, Y.; Ma, X.; Li, X. Compliance analysis of business information system under classified protection 2.0 of cybersecurity. *Procedia Comput. Sci.* 2021, *183*, 87–93.

Trigo, A.; Belfo, F.; Estébanez, R.P. Accounting Information Systems: Evolving towards a Business Process Oriented Accounting. *Procedia Comput. Sci.* 2016, *100*, 987–994.

Ponisciakova, O.; Gogolova, M.; Ivankova, K. The Use of Accounting Information System for the Management of Business Costs. *Procedia Econ. Financ.* 2015, *26*, 418–422.

Azevedo, J.; Duarte, J.; Santos, M.F. Implementing a business intelligence cost accounting solution in a healthcare setting. *Procedia Comput. Sci.* 2021, *198*, 329–334.

Anaya, L.; Qutaishat, F. ERP systems drive businesses towards growth and sustainability. *Procedia Comput. Sci.* 2022, *204*, 854–861.

Molina-Castillo, F.-J.; Rodríguez, R.; López-Nicolas, C.; Bouwman, H. The role of ERP in business model innovation: Impetus or impediment. *Digit. Bus.* 2022, *2*, 100024.

Coşkun, E.; Gezici, B.; Aydos, M.; Tarhan, A.K.; Garousi, V. ERP failure: A systematic mapping of the literature. *Data Knowl. Eng.* 2022, *142*, 102090.

Bernroider EW, N.; Wong CW, Y.; Lai, K.H. From dynamic capabilities to ERP enabled business improvements: The mediating effect of the implementation project. *Int. J. Proj. Manag.* 2014, *32*, 350–362.

Hagel, J. Bringing analytics to life. *J. Account.* 2015, *219*, 24. Available online: https://www. journalofaccountancy .com/ issues/2015/ feb/ big-data-analytics- management-accounting. html (accessed on 2 July 2022).

Ahmed, R.; Shaheen, S.; Philbin, S.P. The role of big data analytics and decision-making in achieving project success. *J. Eng. Technol. Manag. JET-M* 2022, *65*, 101697.

Li, L.; Lin, J.; Ouyang, Y.; Luo, X. Evaluating the impact of big data analytics usage on the decision-making quality of organizations. *Technol. Forecast. Soc. Chang.* 2022, *175*, 121355.

Barton, D.; Court, D. Making advanced analytics work for you. *Harv. Bus. Rev.* 2012, *90*, 78–83.

Shah, S.; Horne, A.; Capella, J. Good Data Won't Guarantee Good Decisions. *Harv. Bus. Rev.* 2012, *90*, 23–25.

Li, C.; Chen, Y.; Shang, Y. A review of industrial big data for decision making in intelligent manufacturing. *Eng. Sci. Technol. Int. J.* 2022, *29*, 101021.

Ulrich, P.; Becker, W.; Fibitz, A.; Reitelshöfer, E.; Schuhknecht, F. Data Analytics Systems and SME type—A Design Science Approach. *Procedia Comput. Sci.* 2018, *126*, 1162–1170.

Brunnschweiler, C.; Edjekumhene, I.; Lujala, P. Does information matter? Transparency and demand for accountability in Ghana's natural resource revenue management. *Ecol. Econ.* 2021, *181*, 106903.

Do, H.; Budhwar, P.; Shipton, H.; Nguyen, H.D.; Nguyen, B. Building organizational resilience, innovation through resource-based management initiatives, organizational learning and environmental dynamism. *J. Bus. Res.* 2022, *141*, 808–821.

Ma, S.; Ding, W.; Liu, Y.; Ren, S.; Yang, H. Digital twin and big data-driven sustainable smart manufacturing based on information management systems for energy-intensive industries. *Appl. Energy* 2022, *326*, 119986.

Wang, B.; Wang, Y.; Yan, F.; Zhao, W. Safety intelligence toward safety management in a big-data environment: A general model and its application in urban safety management. *Safety Sci.* 2022, *154*, 105840.

Aria, M.; Cuccurullo, C. Bibliometrix: An R-tool for comprehensive science mapping analysis. *J. Informetr.* 2017, *11*, 959–975.

Tamala, J.K.; Maramag, E.I.; Simeon, K.A.; Ignacio, J.J. A bibliometric analysis of sustainable oil and gas production research using VOSviewer. *Clean. Eng. Technol.* 2022, *7*, 100437.

Niknejad, N.; Ismail, W.; Bahari, M.; Hendradi, R.; Salleh, A.Z. Mapping the research trends on blockchain technology in food and agriculture industry: A bibliometric analysis. *Environ. Technol. Innov.* 2021, *21*, 101272.

Huber, J.C. The underlying process generating Lotka's Law and the statistics of exceedances. *Inf. Process. Manag.* 1998, *34*, 471–487.

Kumar, S.; Sharma, P.; Garg, K.C. Lotka's law and institutional productivity. *Inf. Process. Manag.* 1998, *34*, 775–783.

Egghe, L. Consequences of Lotka's law in the case of fractional counting of authorship and of first author counts. *Math. Comput. Model.* 1993, *18*, 63–77.

Amodio, P.; Brugnano, L.; Scarselli, F. Implementation of the PaperRank and AuthorRank indices in the Scopus database. *J. Informetr.* 2021, *15*, 101206.

Marcucci, G.; Ciarapica, F.; Poler, R.; Sanchis, R. A bibliometric analysis of the emerging trends in silver economy. *IFAC-Pap.* 2021, *54*, 936–941.

Chen, H.; Jin, Q.; Wang, X.; Xiong, F. Profiling academic-industrial collaborations in bibliometric-enhanced topic networks: A case study on digitalization research. *Technol. Forecast. Soc. Chang.* 2022, *175*, 121402.

Sivarajah, U.; Kamal, M.M.; Irani, Z.; Weerakkody, V. Critical analysis of Big Data challenges and analytical methods. *J. Bus. Res.* 2017, *70*, 263–286.

Akter, S.; Wamba, S.F. Big data analytics in E-commerce: A systematic review and agenda for future research. *Electron. Mark.* 2016, *26*, 173–194.

Ng, I.C.L.; Wakenshaw, S.Y.L. The Internet-of-Things: Review and research directions. *Int. J. Res. Mark.* 2017, *34*, 3–21.

Côrte-Real, N.; Oliveira, T.; Ruivo, P. Assessing business value of Big Data Analytics in European firms. *J. Bus. Res.* 2017, *70*, 379–390.

Mikalef, P.; Krogstie, J.; Pappas, I.O.; Pavlou, P. Exploring the relationship between big data analytics capability and competitive performance: The mediating roles of dynamic and operational capabilities. *Inf. Manag.* 2020, *57*, 103169.

Lezoche, M.; Panetto, H.; Kacprzyk, J.; Hernandez, J.E.; Díaz, M.M.E.A. Agri-food 4.0: A survey of the supply chains and technologies for the future agriculture. *Comput. Ind.* 2020, *117*, 103187.

Holsapple, C.; Lee-Post, A.; Pakath, R. A unified foundation for business analytics. *Decis. Support Syst.* 2014, *64*, 130–141.

Mikalef, P.; Boura, M.; Lekakos, G.; Krogstie, J. Big Data Analytics Capabilities and Innovation: The Mediating Role of Dynamic Capabilities and Moderating Effect of the Environment. *Br. J. Manag.* 2019, *30*, 272–298.

Mikalef, P.; Boura, M.; Lekakos, G.; Krogstie, J. Big data analytics and firm performance: Findings from a mixed-method approach. *J. Bus. Res.* 2019, *98*, 261–276.

Müller, O.; Fay, M.; vom Brocke, J. The Effect of Big Data and Analytics on Firm Performance: An Econometric Analysis Considering Industry Characteristics. *J. Manag. Inf. Syst.* 2018, *35*, 488–509.

Pan, Y.; Zhang, L. Roles of artificial intelligence in construction engineering and management: A critical review and future trends. *Autom. Constr.* 2021, *122*, 103517.

Moeuf, A.; Lamouri, S.; Pellerin, R.; Tamayo-Giraldo, S.; Tobon-Valencia, E.; Eburdy, R. Identification of critical success factors, risks and opportunities of Industry 4.0 in SMEs. *Int. J. Prod. Res.* 2020, *58*, 1384–1400.

Chen, Y. Industrial information integration—A literature review 2006–2015. *J. Ind. Inf. Integr.* 2016, *2*, 30–64.

Mortenson, M.J.; Doherty, N.F.; Robinson, S. Operational research from Taylorism to Terabytes: A research agenda for the analytics age. *Eur. J. Oper. Res.* 2015, *241*, 583–595.

Trieu, V.H. Getting value from Business Intelligence systems: A review and research agenda. *Decis. Support Syst.* 2017, *93*, 111–124.

Zhang, Y.; Ren, S.; Liu, Y.; Sakao, T.; Huisingh, D. A framework for Big Data driven product lifecycle management. *J. Clean. Prod.* 2017, *159*, 229–240.

Popovič, A.; Hackney, R.; Tassabehji, R.; Castelli, M. The impact of big data analytics on firms' high value business performance. *Inf. Syst. Front.* 2018, *20*, 209–222.

Saldanha TJ, V.; Mithas, S.; Krishnan, M.S. Leveraging Customer Involvement for Fueling Innovation: The Role of Relational and Analytical Information Processing Capabilities. *MIS Q.* 2017, *41*, 367–396.

Lăzăroiu, G.; Neguriță, O.; Grecu, I.; Grecu, G.; Mitran, P.C. Consumers' Decision-Making Process on Social Commerce Platforms: Online Trust, Perceived Risk, and Purchase Intentions. *Front. Psychol.* 2020, *11*, 890.

Lai, Y.; Sun, H.; Ren, J. Understanding the determinants of big data analytics (BDA) adoption in logistics and supply chain management: An empirical investigation. *Int. J. Logist. Manag.* 2018, *29*, 676–703.

Oraee, M.; Hosseini, M.R.; Papadonikolaki, E.; Palliyaguru, R.; Arashpour, M. Collaboration in BIM-based construction networks: A bibliometric-qualitative literature review. *Int. J. Proj. Manag.* 2017, *35*, 1288–1301.

Sinha, A.; Priyadarshi, P.; Bhushan, M.; Debbarma, D. Worldwide trends in the scientific production of literature on traceability in food safety: A bibliometric analysis. *Artif. Intell. Agric.* 2021, *5*, 252–261.

Mühl, D.D.; de Oliveira, L. A bibliometric and thematic approach to agriculture 4.0. *Heliyon* 2022, *8*, e09369.

Kim, H.; So, K.K.F. Two decades of customer experience research in hospitality and tourism: A bibliometric analysis and thematic content analysis. *Int. J. Hosp. Manag.* 2022, *100*, 103082.

Ampese, L.C.; Sganzerla, W.G.; Di Domenico Ziero, H.; Mudhoo, A.; Martins, G.; Forster-Carneiro, T. Research progress, trends, and updates on anaerobic digestion technology: A bibliometric analysis. *J. Clean. Prod.* 2022, *331*, 130004.

Valderrama-Zurián, J.C.; García-Zorita, C.; Marugán-Lázaro, S.; Sanz-Casado, E. Comparison of MeSH terms and KeyWords Plus terms for more accurate classification in medical research fields. A case study in cannabis research. *Inf. Process. Manag.* 2021, *58*, 102658.

Lu, W.; Liu, Z.; Huang, Y.; Bu, Y.; Li, X.; Cheng, Q. How do authors select keywords? A preliminary study of author keyword selection behavior. *J. Informetr.* 2020, *14*, 101066.

Karimanzira, D.; Rauschenbach, T. Enhancing aquaponics management with IoT-based Predictive Analytics for efficient information utilization. *Inf. Process. Agric.* 2019, *6*, 375–385.

Park, G.; Song, M. Predicting performances in business processes using deep neural networks. *Decis. Support Syst.* 2020, *129*, 113191.

Tkáč, M.; Verner, R. Artificial neural networks in business: Two decades of research. *Appl. Soft Comput. J.* 2016, *38*, 788–804.

Shamim, S.; Zeng, J.; Khan, Z.; Zia, N.U. Big data analytics capability and decision making performance in emerging market firms: The role of contractual and relational governance mechanisms. *Technol. Forecast. Soc. Chang.* 2020, *161*, 120315.

Boakye, E.A.; Zhao, H.; Ahia, B.N.K. Emerging research on blockchain technology in finance; a conveyed evidence of bibliometric-based evaluations. *J. High Technol. Manag. Res.* 2022, *33*, 100437.

Papi, F.G.; Hübner, J.F.; de Brito, M. A Blockchain integration to support transactions of assets in multi-agent systems. *Eng. Appl. Artif. Intell.* 2022, *107*, 104534.

Perdana, A.; Lee, H.H.; Koh, S.K.; Arisandi, D. Data analytics in small and mid-size enterprises: Enablers and inhibitors for business value and firm performance. *Int. J. Account. Inf. Syst.* 2022, *44*, 100547.

Koltai, T.; Tamás, A. Performance evaluation of teams in business simulation games with weight restricted data envelopment analysis models. *Int. J. Manag. Educ.* 2022, *20*, 100688.

Hadjielias, E.; Christofi, M.; Christou, P.; Hadjielia Drotarova, M. Digitalization, agility, and customer value in tourism. *Technol. Forecast. Soc. Chang.* 2022, *175*, 121334.

Vroon, T.; Teunissen, E.; Drent, M.; Negro, S.O.; van Sark, W.G.J.H.M. Escaping the niche market: An innovation system analysis of the Dutch building integrated photovoltaics (BIPV) sector. *Renew. Sustain. Energy Rev.* 2022, *155*, 111912.

Bui, Q.-T.; Lo, F.-Y. Technology multinational enterprises from emerging markets: Competitive interplay of international entry timing decisions. *Sustain. Technol. Entrep.* 2022, *1*, 100019.

Lee, C.K.M.; Ng KK, H.; Jiao, R.J.; Yang, Z. Editorial Notes: Emerging intelligent automation and optimisation methods for adaptive decision making. *Adv. Eng. Inform.* 2022, *51*, 101500.

Alwis SDe Hou, Z.; Zhang, Y.; Na, M.H.; Ofoghi, B.; Sajjanhar, A. A survey on smart farming data, applications and techniques. *Comput. Ind.* 2022, *138*, 103624.

Cottu, P.; Ramsey, S.D.; Solà-Morales, O.; Spears, P.A.; Taylor, L. The emerging role of real-world data in advanced breast cancer therapy: Recommendations for collaborative decision-making. *Breast* 2022, *61*, 118–122.

Stevens, J.L.; Spaid, B.I.; Breazeale, M.; Esmark Jones, C.L. Timeliness, transparency, and trust: A framework for managing online customer complaints. *Bus. Horiz.* 2018, *61*, 375–384.

Dyussembayeva, S.; Viglia, G.; Nieto-Garcia, M.; Invernizzi, A.C. It makes me feel vulnerable! The impact of public self-disclosure on online complaint behavior. *Int. J. Hosp. Manag.* 2020, *88*, 102512.

Hutzinger, C.; Weitzl, W.J. Co-creation of online service recoveries and its effects on complaint bystanders. *J. Bus. Res.* 2021, *130*, 525–538.

Wu, J.; Wood, G.; Chen, X.; Meyer, M.; Liu, Z. Strategic ambidexterity and innovation in Chinese multinational vs. indigenous firms: The role of managerial capability. *Int. Bus. Rev.* 2020, *29*, 101652.

Ardito, L.; Messeni Petruzzelli, A.; Dezi, L.; Castellano, S. The influence of inbound open innovation on ambidexterity performance: Does it pay to source knowledge from supply chain stakeholders? *J. Bus. Res.* 2020, *119*, 321–329.

Sangeetha, M.; Hoti, A.; Bansal, R.; Faez Hasan, M.; Gajjar, K.; Srivastava, K. Facilitating artificial intelligence supply chain analytics through finance management during the pandemic crises. *Mater. Today Proc.* 2021, *56*, 2092–2095.

Mediavilla, M.A.; Dietrich, F.; Palm, D. Review and analysis of artificial intelligence methods for demand forecasting in supply chain management. *Procedia CIRP* 2022, *107*, 1126–1131.

4

Adoption of Digital Technologies and Backshoring Decisions

Is There a Link?

Bart Kamp & Juan José Gibaja

Deusto University, Orkestra-Basque Institute of Competitiveness and Deusto Business School, Kalea Mundaiz 50, 20012, Donostia/San Sebastian, Spain

Abstract

The present paper assesses whether the adoption of Industry 4.0 technologies can be related to backshoring. It does so by -firstly- investigating the implementation of such technologies by industrial firms with foreign production plants, the experiences and intentions of these firms regarding the location of production activities, and -secondly- by analyzing backshoring cases among them.

It finds that backshoring is a rare phenomenon, and it is questionable whether there is a correlation, left alone causality, between the adoption of digital technologies in home-based manufacturing sites and backshoring hitherto. And while the future may hold more backshoring movements in store, they may not be primarily due to the adoption of Industry 4.0 technologies at home-based plants. Instead, other (foreign) location-specific factors seem to have greater weight in the decision-making processes around backshoring operations. I.e., deteriorating sales forecasts in offshore places where firms have production activities, increases in institutional uncertainty in such places, rationalization of global production apparatuses, and/or a lack of possibilities to deploy foreign manufacturing activities and output for third markets. Also against the backdrop of events like the outbreak of Covid19 and the uncertainty-raising effect it has on international business, the trade-off between producing off-shore or bringing manufacturing activities back home is not likely to depend on technology adoption levels at home and abroad either.

Keywords: *Industry 4.0 · Backshoring · Production location · International business · Global value chains*

1 Introduction

A growing body of literature is looking into the impact of digital technologies on the course of international business (Van Tulder et al. 2018). As part of this stream of research, there is growing scholarly interest in investigating how advanced manufacturing technologies influence the geographical location of production activities. In this regard, Bals et al. (2015) and Fratocchi et al. (2014) study to what extent the application of productivity-enhancing technologies in developed countries may facilitate the backshoring of production activities from emerging economies.

Similarly, Ancarani and Di Mauro (2018, 2019) as well as Fratocchi and Di Stefano (2019) examine whether the adoption of Industry 4.0 bears any relationship to reshoring decisions. In addition, also Dachs et al. (2019) and Chiarvesio and Romanello (2018) explore the link between Industry 4.0 and backshoring of production activities.

Dachs et al. (2019) assert that Industry 4.0 and local manufacturing strategies could have a substantial impact on backshoring in upcoming years. Consequently, they call for new insights to evaluate the relationship between backshoring of production activities and investment in Industry 4.0 technologies at European manufacturing firms.

Despite the importance of assessing whether the uptake of advanced manufacturing technologies influences the backshoring phenomenon, when reviewing the corresponding state-of-the-art, it turns out that publications referring to the concept of Industry 4.0 either lack a clear operationalization of it (Chiarvesio and Romanello 2018) and/or reduce it to a limited set of representative technologies (Dachs et al. 2019; Ancarani and Di Mauro 2018, 2019; Fratocchi and Di Stefano 2019).

Instead of the former, the present paper adheres to a comprehensive breakdown of Industry 4.0 into a broad range of technologies, as introduced by Rüßmann et al. (2015).Footnote1 The former technology breakdown is probably the one that has received most following among academic scholars (see e.g. Gilchrist 2016; Chiarvesio and Romanello 2018; Saucedo-Martinez et al. 2016; Alcacer and Cruz-Machado 2019; Hernandez-de-Menendez et al. 2020; Stentoft et al. 2020). Hence, it serves as our point of reference. Afterwards, we use this breakdown to assess whether and how the adoption of the respective technologies is intertwined with backshoring dynamics.

To that end, the rest of the paper is structured as follows: Sect. 2 outlines the research context and reviews the extant literature, Sect. 3 introduces the methods and data used to conduct our research, Sect. 4 presents the research findings, Sect. 5 discusses the results obtained, Sect. 6 discusses the implications, and Sect. 7 highlights the limitations of the results and insights generated by our research.

2 Research context

The term Industry 4.0 refers to a family of technologies that entail the use and coordination of information, automation, computation and sensing devices for the sake of advanced manufacturing activities (Acatech 2015; Posada et al. 2015; Kagermann 2015).

From an international business and production operations perspective, the adoption of these technologies can influence the decisions regarding the (future) location of production activities (Gray et al. 2013; Chiarvesio and Romanello 2018). As such, the adoption of digital technologies could provide a counterweight against the process of offshoring and the articulation of supply or value chains on a global level. That is: if they are unilaterally -or more intensely- adopted in the home base of companies that have previously offshored production. The way that Industry 4.0 technologies can impact on location decisions, and could have a backshoring effect, stems roughly from the following mechanisms. They can:

- equalize cost levels between high- and low-cost countries (Tate 2014; Bals et al. 2016),
- generate benefits from bringing production activities closer to the end market, thus endowing production processes with superior possibilities in terms of planning flexibility and delivery compliance (Kinkel and Maloca 2009; Lu 2017; Johansson and Olhager 2018; Dachs et al. 2019)
- create synergies through (re)coupling manufacturing to a company's hotspots for R&D, design and product development (Brettel et al. 2014; Rezk et al. 2016; Fratocchi et al. 2014; Lu 2017; Di Mauro et al. 2018; Johansson et al. 2019),
- and/or raise quality standards and customization possibilities for products and operations (Stentoft et al. 2016a, b; Johansson et al. 2019; Ancarani et al. 2019; Dachs et al. 2019).

Consequently, scholars have started to explore the so-called backshoring or reshoring phenomenon (Kinkel 2012, 2014; Gray et al. 2013; Di Mauro et al. 2018).

While research on Industry 4.0, on the one hand, and backshoring, on the other, is growing; publications that look at both simultaneously are still rare, with Chiarvesio and Romanello (2018), Ancarani and Di Mauro (2018, 2019), Dachs et al. (2019) and Fratocchi and Di Stefano (2019) being the exceptions. As such, this field of research is still in a nascent phase (Edmonson and McManus 2007). A typical feature of research domains that are in the early stages is that they face several loose ends. Against this backdrop the present paper sets out to make contributions in the following areas:

1. Adopt a neater approach to Industry 4.0 than has been done so far around backshoring analyses. Instead of treating it as an umbrella term or in a *pars pro totum* manner, propose a comprehensive breakdown into underlying technologies for the sake of research in the backshoring realm (Sect. 2.1).
2. Build on research that points at the relevance of certain technologies for specific backshoring rationales, by examining such relevance and by broadening the base of Industry 4.0 technologies that can be looked into (Sect. 2.2).
3. Build on research that looks beyond technology as a factor for relocation decisions, to provide relief to the role that Industry 4.0 technologies play in such decisions (Sect. 2.3).

2.1 Operationalization of industry 4.0 adoption

Extant research on Industry 4.0 and backshoring has delivered thus far rather inconclusive results. For starters, because the few publications available do not lead to the same conclusions. Rather, they have produced opposite results.

To begin with, the results of Dachs et al. (2019 p. 1) support the idea that the adoption of advanced manufacturing technologies in the home base stimulates backshoring: "Descriptive statistics as well as regression results indicate a positive correlation between the adoption of Industry 4.0 technologies and companies' backshoring propensity."

However, there is counterproof coming from Ancarani et al. (2019 p. 368) who state that: "to date backshoring has largely taken place without investment in new technologies" and from Chiarvesio and Romanello (2018 p. 371) when they state that they "cannot identify a clear and direct relationship among investments in Industry 4.0 technologies and international activities, neither declared by the companies, nor indirectly identified during data collection." Also Müller et al. (2017 p. 165) conclude that "the general estimation for the importance of reshoring of Industry 4.0 remains questionable".

In turn, Fratocchi and Di Stefano (2019) offer mixed results, indicating that automated machinery technologies are relevant for backshoring in case they are applied to repatriation of production activities that were previously offshored for cost motives. Conversely, as regards 3D printing (or additive manufacturing) they only find very weak indices that this technology plays a role in backshoring decisions. Interestingly, Ancarani and Di Mauro (2018) argue that robotics (rather close to automated machinery) is not really an enabler for reshoring, while they argue at the same time that additive manufacturing can be an effective enabler of reshoring moves.

Evidently, there is a big variation in the sources from which these scholars depart (European Manufacturing Survey, Univaq Manufacturing Reshoring dataset focused either on European backshoring cases only or on European and North American cases or case studies) and the number of instances that they work with: 1705 in the case of Dachs et al. (2019), 495 on behalf of Ancarani et al. (2019), 840 in the case of Ancarani and Di Mauro (2018), 816 on behalf of Fratocchi and Di Stefano (2019), 50 for Müller et al. (2017) and 16 in the case of Chiarvesio and Romanello (2018). So do the data analysis techniques deployed: regression analysis in the case of Dachs et al. (2019) and Ancarani et al. (2019), descriptive statistics in the case of Müller et al. (2017), Ancarani and Di Mauro (2018) as well as Fratocchi and Di Stefano (2019), and qualitative analyses in the case of Chiarvesio and Romanello (2018). Finally, there is also a broad variety regarding the data character behind the sources employed: primary data from own survey in the case of Müller et al. (2017) and Dachs et al. (2019), whereas Ancarani and Di Mauro (2018), Ancarani et al. (2019 and Fratocchi and Di Stefano (2019) employ secondary data, and Chiarvesio and Romanello (2018) recur to cases for their primary data.

The former helps to explain why the "results of these studies are difficult to compare" (Müller et al. 2017 p. 169), but it does not change the inconsistency among the different findings.

Most importantly perhaps, while there is consensus on what backshoring or reshoring stands for and how it can be segmented (following e.g. seminal frameworks by Gray et al. 2013, p. 28),[Footnote2] the same can not be said about Industry 4.0. That is: from a perspective of the technologies concerned. Only two of the seven extant publications that examine the phenomenon of backshoring from an Industry 4.0 angle consider the entire set of technologies from Rüßmann et al. (2015). These are Chiarvesio and Romanello (2018) and Stentoft et al. (2020). The remaining publications apply a rather selective or open approaches regarding the Industry 4.0 technologies that they focus on. Among the selective approaches, we find Dachs et al. (2019) who look at eight technologies of which only three bear a clear relationship with the framework for Industry 4.0 as introduced by Rüßmann et al. (2015).Footnote3 The other onesFootnote4 are indeed digital technologies or exponents thereof, but they are "exogenous" to the Industry 4.0 framework of reference that is used for this paper. Ancarani and Di Mauro (2018), for their part, consider three technologies, of which two can be considered "endogenous" to Industry 4.0.Footnote5 Fratocchi and Di Stefano (2019) look at four types of technology, of which two adhere to the Rüßmann et al. (2015) framework.Footnote6 Among the open approaches, Ancarani et al. (2019, p. 365) use "keywords such as Industry 4.0, robotics, automation, additive manufacturing, 3DP, smart manufacturing, digitalization, advanced manufacturing, etc." to assess whether new technology adoption can be related to backshoring. However, this seems to have served for detecting cases of backshoring where some kind of advanced manufacturing technology was involved, instead of a one-by-one probing of the involvement of specific Industry 4.0 technologies in backshoring cases. Similarly, Müller et al. (2017), do not break down Industry 4.0 into specific technologies for their survey, and just use Industry 4.0 as an umbrella term to ask questions to their respondents. Moreover, they treat Industry 4.0 and reshoring in a rather disjointed manner, without manifest attempts to interlink the two concepts.

Finally, Chiarvesio and Romanello (2018 p. 361) and Stentoft et al. (2020)Footnote7 look at the entire range of Industry 4.0 technologies, based on the classification of Rüßmann et al. (2015).Footnote8 However, they do not come to concrete verdicts as to how the respective technologies relate to backshoring behavior. Instead, they come up with more aggregate statements and insights.

2.2 Relevance of respective digital technologies for specific backshoring rationales

Ancarani and Di Mauro (2018), as well as Fratocchi and Di Stefano (2019), postulate certain "production strategy-technology preference" combinations in their publications (see Table 1).

I.e., Fratocchi and Di Stefano (2019) relate « automated machinery» to backshoring that focuses on cost savings in the first place. As such, this type of machinery tends to be connected to production activities that were offshored to seize low cost advantages overseas. In addition, they argue that investments in automated machinery can form part of backshoring decisions that are flexibility-oriented, as they allow firms to adapt products for different customer types.

Conversely, they attribute a quality-orientation feature to 3D printing: when relocation to the home country is aimed at product upgrade, it is indicated to leverage 3D printing.

In a similar style, Ancarani and Di Mauro (2018) relate robotics (and automated machinery) to cost-oriented reshoring, and 3D printing and Cyber-Physical Systems (CPS) to quality-oriented reshoring.

Table 1 Technologies as levers for backshoring according to specific production strategies

Production strategy	**Corresponding technologies according to Ancarani and Di Mauro (2018)**	**Corresponding technologies according to Fratocchi and Di Stefano (2019)**
Cost-oriented	Robotics, automated machinery	Automated machinery
Flexibility-oriented	Robotics, automated machinery	Robotics, automated machinery
Quality-oriented	3D printing	3D printing, CPS

own elaboration

Finally, both Fratocchi and Di Stefano (2019) and Ancarani and Di Mauro (2018) attribute flexibility virtues to robotics and automated machinery, and view them as appropriate for flexibility-oriented reshoring decisions, consequently.

Stentoft et al. (2020) focus on backshoring for cost reasons, but do not look into specific Industry 4.0 technologies and the distinct role they may play in this regard.

2.3 Contextualizing the role of technology in backshoring decisions

While the use of Industry 4.0 technologies may have explanatory power for understanding backshoring movements, clearly there can also be other considerations or factors that add to the explanation of backshoring moves. In other words, when discovering that the adoption of Industry 4.0 technologies coincides or is intertwined with backshoring decisions, this does not entail that it constitutes the main or only driver behind such decisions.

In this sense, Gray et al. (2013), Johansson et al. (2019) and Dachs et al. (2019) argue that offshoring or reshoring decisions can be reviewed through the OLI paradigm (Dunning 2001)[Footnote9] and Transaction Cost Economics (Williamson 1985). Notably by looking at a company's (in)ability to exploit its "organization-specific advantages" (like a competitive product or a sought-after recipe or brand); at the "location-specific (dis)advantages" of the offshore location where production activities are undertaken at a given moment, from e.g. a market access,[Footnote10] technology, skilled labour and suppliers availability; at the "behavioral (un)certainties" with regard to the demand side and of personnel in the host country; at the "environmental (un)certainties" *sur place* in the sense of institutional (in)stability, (un)favorable fiscal and international trade regimes and (lack of) respect for (intellectual/private) property rights; and at the possibilities to coordinate and integrate offshore assets within the overall business of a multinational (cfr. "internalization (dis)advantages"). Whereas Johansson et al. (2019) find through exploratory factor analysis that access to technology -as part of their development "bundle"- is important for backshoring decisions, and the descriptive results from Dachs et al. (2019) reveal that backshoring occurs most frequent in high-technology industries where firms may react fast to changing technology conditions across the globe, Gray et al. (2013) do not refer to technology as a possible factor for backshoring at all.

3 Methods

3.1 Empirical setting

The empirical research setting from which we draw data is the Basque Country. We posit that it provides a relevant testing ground since the Basque economy has an above-average reliance on industrial activities. Manufacturing activities represent almost a quarter of the economy's gross value added, which is clearly higher than the Spanish and EU ratio (Kamp and Ruiz de Apodaca 2017). In fact, this region is a traditional industrial heartland of the Iberian Peninsula, and although it has undergone significant industrial conversion in recent decades, it has demonstrated an ongoing political commitment to maintaining industry at the center of the regional economy (Konstantynova 2017). As such, it can be expected to house an active landscape of manufacturing firms with an interest in adopting the latest production technologies, e.g. in the form of Industry 4.0.

3.2 Research activities

Two research objectives guided the undertaken investigation, namely: 1) whether the adoption of Industry 4.0, or digital technologies, bears a relation to backshoring decisions and their rationales (bullet points 1 and 2 at the end of Sect. 2), and 2) the role of Industry 4.0 technologies among other possible factors influencing such decisions (bullet point 3 at the end of Sect. 2).

The first objective has a rather analytical (theory-testing) character, whereas the second is more exploratory (theory-developing) in nature. Hence, we adopt a two-stage research approach and organized a comprehensive survey in view of the first objective, followed by in-depth case analyses to attain the second (Dul and Hak 2008). The first stage is in line with Dachs et al. (2019) who also apply a survey to investigate the relationship between backshoring of production activities and the use of digital technologies. The second stage aligns with Joubioux and Vanpoucke (2016) and Benstead et al. (2017) who likewise conducted in-depth case studies to study reshoring decision-making processes and to explore how backshoring unfolds. The combination of surveying companies and conducting case analysis also has the advantage that it can help shedding light on eventual causalities between the adoption of Industry 4.0 technologies and backshoring dynamics.

Given that Industry 4.0 and backshoring are relatively new phenomena, it is challenging to probe whether it is Industry 4.0 adoption that leads to backshoring or the other way around (Martinsuo and Chaoji 2017). Therefore, to go beyond revealing patterns or correlations between digital technology adoption and backshoring decisions (as per the survey activities), in-depth case analyses are useful to get an idea of eventual causalities between the former and the latter (Stentoft et al. 2016a, b).

3.2.1 Survey-based research activities

To attain research objectives 1 and 2 (see Image 1 above), a large-scale survey was organized supported by a structured questionnaire.

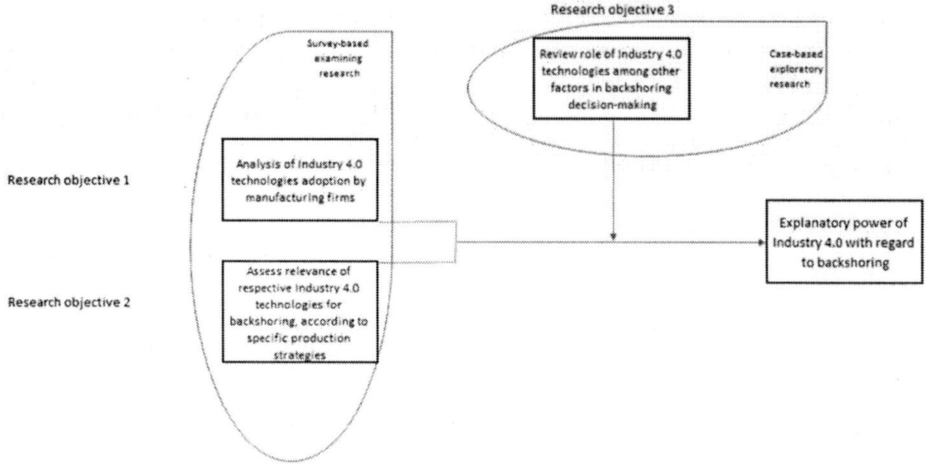

Image – 1 *Interrelations between research objectives and methods applied. Source: own elaboration.*

For the questionnaire design and to operationalize what Industry 4.0 stands for, the Rüßmann et al. (2015) classification was used as well as the Digital Transformation Monitor of the European Commission (DTM 2018). The reason for the latter was that the survey was backed up by the Industrial Agency of the Basque Government (SPRI) who had an interest in comparing the survey results with the DTM (2018). This led to the inclusion of a list of technologies in the survey questionnaire that does not align completely with the Rüßmann et al. (2015) classification, although we did manage to cover it almost entirely by making use of a proxy and a "composite indicator".

As for the "composite indicator"; to cover Horizontal and Vertical systems integration (HVSI), we assessed whether companies had adopted machine-to-machine (M2M) communication both at an intra-firm and inter-firm (together with clients and/or supplier) level. While this may not always be the same as what Rüßmann et al. (2015) portray by HVSI, it should come close. Moreover, it is arguably a more operational yardstick, which makes it more plausible that respondents answer correctly when asked about having implemented this concept at an intra and inter-firm level, than the platform that Rüßmann et al. (2015) refer to. Furthermore, as Chiarvesio and Romanello (2018, p. 361) explicate: M2M communication serves the purpose of HVSI. That is: manufacturing and machine data feed collaboration platforms from production to corporate, within the company, and with suppliers or clients. Consequently, we deem that our proxy is a valuable substitute for the original term.

Finally, we applied the term "robotics", which is not necessarily the same as "autonomous robots" and can thus only serve as a proxy.

For a complete overview of the Industry 4.0 technologies that Rüßmann et al. (2015) consider, how our research dealt with those (and others), as well as the technology sets that other (backshoring) scholars considered, see Table 2.

Table 2 Industry 4.0 technologies considered in backshoring publications

Rüßmann et al. (2015)	**Digital Transformation Monitor of the European Commission**	**This paper**	**Ancarani and Di Mauro (2018)**	**Dachs et al. (2019)**	**Fratocchi and Di Stefano (2019)**	**Chiarvesio and Romanello (2018)**	**Stentoft et al. (2020)**
1-Internet of Things	X	x			Stentoft et al. (2020)	X	X
2-Cloud Technologies	X	x				X	X
3-Big Data Analytics	X	x				X	X
4-Virtual Simulation Systems		x				X	Proxy = Simulation
5-Augmented Reality		x				X	X
6-Additive manufacturing / 3D Printing	X	x	X	X	X	X	X
7-Horizontal and Vertical systems integration		Proxy = Machine-to-Machine communication in cooperation with suppliers and/or clients		Proxy = Digital exchange of data with suppliers / customers + Near real-time production control systems		x	x
8-Autonomous robots	Proxy = robotics	Proxy = robotics	Proxy = robotics		Proxy = robotics	Proxy = Autonomous and collaborative robots	x
9-Cybersecurity	X	x				X	X
Additional technologies							
Artificial Intelligence	x	x					X
Automated Machinery	x	x			X		

Rüßmann et al. (2015)	**Digital Transformation Monitor of the European Commission**	**This paper**	**Ancarani and Di Mauro (2018)**	**Dachs et al. (2019)**	**Fratocchi and Di Stefano (2019)**	**Chiarvesio and Romanello (2018)**	**Stentoft et al. (2020)**
Cyber-Physical Systems		x	X	Proxy = Technologies for human–machine interaction			
Digital Visualization				x			
Mobile Services	X	x		Mobile / wireless devices for providing services			Mobile technologies
Product-Lifecycle Management Systems				X			
RFID and Real-Time-Location Systems (RTLS) technologies							x
Social Media	X	x					
Systems for automation of internal logistics				X			

own elaboration

The survey included questions to determine the participating companies':

- Size in terms of revenue and employees
- Value chain position
- Principal products and market offerings
- Foreign branch plants
- Adoption of digital technologies
- Intentions to backshore manufacturing activities

Apart from asking the survey participants whether they had adopted any of the listed technologies during the last 3 years (Research objective 1), they were asked whether the adoption of Industry 4.0 technologies could lead to backshoring maneuvers by their company and the likelihood of taking such decisions (Research objective 2). To distinguish between the degree of certainty with which they expected this to happen, we provided respondents with the possibility of answering either: "Yes, in fact, such decisions have been made", "Yes, this is a real possibility", or "No".

Take note that we asked after "in-house reshoring" experiences or intentions thereto (see Gray et al. 2013 p. 28; Engström et al. 2018), and not after other forms of backshoring, like outsourced production to an overseas supplier that could be brought back to the home base via an internalization or insourcing action.

The base population for the survey consisted of some 2,000 firms that SPRI had recently interacted with due to expressions of interest or applications by these firms for innovation, R&D, and internationalization support programs offered by the Basque Government. As such, the base population may not be representative of the entire universe of firms in the Basque Country. However, since we are primarily interested in the adoption of Industry 4.0 technologies (related to innovation) and decisions in the realm of international business (related to backshoring), it can be argued that we targeted a relevant set of "likely instances" from which to source insights.

The survey was launched at the end of January 2019 and was closed in late February 2019, resulting in 475 valid answer sets. The answers from these 475 companies were screened to, firstly, retain the companies that engaged in production activities abroad through foreign manufacturing subsidiaries. A procedure that was also followed by Dachs et al. (2019)

Secondly, we considered only companies that operate in B2B markets and that are industrial in nature, being a:

- "manufacturer of finished products for other industrial firms,"
- "supplier of parts or components to other industrial users,"
- "system provider to other industrial users" or
- "provider of industrial services."

Companies that are chiefly a distributor of goods or active in B2C markets were thus left out.

This led to a final sample of 63 companies able to make informed judgments on backshoring issues.[Footnote11] In terms of number of employees, the sample has the following characteristics (see Table 3):

Similarly, Table 4 shows the main business activity of the sample members:

3.2.2 Case-based research activities

To attain research objective 3 (contextualizing the role of technology in backshoring decisions), we tracked companies that have already backshored manufacturing activities to analyze their experiences and motives. To identify such companies, we consulted the representatives of foreign offices that SPRI maintains across the world. This network of offices supports Basque businesses abroad, but also keeps track of Basque companies closing overseas factories. As such, it is a privileged observer of backshoring cases. Consultations with these representatives led to the identification of nine Basque companies with backshoring experiences.

Table 3 Characterization of the sample in terms of number of employees

Number of employees	% of sample
Less than 10	0%
Between 10 and 49	13%
Between 50 and 249	46%
More than 250	41%

N = 63

Table 4 Characterization of the sample in terms of business activity

Business activity	% of sample
Manufacturer of finished goods for industrial customers	54%
Supplier of parts or components for industrial customers	27%
Systems provider for industrial customers	10%
Provider of industrial services	10%

N = 63

In Table 5, essential features of these nine companies are presented.

Contact was established with the above companies and seven of them agreed to an on-site interview.Footnote12 The visits were held in late February 2019. In four cases, the interviewees were general managers, whereas in the other cases the contact person was the company's international business director, a senior advisor to the company's president and a chief technology officer, respectively. To prepare for the interviews, desk research activities were undertaken with regard to these seven companies, notably by going through company websites, corporate presentations, press articles and archives from SPRI.

On-site interviews were conducted in an inductive manner. We informed the interviewees of our interest in the role of Industry 4.0 technologies in relation to backshoring moves. However, we did not direct the conversations towards the role of technology in those processes. Instead, we followed an open approach, giving free rein to the speakers without limiting them through directed or closed questions. During these semi-structured

Table 5 Basque companies with backshoring experience

Company	Approximate turnover in 2018 in million euros	Industry	Backshoring from/to
A	250	Electric power systems	Brazil to Spain
B	125	Bicycles	China to Spain (and Portugal)
C	200	Home appliances	Brazil to Spain
F	250	Kitchen equipment	China and Turkey to Spain
I	700	Vehicles	China and India to Spain
N	25	Metal mechanics	China to Spain
O	400	Electric power systems	Brazil and Turkey to Spain
S	100	Hand tools	Argentina and China to Spain
T	10	Casting technologies	China to Spain

own elaboration

interviews, which lasted between 60 and 90 min each, we "elicited" narratives from the company representatives. From a coding point-of-view, we first tried to comprehend what had led the companies to set up production activities in the foreign places from which they had meanwhile withdrawn. I.e., whether they pursued access to specific resources, whether they targeted cost-efficiency motives, whether they served market-seeking goals, and/or whether they went after strategic asset-seeking advantages (Dunning 1998). Next, we tried to find out why the company had backshored these production activities. For example, because it was not achieving the foreseen objectives, because the company had changed its (international business) priorities or strategy, because certain circumstances had changed and/or because the overseas branch plant had fulfilled its mission. To categorize the key factors behind the backshoring decisions, a taxonomy rooted in the OLI paradigm and Transaction Cost Economics was used (see Sect. 2.3). I.e., to digest our interviews we apply an "eclectic" framework made up of the three tiers from the OLI paradigm (Organization-specific, Location-specific and Internalization-specific advantages), and add the "behavioral uncertainty" and environmental uncertainty" components from TCE (Williamson 1985). We argue that this can help to provide relief to the reasons for backshoring compared to when these types of uncertainties are treated as (implicit) elements of internalization (dis)advantages or location-specific (dis)advantages.

As a follow-up to the interviews, a summary of the take-aways and our interpretation of the factors that played a role in the off- and backshoring decisions were presented to the respective companies to enhance a correct reflection of their experiences. This led some of the interviewees to propose modifications and additions, which helped to put each case into a more correct perspective (Creswell and Miller 2000).

4 Findings

4.1 Descriptive survey-based results

4.1.1 Adoption level of digital technologies

As regards the adoption of digital technologies on behalf of the 63 companies that make up our sample, we found the following:

With regard to the nine technologies that were considered, over 95% has adopted at least one of them and close to two-thirds of the companies had implemented four or more Industry 4.0 technologies (See Fig. 1).

Cybersecurity is the most widely implemented technology, with around 75% of the firms making use of it, followed by Internet of Things and Cloud computing. These two technologies have been implemented by close to 60% of the companies. The least implemented is augmented reality, with below 15% of the respondents making use of it. Robotics, big data analytics and 3D printing occupy middle positions, with some 45–50% of the respondents using these technologies.

In addition, if we look at the technology inventory that the DTM considers (see also Table 2),Footnote13 we conclude that approximately 98% has adopted at least two of them and close to 75% of the companies had implemented four or more technologies. Interestingly, the percentages are slightly higher than for the Industry 4.0 technology selection, which is arguably related to the fact that some technologies are more mature or lower entry (like automated machinery and social media). Indeed, automated machinery is implemented by 75% of the firms, whereas social media is adopted by more than 60% of the sample.

4.1.2 Interaction between adoption of digital technologies and backshoring decisions

Regarding the question whether adoption of the listed digital technologies may lead to backshoring maneuvers, 6% of the sub-sample agreed with this assertion and indicated that they had made concrete decisions to backshore production activities.Footnote14 Another 21% likewise agreed with this viewpoint, but from a forward-looking perspective, indicating that the adoption of Industry 4.0 technologies could make future backshoring decisions plausible. The rest of the respondents, 73%, opined that the adoption of digital technologies would not lead to backshoring decisions by their firm.

In addition, based on the answers to the question of whether "the adoption of digital technologies may lead to backshoring maneuvers" (see Fig. 2), we looked at the average

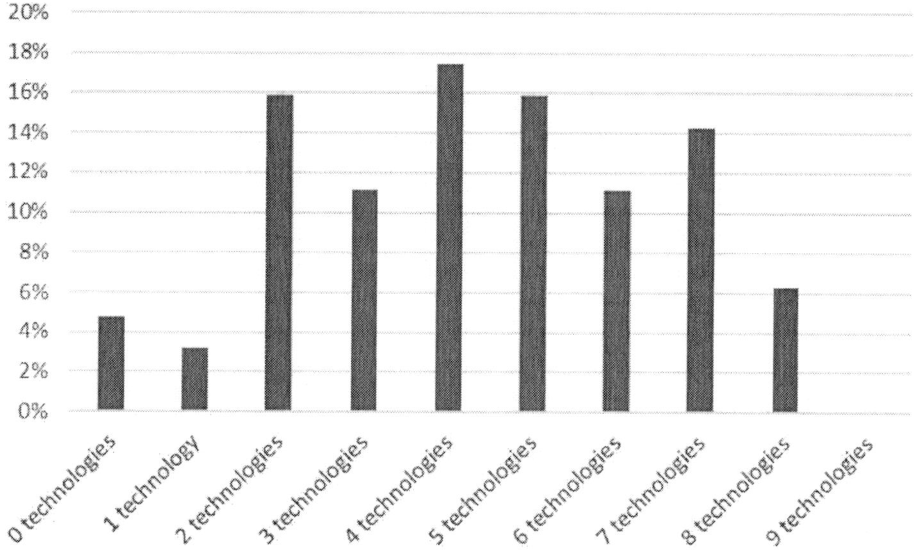

Fig. 1-*Adoption level of the nine technology pillars supporting Industry 4.0. N = 63*

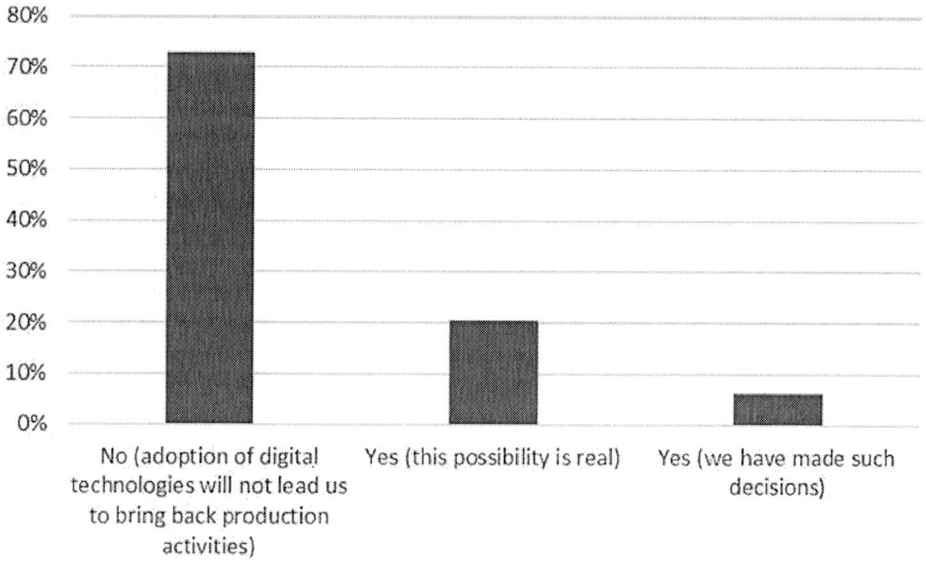

Fig. 2 *Expectations regarding the impact of adopting digital technologies on the backshoring of production activities. N = 63*

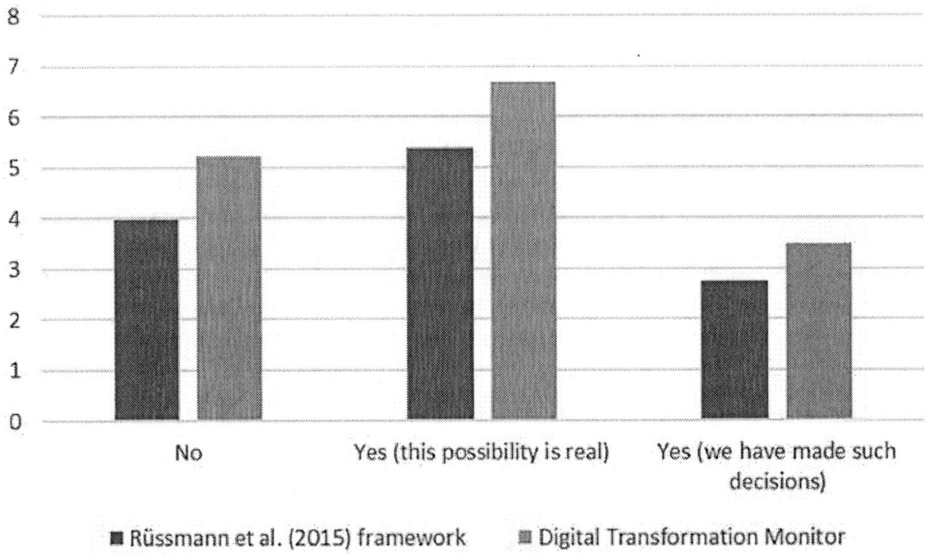

***Fig. 3** Number of digital technologies adopted in comparison to companies' production backshoring postures. N = 63*

number of technologies from the Rüßmann et al. (2015) framework and the ones from the DTM inventory. This led to the following picture:

Figure 3 reveals that the firms that actually took the decision to backshore (answers on the right-hand side of the graph) are not the most prolific adopters of digital technologies. I.e., their adoption scores regarding the Industry 4.0 technologies according to Rüßmann et al. (2015) as well as from the DTM are lower than those for the group of firms that consider backshoring decisions to be a realistic prospect (answers in the center). Even more striking, their technology adoption scores are also outperformed by the group that does not expect to take production backshoring decisions (answers on the left-hand side of the graph).

Take note that while the technology adoption scores on the DTM inventory exceed those of the Industry 4.0 framework of Rüßmann et al. (2015), it is also true that the DTM considers 10 technologies, whereas Rüßmann et al. (2015) focus on 9.

4.2 Regression results based on survey data

4.2.1 Testing at the aggregated level of the Industry 4.0 technology set

Using the respondents' data on technology uptake and backshoring intentions / decisions for non-parametric testing led to the following results. Firstly, we looked separately at the data and scores for the three sub-groups (Yes, we have made backshoring decisions; Yes, this possibility is real; and No). Then, we carried out a One-Way ANOVA Kruskal–Wallis test. This revealed a significant relation ($p = 0.036$) between the adoption of Industry 4.0 technologies and backshoring (p-value threshold: below 0.05).

A first check to see whether we actually were onto something, was to plot the data based on a Tukey post-hoc test (see Fig. 4). When doing this, it became obvious that there is a lot of overlap between the answer range of the firms without backshoring intentions (vertical bar 2) and the answer range of those with backshoring intentions (1) or who had taken decisions to repatriate activities in the (near) future (0). I.e., from a horizontal perspective, the vertical bars coincide partly. This basically implies that we can not affirm that the adoption of a larger amount of Industry 4.0 technologies changes' companies posture towards backshoring and/or that it leads to a bigger chance on backshoring.

A further post-hoc test that we carried out was a -more granular and demanding- Dwass-Steel-Critchlow-Fligner pairwise comparison (p-value threshold: below 0.05). These comparisons neither backed up the previous Kruskal–Wallis tests. Rather, they weakened the signs of a significant correlation between the variables considered.

Dwass-Steel-Critchlow-Fligner pairwise comparison results.

Sub-group 0 versus sub-group 1 $p = 0.091$.

Sub-group 0 versus sub-group 2 $p = 0.315$.

Sub-group 1 versus sub-group 2 $p = 0.157$.

Afterwards, we regrouped the original three sub-groups into two. A first one containing the companies with backshoring intentions (Yes, this possibility is real) and effectively taken decisions towards the (near) future (Yes, we have made such decisions), and a second one made up by the companies that did not expect to backshore production activities (No). This regrouping was done to give some substance to the "Yes"-group, as with only 4 companies counting with firm backshoring decisions, comparisons on a trilateral basis would quickly become meaningless.Footnote15 The subsequent Welch One-Way ANOVA test also delivered a non-significant result ($p = 0.372$) regarding the relationship between the nine Industry 4.0 technologies and backshoring postures (p-value threshold: below 0.05).

Altogether then, the tests at an aggregated level for the Industry 4.0 technologies did not show a convincing relation with backshoring behavior of the sampled firms.

4.2.2 Testing the relevance of individual technologies for backshoring

Next, tests were conducted on the respective, individual, technologies that make up the Industry 4.0 technology set and whether the implementation of one or more of them is (significantly) more abundant among firms with backshoring intentions/decisions versus those without such intentions/decisions. This way, we avoid that a grouping of technologies blurs the sight on individual technologies that matter more than others for backshoring dynamics.

The individual tests revealed the following P values (threshold value: below 0.05) for the Industry 4.0 technologies:

1. Internet of Things: not significant (0.253)
2. Cloud Technologies: not significant (0.190)

3. Big Data Analytics: not significant (P = 0.800)
4. Virtual Simulation Systems: not significant (0.388)
5. Augmented Reality: not significant (0.136)
6. 3D Printing: not significant (0.836)
7. Horizontal and Vertical Systems Integration: almost significant (0.064)
8. Robotics: almost significant (0.071)
9. Cybersecurity: not significant (0.485)

In addition, we carried out the same tests for a series of additional technologies. This resulted in the following findings:

- Artificial Intelligence: not significant (0.815)
- Automated Machinery: not significant (0.707)
- Cyber-Physical Systems: not significant (0.202)
- Mobile Services: not significant (0.870)
- Social Media: not significant (0.148)

From the above results, it turns out that there are just two technologies that show signs of association with backshoring decisions: Horizontal and Vertical Systems Integration and Robotics. None of the others do.

4.2.3 Testing the relevance of individual technologies for specific backshoring rationales

Apart from asking the survey participants whether "the adoption of digital technologies may lead to in-house backshoring maneuvers", we also asked the companies whether they thought that the use of the digital technologies they had implemented could lead to a reallocation of production activities via other 'mechanisms'? I.e., by means of not/less offshoring of production, or by substituting foreign suppliers by national ones. The answers to this question serve as an indication of whether Industry 4.0 technologies can have indirect backshoring effects.

In response to this more broadly framed question, 49 companies indicated that they could foresee this kind of consequences from the adoption of Industry 4.0 technologies. The remaining 14 companies did not expect this to happen.

Against this backdrop, a follow-on question was posed to the sub-sample of 49 companies. They were asked in which way the adopted digital technologies would influence production location and supplier selection decisions?

As answer options they were presented a cost-oriented and a quality-oriented rationale. The first option referred to the ability of digital technologies to make production activities in the home base more cost-competitive compared to offshore locations. The second option referred to the ability of digital technologies to improve the quality of production processes and of tying production steps together, diminishing the interest in delocalizing or fragmenting production steps to/across foreign places.

Take note that companies were able to tick multiple options. That is: they could argue in favour of one of the rationales presented to them or to both. As regards the respective rationales, the firms were asked with which extent these applied according to them (1: very strongly, 2: strongly, 3: moderately, 4: in a limited manner or not at all).

Next, we focused on the companies that attributed a 1 or 2 to either one of the rationales, and reviewed the respective technologies that they had adopted. As such, we check whether specific technologies stand out for specific production strategy rationales. I.e., we group the answers according to a cost-oriented and a quality-oriented rationale or production strategy, and then look at the technologies adopted by the respondents from the respective groups.

Consequently, the following P values were obtained (threshold value: below 0.05).

Firstly, we present the results on the cost-oriented rationale for the nine Industry 4.0 technologies:

1. Internet of Things: not significant (0.451)
2. Cloud Technologies: not significant (0.647)
3. Big Data Analytics: significant (0.047)
4. Virtual Simulation Systems: not significant (0.938)
5. Augmented Reality: not significant (0.644)
6. 3D Printing: not significant (0.938)
7. Horizontal and Vertical Systems Integration: 0.831
8. Robotics: not significant (0.830)
9. Cybersecurity: not significant (0.814)

In addition, the same assessment was made for the supplementary technologies

- Artificial Intelligence: not significant (0.414)
- Automated Machinery: not significant (0.339)
- Cyber-Physical Systems: not significant (0.707)
- Mobile Services: not significant (0.938)
- Social Media: not significant (0.181)

From the above it follows that the only technological pillar that companies attribute an important role to for improving the cost-competitiveness of home-based production operations (and influencing production retention decisions and/or local supplier selection positively) is big data analytics.

Secondly, when examining the quality-oriented rationale we get the following results for the nine Industry 4.0 technologies:

1. Internet of Things: not significant (0.165)
2. Cloud Technologies: not significant (0.647)
3. Big Data Analytics: not significant (0.459)
4. Virtual Simulation Systems: not significant (0.938)
5. Augmented Reality: not significant (0.193)
6. 3D Printing: not significant (0.938)
7. Horizontal and Vertical Systems Integration: not significant (0.718)
8. Robotics: not significant (0.830)
9. Cybersecurity: not significant (0.814)

The same assessment for the supplementary technologies from Table 2 yields the following results:

- Artificial Intelligence: not significant (0.962)
- Automated Machinery: not significant (0.339)
- Cyber-Physical Systems: not significant (0.707)
- Mobile Services: not significant (0.580)
- Social Media: not significant (0.938)

Consequently, this test does not reveal any technology that companies who are driven by quality-oriented motives for their location decisions adopt more systematically than those with an opposite posture.

4.3 Case-based research results

4.3.1 The role of technology in backshoring decisions

As can be seen in Table 6, the companies with previous backshoring experiences reveal nowadays a rather pronounced technology adoption profile. The average number of technologies adopted from the Industry 4.0 framework is 4.57 (higher than the average for effective backshoring firms shown in Fig. 3) and 2.43 for the additional technologies from Table 2).

Table 6 Adoption of digital technologies among case companies with previous backshoring experience

Industry 4.0 technologies	**Company A**	**Company B**	**Company F**	**Company I**	**Company N**	**Company O**	**Company S**
Internet of Things	X		X	X		X	X
Cloud Technologies	X			X		X	
Big Data Analytics	X			X		X	
Virtual Simulation Systems				X			
Augmented Reality							X
Additive manufacturing / 3D Printing	X	X				X	X
Horizontal and Vertical Systems Integration	X		X			X	X
Robotics	X	X	X	X		X	X
Cybersecurity	X	X	X			X	X
Additional technologies							
Artificial Intelligence				X			X
Automated Machinery	X	X	X	X	X	X	X
Cyber-Physical Systems							
Mobile Services	X	X	X		X		
Social Media	X	X	X	X		X	X

Own elaboration based on inputs from companies

As such, this might be somewhat at odds with the results from Sect. 4.2. However, practically all of the backshoring cases we review took place before the adoption of Industry 4.0 technologies came on steam, so the role of these specific technologies certainly has to be relativized. Moreover, past backshoring behavior on behalf of specific firms does not imply that these same companies will repeat such decisions, even if they maintain (several) production plants overseas (which is the case for all case companies except for Company N). In fact, five of the companies with previous backshoring experience participated in our survey and all of them indicated that they did not expect to undertake further backshoring actions. Hence, their answers form part of the "no firms" in Figs. 2, 3 as well as the subsequent regression analyses.

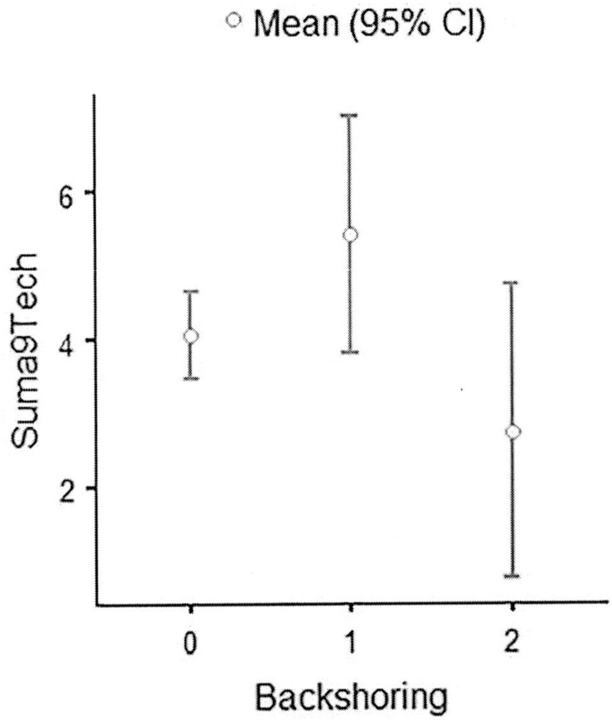

Fig. 4 *Plotting range of answers and average scores on Industry 4.0 technologies adoption versus backshoring postures based on Tukey post-hoc test.*

The seven firms that were interviewed provided insights into 11 backshoring cases where overseas plants of Basque companies were closed or saw their production activities drastically reduced through a transfer of manufacturing activities to the home base.[Footnote16] Five of the firms had undertaken a single backshoring operation, whereas two others had backshored twice. In Table 7, we set out the details of the respective experiences.

In five cases the country from which production activities were backshored was China, whereas there were two backshoring experiences from Brazil and also two from Turkey. In addition, there was one backshoring case from India and one from Argentina.

On average, the time that the overseas plants were operational until backshoring decisions were taken was 15 years, although this number lowers to 11 years if we do not consider the Argentinian plant of Company S. This plant forms an outlier as it was created in 1963 and had been producing for over 50 years before it devolved production activities to the Basque Country via backshoring decisions taken by its owner.

Table 7 Specifics on backshoring cases

Company and country where it set up production	Year of opening / acquisition of plant and year of closure / sell-off / reduction of activity	Entry mode	Why offshore?	Why backshore?
Company B-China **Company F-China** **Company I-China**	2007–2015 2007–2015 1995–2012	Greenfield FDI Greenfield FDI Greenfield FDI	Expectation that the Asian market for premium bicycles, robust kitchen equipment and high-end buses would grow "Market-seeking" Company B and F form part of an industrial cooperative and together with several fellow cooperative firms these two companies decided to set up shop in an industrial park that would only shelter affiliates of this Basque cooperative "Bandwagon effect"	Companies B and I targeted premium market segments whose sales results in the Chinese and adjacent markets remained below expectations Company F's products did match local pockets of demand, but the company found it hard to stand out among local producers of similar products, so the lack of competitive advantage or the lack of appreciation for its superior value caused it to lose ground in the market Consequently, the plants of companies B and F ended up producing for export markets, although they were intended to produce for local markets
Company N- China	2004–2015	Greenfield FDI	Chop up the value chain by locating design activities in Europe and production activities in China. Seize cost advantages through offshoring manufacturing "Efficiency-seeking"	The Chinese plant of Company N produced a lot for the European and the North American market Over time, manufacturing in the Eurozone became more attractive, as producing in China started to get more expensive. Also, from a trade perspective, it became of increasingly greater interest to produce within the Eurozone, as the United

Company and country where it set up production	Year of opening / acquisition of plant and year of closure / sell-off / reduction of activity	Entry mode	Why offshore?	Why backshore?
				States taxes imported bearings from China more heavily than when they are produced in Europe Company N also pointed out internal financial and investment issues: due to a lack of resources to keep the multinational structure that the firm had created intact, it was forced to reconsider its international strategy and overseas production activities Similarly, as the company opted for more R&D-intensive and high-end products, it decided to pull back into its home base and concentrate its activities in the Basque Country
Company S-China	2008 to present (although production has been transferred to Europe)	Greenfield FDI supplemented by takeover of local player with multiple plants	Company S merged with peers from Northern Europe and the United States. The joint holding counted with an own Chinese factory and went on a take-over spree in China. The outcome was an ensemble of plants in China and a sub-optimal distribution of "which plant produces what for which markets" "Strategic asset-seeking"	In this case, restructuring and rationalization of the global production apparatus and the respective "origin" (where they produced)–"destination" (which markets they supplied) relations constituted the trigger for backshoring operations This meant that Company S decided that part of the Chinese production for the Northern European market would be manufactured within Europe

Company and country where it set up production	Year of opening / acquisition of plant and year of closure / sell-off / reduction of activity	Entry mode	Why offshore?	Why backshore?
				This was done for reasons of both logistics and quality, but also since the advanced adoption of new production technologies at European production sites made them more cost competitive than before
Company I-India	2001–2015	Joint venture with two local partners, making use of existing production facilities at first and adding a greenfield plant in 2010	Expectation that the Asian market for high-end buses would grow "Market-seeking"	Company I suffered from a lack of appreciation of its premium products and high-safety buses, as well as disappointing forecasts for the high-end coachwork segment in the Indian market Admittedly, the firm may not have planned the market entry very well, in the belief that having a production presence in the (BR)IC countries was a must and being advised by third parties that the growth possibilities for its product line in the Indian market would be substantial
Company F-Turkey **Company O-Turkey**	2006–2016 1999–2006	Greenfield FDI Greenfield FDI	Sales potential on the domestic (hotel) market "Market-seeking" Relatively well-skilled human resources and supply chain "Resource-seeking"	Company F and Company O blamed turmoil in the domestic (Turkish) market—both from an institutional point of view and as regards sales forecasts—for their decisions to withdraw Both also suffered from a lack of appreciation for

Company and country where it set up production	Year of opening / acquisition of plant and year of closure / sell-off / reduction of activity	Entry mode	Why offshore?	Why backshore?
				their products by local customers, who generally showed a low willingness-to-pay and a tendency to settle for copycat products On top of this, both Company F and Company O indicated that their products manufactured in Turkey were not suitable for other markets, reducing the possibility of fitting the Turkish plant into their overall international business strategy Over time, declining sales meant that maintaining a dedicated plant for the Turkish market became unsustainable for both companies
Company A-Brazil **Company O-Brazil**	2003–2017 (sell-off to a competitor) 2005–severe reduction in activities since 2016	Take-over of existing local company Greenfield FDI	Take-over of diverse kernels of knowledge and technology bases for subsequent transfer and roll-out across the globe "Strategic asset-seeking" (Company A only) Entry to seize sales potential on domestic market "Market-seeking" (both companies)	Both cases suffered from a worsening of domestic market conditions and sales outlooks At the same time, the Brazilian plants were faced with growing environmental uncertainties, including: union pressure, tariffs on parts imports, ineffective functioning of local (segments of the) supply chain The two companies characterized Brazil as a challenging country, administratively speaking, with a lot of

Company and country where it set up production	Year of opening / acquisition of plant and year of closure / sell-off / reduction of activity	Entry mode	Why offshore?	Why backshore?
				red tape and a highly politicized business life The subsequent institutional uncertainties made it unattractive to continue producing in Brazil Furthermore, Company A and Company O pointed to a lack of strategic fit between their Brazilian products/manufacturing activities and their evolving core business and international business activity. In the end, the Brazilian activities became increasingly disconnected from the companies' product and technology portfolio, leading to a phasing out of Brazilian production operations
Company S-Argentina	1963 to present (although production has been transferred to Europe)	Greenfield FDI	Company S merged with peers from Northern Europe and the United States. While Company S already had a branch plant in Argentina since decades, the joint holding also took over an additional factory in Argentina. The outcome was a redundancy in production capacity and a sub-optimal distribution of "which plant	Similar to the experience of Company S in China, the Argentinian backshoring case is a consequence of restructuring and rationalization of the company's global production apparatus and its respective "origin"–"destination" relations Within this context, it was decided that the Argentinian production for the US market would be manufactured in Europe The decision to transfer

Company and country where it set up production	Year of opening / acquisition of plant and year of closure / sell-off / reduction of activity	Entry mode	Why offshore?	Why backshore?
			produces what for which markets" "Strategic asset-seeking"	US-bound production out of Argentina was based on logistics, quality and cost arguments. As far as cost reductions were to be gained from this transfer, they were fueled by the superior level of automation and technological progress at the European plants compared to the one in Argentina

Own elaboration based on interviews and desk research

Building on the previous table, it turns out that disappointing sales in the markets that offshore factories were intended to supply was typically the motivation for backshoring (Company A, B, F and O). In the case of Company B and F backshoring was also due to erroneous forecasts of the offshore market sales potential. Company I also suffered from this. In the case of Company S, a difference in technological sophistication of manufacturing in Spain compared to the technology level of Company S' plants in Argentina and China did function as a catalyzer for backshoring decisions. Particularly as this translated into a cost disadvantage for the Argentinian and Chinese plants versus the Basque plant. Hence, through intra-firm competition for production orders, the Basque factory was assigned manufacturing activities that used to be carried out in either Argentina or China. Company N also testified that as they were facing (labour) cost increases at their Chinese plant, this formed a trigger for backshoring. Problems with product quality was mentioned by Company N and S. Too long delivery times and logistics complexity to serve the end markets also resounded in the case of Companies N and S, as their offshore plants produced for clients on other continents. Eventually, this also played a role for Companies B and F as their offshore plants shifted their focus from selling on-site to producing for Europe. In a similar vein, companies A, B, F, I and O suffered from an overengineered or too high-end product offer for the markets they were supposed to serve. Hence, their plants gradually lost their reason for being in the countries they were located. Lack of ability to manage and integrate the overseas activities properly with the rest of the company's business, was mentioned by Company N. Additionally, Company N suffered from financial constraints. Finally, contextual factors like trade barriers, taxes on products manufactured in China to be shipped to other continents, tense industrial relations and political instability played a role in the backshoring decisions of Companies A, F, N and O.

5 Discussion

5.1 Level of digital technology adoption

Overall, the 63 companies from the survey sample reveal a considerable level of digital technology adoption. If we compare our findings with those of BCG (2016), it seems fair to state that our sample is reporting a considerable adoption rate for Industry 4.0 technologies. That is, BCG (2016) established that 19% of some 300 firms from Germany and 16% of around 300 US firms had either implemented a full Industry 4.0 concept (such as running a smart factory) or initial measures toward this concept (such as the introduction of autonomous robots). Similarly, Ancarani and Di Mauro (2018, pp. 5–6) and Ancarani et al. (2019, p. 367) come to an adoption percentage that is in line with the results from BCG (2016). Against this backdrop, the adoption of robotics, automated machinery or horizontal and vertical system integration on behalf of our sample easily doubles those percentages.

5.2 Frequency of backshoring

Our research revealed 13 backshoring experiences on behalf of 9 firms. On a total of 666 foreign plant locations held by Basque firms overseas (SPRI data from 2019), these 13 backshoring cases represent 2.0%. Similarly, if we compare the fact that there are an estimated 296 Basque firms (data from SPRI) that have one or more overseas production plants and only 9 of them have undertaken backshoring, this represents a maximum of around 3.0% of the total.

This range of backshoring experiences is quite in line with the 4.3% that Dachs et al. (2019, p. 4) establish based on data from the European Manufacturing Survey. It is also in line with the percentage that can be reconstructed from Johansson et al. (2019). They identify 160 backshoring projects out of 4601 plant locations, representing 3.5%.

5.3 Interdependences between digital technology adoption and backshoring decisions

When comparing the survey results on digital technology adoption with findings from other sources (see Sect. 5.1), it seems fair to state that our sample is characterized by a pronounced uptake of digital technologies. However, the survey respondents provide mixed results when it comes to backshoring decisions and intentions towards the (near) future.

Whereas a small percentage (± 6%) of the participants declared to have taken decisions with a view to repatriate activities, there was a larger group (± 20%) who indicated that they may take such decisions. Still, the lion share of companies asserted that they would not take backshoring actions.

While the Dwass-Steel-Critchlow-Fligner pairwise comparisons revealed no significant correlation between backshoring and Industry 4.0 technologies adoption, it is interesting to note that the ones with future intentions to backshore display the highest digital technology adoption rate (see Fig. 3). Therefore, if we relate our results to the following statement of Ancarani et al. (2019, p. 367): "The data collected suggest that the diffusion of Industry 4.0 among companies backshoring to Europe is not widespread (14%)", they provide rather ambiguous support. On the one hand, the participants to our survey who have decided to backshore in the (near) future score lower on digital technology uptake than those who consider taking backshoring decisions and those who do not plan any backshoring operation. As such, this appears to be in line with the above statement. On the other hand, precisely as our survey data indicate that the firms who consider backshoring as a future option are the ones with the highest adoption rate of Industry 4.0 technologies implies that future cases of backshoring could be carried out by firms with a pronounced Industry 4.0 profile.

Moreover, even if the implementation of Industry 4.0 technologies does not seem to be the root cause for backshoring dynamics, it can strengthen them. The fact that almost 20% of the surveyed companies indicated that the use of digital technologies turns 'taking backshoring decisions' into a real possibility (versus only 6% of the survey participants with firm backshoring decisions), could point in this direction. It would also hint at a trend rupture (in line with Dachs et al. 2019) between past and prospective backshoring. In support of this trend rupture idea one can argue that the adoption of digital technologies is a recent phenomenon and its effects on production and plant location decisions can only become visible with time.

5.4 The role of individual digital technologies for backshoring

When assessing whether specific technologies hold a relationship with backshoring attitudes, we find that robotics and horizontal and vertical systems integration are the only ones that reveal a nearly significant correlation with backshoring. The finding regarding robotics is in line with postulations of Ancarani and Di Mauro (2018) and Fratocchi and Di Stefano (2019). Studies that have focused on the individual role of horizontal and vertical systems integration vis-à-vis are not available, but our finding makes sense from an embeddedness perspective. That is: the fact that this technology -via its horizontal dimension- has an inter-firm character that implies coordination with surrounding companies, could lead to backshoring activities to places where the focal firm interacts closely with suppliers and (lead) users (Forsgren et al. 2005).

When checking whether robotics and automated machinery, on the one hand, and 3D printing and Cyber-Physical Systems, on the other, are more pronouncedly adopted by firms that adhere respectively to a cost or quality production strategy, our data do not provide back-up to the postulations that Ancarani and Di Mauro (2018) and Fratocchi and Di Stefano (2019) issue. While this does not exclude that certain technologies can be useful from a cost reduction or quality improvement rationale (or a pursuit of raising flexibility, delivery or customization levels, for that matter), one should also realize that their usefulness will depend on the type of production activities to be backshored. I.e., if large scale production activities are brought back to the home base, the chance that 3D printing will play a crucial role is not so big. In fact, even when looking at firms that manufacture high-end or premium quality products (like Company I and O from our case studies), its relevance may be reduced and it may be largely limited to (rapid) prototyping or the production of accessories and optional features.

5.5 Contextualizing the role of technology in backshoring decisions

When looking at the findings from the historic backshoring cases, technology does not appear to have acted as a meaningful driver for the repatriation decisions taken. Take note that this goes for technology in general and not for specific Industry 4.0 technologies in particular, as most of the backshoring decisions by our case companies were taken at a time that Industry 4.0 technologies were not around. Only in the case of Company S did the difference in technological sophistication of manufacturing in Spain compared to the technology level of Company S' plants in Argentina and China contribute to backshoring decisions. Beyond the experiences of Company S, it seems that other factors played a more determining role when the reviewed companies took their backshoring decisions (see Table 8).

Table 8 Classifying backshoring motives according to OLI-TCE scheme

	Organization-specific disadvantages	Location-specific disadvantages of offshore production sites						Behavioral uncertainties		Environmental uncertainties	Internalization disadvantages	
Company	Product-market mismatch	Eroding sales in markets that the offshore site is intended to serve	Lagging production technology level compared to plants elsewhere (notably in the home base)	Rising cost level	Quality issues	Distance to (unforeseen) end markets	Distance to corporate R&D or design assets	Erroneous forecasting	Predictability of local staff behavior and performance	Institutional uncertainty (political instability, turbulent industrial relations, trade barriers)	Rationalizing product(ion) portfolio across manufacturing sites	Resource shortages (finance, staff) to coordinate foreign operations
A	X	X						(X)		X	X	
B	X	X				(X)		X				
F	X	X				(X)		X		X		
I	X							X				
N				X		X				X		X
O	X	X						(X)		X	X	
S			X	X	X	X					X	

Own elaboration

To start with, Companies A, B, F, I and O seemed unable to exploit their "organization-specific advantages" in the sense that they discovered ± to be offering the right product to the wrong market. That is, they ended up offering over-engineered products and/or were targeting marginal market segments in the countries they had set their sights on. This type of product-market mismatch as an ingredient for backshoring has also been referred to by Di Mauro et al. (2018).

When considering "location-specific (dis)advantages", beyond the mentioned technology differential that Company S referred to, the following factors came to the surface. Rising cost levels as a sign of fleeting advantages of offshore locations (Bals et al. 2016) were reported by Company S, allowing its Basque plant to take over production assignments from its counterparts in Argentina and China. Company N also reported this, which - together with financial shortages that it was suffering from after the credit crunch- prompted it to divest of its Chinese plant and backshore its production activities. Quality issues were only declared by Company S as a reason for backshoring (Stentoft et al. 2016a, b). The distance and logistics to end markets became an issue for Companies B and F as a lack of success on their host markets led them to manufacture products for export to Europe. As this was an unforeseen downside, it influenced their backshoring decisions. As such, the argument that backshoring can serve to bring production closer to the end market (Johansson and Olhager 2018) applies to Companies B and F.

In terms of "behavioral uncertainties" we see that Companies B, F and I were forced to correct or revoke their prior internationalization decisions" (Kinkel and Maloca 2009; Dachs and Kinkel 2013) due to erroneous or overoptimistic forecasting. Also Companies A and O were confronted with deteriorating or disappointing sales in the markets that their offshore factories were intended to supply, and this motivated their backshoring decisions. Ultimately, these decisions can be related to the fact that market-seeking motives formed the primary motive to go abroad for the companies considered. Behavioral uncertainties in terms of deficient or opportunistic behavior of staff or suppliers was not explicitly reported.

"Environmental uncertainty" (e.g. in the form of institutional instability, political turmoil, tense labour relations) played a role in the backshoring decisions of Company A and Company O out of Brazil, and Company F and O out of Turkey. By extension, Company O argued that plant closures tend to be linked to moving out of unstable (commercial, political) markets rather than to production (technology)-related motives. Company N, for its part, referred to rising trade barriers hampering it to ship products from China to other continents in a competitive manner. This type of changing exogenous circumstances as a reason for exiting foreign investments align with findings from Anderson and Gatignon (1986), as well as Gylling et al. (2015), Mugurusi and De Boer (2014) and Barbieri et al. (2018).

As for "internalization disadvantages", Company N reported a lack of coordination and oversight capacities as a catalyzer for backshoring, which resonates with findings from Brouthers and Nakos (2004), Müller et al. (2017) or Dachs et al. (2019). Rationalizing product(ion) portfolios across internal manufacturing sites and optimizing was an issue for Company A, O and S. As such, for them backshoring was also the outcome of a deliberate strategic intent. In the case of Company A, their production was increasingly spread out across the world (particularly in South America) to comply with local content rules in different markets. Recently, they decided to divest several of their earlier acquisitions as the products that these plants manufactured were insufficiently marketable across the globe, making them less interesting from a strategic business perspective. Ultimately, this led to the sell-off of Company A's Brazilian subsidiary. This aligns with the observation of Di Mauro et al. (2018) that if products manufactured in offshore locations end up being poorly adjusted to the owner's portfolio, this can give rise to a firm's withdrawal from such production places. In the case of Company S and its plants in China and Argentina, the transfer of production to Europe clearly reflects the desire to streamline the product–market combinations the respective plants serve. Similarly, Company O argued that they scrutinize their global production apparatus regularly and try to move to places of strategic importance and where there is a stable and sizeable market available. This is a kind of "strategic asset retention" behavior, which certainly in the case of Company S and A aligns with their strategic asset-seeking motives to create or acquire foreign production capacity in the first place. As such, this is in line with assertions by Grandinetti and Tabacco (2015) or Robinson and Hsieh (2016) that global reorganization rounds can unlock backshoring movements.

Altogether then, technology seems to form part of the backshoring equation, but it certainly did not appear to constitute a preponderant variable. Accordingly, during the company interviews, it became clear that if backshoring takes place, it is often due to multiple factors. And when backshoring is being considered, (digital) technologies can act as a catalyst or accelerator for a backshoring decision that made sense all along. Hence, in the cases under review seemed to have been a catalyzer, rather than an instigator, trigger or driver.

6 Implications

6.1 Conceptual implications

It seems fair to state that while a growing body of backshoring research is taking shape, including research that looks at it from an Industry 4.0 perspective, the range of technologies considered in such studies tends to be small. In furtherance to Stentoft et al. (2020), the present study underlines that reviewing companies' adoption of digital technologies can and should be expanded to understand the dynamics between Industry 4.0 and backshoring. One, because there is more to Industry 4.0 than just two or three of the most adopted digital technologies among manufacturing firms. Two, to paraphrase Gray et al. (2013), because it is important to define what Industry 4.0 is, which digital technologies go underneath this umbrella term, and how their uptake might evolve. These issues matter to avoid that Industry 4.0 is considered as a black box or that (backshoring) analysis in relation to Industry 4.0 focus on mere "digital technology mixes". Consequently, breaking Industry 4.0 down into concrete technologies and assessing the joint and individual relation of the respective technologies with backshoring offers analytical surplus value.

In addition, the present paper's consideration of behavioral and environmental uncertainties (from the TCE toolbox to predict governance arrangements) as separate categories next to the classic trichotomy of OLI (dis)advantages to foreign market entry/exit decisions (instead of treating them as parts of location-specific or internalization advantages) served to break further conceptual ground. I.e., it helped to segment the motives behind backshoring decisions in a more granular manner and expand the variety of factors or drivers, as well as bundles of them, affecting backshoring operations (Dachs et al. 2019; Johansson et al. 2019).

6.2 Practical implications

The impact of Industry 4.0 technologies on backshoring operations is not clear-cut. While we did not find significant evidence that the adoption of digital technologies has stimulated backshoring so far, in the future this may happen. At least, the stated evidence we obtained on possible future backshoring in association to Industry 4.0 clearly supersedes the revealed evidence on past and present backshoring in relation to the adoption of digital technologies. Furthermore, happenings like the outbreak of COVID19 could foster additional backshoring activity (Barbieri et al. 2020; Strange 2020; UNCTAD 2020). Conversely, it is also possible that making supply chains more robust could be their preferred response to continue reaping the advantages of international trade and global value chains (Miroudot 2020). In fact, precisely Industry 4.0 technologies like Big Data Analytics can be leveraged to deal better with supply chain risks (Birkel and Hartmann 2020). Moreover, the idea that nearby sourcing will bring more stability and certainty is not so evident. In this regard, a recent OECD (2020) study highlights that in addition to higher costs, recurring to local sourcing can lead to higher volatility in securing supplies, as there are fewer channels for adjusting input provision. Such insights would then neither make it likely that we will witness some kind of de-globalization process nor that Industry 4.0 technologies would drive such a process forward.

In a similar vein, we obtained indications from our survey that the implementation of digital technologies may have a stronger dissuasive effect on possible offshoring decisions than on the inclination of firms to backshore production activities. This aligns with results from Müller et al. (2017) and Stentoft et al. (2020). Consequently, policy makers may have more interest in pursuing production retention initiatives than in creating backshoring agencies. The variety of factors in play for backshoring, as revealed by our case analyses, also hints at the importance of broader framework conditions compared to the adoption of digital technologies itself. This implies that place-based cluster and value chain development as part of industrial policies may also be important tools to foster backshoring (Nujen and Halse, 2017). Take note that the relevance of ecosystem quality in the home base is also echoed by Tate (2014), Baraldi et al. (2018) and Di Mauro et al. (2018). Consequently, backshoring firms should seek out places where an adequate supply chain and technological milieu is available for the production activities to be repatriated.

7 Limitations and suggestions for future research

Evidently, the present paper does not come without limitations. First, our research has been based on a relatively small number of company observations from a restricted geographical area. As such, the possibility for generalizing our results is reduced.

Second, the fact that we worked with a reduced sample also generated methodological constraints. I.e., given that our survey only counted with four companies with firm backshoring decisions led us to combine this sub-sample with the one for companies with future backshoring intentions. While this was done with the purpose to enable the statistical analyses that we presented in Sect. 4.2, it reduces the purity of our comparisons.

Third, our case studies on companies with backshoring experience to assess the role of technology behind such decisions has limitations for appraising the relevance of Industry 4.0 technologies amidst those decisions. That is, the reviewed backshoring experiences took place during a period (2006–2017) in which Industry 4.0 and the uptake of corresponding digital technologies was largely absent. This implies that they only serve to assess the role of technology at large, but not of specific Industry 4.0 technologies, for backshoring. Additionally, it can be argued that instead of our mixed method of combining a questionnaire-based survey with case studies, full-fledged case studying could reveal more insights into this question.

Fourth, for a couple of the independent variables, we recurred to proxies that can certainly deviate from the original concepts in the Industry 4.0 framework we adhered to. Although this is common and also applies to other publications, it shows that it is important to set common definitions for concepts like Industry 4.0 and to operationalize its underlying technological building blocks in order to come to research results that are comparable and interoperable with other analyses. At present, such lack of commonality hampers the comparability of our findings with other studies.

The former are lessons to take into account for future research. In addition, we deem that further testing of which Industry 4.0 technologies matter for respective types of backshoring rationales or production strategies (as per Ancarani and Di Mauro 2018, and Fratocchi and Di Stefano 2019) is indicated.

Furthermore, looking at the adoption of Industry 4.0 technologies amidst other factors that play a role in decision-making around backshoring deserves following. Either by looking at practice-based bundles of relocation drivers (Johansson et al. 2019) or through a conceptual lens to such processes, like TCE and the OLI paradigm (Dachs et al. 2019; Johansson et al. 2019).

Finally, similar to how we treated behavioral and environmental uncertainties next to the classical OLI pillars, other central components from TCE like asset specificity of foreign investments or frequency of interaction between an offshore site and corporate Headquarters (closely related to coordination costs of foreign operations) may receive separate attention in backshoring studies.

Notes

1. It considers the following nine technologies as "endogenous" to Industry 4.0: Internet of Things, Cloud technologies, Big data analytics, Virtual simulation systems, Augmented reality, Additive manufacturing / 3D Printing, Horizontal and Vertical systems integration, Autonomous robots and Cybersecurity.

2. Gray et al. (2013) recognize 4 reshoring options in function of whether the original off-shored activity was performed in-house or outsourced and whether the back-shored activity will be performed in-house or by third parties. In the present paper, we focus on what they call "in-house reshoring".

3. These are: Additive manufacturing, and Digital exchange of data with suppliers / customers in combination with Near real-time production control systems as a proxy for Horizontal and Vertical Systems Integration.

4. I.e., Product-Lifecycle-Management Systems, Systems for automation of internal logistics, Mobile/wireless devices to provide services, Technologies for human–machine interaction, and Digital visualization.

5. Robotics and 3D printing adhere to the Rüßmann et al. (2015) framework, whereas automated machinery falls aside.
6. That is: 3D printing and Robotics, whereas Automated machinery and Cyber-Physical Systems fall aside.
7. Take note that Stentoft et al. (2020) do not look at backshoring per sé, but at relocating production activities abroad.
8. See Table 2.
9. OLI stands for: Organization-specific, Location-specific and Internalization advantages.
10. Due to the COVID-19 pandemic, attention has grown for the disadvantages and risks that disruptions in (long haul) supply chains may suffer (OECD, 2020).
11. These 63 companies represent around 20% of the totality of Basque companies with overseas production plants (see Sect. 5.1).
12. Companies A, B, F, I, N, O and S were visited.
13. Big Data Analytics, Cloud Computing, Cybersecurity, Internet of Things, Automated Machinery, Robotics, 3D Printing, Artificial Intelligence, Mobile Services and Social Media.
14. Take note that the companies which declared that they have taken backshoring decisions referred to decisions in the here and now. So, recently taken decisions to come into effect in the (near) future. That is: around the time of the survey they had taken such decisions, but the repatriation of activities was to take place in future tense.
15. Off course, the decision to combine "Yes, indeed" and "Yes, maybe" also has its drawbacks, and this is something that we acknowledge.
16. In one case, the backshoring operation had a dual character, bringing one part of the production activities back to the Basque Country and another part to Portugal (nearshoring).

References

Acatech (2015) Smart Service Welt. Acatech, Frankfurt am Main

Alcácer V, Cruz-Machado V (2019) Scanning the Industry 4.0: A Literature Review on Technologies for Manufacturing Systems. Eng Sci Technol Int J 22:899–919

Ancarani A, Di Mauro C (2018) Reshoring and Industry 4.0: how often do they go together? IEEE Eng Manag Rev 46(2):87–96

Ancarani A, Di Mauro C, Mascali F (2019) Backshoring strategy and the adoption of Industry 4.0: Evidence from Europe. J World Bus 54:360–371

Anderson E, Gatignon H (1986) Modes of Foreign Entry: A Transaction Cost Analysis and Propositions. J Int Bus Stud 17(3):1–26

Bals L, Daum A, Tate W (2015) From offshoring to rightshoring: Focus on the backshoring phenomenon. AIB Insights 15(4):3

Bals L, Kirchoff JF, Foerstl K (2016) Exploring the reshoring and insourcing decision-making process: toward an agenda for future research. Oper Manag Res 9:102–116

Baraldi E, Ciabuschi F, Lindahl O, Fratocchi L (2018) A network perspective on the reshoring process: The relevance of the home-and the host-country contexts. Ind Mark Manage 70:156–166

Barbieri P, Ciabuschi F, Fratocchi F, Vignoli M (2018) What do we know about manufacturing reshoring? J Glob Oper Strateg Sourc 11(1):79–122

Barbieri P, Boffelli A, Elia S, Fratocchi L, Kalchschmidt M, Samson D (2020) What can we learn about reshoring after Covid-19? Oper Manag Res. https://doi.org/10.1007/s12063-020-00160-1

Benstead A, Stevenson M, Hendry L (2017) Why and how do firms reshore? A contingency-based conceptual framework. Oper Manag Res 10:85–103

Birkel HS, Hartmann E (2020) Internet of Things – The future of managing supply chain risks. Supply Chain Manag 25(5):535–548

Boston Consulting Group (2016) Time to accelerate in the race toward Industry 4.0. BCG Perspectives. https://www.bcg.com/publications/2016/lean-manufacturing-operations-time-accelerate-race-toward-industry-4.aspx

Brettel M, Friederichsen N, Keller M, Rosenberg M (2014) How virtualization, decentralization and network building change the manufacturing landscape: An Industry 4.0 perspective. Int J Mech, Industrial Sci Eng 8(1):37–44

Brouthers K, Nakos G (2004) SME entry mode choice and performance: a transaction cost perspective. Entrepreneurship Theory & Practice, Spring: 229–247

Chiarvesio M, Romanello R (2018) Industry 4.0 Technologies and Internationalization: Insights from Italian Companies. In: R. Van Tulder, A. Verbeke, L. Piscitello (ed) Int Bus Inf Digital Age, Emerald, Bingley, pp 357–378

Creswell J, Miller D (2000) Determining validity in qualitative inquiry. Theory Pract 39(3):124–130

Dachs B, Kinkel S (2013) Backshoring of production activities in European manufacturing. Evidence from a large-scale survey. In: Proceedings of the 20th European Operations Management Association Conference, Dublin, Ireland

Dachs B, Kinkel S, Jäger A (2019) Bringing it all back home? Backshoring of manufacturing activities and the adoption of Industry 4.0 technologies. J World Bus 54:101017

Digital Transformation Monitor of the European Commission (2018) https://ec. europa. eu/ growth/tools-databases/dem/monitor/sites/default/files/Digital%20Transformation% 20S coreboard % 202018_0.pdf

Di Mauro C, Fratocchi L, Orzes G, Sartor M (2018) Offshoring and backshoring: A multiple case study analysis. J Purch Supply Manag 24(2):108–134

Dul T, Hak J (2008) Case Study Research Methodology in Business Research. Butterworth-Heinemann, Oxford

Dunning J (1998) Location and the multinational enterprise: a neglected factor? J Int Bus Stud 29(1):45–66

Dunning JH (2001) The eclectic (OLI) paradigm of international production: past, present and future. Int J Econ Bus 8(2):173–190

Edmondson A, McManus S (2007) Methodological fit in management field research. Acad Manag Rev 32(4):1155–1179

Engström G, Sollander K, Hilletofth P (2018) Reshoring drivers and barriers in the Swedish manufacturing industry. J Glob Operations Strateg Sourcing 11(2):174–201

Fratocchi L, Di Mauro C, Barbieri P, Nassimbeni G, Zanoni A (2014) When manufacturing moves back: Concepts and questions. J Purch Supply Manag 20(1):54–59

Fratocchi L, Di Stefano C (2019) Do Industry 4.0 technologies matter when companies evaluate reshoring decisions? IEEE International Workshop on Metrology for Industry 4.0 and IoT, MetroInd 4.0 and IoT 2019 - Proceedings, art. no. 8792897, pp 376–381

Forsgren M, Holm U, Johanson J (2005) Managing the Embedded Multinational - A Business Network View. Edward Elgar, Aldershot

Gilchrist A (2016) Industry 4.0: The Industrial Internet of Things. Springer, Nonthaburi

Grandinetti R, Tabacco R (2015) A return to spatial proximity: combining global suppliers with local subcontractors. Int J Glob Small Bus 7(2):139–161

Gray JV, Skowronski K, Esenduran G, Rungtusanatham MJ (2013) The reshoring phenomenon: what supply chain academics ought to know and should do. J Supply Chain Manag 49:27–33

Gylling M, Heikkilä J, Jussila K, Saarinen M (2015) Making decisions on offshore outsourcing and backshoring. Int J Prod Econ 162:92–100

Hernandez-de-Menendez M, Morales-Menendez R, Escobar C, McGovern M (2020) Competencies for Industry 4.0. Int J Interac Des Manuf (IJIDeM) (2020) 14:1511–1524

Johansson M, Olhager J (2018) Manufacturing relocation through offshoring and backshoring: the case of Sweden. J Manuf Technol Manag 29(4):637–657. https://doi.org/10.1108/JMTM-01-2017-0006

Johansson M, Olhager J, Heikkiläb J, Stentoft J (2019) Offshoring versus backshoring: Empirically derived bundles of relocation drivers, and their relationship with benefits. J Purch Supply Manag. https:// doi.org/10.1016/j.pursup.2018.07.003

Joubioux C, Vanpoucke E (2016) Towards right-shoring: a framework for off-and re-shoring decision making. Oper Manag Res 9:117–132

Kagermann H (2015) Change through digitization—value creation in the age of ndustry 4.0. In: Albach H, Meffert H, Pinkwart A, Reichwald R (eds) Management of permanent change. Springer Gabler, Wiesbaden, pp 23–45. https://doi.org/10.1007/978-3-658-05014-6_2

Kamp B, Ruiz de Apodaca I (2017) Are KIBS beneficial to international business performance? Competitiveness Review: Int Bus J 27(1):80–95

Kinkel S (2012) Trends in production relocation and backshoring activities. Int J Oper Prod Manag 32(6):696–720

Kinkel S (2014) Future and impact of backshoring—some conclusions from 15 years of research on German practices. J Purch Supply Manag 20(1):63–65

Kinkel S, Maloca S (2009) Drivers and antecedents of manufacturing offshoring and backshoring - A German perspective. J Purch Supply Manag 15:154–165

Konstantynova A (2017) Basque Country cluster policy: the road of 25 years. Reg Stud Reg Sci 4(1):109–116

Lu Y (2017) Industry 4.0: A survey on technologies, applications and open research issues. J Ind Inf Integr 6:1–10

Martinsuo M, Chaoji P (2017) Manufacturing innovations and their implications for manufacturing relocation. In: Heikkilä J (ed) Relocation of Nordic manufacturing. Tampere University of Technology, Tampere

Miroudot S (2020) Reshaping the policy debate on the implications of COVID-19 for global supply chains. J Int Bus Policy 3:430–442

Mugurusi G, de Boer L (2014) Conceptualising the production offshoring organisation using the viable systems model (VSM). Strategic Outsourcing: An International Journal. 7(3):275–298. https: //doi. org/10.1108/SO-10-2014-0026

Müller J, Dotzauer V, Voigt K (2017). Industry 4.0 and its Impact on Reshoring Decisions of German Manufacturing Enterprises. In: Bode C, Bogaschewsky R, Eßig, M et al (eds) Supply Chain Research. Springer, Heidelberg

Nujen B, Halse L (2017) Global shift-back's: A strategy for reviving manufacturing competences, in: Breaking up the Global Value Chain, pp 245–267. https://doi.org/10.1108/ S1571-50272017 0000030010

OECD (2020) Shocks, risks and global value chains: Insights from the OECD METRO model. OECD, Paris

Posada J, Toro C, Barandiaran I, Oyarzun D, Stricker D, de Amicis R, Pinto E, Eisert P, Dollner J, Vallarino I (2015) Visual computing as a key enabling technology for industrie 4.0 and industrial internet. IEEE Comput Graphics Appl 35(2):26–40

Rezk R, Srai J, Williamson P (2016) The impact of product attributes and emerging technologies on firms' international configuration. J Int Bus Stud 47(5):610–618

Robinson P, Hsieh L (2016) Reshoring: a strategic renewal of luxury clothing supply chains. Oper Manag Res 9(3):89–101

Rüßmann M, Lorenz M, Gerbert P, Waldner M, Justus J, Engel P, Harnisch M (2015) Industry 4.0: The future of productivity and growth in manufacturing industries. Boston Consulting Group, 1–9

Saucedo-Martínez J, Pérez-Lara M, Marmolejo-Saucedo J, Salais-Fierro T, Vasant P (2016) Industry 4.0 framework for management and operations: a review. J Ambient Intell Human Comput (2018) 9:789–801

Stentoft J, Mikkelsen O, Jensen J (2016) Offshoring and backshoring manufacturing from a supply chain innovation perspective. Supply Chain Forum: Int J 17(4):190–204

Stentoft J, Olhager J, Heikkilä J, Thoms L (2016b) Manufacturing backshoring: a systematic literature review. Oper Manag Res 9(3):53–61

Stentoft J, Wickstroem K, Haug A, Philipsen K (2020) Cost-driven motives to relocate manufacturing abroad among small- and medium-sized manufacturers: The influence of Industry 4.0. J Manuf Technol Manag. https://doi.org/10.1108/JMTM-07-2019-0283

Strange R (2020) The 2020 Covid-19 pandemic and global value chains. J Ind Bus Econ 47:455–465

Tate W (2014) Offshoring and reshoring: US insights and research challenges. J Purch Supply Manag 20(1):66–68

UNCTAD (2020) World Investment Report, 2020 – International production beyond the pandemic. Geneva: UNCTAD

Van Tulder R, Verbeke A, Piscitello L (ed) (2018) International business in the information and digital age (Progress in International Business Research, Volume 13). Emerald, Bingley

Williamson OE (1985) The economic institutions of capitalism. Free Press, New York

5

Blockchain as Enabling Factor for Implementing RFID and IoT Technologies in VMI

A Simulation on the Parmigiano Reggiano Supply Chain

Antonello Cammarano, Vincenzo Varriale, Francesca Michelino & Mauro Caputo

Department of Industrial Engineering, University of Salerno, Fisciano, Italy

Abstract

Blockchain has recently been associated to Supply Chain Management to solve several problems and change operations management processes. The study proposes to analyse three different scenarios of the Parmigiano Reggiano supply chain considering blockchain technology as an enabler for the use of other technologies such as RFID and the Internet of Things (IoT) and for the exploitation of the Vendor Managed Inventory (VMI) strategy. The study is based on the evaluation of three agent-based simulation scenarios, a traditional "as is" scenario, a second "to be" scenario implementing emerging technologies including blockchain, and a third "to be" scenario that combines the second one with the VMI optimization strategy. The results show how the combined adoption of these technologies improves the procurement process and customer satisfaction. Findings highlight the impacts that the different scenarios have on the supply chain operations in a quantitative way and allows to evaluate the changes in supply chain processes. By employing emerging technologies, order management activities are more automated and time to order and lead time order preparation are reduced. However, to achieve these performances, other data capture tools such as RFID and IoT are needed. Finally, the introduction of the VMI strategy, when enabled by blockchain technology, improves the procurement performances and significantly reduces unfilled orders.

Keywords: *Blockchain · Supply chain · Vendor managed inventory · RFID · Internet of things*

1 Introduction

Nowadays, supply chains face several problems in terms of ecosystem complexity (Jaeger et al. 2021; Serdarasan 2013), sustainability (Jaeger and Upadhyay 2020; Sharma et al. 2022; Siddh et al. 2021; Upadhyay et al. 2021a), international logistics (Stojanović and Ivetić 2020), collaboration between the network players (Cammarano et al. 2019; Jraisat et al. 2021; Ralston et al. 2020), demand management (Wang et al. 2015), transparency (Xu et al. 2021), disruptions (Yu et al. 2021) and distortion of information (Xue et al. 2020). These multiple challenges lead companies to constantly innovate and implement systems that use emerging technologies (Agrawal et al. 2022). In particular, one of the purposes of the supply chain is to manage the processes and the transactions between buyers and suppliers, optimizing costs and times but at the same time guaranteeing high quality of the service and the products supplied (Mukhuty et al. 2022). This scenario includes the new Industry 4.0 plans that are based on the connection among new technologies automating different procedures in order to optimize manufacturing and logistics processes of each company in the ecosystem (Li et al. 2021a; Srivastava et al. 2022). Indeed, the effective and efficient supply chain management improves the coordination between supply and demand by reducing costs (Ketokivi and Mahoney 2020). In addition, the challenges of supply chain management have further amplified with the Covid-19 pandemic (Hald and Coslugeanu 2021; Joshi et al. 2022; Sharma et al. 2021). Taking control over data is essential in this scenario as it allows to make decisions that can improve business performance.

Currently, there are several strategies to solve these challenges, such as Collaborative Planning, Forecasting and Replenishment (CPFR) (Singhry and Abd Rahman 2019) or Just in Time (JIT) (Alfayad 2020). There has been an exponential increase in the availability of data and for the implementation of new technological solutions that allow to improve efficient inventory and supply policies (Cammarano et al. 2020). One of the strategies used in this area is VMI which permits upstream actors to manage the goods of downstream players. VMI effectively reduces inventory costs and improves collaboration between buyers and suppliers (Disney and Towill 2003). However, this strategy faces many challenges when collecting data. Some of these challenges include data integrity, accessibility, information delay, data transparency, server centralization, and traceability within the system's stakeholders (Kolb et al. 2018).

To solve these problems, the development and use of emerging technologies is necessary to improve the effectiveness and efficiency of the entire supply chain. For example, data collection can be done by sensors and drones (Sharma et al. 2020). Consequently, by using IoT, this information can be sent to servers for data processing to make more accurate decisions (Lezoche et al. 2020). However, these systems are based on the centralized server-client paradigm which could be easily tampered by hackers (Feng et al. 2020). To solve such huge problems, many scholars are studying the use of distributed ledgers technologies, and specifically blockchain. This technology is based on a distributed and encrypted ledger that allows the transactions to be securely stored and ensures greater transparency between the actors in the chain. Hence, blockchain technology could expand the use cases of VMI (Casino et al. 2019a). There is a high interest of scholars on the combined and connected use of these technologies in the food supply chain (Astill et al. 2019; Lezoche et al. 2020). Several scholars claim that blockchain can enable process management in a more effective and efficient way (Saberi et al. 2019; Upadhyay et al. 2021b; Vu et al. 2021).

However, few works evaluated and compared the efficiency of operations management for the supply chains by integrating or not the blockchain with other technologies. The research focused mainly on improving and measuring the technological performance of blockchain technology—such as latency time, throughput and number of transactions—and less on response times for the supply chain operations (Alonso et al. 2020; Yoon et al. 2020). To be used in supply chain operations, blockchain technology should be driven by external tools and technologies to collect input data. In this way it is possible to carry out concrete, secure, precise and efficient decisions. Current literature little explored the combined effect of blockchain with other emerging technologies to improve the overall supply chain operations. On the one hand, there are no real case studies that combine different technologies on multiple areas of supply chain management; on the other hand, literature focuses on the analysis of single technologies in different areas of the supply chain (Lohmer et al. 2020; Longo et al. 2019; Manupati et al. 2020).

Hence, the purpose of the paper is to evaluate blockchain integrated with other technologies in a food supply chain using a simulation tool. Simulation is a powerful descriptive tool for experimenting, evaluating and comparing different alternatives of new system designs. The key results allow predicting system performance and identifying potential issues. In the absence of a real system model, simulation allows to experiment and compare different alternative models. Moreover, the simulation reproduces new projects avoiding big investments in new systems for which there is a little or no experience, reducing the potential implementation risks. Finally, the simulation models provide numerical and detailed measures of system performance (Carson 2004). Specifically, a comparison is proposed, within the Parmigiano Reggiano cheese supply chain, an excellent Made in Italy product, between a traditional scenario and one with the use of emerging technologies, such as: blockchain, IoT, RFID and smart contracts. Differences in terms of efficiency indicators regarding process times are highlighted. Thereafter, a further scenario is proposed that implements the VMI strategy connected to the use of the blockchain, highlighting further improvements in terms of time performance and customer satisfaction by exploiting the potentials of the shared distributed ledger and smart contracts.

This research addresses the aforementioned gap in both literature and industrial practice of operations management. In order to quantitatively show the advantages that supply chain players can obtain by combining different emerging technologies, the simulation scenarios were developed considering a producer, a delivery company, a wholesaler, three retailers and the customers. The areas and operations considered in the simulation models include all the main organizational, production and delivery processes such as: order management, inventory management and logistics. This article aims to clarify the following research questions:

1. On which supply chain operations can blockchain, IoT, RFID and smart contract derive operational time benefits for organizations?
2. What are the benefits for each participant of supply chain in the various scenarios considered?

The rest of the article is organized as follows: Sect. 2 provides a framework conceptualization of the work. Then, Sect. 3 illustrates a background on blockchain technology and its use in the food supply chain. In addition, the perspective of blockchain technology as an enabler of the VMI strategy is clarified. Section 4 describes the three proposed simulation scenarios, while Sect. 5 shows the output results from the three scenarios. Section 6 discusses the results for the three scenarios and clarifies the practical and managerial implications of the combined use of these technologies. The conclusions will close the work.

2 Framework conceptualization

Scientific literature widely highlighted how trust and information sharing are crucial for improving supply chain performances such as flexibility and resilience, especially in an era of globalization (Kasemsap 2017). Trust among players promotes costs reduction and better collaborative relationship among partners (Kim and Chai 2017). In addition, it is important that the actors of supply chains plan production activities and monitor own inventory in a precise, accurate and timely manner. This enables to mitigate the bullwhip effect and reduce issues such as increased inventories, logistics costs and inefficiencies. The phenomenon has significantly reduced with the information and communication technologies (Hofmann 2017; Varriale et al. 2021a). However, when the supply chain expands to other countries, sharing information becomes more complex (Shore 2001). In low-trust scenarios, it is difficult to establish collaborative relationships where data access is essential to efficiently manage supply chain operations (Ebrahim-Khanjari et al. 2012; Michelino et al. 2015). Despite the information technology has reduced information asymmetry, further investments are needed in these fields (Zhong et al. 2016).

Through literature review, conceptual studies, pilot projects and surveys, scientific literature hypothesizes a time reduction for the supply chain operations employing different technologies, included blockchain, without being able to actually verify it since real cases studies are still few. Several authors claim that "stand-alone" blockchain can automate various supply chain operations. For example, Walmart used blockchain to reduce tracking time for its pilot projects (Astill et al. 2019). Casino et al. (2020) analysed a pilot case of a private blockchain that uses smart contact to improve the traceability of dairy products. Other studies focused on improving collaborative and trusting relationships between partners which allows the optimization of information exchange via blockchain (Longo et al. 2019). For example, companies can obtain comprehensive information on the shelf life of food products to manage inventory and plan transportation by reducing waste (Astill et al. 2019; Roeck et al. 2020). Some studies suggest systems for processing complaints to optimize the supply chain resilience among different entities of the network (Kamilaris et al. 2019; Kumar et al. 2020).

Figure 1 shows the framework conceptualization. In scheme a) the partners manage the relationships with the closest actors upstream and downstream. The information is managed internally using the historical data for sales forecasts. Scheme b) provides the integration of different technologies such as RFID, IoT, blockchain and smart contracts for each player. Blockchain becomes an enabler of information sharing by strengthening the resilience of supply chain operations between different actors.

3 Literature review

3.1 Blockchain technology

Blockchain technology is a distributed and decentralized ledger that enables data sharing in a transparent and certified way (Choi 2019). The blockchain has had great success in the financial sector with the introduction of the Bitcoin platform (Fosso Wamba et al. 2020). However, its growing focus has also shifted to other areas including the supply chain (Queiroz et al. 2019). Blockchain solutions for supply chains are on the rise as they can improve some of the business and organizational processes (Varriale et al. 2021b). Blockchain technology is presented as an ordered set of blocks containing transactions recorded through consensus mechanisms. Blockchain is tamper-proof: any information recorded in the distributed ledger is unalterable and cannot be changed. The literature divides blockchains into three types: public, private and consortium (Gourisetti et al. 2020). Depending on the information to be shared, the appropriate type is used. In particular, in a public blockchain anyone can connect to the platform and read the stored data (Chang et al. 2020). Instead, in a private blockchain only authorized users can access (Assaqty et al. 2020). Finally, consortium blockchains admit partial authorizations on certain areas for certain users (Qiao et al. 2018). These three types allow different levels of privacy depending on the transactions and information recorded in the distributed ledger. A connected and relevant aspect of the technology is the use of smart contracts, programs that can perform calculations by automating processes and operating as a decentralized machine. Smart contracts are agreements between network participants that can be activated when specific events occur (Christidis and Devetsikiotis 2016). These capabilities are set to improve supply chain management in different steps and processes.

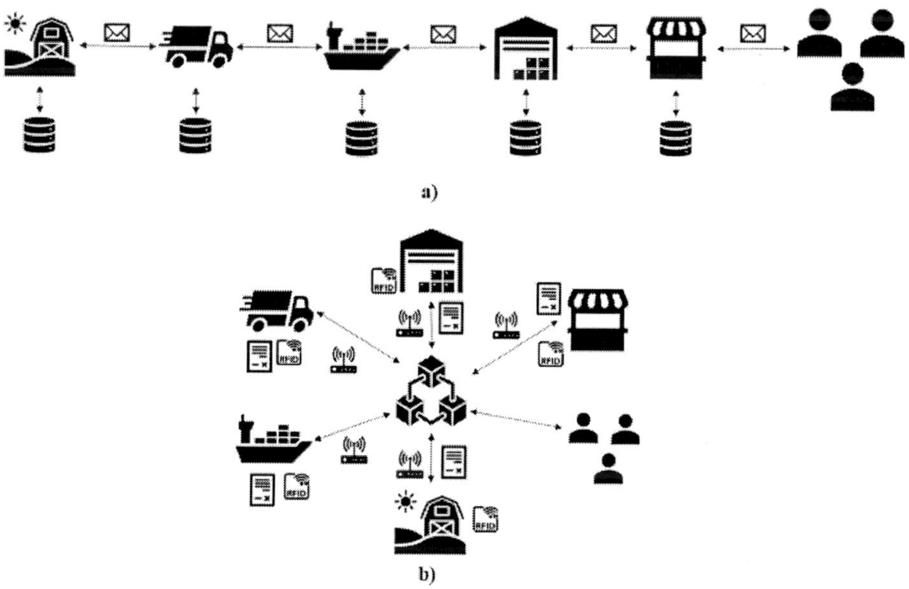

***Fig. 1** Framework conceptualization of the scenarios considered: a) schematization of traditional supply chain; b) schematization of emerging technologies integration for the supply chains*

3.2 Blockchain and food supply chain

In recent years, research on the food supply chain has been moving towards innovative technologies and optimization methods (Kamble et al. 2020). The reasons why it is pushing towards innovation in this area are mainly related to risk management (Zhou et al. 2021). The issues affecting the food sector concern: inadequate demand management (Kittipanya-ngam and Tan 2020), incorrect information management (Kouhizadeh et al. 2020), lack of collaboration between the players in the supply chain (Guggenberger et al. 2020) and lack of regulations for controlling food safety and quality (Tse et al. 2018). In addition, more and more consumers demand up-to-date, real-time information on the foods they purchase (Astill et al. 2019). The factors that have greater importance regard the complete transparency and visibility of the supply chain for each participants (Kayikci et al. 2020). Regulatory authorities have imposed standards and certifications on food producers to ensure integrity of food and safety for consumers (Kamble et al. 2020). These certifications improve aspects such as transparency and quality of the food supply chain. However, suppliers, producers, distributors and retailers should exploit alternative approaches, methods and technologies to improve consumer trust in the products purchased (Kittipanya-ngam and Tan 2020). One of the ways to improve these aspects is to move towards a complete digitalization of the entire chain, from the raw materials to the finished product (Bhatti et al. 2021). However, the digitization of a traditional supply chain is a complex and an expensive operation and requires the availability of several resources, both human and digital (Ivanov et al. 2019).

The implementation of IT systems has helped to reduce inventory costs human error and improved the efficiency of communications. Consumer needs regarding the traceability of the entire supply chain are pressing (Hastig and Sodhi 2020). Researchers are investigating tracking and tracing issues, using emerging technologies such as: IoT, GPS, RFID tags and other sensors. These new technologies store information in real time and send it to servers. However, managing data with centralized systems via the IoT has several privacy and security problems (Feng et al. 2020). In this scenario, blockchain technology can be exploited thanks to its peculiarities. The blockchain is the suitable technology to collect data from external devices being a distributed ledger that uses encryption schemes to ensure the security of the system. Since blockchain technology is an immutable ledger, it allows to trace the phases of a product (Pedersen et al. 2019). In addition, another tool that contributes to the overall optimization of the supply chain is the use of smart contracts that can transfer data and information within the blockchain depending on specific conditions. Smart contracts can be implemented to improve order management or to speed up bureaucratic and administrative processes at customs and in international transport (Hasan et al. 2019). Several researchers argue how blockchain can be used in food supply chains to improve process sustainability (Bai and Sarkis 2020; Mukherjee et al. 2021; Upadhyay et al. 2021c; Varriale et al. 2020). Yet, to date main issues of implementing this technology are related to the cost of implementation and the limits of the technological performance (Kouhizadeh et al. 2021).

As shown in Table 1, benefits, challenges and future directions of blockchain have been mainly discussed in the food supply chain sector through systematic literature reviews (SLR). Additionally, scholars have analysed blockchain technology for the food supply chain using manager interviews and case studies. Many articles discuss about the implementation of the technical architecture and how the stakeholders will manage these new digital platforms. However, these changes are still not quantifiable with real data and are difficult to measure for the current state of the art. For example, through a literature review, Vu et al. (2021) show that only 10% of the, sample under analysis concerned documents that quantitatively measured the impacts of blockchain for the food supply chain.

Hence, the study aims to measure the impacts that blockchain connected to other technologies has on supply chain operations. Starting from previous studies, that have conceptually designed the different food supply chain configurations through the adoption of blockchain and other technologies without demonstrating their possible effects on supply chain operations, the study aims to measure what are the long-term impacts on time performances and relative customer satisfaction that these technologies carry out for a food supply chain.

Table 1 Studies of blockchain for the food supply chains

#	Authors	Research Method	Sector	Study Nature	Description
1	(Zhao et al. 2019)	SLR	Agri-food	Qualitative and Quantitative	The study analyses 62 academic articles from 2008 to 2018 and identifies four aspects that improve the agri-food supply chain management: traceability, information security, production and sustainable management of water. Additionally, six challenges are identified such as: storage capacity and scalability, loss of privacy, high cost, regulatory issues, speed and latency issues, and lack of skills
2	(Gopi et al. 2019)	SLR	Seafood	Qualitative	The study summarizes the emerging methodologies for determining the provenance and authenticity of seafood. The aim of this review is to provide an overview of the methods that could be used by authorities to enforce regulations and contain risks for the fishing industry to self-regulate and protect from food fraud
3	(George et al. 2019)	Mathematical model	Restaurant	Quantitative	This paper examines the main existing food traceability methods and proposes a restaurant prototype to implement more reliable food traceability using Blockchain and product identifiers. The prototype captures data from various stakeholders along the

#	Authors	Research Method	Sector	Study Nature	Description
					food supply chain and applies the Food Quality Index algorithm to assess quality performance. The prototype classifies the quality of food for human consumption as well as strengthening the traceability of food
4	(Spadoni et al. 2019)	Case study	Wine	Qualitative	The study is a storytelling of a start-up that adopts blockchain technology to track wine
5	(Kamilaris et al. 2019)	SLR	Agri-food	Qualitative	The article analyses 29 articles and 49 initiatives to outline the state of the art of research and the challenges of adopting the blockchain
6	(Astill et al. 2019)	Conceptual	Food	Qualitative	The article aims to examine technologies for the data management within the food supply chain, such as blockchain and Big Data analysis. In addition, the work considers IoT as a technology that collect data from multiple stages within supply chains and lead to transparent data-driven food production systems
7	(Kamble et al. 2020)	SLR	Agri-food	Qualitative	The article analyses 84 academic articles from 2000 to 2017 proposing an application framework for managers involved in the agri-food supply chain to achieve sustainable performance
8	(Kittipanya-ngam and Tan 2020)	Case study	Food	Qualitative	The article proposes a framework for the digitalization of the food supply chain based on four case studies of Thai companies
9	(Lezoche et al. 2020)	SLR	Agri-food	Qualitative	The article investigates and compares more than one hundred articles on new technologies, including blockchain, to understand the future paths of the agri-food sector
10	(Alonso et al. 2020)	Technical Implementati on	Food	Quantitative	The study presents a platform geared for the application of IoT, Edge Computing, Artificial Intelligence and Blockchain in Smart Farming environments, to

#	Authors	Research Method	Sector	Study Nature	Description
					monitor the status of dairy cattle and forage cereals in real time, as well as ensuring the traceability and sustainability of the several processes involved in production
11	(Klerkx and Rose 2020)	Conceptual	Agri-food	Qualitative	The study presents a theoretical framework on how enabling technologies of agri-food 4.0 can have potential impacts on the agri-food supply chain management
12	(Ciruela-Lorenzo et al. 2020)	Case study	Agri-food	Qualitative	The article provides a review of main digital technologies, such as the Internet of Things, robots, Artificial Intelligence, Big Data and Blockchain, and how these technologies could help decision-making actors. These theories are described through two case studies of agricultural cooperatives in Spain
13	(Feng et al. 2020)	Technical Implementati on	Agri-food	Quantitative	The article proposes an architecture design framework and flowchart for blockchain-based food traceability to highlight the benefits and challenges of implementing blockchain
14	(Köhler and Pizzol 2020)	Case study	Food	Qualitative	The study analyses six food supply chain case studies by evaluating four different components of technology: technique, knowledge, organization and product. The study provides new insights into how blockchain can be implemented in food supply chains
15	(Osmanoglu et al. 2020)	Mathematical Model	Agri-food	Qualitative	The study proposes a blockchain-based solution that estimates the yield of agricultural products
16	(Shahid et al. 2020)	Technical implementati on	Agri-food	Quantitative	The study proposes technology efficiency solutions to improve information recording performance by exploiting optimization algorithms. In this work, simulations and evaluations of smart contracts are presented along with security and

#	Authors	Research Method	Sector	Study Nature	Description
					vulnerability analysis
17	(Kayikci et al. 2020)	SLR	Food	Qualitative	The study analyses 125 articles from 2008 to 2020 and investigates the suitability of blockchain technology in solving the main challenges, such as traceability, trust and accountability in the food industry
18	(Della Valle and Oliver 2020)	Interviews	Food	Qualitative	The study features 18 interviews with experienced blockchain managers for supply chains. Analysis shows that blockchain does not appear to be a disruptive technology. Five enablers are presented that can foster rapid blockchain adoption in the industry
19	(Stranieri et al. 2021)	Case study and interviews	Agri-food	Qualitative	The study proposes a conceptual framework that includes performances discussed in literature: efficiency, flexibility, responsiveness, food quality and transparency of supply chains. These dimensions are assessed using a case study. The data were collected through semi-structured interviews with key managers in the different phases of the three supply chains and were systematically analysed through a thematic analysis
20	(Rainero and Modarelli 2 021)	Interviews	Food	Quantitative	The article is an exploratory analysis of customer perceptions and real knowledge of the blockchain in the food and beverage sector. The study is based on 80 surveys and interviews
21	(Mishra and Maheshwari 2021)	Conceptual	Food	Qualitative	The study proposes a conceptual framework for the application of blockchain in the Public Distribution System in India to manage the grains supply chain
22	(Vu et al. 2021)	SLR	Food	Qualitative	The study analysis 69 articles to assess the barriers, applications and implementation stages of Blockchain within food supply chains

#	Authors	Research Method	Sector	Study Nature	Description
23	(Sharma et al. 2021)	Interviews	Food	Quantitative	This study provides insights to decision makers, managers to make meaningful decisions during an emergency using blockchain technology via multi-criteria approaches
24	(Bechtsis et al. 2021)	SLR and case study	Food	Qualitative	This article highlights through a literature review and the evaluation of a case study how blockchain technology can improve the security and resilience of the supply chain
25	(Yi et al. 2021)	Interviews	Food	Qualitative	The enabling factors of blockchain are highlighted and understood through the interview of 21 members of the food supply chain in China
26	(Li et al. 2021b)	SLR	Food	Qualitative	The paper analysis the main blockchain platforms used in food supply chains and conducts an analysis to explore the benefits and challenges of the technology
27	(Kramer et al. 2021)	SLR	Food	Qualitative	The research is based on a broad overview of the literature review and exploratory use cases of blockchain implementations in the agri-food industry
28	(Saurabh and Dey 2021)	Conceptual and Technical implementation	Wine	Quantitative	The study proposes what are the factors driving the adoption of blockchain and shows qualitative implementation scenarios for the wine supply chain
29	(Galanakis et al. 2021)	Conceptual	Food	Qualitative	The article theoretically investigates how technologies, including blockchain, can mitigate the effects of the post lockdown of COVID-19
30	(Nurgazina et al. 2021)	SLR	Food	Qualitative	The study analyses 69 articles to understand the effect that blockchain and IoT can have on the sustainability of food supply chains
31	(Tsolakis et al. 2021)	Case study and interviews	Fish	Qualitative and Quantitative	The study proposes the design of blockchain on food supply chains that promote sustainable development goals, in the context

#	Authors	Research Method	Sector	Study Nature	Description
					of the Thai seafood industry. A possible implementation of blockchain is shown through the analysis of fish case studies
32	(Ali et al. 2021)	Case study	Food	Qualitative and Quantitative	The study proposes the analysis of five case studies to show how certain challenges for the halal food supply chain have been overcome
33	(Yang et al. 2021)	Mathematical model	Food	Quantitative	The study analyses, through game theory, operational decisions and blockchain adoption strategies for a food supply chain consisting of a platform and a supplier
34	(Joo and Han 2021)	Mathematical model	Food	Quantitative	The article examines the features of distributed trust in the blockchain-based food supply chain and tests seven hypotheses using a structural equation model that integrates distributed trust (i.e. transparency, traceability and security) and user satisfaction
35	(Rana et al. 2021)	SLR	Agri-food	Qualitative	The study analyses academic journals from 2010 to 2020 that discuss blockchain applications in the food supply chain to determine future directions
36	(Benyam et al. 2021)	SLR	Food	Qualitative	The study analyses 24 articles to investigate the role of digital agricultural technologies in enabling the prevention / reduction of food and waste loss from a global perspective

3.3 The combination of VMI and blockchain

VMI strategy has been extensively studied in literature (Salem and Elomri 2017). Several authors focused on the success factors for its effective implementation, such as the exchange of information and collaboration between the actors in the chain (Ryu 2016). VMI is used to reduce the bullwhip effect (Disney and Towill 2003), manage orders (Yao et al. 2010), improve the service level (Shi and Xiao 2015), reduce costs (Zhang et al. 2007) and reduce the inventory (Lee et al. 2016). Obtaining precise information on the demand in advance would allow the seller to respond quickly to unexpected orders and improve supply planning (Dong et al. 2014). Furthermore, VMI allows to stabilize the frequency of purchase orders as the seller has a complete knowledge of the downstream demand (Taleizadeh et al. 2015). On the one hand, VMI encourages collaboration with other players in the supply chain, on the other hand, shared knowledge could harm the other players in the chain (Disney and Towill 2003). Currently, the information exchange with traditional technologies could be tampered with, corrupted and not certified. The actors in the supply chain could have opportunistic behaviours or they can make mistakes such as misalignments of real inventory and IT inventory (Kamilaris et al. 2019). For this reasons, blockchain technology would more easily enable the VMI strategy. Indeed, the use of blockchain technology and smart contracts for VMI operations would reduce the need for human intervention (Omar et al. 2020). Features such as data integrity, security and immutability help to trust the mechanism in which the technology works rather than the relationships between network partners (Pedersen et al. 2019). In this way, actors operating with blockchains can trust the information stored in the distributed ledger and they can plan order management (Casino et al. 2019b). Thus, the blockchain enhances the principles of VMI by allowing complete data sharing, traceability and transparency (Guggenberger et al. 2020). Making this information available to those who manage the inventory upstream will enable them to accurately manage the demand by frequently monitoring the stock level. In this way, buyers will place more frequent and smaller orders and consequently have cost savings. At the same time, blockchain will ensure better collaboration between stakeholders as the secure bidirectional exchange of data will increase trust between parties (Chang et al. 2020). Using blockchain, the producer can access to the data shared by wholesalers and retailers. It allows to identify exactly when their downstream customers have reached the reorder level. The combination of the VMI strategy with blockchain technology creates an agile and responsive supply chain. Some researchers are investigating the binomial blockchain and VMI (Kolb et al. 2018). Some propose solutions from a conceptual and theoretical point of view (Casino et al. 2019b). Others suggest solutions in which they show the mechanisms of smart contracts and the security performances of the system (Omar et al. 2020). This article differs from the others because the aim of the research is to evaluate *ex-ante* the possible impact that combination of emerging technologies could obtain on the traditional business processes operations of a food supply chain. The purpose of the article is to evaluate how the visibility of the chain by the actors, the information sharing and the management of integrated emerging technologies can have an impact on the operational supply chain performance.

4 Research methodology

In the last five years, research on blockchain for supply chain management has increased exponentially, however few papers have evaluated the performance of the technology in managing supply chains operations. Exploratory research based on case studies allows a better understanding of the phenomenon that can lead to the development of new theories through processing (Gehman et al. 2018). The study of Parmigiano Reggiano cheese production and distribution case is fundamental for easy data access and the close proximity of the phenomenon (Eisenhardt 1989). Simulation provides an experimentation platform that emulate real conditions through a dynamic set of objects and variables (Weick 1989). Table 2 reports a list of simulation works considering the blockchain adoption for supply chains. From this table, the articles that highlight the potential of blockchain within supply chain processes measuring its benefits and disadvantages are relatively few, despite how much this topic has been discussed in the last period. Few

Table 2 Simulation studies of blockchain for the supply chains

Reference	Other technologies/strategies	Area	Sector	Topic	Software	Technological Performance of Blockchain						Operations Performance of Blockchain for the supply chains				
						Smart contract	N. of transactions	Architecture cost	Speed of transactions	Time consuming	Transaction costs	Time performance	Costs	Stock performance	Demand volatility	Carbon tax
(Dasaklis and Casino 2019)	RFID, IoT, VMI	Inventory management	Manufacturing	Inventory strategy	Ethereum	x										
(Omar et al. 2020)	VMI	Inventory management	No declared	Inventory strategy	Ethereum	x			x		x					
(Helo and Shamsuzzoha 2020)	RFID, IoT	Logistics	Manufacturing	Shipping, tracking & tracing	Ethereum	x										
(Yoon et al. 2020)	No other technologies	Logistics	Manufacturing	International trades	No declared (Mathematical models)		x								x	
(Longo et al. 2019)	No other technologies	Inventory management	No declared	Information sharing	Unicalcoin and Java			x	x		x		x			
(Hasan et al. 2019)	IoT, RFID	Logistics	No declared	Shipping	Ethereum	x										
(Casino et al. 2019a)	IoT, RFID	No specific area	Food	Tracking & Tracing	Ethereum	x										
(Martinez et al. 2019)	No other technologies	Order management	Manufacturing	System architecture & performance	Simul8							x				
(Manupati et al. 2020)	No other technologies	Inventory management	Manufacturing	Shipping and market demand	Matlab					x	x		x		x	x
(Lohmer et al. 2020)	No other technologies	No specific area	No declared	Risk management	AnyLogic 8.5.0							x		x	x	
(Dolgui et al. 2020)	No other technologies	Logistics	Manufacturing	System architecture & performance	Hyperledger Fabric	x										
(Tozanli et al. 2020b)	No other technologies	Production	High-tech	System architecture & performance	No declared (Discret-Event Simulation)								x			
(Alonso et al. 2020)	Edge Computing, RFID, IoT, QR Code	Production	Dairy farming	System architecture & performance	No declared				x	x						
(Sund et al. 2020)	No other technologies	Logistics	Furniture retailer	Shipping	Quorum	x	x		x	x						
(Shahid et al. 2020)	No other technologies	No specific area	Agri-food	Tracking & Tracing	Remix Integrated Development Environment (IDE) Ganache and Metamask	x	x				x					
(Bai et al. 2021)	No other technologies	Production	Agriculture	Tracking	Phyton 3.5		x									
(Tozanli et al. 2020a)	RFID, IoT	Waste management	Electronic	Disassembly-to-order	Arena v15.1								x			
This article	**RFID, IoT, VMI**	**Order management, logistics and inventory management**	**Food**	**Inventory strategy and market demand**	**Anylogic 7.0.2**							**x**		**x**		

works have assessed the impacts that blockchain, alone or integrated with other technologies, could carry out in terms of improving processes within supply chain operations. Previous studies evaluated technology challenges such as scalability, privacy, and security issues (Alonso et al. 2020; Omar et al. 2020; Shahid et al. 2020), others on costs issues (Longo et al. 2019; Manupati et al. 2020; Tozanlı et al. 2020a). Some authors analysed time performances, but only on single case studies and in specific areas of order management (Martinez et al. 2019). Others have used the times to evaluate how the volatility of demand fluctuates and how much stock is needed for the actors in the network (Lohmer et al. 2020). Our work differs from the others because it evaluates the times on all the operations processes of the Parmigiano Reggiano supply chain for all the actors involved. Furthermore, our work evaluates ex-ante the promising impacts that blockchain, IoT, RFID and VMI could have on the Parmigiano Reggiano supply chain. This work aims to explore, quantify and test what the literature has promoted in this research area in recent years. The ability to simulate and perform a cost–benefit analysis is essential to gain adoption by more participants and not just by multinationals where profits are greater.

The simulation approach used is discrete events because it provides a detailed analysis of all phases and is precise, reliable and easy to program. In particular, starting from the most accredited literature on the use of simulation, three scenarios of the cheese supply chain have been developed: a first traditional scenario "as is", without the use of blockchain and other technologies (Bottani and Montanari 2010; Muravev et al. 2019); a second scenario "to be" with the combined use of blockchain technology, IoT and RFID without VMI strategy (Lohmer et al. 2020; Longo et al. 2019; Martinez et al. 2019); and, finally, a third scenario "to be" with the addition of the VMI optimization strategy (Casino et al. 2019b; Omar et al. 2020). Anylogic 7.0.2 Professional was used for simulations2. Figure 2 shows the methods and steps that allowed the construction of the entire architecture.

4.1 Simulation study and data collection

In order to improve the state of the art of the existing literature and validate the work, a simulation study of an Italian factory of Parmigiano Reggiano that exports cheese abroad was considered. In particular, the supply chain was simulated starting from the producer to the final retailer. The phases of warehousing, logistics and order management were considered. In this way it was possible to compare the results and provide a good representation of what blockchain can change. Secondary sources were used for data collection: statistical reports (ISTAT 2022), consortium reports (Parmigiano 2022), scientific articles presented in Table 2 and online reports.

4.2 Design of the simulation study

The following aspects should be specified in a simulation study: input parameters to vary, output parameters, duration of the warm-up phase and execution time of the model and number of replication (Carson 2004). The detailed parameters of our simulation study are shown in Table 3.

4.3 Traditional food supply chain model

The network is composed by a producer (P), a delivery company (DC), a wholesaler (W), and three retailers (RA, RB and RC). The network structure and materials flow are presented in Fig. 3. The producer supplies the wholesaler, which, in turn, supplies the three retailers. The network is based on the export of 12 months aged Parmigiano Reggiano from Italy to Spain. The producer is located in Reggio Emilia (Italy), the wholesaler is located in the industrial area of Barcelona and the three retailers at different distances in the metropolitan city of Barcelona.

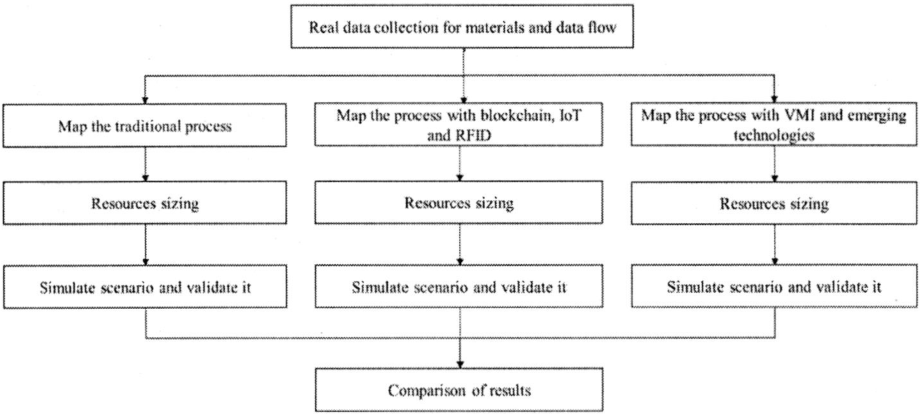

Fig. 2 *Steps and techniques for the construction of the three scenarios*

Table 3 Parameter of simulation experiments

Model runtime	**0–18 months. The simulation model starts without a warm-up phase as it has been preloaded**
Varying input parameters	Phases of order management for each actor in the supply chain and phase of loading / unloading of the goods managed by the delivery company
Output parameters	There are 12 output parameters divided between the different actors •lead time order preparation for the producer; •shipping time for the delivery company; •time to order for the wholesaler; •Unfilled orders, service level and lead time for each retailer
Number of runs	10 replications for each model with relative precision 0.01

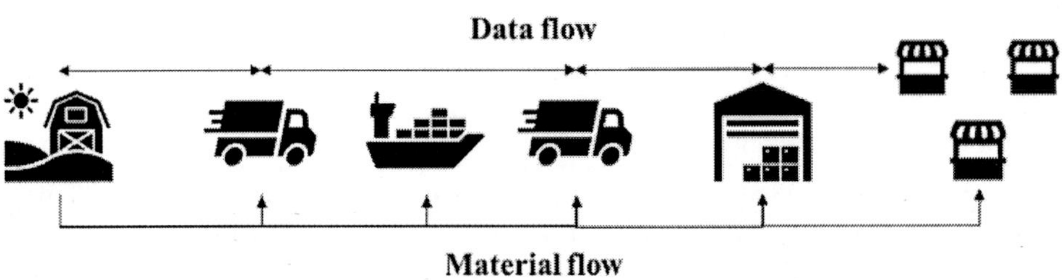

Fig. 3 *Traditional scenario scheme. The material flow goes from upstream to downstream while the data flow is exchanged by each actor in the supply chain*

The daily number of potential customers of each retailer changes based on the inter-arrival times modelled with an exponential distribution according to the opening hours of the retailers (see Appendix A). In addition, each retailer divides the cheese wheel into 200 pieces of 200 g and the purchase percentages have been modelled with a triangular distribution. The system was preloaded to eliminate the transitory: in this way the products are already available in stock. In addition to the aging time, the storing, checking, packing and picking times of the producer and wholesaler were also estimated. The wholesaler and the retailers order the products when they reach a limit value, in this way a reorder time is defined. Specifically, RA reorders four cheese wheels if it has a stock level below two cheese wheels after a five-day manual check, while RB and RC reorder three cheese wheels if they have a stock level below two cheese wheels every five days. Finally, the wholesaler periodically replenishes 275 cheese wheels every eight days, as it supplies other retailers that have not been modelled. The shipment from the producer to the wholesaler is based on an intermodal transport (truck-ship-truck) performed by a delivery company. Once the shipment has been designed according to the agreements made and what has been defined, the carrier will go to the producer's warehouse to load the products. Before proceeding with loading, the carrier checks whether the goods placed in the warehouse shipping zone reflect what is defined in the order. After this operation the goods are loaded, and the seal is affixed. Each seal has a unique identification code which is also reported on the documentation. After applying the seal, the documents that will accompany the goods throughout the shipment are signed. The loading takes place in Full Truck Load mode to minimize shipping costs, therefore the truck load is 275 units. Upon arrival of the goods at the wholesaler, an operator verifies the integrity of the seal, the documentation and the condition of the goods. Following these operations there is the signature of the documents certifying the successful delivery. Any reservations will also be placed on these documents in the event of goods damage. To close the order the documentation must be delivered to the administrative office for the billing. In a traditional process it is necessary to wait that the carrier returns to the delivery company headquarters and delivers the documents. Finally, depending on the orders received by the wholesaler, the goods are shipped to the retailers. From Monday to Friday, a unit of each partner keeps track of data such as stock levels, the quantity of goods sold and the quantity of unfilled orders. Since the orders have been shipped, the stock level must be updated. This process is carried out by an operator periodically at regular intervals of five days. This modelling has been implemented for each player in the supply chain.

Table 4 illustrates the areas, resources and equipment considered in this scenario for each actor with the relative description.

4.4 Simulation model with blockchain, IoT and RFID within the food supply chain

The second simulation scenario regards the combined use of emerging blockchain, IoT and RFID technologies. These technologies will allow the real-time control of the storage of products and the transactions that have taken place between the network players. The events are collected by the sensors and are consequently stored within the blockchain. The technologies are installed in the warehouses of each actor and in the truck of the DC in order to constantly monitor every single phase (Fig. 4). The orders management between the actors is automated using smart contracts. The simulation scenario is based on a private blockchain using Hyperledger Fabric (Hyperledger 2022). Private blockchains can be used for the respective relationships between entities. The only advantage of blockchain over a conventional solution that uses other IT methods in this scenario is its immutability.

Table 4 Area, resources, equipment and activities involved in the traditional supply chain scenario

Area	Activities	Resources	Equipment	Description	P	DC	W	RA	RB	RC
Order management	Order receipt	Order clerk	Excel; e-mail; phone	The order clerk supervises the order management steps. He checks the real availability of the cheese wheels in the warehouse, organizes all the phases and sends the information to the employees who should handle of carrying out the physical operations for the shipping	✓	✓	✓			
	Order processing				✓	✓	✓	✓	✓	✓
	Order generation					✓	✓	✓	✓	✓
Inventory management	Storing	Warehouse worker	Stacker crane	Worker that deals with the cheese wheels transportation from the reception area to the stacker crane for loading into the shelving	✓		✓			
	Picking		Forklift	Worker that deals with the cheese wheels transportation for quality control	✓		✓			
	Checking			Worker selected for the quality control of cheese wheels	✓					
	Packing			Worker that deals with both the cheese wheels packaging and the creation of the shipment batch. In addition, he provides the cheese wheels transportation for loading on the truck to be used for the transportation step	✓		✓			
Logistics	Checking pallet	Truck Driver	Truck	Driver in charge of checking the quality of cheese wheel packages		✓	✓			
	Loading pallet			Driver in charge of loading goods		✓	✓			
	Signing pallet			Driver in charge of verifying the documentation		✓	✓			
	Shipping			Driver in charge of shipping goods		✓	✓			
	Unloading pallet			Driver in charge of unloading goods		✓	✓			

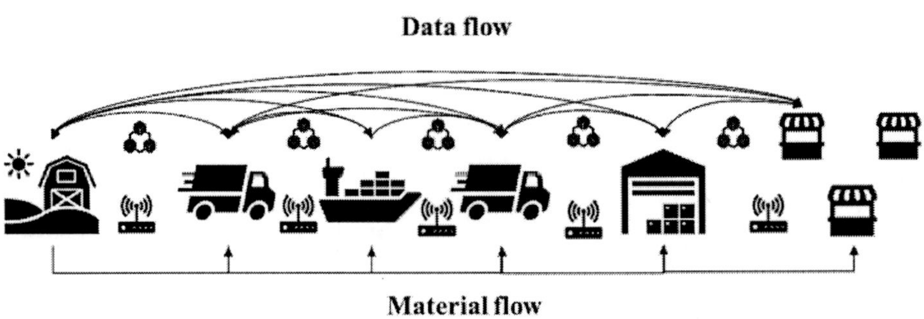

Fig. 4 *Scenario with the use of technologies such as IoT, RFID and blockchain. The data flow is shared between the partners of the chain using blockchain*

In this scenario each actor has its key pair for transaction access, depending on its role. The use of these new technologies leads to a constant track of stock levels and the quantities of the goods sold. The stock level is updated in real time. In this case, the alignment and coordination phase of IT and real warehouses is reduced. In particular, the reordering process is not based on a periodic manual check on the quantity available in the warehouse for both retailers and wholesalers. The data monitoring activities are carried out by the RFID sensors and the IoT infrastructure that capture the data constantly. The order management unit will have an alert signal whenever the quantities in the warehouse reach the limit below the pre-established stock quantity, which is the same as in the traditional scenario. Other players, such as the DC, can participate in the smart contract and have permissions to update and change product status. When goods arrive at destination, the receiver checks the smart contract data and accepts them, confirming the transaction. Finally, the product is delivered to the final actor. The status of the goods including location, transport conditions, delivery times and temperature will be updated within the distributed register to keep track of events in real time.

Table 5 illustrates the areas, resources and equipment considered in this scenario for each actor with the relative description.

4.5 VMI and emerging technologies model within the food supply chain

The third scenario regards the combined use of VMI strategies and digital technologies to obtain a further optimization of the chain. In this case, the wholesaler's and retailers' warehouses are managed by the producer. Indeed, using the blockchain technology, the producer could know the storage units of each downstream actor. The retailers and the wholesaler keep an up-to-date track of their inventory through sensors and IoT infrastructure and record these data to the distributed ledger. The producer controls the inventory of the actors via blockchain and, when needed, activates a smart contract with a new order to reload the downstream actors based on previously identified conditions and information (Fig. 5). In addition, the orders management and the activities to be carried out between the players are automated through the use of smart contracts. Also, in this case the reordering process of the cheese wheels for the downstream actors is based on the same previous input data. The actors send their inventory status to the blockchain daily using off-chain storage such as the InterPlanetary File System (IPFS) (Baumgart and Mies 2007; Casino et al. 2019b). Table 6 illustrates the areas, resources and equipment considered in this scenario for each actor with the relative activities description.

4.6 Comparison between the three scenarios

In the traditional scenario the order management is based on exchanges of emails, phone calls, the use of Excel and different IT systems. The lack of standardization of the activities requires more time for the practices. The orders between several players are highly manual and consequently there is a cost associated with human resources. Also, due to the laborious manual tasks required for each order, processing and response times are long. In addition, each customer (wholesaler and retailers) sends an order request to the order management unit, then this unit checks the stock in the warehouse, solves any problem and finally approves the order request. Consequently, the order management unit transmits the order specifications to the operators to carry out the delivery. The order management of the scenario with blockchain, RFID and IoT is automated through a smart contract that will allow to carry out the order upon the occurrence of specific conditions depending on the presence of the goods in the warehouse provided by the real-time control via RFID sensors of the inventory. In this case, the use of human resources and process time are reduced as the smart contract was previously implemented in accordance

Table 5 Area, resources, equipment and activities involved in the supply chain scenario with IoT, RFID, blockchain and smart contract

Area	Activities	Resources	Equipment	Description	P	DC	W	RA	RB	RC
Order management	Order receipt	Order clerk	Blockchain; Smart Contract	The order clerk supervises the order management steps. He checks the real availability of the cheese wheels in the warehouse using blockchain, organizes all the steps and sends the information to the worker who should handle of carrying out the physical operations for the shipping	✓	✓	✓			
	Order processing				✓	✓	✓	✓	✓	✓
	Order generation					✓	✓	✓	✓	✓
Inventory management	Storing	Warehouse worker	Stacker crane; RFID; IoT; Blockchain	Worker that deals with the cheese wheels transportation from the reception area to the stacker crane for loading into the shelving. Inside the shelves there are RFID and IoT infrastructure to monitor the goods in the warehouse	✓		✓			
	Picking		Forklift	Worker that deals with the cheese wheels transportation for quality control	✓		✓			
	Checking			Worker selected for the quality control of cheese wheels	✓					
	Packing		RFID	Worker that deals with both the cheese wheels packaging and the creation of the shipment batch. An RFID sensor is applied to each package. The quality of the batch is tracked via a blockchain transaction. In addition, he provides the cheese wheels transportation for loading on the truck to be used for the transportation step	✓		✓			
Logistics	Checking pallet	Truck Driver	Truck; Blockchain	Driver in charge of checking the quality of cheese wheel packages. The driver checks that the packages are guaranteed by viewing the transaction in blockchain		✓	✓			
	Loading pallet			Driver in charge of loading goods		✓	✓			
	Signing pallet		Blockchain	Driver in charge of verifying the documentation through the pair keys		✓	✓			
	Shipping		RFID; IoT	Driver in charge of the shipment of the goods constantly monitored along the route with RFID and IoT infrastructure		✓	✓			
	Unloading pallet			Driver in charge of unloading goods		✓	✓			

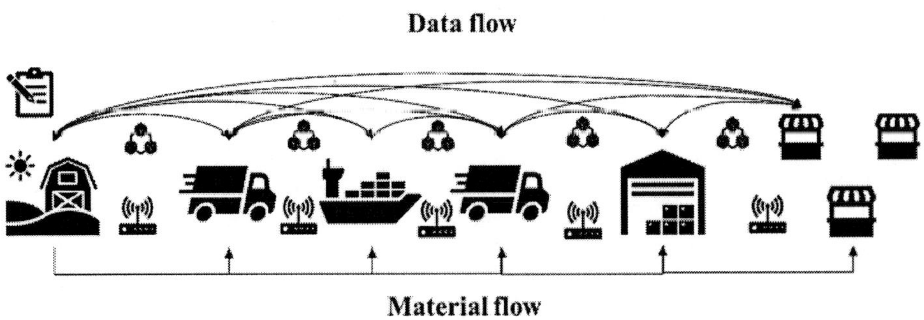

Fig. 5 *The third scenario concern the VMI strategy combined with emerging technologies. The producer manages the orders downstream thanks to the complete visibility of the blockchain*

Table 6 Area, resources, equipment and activities involved in the supply chain scenario with VMI

Area	Activities	Resources	Equipment	Description	P	DC	W	RA	RB	RC
Order management	Order receipt	Order clerk	Blockchain; Smart Contract	The order clerk supervises the order management steps. He checks the real availability of the cheese wheels in the warehouse using blockchain, organizes all the steps and sends the information to the worker who should handle of carrying out the physical operations for the shipping. He oversees the relations with the downstream players in the supply chain network employing a smart contract	✓	✓				
	Order processing				✓	✓				
	Order generation				✓	✓				
Inventory management	Storing	Warehouse worker	Stacker crane; RFID; IoT; Blockchain	Worker that deals with the cheese wheels transportation from the reception area to the stacker crane for loading into the shelving. Inside the shelves there are RFID and IoT infrastructure to monitor the goods in the warehouse	✓		✓			
	Picking	Warehouse worker	Forklift	Worker that deals with the cheese wheels transportation for quality control	✓		✓			
	Checking	Warehouse worker		Worker selected for the quality control of cheese wheels	✓					
	Packing	Warehouse worker	RFID	Worker that deals with both the cheese wheels packaging and the creation of the shipment batch. An RFID sensor is applied to each package. The quality of the batch is tracked via a blockchain transaction. In addition, he provides the cheese wheels transportation for loading on the truck to be used for the transportation step	✓		✓			
Logistics	Checking pallet	Truck Driver	Truck; Blockchain	Driver in charge of checking the quality of cheese wheel packages. The driver checks that the packages are guaranteed by viewing the transaction in blockchain		✓	✓			
	Loading pallet			Driver in charge of loading goods		✓	✓			
	Signing pallet		Blockchain	Driver in charge of verifying the documentation through the pair keys		✓	✓			
	Shipping		RFID; IoT	Driver in charge of the shipment of the goods constantly monitored along the route with RFID and IoT infrastructure		✓	✓			
	Unloading pallet			Driver in charge of unloading goods		✓	✓			

with contractual agreements. However, in the third scenario the order management is further optimized with the VMI strategy. In fact, thanks to the safe and certified visibility of the goods in the inventories of the different players, the producer can activate the smart contract when necessary since he can view all the transactions and know the level of stock available. In this case, having visibility on sales, the producer supplies the actors downstream.

Regarding inventory checking time, the monitoring of the goods in the warehouse for each actor is carried out by the operators on a pre-established periodic basis. Obviously, this can lead to inefficiencies and generate unfilled orders. However, in the second and third scenarios, the monitoring between the real and the virtual warehouse is carried out in real time by using RFID sensors and the IoT infrastructure that allows information to be sent to the distributed ledger. In this way the actors involved view the product status in real time. In addition, the complete visibility of the stock level allows the producer to make autonomous decisions.

Finally, the documentation sign step in the traditional solution is manual. Very often this phase can generate problems of authenticity and incorrect documentation and consequently the processing time for the monitoring can be longer. Instead, in the second and third scenarios, the documentation management is carried out through a digital certification in which the signatures management is based on public and private keys. This allows for greater safety and speed of delivery operations. Table 7 summarizes the main differences between the three scenarios. The Appendix A shows the data input for each actor and simulation step (see Tables 10, 11, 12, 13 and 14).

Table 7 - Schematization of comparison between the three different scenarios

	Traditional scenario	Blockchain, Rfid and IoT scenario	VMI and emerging technologies scenario
Order management	Manual order management with tools such as Excel, email, fax, telephone and different IT systems by the players in the supply chain	Automated order management through smart contracts between all the players in the supply chain	Automated order management with smart contract controlled by the producer
Inventory checking time	Manual periodic monitoring of the level of stock in the warehouse carried out by the operators	Real time control and total tracking of products during all phases carried out by RFID sensors	The same of second scenario
Sign documentation time	Paper management of transport documentation	Digital documentation management in a certified way using blockchain	The same of second scenario

5 Results

Table 8 shows the results of the three simulation models. The time to order was defined as the time needed to have the required quantity of goods in stock and was evaluated between the producer and the wholesaler. This indicator includes the phases in which the commercial unit of the wholesaler defines the order to be executed until the goods arrive in its warehouse. The first step consists in the analysis of the needs in which the wholesaler's order management department defines the request for goods. Then, there is the order fulfilment phase where the wholesaler's staff prepares the documentation and contacts for the producer. The order arrives at the producer and the order acceptance and processing step begins. After accepting the order, the producer will contact the delivery company agreeing on times and transport methods. Finally, the order is prepared and shipped on the agreed day and then there will be the transport phase. The last step concerns the checking of the wholesaler regarding the goods supplied. The difference between the traditional scenario and the one with the use of the technology consists in a

Table 8 Output parameters analysed

	Unit	Traditional Model (Mean)	Blockchain, IoT and RFID Model (Mean)	VMI and emerging technologies model (mean)	%Δ (1–2)	%Δ (1–3)	%Δ (2–3)
Time to order (P-W)	hour	162	142	140	12.63%	13.29%	0.75 %
Lead time order preparation (P)	hour	89	80	78	10.64%	12.24%	1.79 %
Shipping time (DC)	hour	36	36	36	0.78%	0.83%	0.00 %
Consumers (RA)		43,630	43,743	43,804	0.26%	0.40%	0.14 %
Unfilled orders (RA)	item	1745	201	120	88.48%	93.14%	40.46 %
Service level (RA)	%	96.00%	99.51%	99.73%	3.66%	3.88%	0.22 %
Lead Time (RA)	hour	29	17	18	42.20%	40.18%	3.50 %
Consumers (RB)		32,871	32,907	32,880	0.11%	0.03%	0.08 %
Unfilled orders (RB)	item	1644	99	16	93.98%	99.03%	83.84 %
Service level (RB)	%	95.00%	99.70%	99.95%	4.95%	5.21%	0.25 %
Lead Time (RB)	hour	34	17	18	48.93%	46.73%	4.31 %
Consumers (RC)		21,910	21,912	21,905	0.01%	0.02%	0.03 %
Unfilled orders (RC)	item	1205	43	6	96.43%	99.50%	86.05 %
Service level (RC)	%	94.50%	99.81%	99.97%	5.62%	5.79%	0.16 %
Lead Time (RC)	hour	36	18	18	49.96%	51.16%	2.40 %

saving times of approximately 20 h and the percentage variation between scenario 1 and 2 and scenario 1 and 3 is approximately 13%. The lead time of the producer's order preparation can be estimated as the sum of the time required to carry out the warehouse activities. The times considered are:

Order management time is the time taken to evaluate whether to fulfil an order and the time needed to organize the warehouse activities;

Picking and checking time is the time taken to pick up the products needed to complete a shipment batch from the storage area and to carry out the quality check of each product;

Pallet packing time is the time required for packing single product and for creating batches to be loaded into trucks for the shipping.

Also in this case, the time is reduced by about 11% between scenario 1–2 and 12% between scenario 1–3. The improvement in terms of effectiveness and efficiency is due to the time savings for the order management and the real-time control of the products stored in the warehouse.

The shipping time is the time from the departure of the producer's goods until delivery to the wholesaler. It considers three times: first, time for checking goods and bureaucratic procedures for verifying the conformity of the goods, documents loading that will accompany the shipment; then, the transit time is the time it takes for the goods to arrive at their destination; finally, the time for unloading goods and bureaucratic procedures, in which it is necessary to check the conformity of the goods, unloading from transport and signing the documents that will certify the delivery.

Finally, unfilled orders are the customers who have not found the product on the retailers' shelf, while the service level is the percentage of these dissatisfied consumers. It is shown that the average unfilled orders have decreased between scenario 1 and 2 by 92%, however between scenario 2 and 3 there is a further optimization of about 70%. The last indicator is the supply lead time, which corresponds to the time that elapses between the sending of the retailer's order to the wholesaler upon arrival of the ordered goods. Moreover, the greatest average variation between scenario 1 and scenario 2 is approximately 47% thanks to the automation of various processes.

The graphs of the most significant output parameters of the simulation are presented below: lead time order preparation, time to order (P-W) and unfilled order. The lead time order preparation (Fig. 6) for the producer order is optimized with the introduction of blockchain as it reduces the order management time using smart contracts. In addition, the VMI strategy further reduces this time as the producer can plan their activities in advance.

The values assumed by the time to order for the second and third scenarios are on average lower than the values of the first scenario (Fig. 7). The result is due to the more streamlined and automated activities, making the processes less random, as human work times are reduced. A lower time to order value allow a greater speed of customer service and less probability of stockout occurring. For the producer, the benefits of a reduction in delivery time are twofold. First, faster processes allow for economic savings as the time spent by human resources is less. The second aspect concerns greater customer satisfaction as the goods manage to arrive earlier at their destination having better control and traceability of processes.

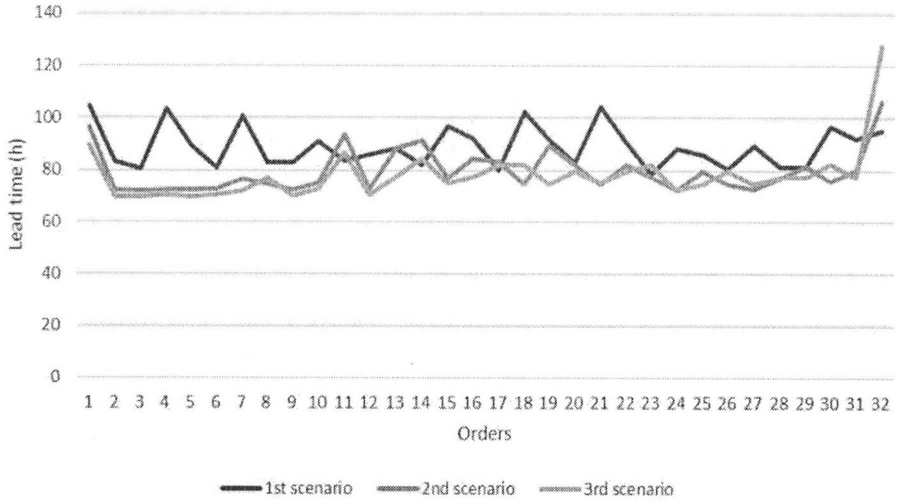

Fig. 6 *Lead time order preparation for the producer*

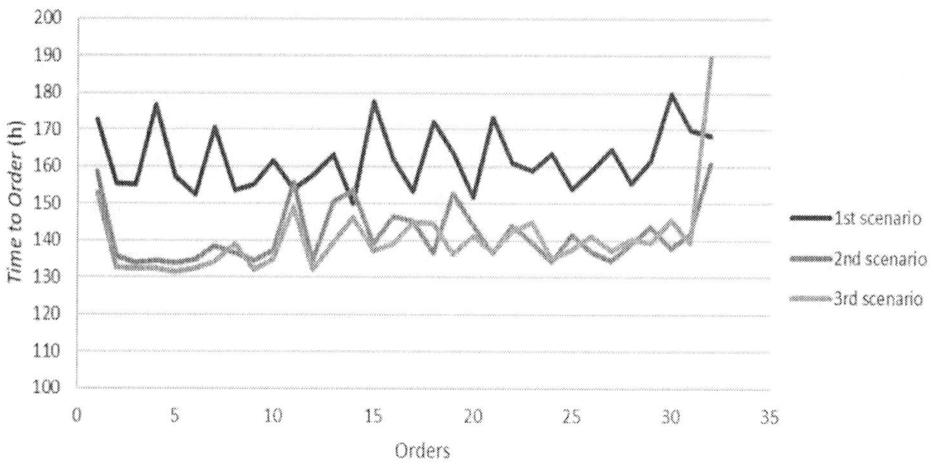

Fig. *7 Time to order between the producer and the wholesaler*

These output parameters optimize the activities within the supply chain, consequently allowing greater satisfaction of retailers' customers. The graph in Fig. 8 shows how on ten simulations the percentage of filled orders in the second and especially in the third scenario has significantly improved.

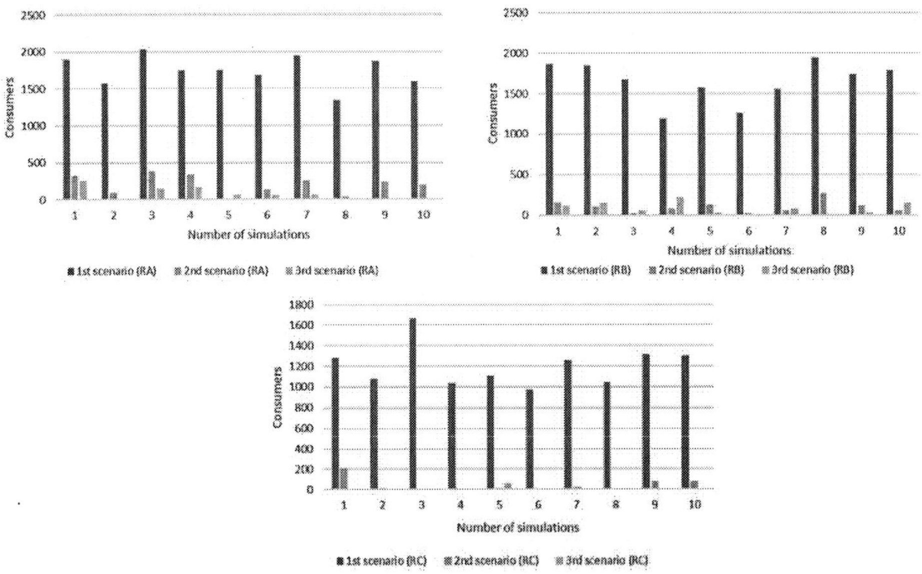

Fig. 8 *Average unfilled orders among the three retailers*

Table 9 Results of the sensitivity analysis considering the unfilled orders variations

Parameter	**Value**	**%Δ1–2**	**%Δ1–3**	**%Δ2–3**
Delivery time (DC)	-20%	81%	86%	24%
	-10%	78%	78%	0%
	10%	69%	86%	54%
	20%	77%	78%	8%
%Product purchase	-20%	99%	100%	100%
	-10%	90%	91%	10%
	10%	31%	37%	8%
	20%	17%	24%	9%
Ageing time	-20%	89%	100%	100%
	-10%	84%	89%	31%
	10%	96%	97%	20%
	20%	81%	83%	12%

5.1 Sensitivity analysis

A sensitivity analysis is carried out to consider the influence of structural parameters on the model outputs. There are different types of sensitivity analysis, depending on the target of the analysis (Borgonovo and Plischke 2016). In particular, factor prioritization was chosen to study the influence of the different parameters of the model. Three structural parameters were considered: delivery time of DC, % product purchase and ageing time. These parameters were varied from -20% to + 20% in four steps. The variations of these parameters carry out evaluations on the unfilled orders. Table 9 shows the values of such variations.

Results show that the variations in the percentage of product purchase have a significant influence on fulfilled orders. In particular, the higher the percentage of products purchase, the greater the reactivity to satisfy the demand for the second and third scenarios. Scenarios 2 and 3 show how the technologies and VMI strategy significantly limit these problems. A solution with blockchain and smart contract enables the optimization of the supply chain allowing an improvement in the resilience of the supply chain. However, the variation in timing parameters such as the delivery time of DC and the ageing time of the cheese do not show any significant variation for the unfilled orders.

6 Discussion

This section deepens the research results to answer the two questions that guided this work and provides some research implications.

6.1 On which supply chain operations can blockchain, IoT, RFID and smart contract derive operational time benefits for organizations?

The study showed the impact in terms of time performances that blockchain, connected to other technologies, has on supply chain operations from a numerical point of view. Starting from previous studies combining VMI and blockchain (Dasaklis and Casino 2019; Guggenberger et al. 2020; Omar et al. 2020), the study derived the time impacts on the Parmigiano Reggiano supply chain. The results in Table 8 show the variations in terms of time performance. The time advantage of the second scenario mainly depends on the technologies that capture the data, i.e. RFID and IoT. In addition, time is reduced because the needs analysis process is optimized by the presence of real-time inventory tracking systems. In this way, the order management unit has better visibility of the inventory in its physical warehouse by consulting the distributed ledger. Consequently, by combining continuous monitoring and exploiting the VMI strategy, the optimization of time and the reduction of unfilled orders is further improved. However, the difference between the time to order and lead time order preparation variables between the three scenarios have not drastically changed. The variation among the three scenarios ranges between 10 and 13%. Blockchain technology and the smart contracts facilitate tracking systems, visibility of the entire supply chain and allow greater trust and collaboration between partners. The VMI strategy, which may be unusable when there are opportunistic behaviours between partners, is implementable and guarantees the achievement of the results since the blockchain guarantees the concept of trust as the transactions within it are safe and immutable. As widely recognized in the literature, VMI regulates the frequency of purchased orders because the seller has a complete visibility of the downstream demand (Taleizadeh et al. 2015). Thus, the bullwhip effect is mitigated by reducing the variance of demand. Furthermore, the benefits of shorter delivery times are twofold for the producer. On the one hand, faster processes allow for economic savings as the time spent by human resources is less. On the other hand, there is greater customer satisfaction as goods arrive earlier at their destination with full process control and traceability. The use of these tools can increase the company's reputation towards the final market.

Note that shipping time is almost unchanged because it is mainly based on material flow operations. Indeed, blockchain impacts on information flows but not on material ones. The order management is more automated and improves time performances for each operation. However, for real optimization it is necessary to equip the other areas such as inventory and logistics with technologies such as IoT and RFID for data capture. As for the output parameters on each retailer, it is evident that the capture of information in real time and implementing the VMI strategy carries out benefits in terms of time advantages and customer satisfaction. As confirmed by the sensitivity analysis, by varying the percentage of product purchase, the scenarios with emerging technologies and the VMI strategy are more reactive to meet demand and make the supply chain resilient. This can be explained by the fact that in the traditional scenario relationships among organizations are performed by neighbouring players and planning is done only on the historical purchase data that each actor receives from their downstream counterparts. For the scenario with both emerging technologies and the use of VMI, the forecasts are more accurate since the data are updated daily on the blockchain and shared among all the players. It is interesting to note the percentage differences between the second and third scenarios (%Δ2-3) in Table 8. The only variables significantly changed in the third scenario compared to the second one are the reduction in unfilled orders of the three retailers which vary from 40 to 86%. The other variables, such as time to order, lead time order preparation and lead time to the retailers in the third scenario do not differ significantly from the second. This implies that emerging technologies enable time reduction on some activities. The adoption of the VMI strategy, enabled by these tools, mainly strengthens the customer satisfaction parameter by reducing the unfilled orders.

The orders planning carried out by the producer improves the overall efficiency of the supply chain thanks to the visibility of downstream demand. The use of blockchain changes the operations processes and organizational models of companies allowing for better data sharing. Therefore, the innovativeness of the model presented consists in measuring *ex-ante* the impacts that integration of different technologies can introduce within the Parmigiano Reggiano supply chain. Blockchain can be considered as an enabling tool for more effective and efficient operations management. The results demonstrate that blockchain technology is a cost-effective tool for overcoming the problems of collaboration and trust in a supply chain and for minimizing the negative impacts of information asymmetry at the supply chain level.

6.2 What are the benefits for each participant for supply chain operations in the various scenarios considered?

The benefits that the second and the third scenarios bring to each participant regard the exchange of information on a single platform among the players. The inaccuracies of the specifications and the lack of clarity that arises in the first scenario are reduced by using blockchain and smart contracts. For example, non-standard order acquisition systems such as emails and phone calls can generate errors and further waste of time by increasing order fulfilment times for each actor. The timing for the order management of the three scenarios is different. With the information sharing of the distributed ledger, there is greater traceability of orders, better visibility for participants and consequently greater trust in operations without the use of other intermediaries. Employing a single platform for the transactions exchange, the orders receipt and processing are carried out in a standardized way with the smart contracts.

In the second and the third scenarios, RFID sensors, IoT infrastructure and blockchain are implemented within the producer and wholesaler's warehouse and during the shipment. Therefore, this system architecture allows to acquire the stock level data in real time through RFID sensors, transfer the data on the blockchain using the IoT infrastructure and finally record them permanently and securely within the blockchain. This configuration saves time for the order management unit and reduces the time it takes for an operator to check, identify and record the position of the product in the warehouse. Finally, retailers request the goods via the blockchain platform by activating a smart contract. In this case, retailers are guaranteed the quality of the goods thanks to the complete traceability and visibility provided by the blockchain. The second and third scenarios solve the communication problems among the actors, reduce the potential waste of time due to human error and the presence of unnecessary bureaucratic activities. In particular, the VMI strategy of the third scenario reduces the workload of the actors downstream of the producer, guaranteeing greater flexibility in satisfying the final consumers.

6.3 Research implications

This is one of the first studies that clarifies and shows *ex-ante* the impacts in terms of time performances on operations that the integration of emerging technologies and the VMI strategy can have on supply chains. The second and third scenarios show how information exchange, control and monitoring on a shared platform can reduce procurement lead times and unfilled order. The research provides various insights into how the supply chains can be reorganized in different areas with the introduction of emerging technologies. It highlights the role of blockchain as an enabler of the VMI strategy for the operations management.

The study provides a first benchmark to managers and practitioners regarding the contribution of new technologies within supply chains and how these emerging technologies can be employed in supply chain operations. Real and pilot cases are currently in development in the real world. The use of simulation as a research tool allows to compare and analyse different alternatives in the absence of a real system model. The study investigates the advantages of applying these technologies by reducing the potential implementation risks through the analysis of quantitative parameters. Models that employ emerging technologies strengthen collaborative relationships and trust between partners as well as automate some operations by increasing the reputation among each participant in the network. The study aims to incentivize the adoption of these technologies which is still slow as the potential benefits are not clear. However, several issues remain open, for example, how to integrate these technologies with other

IT systems or how to reduce the knowledge and technical skills gap to properly manage these emerging tools.

7 Conclusions

The visibility of the chain is one of the problems that most afflicts modern chains. Most of the solutions present are of the one up-one down visibility type, i.e. the partners manage the relationships with the closest players upstream and downstream. However, an end-to-end visibility involves all the actors in the supply chain so that anyone could understand the external dynamics. To date the single source of truth is used, based on the involvement of a trusted third party who takes care of managing information in the supply chain. Alternatively, whoever manages the information can be a leader in the supply chain. However, these two solutions are not always achievable because, on the one hand, the third party may not exist, or the leader company does not want to manage the information of the other stakeholders. Furthermore, the players in the supply chain may have IT systems that are difficult to integrate with each other. Blockchain, being a distributed ledger, converts the concept of single source of truth into common source of truth and allowing a shared and unitary vision of reality. Collaborative environments based on trust and information sharing can be successful using blockchain technology as an intermediary. Several properties of blockchains are beneficial: the decentralized nature of data storage, data validation, immutability and transparency. The process of sharing information and data is more resilient as there is no single point of failure. This will lead to greater transaction confidence and mitigate cybersecurity risks.

This article aims to investigate different scenarios of the Parmigiano Reggiano supply chain with the application of integrated technologies and the combination of the VMI strategy. The work also conducts an in-depth analysis on the use of blockchain as an enabling factor for the VMI strategy. In the three proposed scenarios, the effects that the combined use of smart contracts, IoT blockchains, RFID and VMI have on the efficiency and effectiveness of the considered supply chain are studied. The results show how the capture of information in real time and the total visibility of the chain with the distributed ledger has a positive improvement in terms of time performance and fulfilled orders. The importance of building new organizational models is highlighted, considering the combined use of these techniques and technologies to ensure the achievement of better results.

However, further theoretical, empirical and quantitative studies are needed on the actual benefit of the connected use of these technologies. First, a necessary assessment should be carried out on the cost analysis of the entire technological infrastructure and the impact it has on each actor in the supply chain. In addition, a network with a larger number of participants should be considered in order to evaluate the technological performance of the blockchain in terms of scalability, throughput, storage and latency. Further investigation would be needed on how these technological, cost and time performance together could impact on entire supply chains. Moreover, it is necessary to consider different scenarios with different conditions such as international logistics, the risks of disruption events due to catastrophic phenomena such as the covid-19 pandemic, in order to better understand the real advantages and challenges of these new solutions. It is necessary to investigate how blockchain technology could enable other areas, such as humanitarian activities, to improve collaboration management, information sharing and disruption event management for catastrophic events for a more resilient supply chain.

Appendix A. Data input of the simulation scenarios

Table 10 Data Input (P)

		Traditional model	**Blockchain, IoT and RFID model**	**VMI and emerging technologies model**
		Unit	**Unit**	**Unit**
Production time		**21 Days**	**21 Days**	**21 Days**
Ageing time		12 Months	12 Months	12 Months
Storing time	Triangular distribution—Minimum	18 s	18 s	18 s
	Mode	30 s	30 s	30 s
	Maximum	1 min-	1 min	1 min
Picking and checking time	Triangular distribution—Minimum	1 min	1 min	1 min
	Mode	1,5 min	1,5 min	1,5 min
	Maximum	2 min	2 min	2 min
Packing pallet time	Triangular distribution—Minimum	50 s	50 s	50 s
	Mode	1 min	1 min	1 min
	Maximum	1,20 min	1,20 min	1,20 min

Table 11 Data Input (DC)

Checking pallet time	**Normal distribution—Mean**	**15 min**	**15 min**	**15 min**
	SD	1 min	1 min	1 min
Loading pallet time	Normal distribution—Mean	40 min	40 min	40 min
	SD	2 min	2 min	2 min
Sign documentation time (P—DC)	**Normal distribution—Mean**	**5 min**	**5 s**	**5 s**

Checking pallet time	**Normal distribution—Mean**	**15 min**	**15 min**	**15 min**
	SD	**1 min**	**0.5 s**	**0,5 s**
Shipping time by truck	Triangular distribution—Minimum	4 h	4 h	4 h
	Mode	4 h, 20 min	4 h, 20 min	4 h, 20 min
	Maximum	4 h, 40 min	4 h, 40 min	4 h, 40 min
Shipping time by ship	Normal distribution—Mean	29 h	29 h	29 h
	SD	30 min	30 min	30 min
Shipping time by truck	Normal distribution—Mean	2 h	2 h	2 h
	SD	5 min	5 min	5 min

Table 12 Data Input (W)

Checking pallet time	**Normal distribution—Mean**	**15 min**	**15 min**	**15 min**
	SD	1 min	1 min	1 min
Unloading pallet time	Normal distribution—Mean	40 min	40 min	40 min
	SD	2 min	2 min	2 min
Sign documentation time (DC—W)	**Normal distribution—Mean**	**5 min**	**5 s**	**5 s**
	SD	**1 min**	**0.5 s**	**0.5 s**
Storing time	Triangular distribution—Minimum	4 min	4 min	4 min
	Mode	5 min	5 min	5 min
	Maximum	7 min	7 min	7 min
Picking and packing time	Triangular distribution—Minimum	4 min	4 min	4 min
	Mode	5 min	5 min	5 min
	Maximum	7 min	7 min	7 min

Table 13 Data Input (R)

Shipping time by truck (A)	**Normal distribution—Mean**	**30 min**	**30 min**	**30 min**
	SD	5 min	5 min	5 min
Shipping time by truck (B)	Normal distribution—Mean	50 min	50 min	50 min
	SD	4 min	4 min	4 min
Shipping time by truck (C)	Normal distribution—Mean	60 min	60 min	60 min
	SD	5 min	5 min	5 min
Customers (A)	Interarrival time (Exponential distribution)	1600 customers/day	1600 customers/day	1600 customers/d ay
Customers (B)		1200 customers/day	1200 customers/day	1200 customers/d ay
Customers (C)		800 customers/day	800 customers/day	800 customers/d ay
% Product purchase	Triangular distribution—Minimum	3%	3%	3%
	Mode	5%	5%	5%
	Maximum	7%	7%	7%

Table 14 Data Flow Input

Order management (P)	**Normal distribution—Mean**	**1 h**	**5 min**	**5 min**
	SD	2 min	30 s	30 s
Order management (DC)	Normal distribution—Mean	1 h, 30 min	10 min	10 min
	SD	2 min	30 s	30 s
Order management (W)	Normal distribution—Mean	1 h, 30 min	5 min	
	SD	2 min	30 s	
Order management (R)	Normal distribution—Mean	1 h	5 min	
	SD	2 min	30 s	

Author Contributions

Conceptualization, Vincenzo Varriale and Mauro Caputo; data curation, Antonello Cammarano and Vincenzo Varriale; formal analysis, Antonello Cammarano, Vincenzo Varriale, and Francesca Michelino.; methodology, Antonello Cammarano; project administration, Mauro Caputo; supervision, Francesca Michelino and Mauro Caputo; validation, Francesca Michelino and Mauro Caputo; writing—original draft, Antonello Cammarano and Vincenzo Varriale; writing—review and editing, Francesca Michelino. All authors have read and agreed to the published version of the manuscript.

References

Agrawal R, Wankhede VA, Kumar A, Upadhyay A, Garza-Reyes JA (2022) Nexus of circular economy and sustainable business performance in the era of digitalization. Int J Prod Perf Manag 71(3):748–774. https://doi.org/10.1108/IJPPM-12-2020-0676

Alfayad FS (2020) Reducing just-in-time delivery related cost volatility in the global supply chain: Consumers and blockchain technology. Int J Supply Chain Manag 9(3):963–972

Ali MH, Chung L, Kumar A et al (2021) A sustainable Blockchain framework for the halal food supply chain: Lessons from Malaysia. Technol Forecast Soc Change 170:120870. https://doi. org/ 10.1016/j.techfore.2021.120870

Alonso RS, Sittón-Candanedo I, García Ó et al (2020) An intelligent Edge-IoT platform for monitoring livestock a nd crops in a dairy farming scenario. Ad Hoc Netw 98:102047. https://doi.org/10.1016/j.adhoc.2019.102047

Assaqty MIS, Gao Y, Hu X et al (2020) Private-Blockchain-Based Industrial IoT for Material and Product Tracking in Smart Manufacturing. IEEE Netw 34(5):91–97

Astill J, Dara RA, Campbell M et al (2019) Transparency in food supply chains: A review of enabling technology solutions. Trends Food Sci Technol 91:240–247

Bai C, Sarkis J (2020) A supply chain transparency and sustainability technology appraisal model for blockchain technology. Int J Prod Res 58(7):2142–2162. https://doi.org/10.1080/00207 543.2019.1708989

Bai Y, Fan K, Zhang K et al (2021) Blockchain-based trust management for agricultural green supply: A game theoretic approach. J Clean Prod 310:124707. https://doi. org/10.1016/j.jclepro. 20 21. 127407

Baumgart I, Mies S (2007) IPFS - Content Addressed, Versioned, P2P File System (DRAFT 3). Proc Int Conf Parallel Distrib Syst - ICPADS

Bechtsis D, Tsolakis N, Iakovou E, Vlachos D (2021) Data-driven secure, resilient and sustainable supply chains: gaps, opportunities, and a new generalised data sharing and data monetisation framework. Int J Prod Res. https://doi.org/10.1080/00207543.2021.1957506

Benyam AA, Soma T, Fraser E (2021) Digital agricultural technologies for food loss and waste prevention and reduction: Global trends, adoption opportunities and barriers. J Clean Prod 323:129099

Bhatti A, Malik H, Kamal AZ et al (2021) Much- needed business digital transformation through big data, internet of things and blockchain capabilities: implications for strategic performance in telecommunication sector. Bus Process Manag J 27(6):1854–1873. https: //doi. org/10.1108/BPMJ-12-2020-0553

Borgonovo E, Plischke E (2016) Sensitivity analysis: A review of recent advances. Eur J Oper Res 248(3):869–887

Bottani E, Montanari R (2010) Supply chain design and cost analysis through simulation. Int J Prod Res 48(10):2859–2886. https://doi.org/10.1080/00207540902960299

Cammarano A, Michelino F, Lamberti E, Caputo M (2019) Investigating technological strategy and relevance of knowledge domains in R&D collaborations. Int J Technol Manag 79(1):60–83. https://doi.org/10.1504/IJBCRM.2018.096534

Cammarano A, Michelino F, Vitale MP et al (2020) Technological Strategies and Quality of Invention: The Role of Knowledge Base and Technical Applications. IEEE Trans Eng Manag. https: //doi.org/10.1109/TEM.2020.2973861

Carson JS (2004) Introduction to modeling and simulation. In: Proceedings - Winter Simulation Conference WSC '04, pages 9–16, Piscataway, New Jersey, Institute of Electrical and Electronics Engineers, Inc., available at:https://doi.org/10.1201/b17595-6.

Casino F, Kanakaris V, Dasaklis TK et al (2019a) Modeling food supply chain traceability based on blockchain technology. IFAC-PapersOnLine 52(13):2728–2733. https://doi. org/10.1016/j. ifacol. 2019.11.620

Casino F, Dasaklis TK, Patsakis C (2019b) Enhanced vendor-managed inventory through blockchain. In: 2019b 4th South-East Europe Design Automation, Computer Engineering, Computer Networks and Social Media Conference, SEEDA-CECNSM 2019b, available at https:// doi.org/10.1109/SEEDA-CECNSM.2019.8908481

Casino F, Kanakaris V, Dasaklis TK, Moschuris S, Stachtiaris S, Pagoni M, Rachaniotis NP (2020) Blockchain-based food supply chain traceability: a case study in the dairy sector. Int J Prod Res 59(19):5758–5770. https://doi.org/10.1080/00207543.2020.1789238

Chang Y, Iakovou E, Shi W (2020) Blockchain in global supply chains and cross border trade: a critical synthesis of the state-of-the-art, challenges and opportunities. Int J Prod Res 58(7):2082–2099. https://doi.org/10.1080/00207543.2019.1651946

Choi TM (2019) Blockchain-technology-supported platforms for diamond authentication and certification in luxury supply chains. Transp Res Part E Logist Transp Rev 128:17–29. https://doi. org/10.1016/j.tre.2019.05.011

Christidis K, Devetsikiotis M (2016) Blockchains and Smart Contracts for the Internet of Things. IEEE Access 4:2292–2303. https://doi.org/10.1109/ACCESS.2016.2566339

Ciruela-Lorenzo AM, Del-Aguila-Obra AR, Padilla-Meléndez A, Plaza-Angulo JJ (2020) Digitalization of agri-cooperatives in the smart agriculture context. Proposal of a digital diagnosis tool. Sustain 12(4):1325. https://doi.org/10.3390/su12041325

Dasaklis T, Casino F (2019) Improving Vendor-managed Inventory Strategy Based on Internet of Things (IoT) Applications and Blockchain Technology. In: ICBC 2019 - IEEE International Conference on Blockchain and Cryptocurrency, Seoul, Korea (South), May 14–17, available at: https://doi.org/10.1109/BLOC.2019.8751478

Della Valle F, Oliver M (2020) Blockchain Enablers for Supply Chains: How to Boost Implementation in Industry. IEEE Access 8:209699–209716. https://doi.org/10.1109/ACCESS.2020.3038463

Disney SM, Towill DR (2003) Vendor-managed inventory and bullwhip reduction in a two-level supply chain. Int J Oper Prod Manag 23(6):625–651. https://doi.org/10.1108/01443570310476654

Dolgui A, Ivanov D, Potryasaev S et al (2020) Blockchain-oriented dynamic modelling of smart contract design and execution in the supply chain. Int J Prod Res 58(7):2184–2199. https://doi.org/10.1080/00207543.2019.1627439

Dong Y, Dresner M, Yao Y (2014) Beyond information sharing: An empirical analysis of vendor-managed inventory. Prod Oper Manag 23(5):817–828. https://doi.org /10.1111/poms.12085

Ebrahim-Khanjari N, Hopp W, Iravani SMR (2012) Trust and information sharing in supply chains. Prod Oper Man 21(3):444–464. https://doi.org/10.1111/j.1937-5956.2011.01284.x

Eisenhardt KM (1989) Building Theories from Case Study Research. Acad Manag Rev 14(4):532–550. https://doi.org/10.5465/amr.1989.4308385

Feng H, Wang X, Duan Y et al (2020) Applying blockchain technology to improve agri-food traceability: A review of development methods, benefits and challenges. J Clean Prod 260 (121031):1–15

Fosso Wamba S, Kala Kamdjoug JR, Epie Bawack R, Keogh JG (2020) Bitcoin, Blockchain and Fintech: a systematic review and case studies in the supply chain. Prod Plan Control 31(2–3):115–142. https://doi.org/10.1080/09537287.2019.1631460

Galanakis CM, Rizou M, Aldawoud TMS et al (2021) Innovations and technology disruptions in the food sector within the COVID-19 pandemic and post-lockdown era. Trends Food Sci Technol 110:193–200

Gehman J, Glaser VL, Eisenhardt KM et al (2018) Finding Theory-Method Fit: A Comparison of Three Qualitative Approaches to Theory Building. J Manag Inq 27(3):284–300. https://doi. org/ 10.1177/1056492617706029

George RV, Harsh HO, Ray P, Babu AK (2019) Food quality traceability prototype for restaurants using blockchain and food quality data index. J Clean Prod 240:118021. https://doi.org/ 10.1016/j.jclepro.2019.118021

Gopi K, Mazumder D, Sammut J, Saintilan N (2019) Determining the provenance and authenticity of seafood: A review of current methodologies. Trends Food Sci Technol 91:292–304

Gourisetti SNG, Mylrea M, Patangia H (2020) Evaluation and Demonstration of Blockchain Applicability Framework. IEEE Trans Eng Manag. https://doi.org/10.1109 /TEM.2019.2928280

Guggenberger T, Schweizer A, Urbach N (2020) Improving Interorganizational Information Sharing for Vendor Managed Inventory: Toward a Decentralized Information Hub Using

Blockchain Technology. IEEE Trans Eng Manag 67(4):1074–1085. https://doi.org/10.1109/TEM. 2020.2978628

Hald KS, Coslugeanu P (2021) The preliminary supply chain lessons of the COVID-19 disruption—What is the role of digital technologies? Oper Manag Res. https://doi.org/10.1007/ s12063-021-00207-x

Hasan H, AlHadhrami E, AlDhaheri A et al (2019) Smart contract-based approach for efficient shipment management. Comput Ind Eng 136:149–159. https://doi.org/ 10.1016/j.cie.2019 .07.022

Hastig GM, Sodhi MMS (2020) Blockchain for Supply Chain Traceability: Business Requirements and Critical Success Factors. Prod Oper Manag 29(4):935–954. https://doi. org/10.1111/ poms.13147

Helo P, Shamsuzzoha AHM (2020) Real-time supply chain—A blockchain architecture for project deliveries. Robot Comput Integr Manuf 63:101909. https://doi.org/ 10.1016/j.rcim.2019.101909

Hofmann E (2017) Big data and supply chain decisions: the impact of volume, variety and velocity properties on the bullwhip effect. Int J Prod Res 55(17):5108–5126

Hyperledger (2022) Hyperledger – Open Source Blockchain Technologies. https://www.hyperledger.org/

ISTAT (2022). https://www.dati.istat.it/

Ivanov D, Dolgui A, Sokolov B (2019) The impact of digital technology and Industry 4.0 on the ripple effect and supply chain risk analytics. Int J Prod Res 57(3):829–846. https://doi.org/10. 1080/00207543.2018.1488086

Jæger B, Menebo MM, Upadhyay A (2021) Identification of environmental supply chain bottlenecks: a case study of the Ethiopian healthcare supply chain. Manag Environ Qual Int J 32(6):1233–1254. https://doi.org/10.1108/MEQ-12-2019-0277

Jaeger B, Upadhyay A (2020) Understanding barriers to circular economy: cases from the manufacturing industry. J Enter Inf Man 33(4):729–745

Joo J, Han Y (2021) An evidence of distributed trust in blockchain-based sustainable food supply chain. Sustain 13(19):10980. https://doi.org/10.3390/su131910980

Joshi S, Sharma M, Das RP, Muduli K, Raut R, Narkhede BE, Shee H, Misra A (2022) Assessing Effectiveness of Humanitarian Activities against COVID-19 Disruption: The Role of Blockchain-Enabled Digital Humanitarian Network (BT-DHN). Sustain 14(3):1–22

Jraisat L, Upadhyay A, Ghalia T, Jresseit M, Kumar V, Sarpong D (2021) Triads in sustainable supply-chain perspective: why is a collaboration mechanism needed? Int J Prod Res. https: //doi.org/10.1080/00207543.2021.1936263

Kamble SS, Gunasekaran A, Gawankar SA (2020) Achieving sustainable performance in a data-driven agriculture supply chain: A review for research and applications. Int J Prod Econ 219:179–194

Kamilaris A, Fonts A, Prenafeta-Boldú FX (2019) The rise of blockchain technology in agriculture and food supply chains. Trends Food Sci Technol 91:640–652

Kasemsap K (2017) Advocating information system, information integration, and information sharing in global supply chain. Oper Serv Man. https://doi.org/10.4018/978-1-5225-3909-4.ch070

Kayikci Y, Subramanian N, Dora M, Bhatia MS (2020) Food supply chain in the era of Industry 4.0: blockchain technology implementation opportunities and impediments from the perspective of people, process, performance, and technology. Prod Plan Control 33(2–3):301–321. https://doi. org/10.1080/09537287.2020.1810757

Ketokivi M, Mahoney JT (2020) Transaction Cost Economics As a Theory of Supply Chain Efficiency. Prod Oper Manag 32(5):232–240. https://doi.org/10.1111/poms.13148

Kim M, Chai S (2017) The impact of supplier innovativeness, information sharing and strategic sourcing on improving supply chain agility: Global supply chain perspective. Int J Prod Econ 187:42–52. https://doi.org/10.1016/j.ijpe.2017.02.007

Kittipanya-ngam P, Tan KH (2020) A framework for food supply chain digitalization: lessons from Thailand. Prod Plan Control 31(2–3):158–172. https://doi.org/10. 1080/0953 7287. 2019.1631462

Klerkx L, Rose D (2020) Dealing with the game-changing technologies of Agriculture 4.0: How do we manage diversity and responsibility in food system transition pathways? Glob Food Sec 24, 100347. https://doi.org/10.1016/j.gfs.2019.100347

Köhler S, Pizzol M (2020) Technology assessment of blockchain-based technologies in the food supply chain. J Clean Prod 269:122193. https://doi.org/10.1016/j.jclepro.2020.122193

Kolb J, Hornung DJ, Kraft F, Winkelmann A (2018) Industrial application of blockchain technology - Erasing the weaknesses of vendor managed inventory. In: 26th European Conference on Information Systems: Beyond Digitization - Facets of Socio-Technical Change, ECIS 2018, Portsmouth, UK, 28 November

Kouhizadeh M, Saberi S, Sarkis J (2021) Blockchain technology and the sustainable supply chain: Theoretically exploring adoption barriers. Int J Prod Econ 231(10731):1–21. https: //doi. org/ 10.1016/j.ijpe.2020.107831

Kouhizadeh M, Zhu Q, Sarkis J (2020) Blockchain and the circular economy: potential tensions and critical reflections from practice. Prod Plan Control 31(11–12):950–966. https://doi.org/ 10.1080/09537287.2019.1695925

Kramer MP, Bitsch L, Hanf J (2021) Blockchain and its impacts on agri-food supply chain network management. Sustain 13(4):2168. https://doi.org/10.3390/su13042168

Kumar A, Liu R, Shan Z (2020) Is Blockchain a Silver Bullet for Supply Chain Management? Technical Challenges and Research Opportunities. Dec Scien 51(1):8–37

Lee JY, Cho RK, Paik SK (2016) Supply chain coordination in vendor-managed inventory systems with stockout-cost sharing under limited storage capacity. Eur J Oper Res 248(1):95–106. https: //doi.org/10.1016/j.ejor.2015.06.080

Lezoche M, Panetto H, Kacprzyk J et al (2020) Agri-food 4.0: A survey of the Supply Chains and Technologies for the Future Agriculture. Comput Ind 117:(103187)1–15

Li Z, Zhong RY, Tian ZG et al (2021a) Industrial Blockchain: A state-of-the-art Survey. Robot Comput Integr Manuf 70:102124

Li K, Lee JY, Gharehgozli A (2021b) Blockchain in food supply chains: a literature review and synthesis analysis of platforms, benefits and challenges. Int J Prod Res. https://doi.org/10. 1080 /00207543.2021.1970849

Lohmer J, Bugert N, Lasch R (2020) Analysis of resilience strategies and ripple effect in blockchain-coordinated supply chains: An agent-based simulation study. Int J Prod Econ 228(107882):1–13. https://doi.org/10.1016/j.ijpe.2020.107882

Longo F, Nicoletti L, Padovano A et al (2019) Blockchain-enabled supply chain: An experimental study. Comput Ind Eng 136:57–69. https://doi.org/10.1016/j.cie.2019.07.026

Manupati VK, Schoenherr T, Ramkumar M et al (2020) A blockchain-based approach for a multi-echelon sustainable supply chain. Int J Prod Res 58(7):2222–2241. https://doi. org/10.1080/ 00207543.2019.1683248

Martinez V, Zhao M, Blujdea C et al (2019) Blockchain-driven customer order management. Int J Oper Prod Manag 39(6–7–8):993–1022. https://doi.org/10.1108/IJOPM-01-2019-0100

Michelino F, Lamberti E, Cammarano A, Caputo M (2015) Open models for innovation: An accounting-based perspective. Int J Techn Man 68(1/2):99–121. https://doi. org/10.1504 /IJTM.2015.068778

Mishra H, Maheshwari P (2021) Blockchain in Indian Public Distribution System: a conceptual framework to prevent leakage of the supplies and its enablers and disablers. J Glob Oper Strateg Sourc 14(2):312–335. https://doi.org/10.1108/JGOSS-07-2020-0044

Mukherjee AA, Singh RK, Mishra R, Bag S (2021) Application of blockchain technology for sustainability development in agricultural supply chain: justification framework. Oper Manag Res. https://doi.org/10.1007/s12063-021-00180-5

Mukhuty S, Upadhyay A, Rothwell H (2022) Strategic sustainable development of Industry 4.0 through the lens of social responsibility: The role of human resource practices. Busin Strat Environ. https://doi.org/10.1002/bse.3008

Muravev D, Hu H, Rakhmangulov A, Dai L (2019) Multi-agent simulation of the balanced main parameters of the logistics centers. In: IFAC-PapersOnLine 52(12): 1057–1062

Nurgazina J, Pakdeetrakulwong U, Moser T, Reiner G (2021) Distributed ledger technology applications in food supply chains: A review of challenges and future research directions. Sustain 13(8):4206

Omar IA, Jayaraman R, Salah K et al (2020) Enhancing Vendor Managed Inventory Supply Chain Operations Using Blockchain Smart Contracts. IEEE Access 8:5034–5061. https://doi. org/10. 1109/ access.2020.3028031

Osmanoglu M, Tugrul B, Dogantuna T, Bostanci E (2020) An Effective Yield Estimation System Based on Blockchain Technology. IEEE Trans Eng Manag 67(4):1157–1168. https://doi. org/10.1109/TEM.2020.2978829

Parmigiano Reggiano (2022). https://ar.parmigianoreggiano.it/ar/ar.do

Pedersen AB, Risius M, Beck R (2019) A ten-step decision path to determine when to use blockchain technologies. MIS Q Exec 18 (2): 99–115. https://doi.org/10.17705/2msqe.00010

Qiao R, Zhu S, Wang Q, Qin J (2018) Optimization of dynamic data traceability mechanism in Internet of Things based on consortium blockchain. Int J Distrib Sens Networks 14(12):1–15. https://doi.org/10.1177/1550147718819072

Queiroz MM, Telles R, Bonilla SH (2019) Blockchain and supply chain management integration: a systematic review of the literature. Supply Chain Manag 25(2):241–254

Rainero C, Modarelli G (2021) Food tracking and blockchain-induced knowledge: a corporate social responsibility tool for sustainable decision-making. Br Food J 123(12):4284–4308. https:// doi.org/10.1108/BFJ-10-2020-0921

Ralston PM, Keller SB, Grawe SJ (2020) Collaborative process competence as an enabler of supply chain collaboration in competitive environments and the impact on customer account management. Int J Logist Manag 31(4):905–929. https://doi.org/10.1108/IJLM-11-2019-0310

Rana RL, Tricase C, De Cesare L (2021) Blockchain technology for a sustainable agri-food supply chain. Br Food J 123(11):3471–3485

Roeck D, Sternberg H, Hofmann E (2020) Distributed ledger technology in supply chains: a transaction cost perspective. Int J Prod Res 58(7):2124–2141. https://doi.org/10.1080/00207543. 2019. 1657247

Ryu CS (2016) Review of vendor managed inventory: Investigation on how it improves supply chain performance. J Distrib Sci 14(9):47–64

Saberi S, Kouhizadeh M, Sarkis J, Shen L (2019) Blockchain technology and its relationships to sustainable supply chain management. Int J Prod Res 57(7):2117–2135. https://doi.org/10. 1080 /00207543.2018.1533261

Salem RW, Elomri A (2017) Vendor managed inventory (VMI): From theory to practical implementation a literature review. Int J Supply Chain Manag 6(1):68–93

Saurabh S, Dey K (2021) Blockchain technology adoption, architecture, and sustainable agri-food supply chains. J Clean Prod 284:124731. https://doi.org/10.1016/j.jclepro.2020.124731

Serdarasan S (2013) A review of supply chain complexity drivers. Comput Ind Eng 66(3):533–540. https://doi.org/10.1016/j.cie.2012.12.008

Shahid A, Almogren A, Javaid N et al (2020) Blockchain-Based Agri-Food Supply Chain: A Complete Solution. IEEE Access 8:69230–69243. https://doi.org/10.1109 /ACCESS.2020. 2986 257

Sharma M, Joshi S, Luthra S, Kumar A (2021) Managing disruptions and risks amidst COVID-19 outbreaks: role of blockchain technology in developing resilient food supply chains. Oper Manag Res. https://doi.org/10.1007/s12063-021-00198-9

Sharma R, Kamble SS, Gunasekaran A et al (2020) A systematic literature review on machine learning applications for sustainable agriculture supply chain performance. Comput Oper Res 119(104926):1–17. https://doi.org/10.1016/j.cor.2020.104926

Sharma M, Kumar A, Luthra S, Joshi S, Upadhyay A (2022) The impact of environmental dynamism on low-carbon practices and digital supply chain networks to enhance sustainable performance: An empirical analysis. Busin Strat Environ. https://doi.org/10.1002/bse.2983

Shi J, Xiao T (2015) Service investment and consumer returns policy in a vendor-managed inventory supply chain. J Ind Manag Optim 11(2):439–459. https://doi.org/10.3934/ jimo. 2015. 11.439

Shore B (2001) Information sharing in global supply chain systems. J Glob Inf Tech Man 4(3):27–50. https://doi.org/10.1080/1097198X.2001.10856306

Siddh M, Kumar S, Soni G et al (2021) Impact of agri-fresh food supply chain quality practices on organizational sustainability. Oper Manag Res. https://doi.org/10.1007/s12063-021-00196-x

Singhry HB, Abd Rahman A (2019) Enhancing supply chain performance through collaborative planning, forecasting, and replenishment. Bus Process Manag J 24(4):625–646. https://doi.org /10.1108/BPMJ-03-2017-0052

Spadoni R, Nanetti M, Bondanese A, Rivaroli S (2019) Innovative solutions for the wine sector: The role of startups. Wine Econ Policy 8(2):165–170

Srivastava DK, Kumar V, Ekren BY, Upadhyay A, Tyagi M, Kumari A (2022) Adopting Industry 4.0 by leveraging organisational factors. Technol Forecast Soc Change 176:1–10

Stojanović ĐM, Ivetić J (2020) Macrologistic performance and logistics commitments in sales contracts in international supply chains. Int J Logist Manag 31(1):59–76. https://doi. org/10.1108/ IJLM-12-2018-0323

Stranieri S, Riccardi F, Meuwissen MPM, Soregaroli C (2021) Exploring the impact of blockchain on the performance of agri-food supply chains. Food Control 119:107495. https:// doi.org/10.1016/j.foodcont.2020.107495

Sund T, Lööf C, Nadjm-Tehrani S, Asplund M (2020) Blockchain-based event processing in supply chains—A case study at IKEA. Robot Comput Integr Manuf 65:101971. https://doi.org/ 10.1016/ j.rcim.2020.101971

Taleizadeh AA, Noori-Daryan M, Cárdenas-Barrón LE (2015) Joint optimization of price, replenishment frequency, replenishment cycle and production rate in vendor managed inventory system with deteriorating items. Int J Prod Econ 159:285–295. https://doi.org/ 10.1016/j.ijpe. 2014.09.009

Tozanli Ö, Kongar E, Gupta SM (2020) Evaluation of waste electronic product trade-in strategies in predictive twin disassembly systems in the era of blockchain. Sustain 12(13): 5416. https:// doi.org/10.3390/su12135416

Tozanlı Ö, Kongar E, Gupta SM (2020) Trade-in-to-upgrade as a marketing strategy in disassembly-to-order systems at the edge of blockchain technology. Int J Prod Res 58(23):7183–7200. https://doi.org/10.1080/00207543.2020.1712489

Tse D, Zhang B, Yang Y et al (2018) Blockchain application in food supply information security. In: IEEE International Conference on Industrial Engineering and Engineering

Management Singapore, December 10–13, available at: https://doi.org/10.1 109/IEEM. 2017.8290114

Tsolakis N, Niedenzu D, Simonetto M et al (2021) Supply network design to address United Nations Sustainable Development Goals: A case study of blockchain implementation in Thai fish industry. J Bus Res 131:495–519. https://doi.org/10.1016/j.jbusres.2020.08.003

Upadhyay A, Laing T, Kumar V, Dora M (2021a) Exploring barriers and drivers to the implementation of circular economy practices in the mining industry. Resour Pol 72:1–7. https://doi.org/10.1016/j.resourpol.2021.102037

Upadhyay A, Ayodele JO, Kumar A, Garza-Reyes JA (2021b) A review of challenges and opportunities of blockchain adoption for operational excellence in the UK automotive industry. J Glob Oper Strat Sourc 14(1):7–60. https://doi.org/10.1108/JGOSS-05-2020-0024

Upadhyay A, Mukhuty S, Kumar V, Kazancoglu Y (2021c) Blockchain technology and the circular economy: Implications for sustainability and social responsibility. J Clean Prod 239:1–7. https://doi.org/10.1016/j.jclepro.2021.126130

Varriale V, Cammarano A, Michelino F, Caputo M (2020) The unknown potential of blockchain for sustainable supply chains. Sustain 12(22):1–16. https://doi.org/10. 3390/su12229400

Varriale V, Cammarano A, Michelino F, Caputo M (2021a) The role of supplier innovation performance and strategies on the smartphone supply market. Eur Man J. https://doi.org/ 10.1016/ j.emj.2021.09.010

Varriale V, Cammarano A, Michelino F, Caputo M (2021b) New organizational changes with blockchain: a focus on the supply chain. J Organ Chang Manag 34(2):420–438. https://doi. org/ 10.1108/jocm-08-2020-0249

Vu N, Ghadge A, Bourlakis M (2021) Blockchain adoption in food supply chains: a review and implementation framework. Prod Plan Control. https://doi.org/10.1080/ 09537287. 2021. 1939902

Wang Y, Wallace SW, Shen B, Choi TM (2015) Service supply chain management: A review of operational models. Eur J Oper Res 247(3):685–698

Weick KE (1989) Theory Construction as Disciplined Imagination. Acad Manag Rev 14(4):516–531. https://doi.org/10.5465/amr.1989.4308376

Xu P, Lee J, Barth JR, Richey RG (2021) Blockchain as supply chain technology: considering transparency and security. Int J Phys Distrib Logist Manag 51(3):305–324. https://doi. org/10.1108/ -08-2019-0234

Xue X, Dou J, Shang Y (2020) Blockchain-driven supply chain decentralized operations – information sharing perspective. Bus Process Manag J 27(1):184–203. https://doi. org/10.1 108/ BPMJ-12-2019-0518

Yang L, Zhang J, Shi X (2021) Can blockchain help food supply chains with platform operations during the COVID-19 outbreak? Electron Commer Res Appl 49:101093. https://doi.org/10. 1016/j.elerap.2021.101093

Yao Y, Dong Y, Dresner M (2010) Managing supply chain backorders under vendor managed inventory: An incentive approach and empirical analysis. Eur J Oper Res 44(3):361–378. https: //doi.org/10.1016/j.ejor.2009.08.004

Yi Y, Bremer P, Mather D, Mirosa M (2021) Factors affecting the diffusion of traceability practices in an imported fresh produce supply chain in China. Br Food J. https://doi.org/ 10.1108/BFJ-03-2021-0227

Yoon J, Talluri S, Yildiz H, Sheu C (2020) The value of Blockchain technology implementation in international trades under demand volatility risk. Int J Prod Res 58(7):2163–2183. https://doi. org/10.1080/00207543.2019.1693651

Yu Z, Razzaq A, Rehman A et al (2021) Disruption in global supply chain and socio-economic shocks: a lesson from COVID-19 for sustainable production and consumption. Oper Manag Res. https://doi.org/10.1007/s12063-021-00179-y

Zhang T, Liang L, Yu Y, Yu Y (2007) An integrated vendor-managed inventory model for a two-echelon system with order cost reduction. Int J Prod Econ 109(1–2):241–253. https://doi.org/ 10.1016/j.ijpe.2006.12.051

Zhao G, Liu S, Lopez C et al (2019) Blockchain technology in agri-food value chain management: A synthesis of applications, challenges and future research directions. Comput Ind 109:83–99. https://doi.org/10.1016/j.compind.2019.04.002

Zhong RY, Newman ST, Huang GQ, Lan S (2016) Big Data for supply chain management in the service and manufacturing sectors: Challenges, opportunities, and future perspectives. Comp Ind Engin 101:572–591. https://doi.org/10.1016/j.cie.2016.07.013

Zhou X, Pullman M, Xu Z (2021) The impact of food supply chain traceability on sustainability performance. Oper Manag Res. https://doi.org/10.1007/s12063-021-00189-w

6

Integration of the Buyer

Supplier Interface for Global Sourcing

Lydia Bals & Virpi Turkulainen

Mainz University of Applied Sciences, Lucy-Hillebrand-Str. 2, 55128, Mainz, Germany
EBS University for Business and Law, Oestrich-Winkel, Germany
Copenhagen Business School (CBS), Copenhagen, Denmark

Abstract

While global sourcing often implies that the firm needs to, for example, redesign the procurement organization and make decisions on what to centralize and what to manage locally, global sourcing also has direct implications for management of the buyer–supplier interface. This study takes an organization design focus and addresses global sourcing organization design as well as provides illustrations on how to integrate the buyer–supplier interface for global sourcing. Integration is conceptualized as coordination and cooperation. The paper is based on an embedded unit case study of a global technical industrial product and service systems provider, TechInd (pseudonym). Data was collected from TechInd as well as from six of its suppliers. The findings indicate that the global sourcing organization structure, as well as the differences in the buyer's sourcing and supplier's sales organizations, pose requirements for management of the interface in terms of coordination and cooperation. Challenges arising particularly due to differences in geographical scope and level of centralization can be managed by introducing the key account role and alignment of incentives.

Keywords: *Global sourcing · Buyer–supplier relationship · Integration · Organizational design · Case study · Project-based operations*

1 Introduction

Along with the increasing strategic role and importance of purchasing and supply management (Capon and Senn 2010; Faes et al. 2000; Foerstl et al. 2013; Gadde and Snehota 2000), contemporary companies continue to increase global sourcing of goods and services (Jia et al. 2014; Schleper et al. 2020). Global sourcing[Footnote1] implies that the firm often needs to, for example, redesign the procurement organization and make decisions on what to centralize and what to manage locally (Bals and Turkulainen 2017). Hence, moving towards global sourcing poses organizational implications to the focal firm (Bals and Turkulainen 2017; Jia et al. 2014; Luzzini et al. 2014; Trautmann et al. 2009b), and subsequently, global sourcing directly affects the buyer–supplier interface (Horn et al. 2014; Vanpoucke et al. 2014; Wieland et al. 2020).

The purpose of this study is to develop further understanding of how to integrate the buyer–supplier interface for global sourcing. Global sourcing poses direct managerial challenges as follows. First, global sourcing often means a significant reduction in the supplier base, sometimes as much as by 70 to 90 percent (Capon and Senn 2010), requiring additional strategic intent and attention from buyers and suppliers. Moreover, the suppliers need to market and sell their products and services for the same buyer on a global scale, while addressing potential local variations (Capon and Senn 2010; Swoboda et al. 2012). Finally, aligning the buyer and supplier organization structures might be needed to facilitate effective management of the buyer–supplier relationship (BSR) (Capon and Senn 2010; Guesalaga et al. 2018; Homburg et al. 2000; Toulan et al. 2006), representing an area in need for more research (Guesalaga et al. 2018).

While there is research on global sourcing organization design (e.g. Bals and Turkulainen 2017; Jia et al. 2017; Johnson and Leenders 2001; Narasimhan and Carter 1990), it has mainly addressed the design of the sourcing organization only, paying less attention to the buyer–supplier interface and its management. However, integration of the BSR is one of the fundamental issues in management of the interface (Kaipia and Turkulainen 2017; Sheth and Sharma 1997; Terpend et al. 2008) and it is particularly critical for global sourcing: as stated by Capon and Senn (2010, p. 35f.), "a traditional multinational supplier *cannot* satisfy the needs of a multinational customer that globalizes its procurement, even though both firms operate in similar countries around the world [so] the reality is very clear: for multinational suppliers to survive and grow in the twenty-first century, they must make the necessary investments to address the challenges of multinational customers that are globalizing their procurement operations". In our study, we address this phenomenon and pursue the following research question: *How to integrate the buyer–supplier interface for global sourcing?* We take an organization design perspective and build on Gulati et al. (2005) defining integration as consisting of coordination and alignment of actions (Burton et al. 2006; Galbraith 1973) as well as cooperation and alignment of interests (Yan and Dooley 2013). We analyze empirical data collected from a globally operating firm TechInd (pseudonym), which is a provider of technical industrial product and service systems, as well as from six of its tier-1 suppliers.

Our study provides an illustration of contemporary global sourcing organizational design (Bals and Turkulainen 2017; Jia et al. 2017). We also complement research on BSRs and integration in the buyer–supplier interface in a generic sourcing setting (Ambrose et al. 2008; Revilla and Knoppen 2015; Turkulainen et al. 2017; Vanpoucke et al. 2014), going beyond the implications that global sourcing has on the buyer's organization (Giunipero and Monczka 1997; Jia et al. 2014; Johnson and Leenders 2001; Luzzini et al. 2014; Narasimhan and Carter 1990; Schneider and Wallenburg 2013; Trautmann et al. 2009b). This way our study also provides insight into the calls for research on the interdependence between buyer–supplier organization structures (Bals and Turkulainen 2017; Guesalaga et al. 2018; Toulan et al. 2006) and on the inter-organizational interface in global sourcing (Wieland et al. 2020). The empirical study takes place in the project operations context, which is increasingly characteristic to operations environment (Maylor and Turkulainen 2019) and yet poses additional managerial challenges due to uniqueness and temporal nature of the operations (Burke and Morley 2016; Lundin and Söderholm 1995).

2 Global sourcing and the buyer–supplier interface

We use the term organizational design for the 'organization structure' (i.e. division of tasks and responsibilities) as well as for the 'processes' of managing the organizational interfaces (Mintzberg 1983). These processes are coordination and cooperation as the constituents of integration (Galbraith 1973; Gulati et al. 2005; Lawrence and Lorsch 1967; Yan and Dooley 2013), the concept which we elaborate in this study. Both the 'organization structure' and 'management processes' aspects of organizational design will be further introduced in the next two subsections.

2.1 Global sourcing organization structure

Research on the aspects of organization structure in the global sourcing setting has mainly focused on the *buyer's* global sourcing organization structure. Organization structure is typically characterized by the dimension of centralization, identifying two basic structures of either centralized and decentralized organization (Arnold 1999; Faes et al. 2000; Giunipero and Monczka 1997; Johnson and Leenders 2001; Narasimhan and Carter 1990; Schneider and Wallenburg 2013).As global sourcing develops, organizations tend to move towards more centralized structures to achieve various synergy benefits (Karjalainen 2011). From the supplier's perspective, a centralized structure for global sourcing implies that there is a single interface towards the supplier. Recent trends have tended towards hybrid organization structures (Procurement Strategy Council 2013), combining aspects of centralization and decentralization (Johnson and Leenders 2001). In these hybrid structures, for example, the firm-level office maintains responsibility for the negotiation of longer-term contracts, while local units issue orders against these contracts (Trautmann et al. 2009a). Hybrid structures are especially suitable to capture benefits in terms of economies of scale, economies of processes, and economies of learning, while simultaneously retaining some degree of decentralization (Trautmann et al. 2009a). One of the key challenges in hybrid global sourcing structures is to decide what to centralize and what to decentralize (Matthyssens and Faes 1997). From the supplier perspective, the buyer's hybrid sourcing organization structure makes management of the BSR especially challenging; the supplier is required to manage the customer interface globally, while simultaneously providing variations at the local level.

In addition, research has identified *categories* (homogenous sets of products and services purchased from a common supply market and with similar product and spend characteristics) (Ates et al. 2017; Luzzini et al. 2012, 2014; Trautmann et al. 2009a, 2009b), *geography* (Giunipero and Monczka 1997), and *business units* (Narasimhan and Carter 1990) as the basis of global sourcing organization structure. Recently, Bals and Turkulainen (2017) discussed how the global sourcing organization structure supports outsourcing parts of Purchasing and Supply Management (PSM), while also developing an understanding of the fourth structural alternative of *activity*. Taken together, structural alternatives can be summarized as decisions along the dimensions of category, business unit/customer, geography, and activity, together with the decision on the degree of centralization (Bals et al. 2018). On the supplier side, research reports that the supplier organization structures are moving from being product- or geography-focused, towards more customer-centric (Homburg et al. 2000; Toulan et al. 2006) due to the challenges they create for the management of the customer relationship (Guesalaga et al. 2018).

2.2 Management processes at the buyer–supplier interface

Processes, as the second aspect of organizational design, refer to the integration of the organizational interfaces (Lawrence and Lorsch 1967). Similarly, successful management of the BSRs requires integration of the interface (Ambrose et al. 2008; Kaipia and Turkulainen 2017; Revilla and Knoppen 2015; Terpend et al. 2008; Turkulainen et al. 2017). Integration refers to "the process of achieving unity of effort among the various subsystems in the accomplishment of the organization's task" (Lawrence and Lorsch 1967, p. 4).

Management of the buyer–supplier interface has gained considerable attention in the last couple of decades (Ambrose et al. 2008, 2010; Araujo et al. 1998; Cousins et al. 2006, 2008; Das et al. 2006; Gadde and Snehota 2000; Kaipia and Turkulainen 2017; Kulangara et al. 2016). In particular, there is an increasing trend towards closer BSRs, partnerships, and relational approaches (Araujo et al. 1998; Cousins and Menguc 2006; Gadde and Snehota 2000; Lahdenperä 2012; Quintens et al. 2006; Revilla and Knoppen 2015). Research, for example, suggests that not all BSRs are managed in the same way (Cousins et al. 2006; Kraljic 1983; Vesalainen and Kohtamaki 2015). The underlying idea is that developing relationships is resource-intensive and can be justified only if the benefits are greater than the costs (Kaipia and Turkulainen 2017). In one of the foundational works, Kraljic (1983) suggests that management of the BSR depends on the impact and supply risk of what is purchased.

Integration can be divided into coordination and cooperation (Gulati et al. 2005; Yan and Dooley 2013). The organizational boundary implies two differentiated organizations in terms of, for example, their structure and goals (Lawrence and Lorsch 1967). While the level of differentiation can be high even within the same organization (Lawrence and Lorsch 1967), it is likely higher between firms (Yan and Dooley 2013). Higher levels of differentiation increase the challenge of integration (Lawrence and Lorsch 1967; Turkulainen and Ketokivi 2012), implying that significant managerial effort is needed for the processes of integration.

Coordination refers to 'alignment of actions' and flows of information (Galbraith 1973; Nadler and Tushman 1997), so that the organizational units or organizations arrive at mutually beneficial outcomes (Faes et al. 2000; Pagell 2004; Turkulainen and Ketokivi 2012). Alignment of actions is needed due to a lack of shared knowledge

(Bensaou and Venkatraman 1995; Gulati et al. 2005; Hwang et al. 2019; Yan and Dooley 2013), so coordination then facilitates processing of information and interaction across the organizational boundary (Cousins and Menguc 2006; Foerstl et al. 2013; Galbraith 1973; Nadler and Tushman 1997), thus building on the concept of bounded rationality (March and Simon 1958). In order to facilitate information flows between the organizations, the buyer and the supplier need to establish bi-directional, face-to-face, and multi-channel communication flows with each other to increase the richness of the information (Bensaou and Venkatraman 1995; Foerstl et al. 2013; Hwang et al. 2019). Coordination is essential to global sourcing as, by definition, global sourcing traditionally includes cross-functional coordination (Trent and Monczka 2003a, 2005). In the contemporary context, it potentially also requires external coordination with the suppliers (Wieland et al. 2020).

Second, *cooperation* as an aspect of integration refers to 'alignment of interests', which arise not just due to lack of information, but also various behavioral aspects (Gulati et al. 2005; Yan and Dooley 2013). Cooperation builds on the assumption that behavior is motivated by personal interests and benefits, and that subsequent uncooperative behavior tends to divert shared resources from serving joint needs and benefits to satisfying firms' interests (Gulati et al. 2005). Cooperation and alignment of interests can be facilitated by the development of common goals (Yan and Dooley 2013). If the goals are unified, for example, by developing and implementing incentives, individuals in each organization can be motivated to behave cooperatively, establish commitment, and pursue these common goals (Gulati et al. 2005). Cooperation and alignment of goals is critical in the global sourcing context, as global sourcing often tends to result in cross-functional and inter-organizational conflicts (Horn et al. 2014; Kotabe and Murray 2004; Stanczyk et al. 2015).

2.3 Summary of research on organizational design aspects in the sourcing context

We study how buyer–supplier interfaces are integrated for global sourcing, conceptualizing integration as coordination and cooperation. The following table (Table 1) provides a classification of exemplary research at the intersection of organizational design and sourcing. The intent is to summarize and further clarify the focus and positioning of this study. These examples are studies that have addressed organizational design aspects related to sourcing, both within the buying organization, as well as at the buyer–supplier interface. We have divided research into studies on global sourcing and generic sourcing (i.e. studies without a specific focus on global sourcing).

As Table 1 indicates, research on global sourcing has especially focused on the internal organizational design of the buying company while research on management of the buyer–supplier interface has addressed the generic sourcing setting. Our study links these two streams by focusing on developing understanding of how the buyer–supplier interface is integrated for global sourcing. As mentioned earlier, global sourcing poses a particularly challenging setting for both buyers and suppliers in terms of choosing the right business partner and managing the business relationship. Therefore, integration can be expected to be particularly pronounced and insights on potential structural alignments be more prominent than in the generic sourcing setting.

Table 1 Examples of research at the intersection of organizational design and sourcing

	Intra-organization focus	**Inter-organizational focus on buyer–supplier interface**
Generic sourcing	Centralization and decentralization Rozemeijer et al. (2003) Structural alternatives: categories, geography, BU, activities Bals et al. (2018) Coordination Foerstl et al. (2013); Gonzalez-Zapatero et al. (2016); Pagell (2004); Turkulainen and Swink (2017) Cooperation Bals et al. (2009); Gonzalez-Zapatero et al. (2016); Pagell (2004)	Coordination Ambrose et al. (2008; 2010); Cavinato (1991); Kaipia and Turkulainen (2017); Revilla and Knoppen (2015); Vanpoucke et al. (2014); Haartman and Bengtsson (2015) Cooperation Ambrose et al. (2010); Chae et al. (2019); Caldwell et al. (2009); Cousins et al. (2006, 2008); Revilla and Knoppen (2015); Roehrich and Lewis (2014); Vanpoucke et al. (2014); Vesalainen and Kohtamaki (2015); van de Vijver et al. (2011); Villena et al. (2011); Yan and Dooley (2013, 2014)
Global sourcing	Centralization and decentralization Arnold (1999); Ates et al. (2017); Bals and Turkulainen (2017); Cavinato (1991); Giunipero and Monczka (1997); Jia et al. (2014; 2017); Karjalainen (2011); Luzzini et al. (2014); Narasimhan and Carter (1990); Quintens et al. (2006); Trautmann et al. (2009b); Trent and Monczka (2003b) Structural alternatives: categories, geography, BU, activities Ates et al. (2017); Bals and Turkulainen (2017); Jia et al. (2017); Luzzini et al. (2014); Narasimhan and Carter (1990); Rozemeijer et al. (2003); Trautmann et al. (2009b) Coordination Ates et al. (2017); Faes et al. (2000); Jia et al. (2017); Monczka and Trent (1991); Narasimhan and Carter (1990); Schleper et al. (2020); Trautmann et al. 2009a, 2009b; Trent and Monczka (2003b); Trent and Monczka (2003a, 2005) Cooperation Horn et al. (2014); Kotabe and Murray (2004)	Coordination Bals and Turkulainen (2017); Wieland et al. (2020) Cooperation Horn et al. (2014) The focus of our study: integration of the buyer–supplier interface for global sourcing

*Please note that one study can be presented in several cells of the matrix depending on its focus

Figure 1 below represents the conceptual framework, graphically summarizing the organizational structural elements as well as the processes for integration of the buyer–supplier interface. The level of the analysis is at the organizational level, with the focus on the inter-organizational interface. Figure 1 summarizes the following: (1) understanding global sourcing organization structures requires analysis of the structural alternatives (dimensions of category, activity, geography, or business unit), as well as of the degree of centralization at both the global and local levels; (2) the link between organization structures and buyer–supplier interface and its integration; (3) integration as the processes of coordination and cooperation.

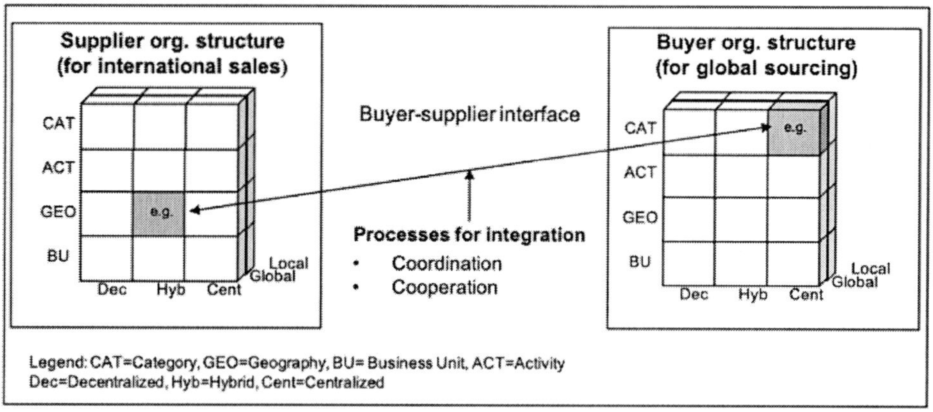

Fig. 1 Conceptual Framework: Global Sourcing and the Buyer–Supplier Interface – Organization Structure and Processes for Integration

3 Methodology

3.1 Research method

In this study, we illustrate how the buyer–supplier interface is integrated for global sourcing, taking an organizational design view. For the purposes of this study, we collected empirical data following *a single embedded unit case study design* (Yin 2009). We selected this for four reasons. First, case studies facilitate the collection of rich data and the development of an understanding of complex organizational design matters (Dubois and Gibbert 2010; Piekkari et al. 2010). Second, case studies are well suited for research questions of "how" (Yin 2009), in line with our focus on how to integrate the buyer–supplier interface for global sourcing. Third, the case study method supports the aim of investigating a contemporary less-explored phenomenon in-depth and within its real-life context (Dubois and Gibbert 2010; Yin 2009). Finally, although a single case study is limited with respect to making generalizations, it fits the illustrative purpose of the empirical study (Ketokivi and Choi 2014). The unit of analysis is a relationship between a buyer engaged in global sourcing and its 1st tier supplier. We consider a single-embedded case study suitable as it allows us to engage in analysis of multiple buyer–supplier relationships, while controlling for the organizational setting. Furthermore, a single case study is also appropriate as the purpose is illustration, not generalizability (Ketokivi and Choi 2014).

3.2 Case selection and description

For the purpose of developing understanding of integration of the buyer–supplier interface for global sourcing, we wanted to analyze a buyer organization that was sourcing globally and had adapted its global organization to facilitate that. The case company we selected is TechInd (pseudonym), which is a large provider of technical industrial product and service systems to, for example, the construction and shipbuilding industries. TechInd is headquartered in Germany and has over 40 subsidiaries in more than 30 countries. In 2018, it had around 25,000 employees and sales of over 1.5 billion Euros. Its core products are insulation, passive fire protection, surface protection, and interior outfitting. The operations of TechInd are project-based (Hayes and Wheelwright 1979) and relate to industrial plants, building construction, offshore platforms, and shipbuilding. We chose to focus the empirical part of the study in the project-based operations context because while integration of the buyer–supplier interface is a major challenge in the ongoing operations context (Vanpoucke et al. 2014), the managerial challenge is even more significant in the context of project-based operations. This is because project-based operations are typically characterized by lack of joint working experience and a pre-determined limited duration of operations and of the entire organizational relationship, as well as by aspects of uniqueness inherent in projects (Burke and Morley 2016; Lundin and Söderholm 1995). The management challenge is further increased by the fact that project-based industries, such as the industries in which TechInd operates, have traditionally been very local and are currently globalizing, allowing us to provide also direct practical value. We started research collaboration with TechInd already in 2016 as part of a larger study on organizational designs.

We selected TechInd for several reasons. First, TechInd had implemented a global sourcing strategy for several categories a number of years prior to our study. Second, we were given multi-year access to collect data to gain a detailed understanding of the organizational implications of global sourcing. Finally, we also got the opportunity to interview direct sales counterparts at six 1st tier suppliers and receive the key account managers views and input on the management of the buyer–supplier interface.

3.3 Data collection

Data were mainly collected by interviews and systematic observations of managerial workshops and meetings over the period of study (2016–2018), as illustrated in Fig. 2. Based on the above conceptual framework developed for this paper, we developed an interview guide and conducted seven interviews at TechInd and six interviews with the suppliers in 2018. The interviewee demographics as well as some company background information for the suppliers are shown in Table 2. The interview guide is shown in Appendix A. It was used to facilitate discussion and as a general guide for the interviews. The interviews resulted in a total of 122 transcribed pages.

The systematic observations (2016–2018) were part of a larger study on buyer organizational designs and therefore particularly centered on understanding the buyer side. We were allowed to attend global sourcing organization design and implementation project workshops and gained access to all presentations, minutes and also took own observational notes. We also collected other material, such as charts and process descriptions. To combine both the observational and interview data allowed us to engage in data triangulation; for example, insights on organization structures were triangulated based on organization charts, workshop observations, and interview data.

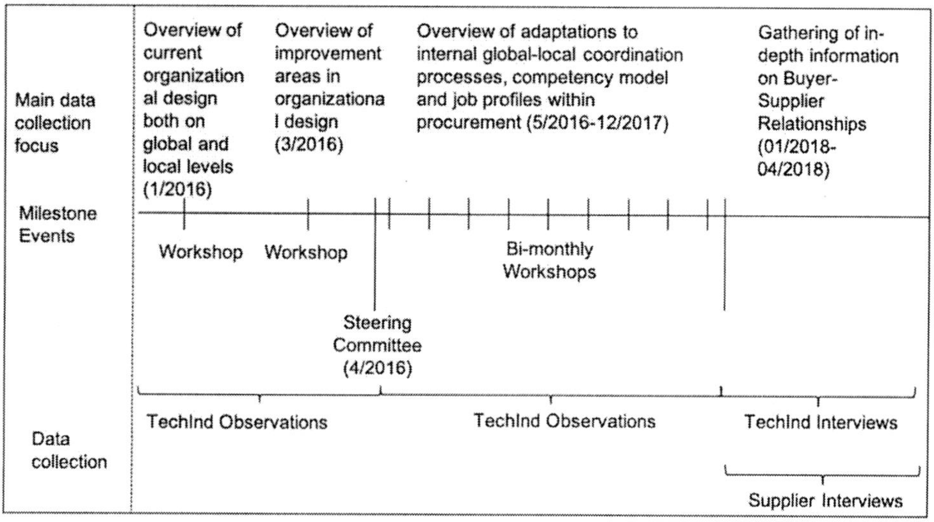

Fig. 2 *Overview on data collection*

Anonymity was ensured to the suppliers from the first contact onwards emphasizing that this is a research study that it is not directed by TechInd in any way. Informed consent was received from all interviewees. Only highly aggregated results (in terms of basic themes) were later reported back to both TechInd and the suppliers, as outlined to both parties before consenting. Moreover, the suppliers were encouraged to discuss their overall experiences related to organizational structures influencing the BSR. In the data analysis, the replies were carefully analyzed for both TechInd and the additional customer examples mentioned, and the display of results also differentiates those.

The interviewee selection and interview process had three major steps. First, we conducted an interview and had a discussion with the CPO about this research project, including purchasing organization, global sourcing, and the identified global sourcing categories. Second, we interviewed six global category managers about the BSRs and their integration. In these interviews, we also asked the interviewees to identify potential suppliers and their respective category for the study. We asked the category managers to position these categories on the Kraljic (1983) matrix because, as mentioned earlier, Kraljic suggests that management of the supplier relationship depends on the impact and supply risk of what is purchased. The choice of suppliers was made so that their category represents a large spend area, positioned as being high in importance (S1, S2 and S4 are classified as 'leverage' and S3, S5 and S6 are classified as 'critical'), as we expected that to be related to intensive interaction. Subsequently, we interviewed the supplier sales representatives.

Table 2 Interviewee demographics

Interviewee	Category	Position	Tenure within position (in years)	Practical experience (in years)				
Buyer (TechInd) representatives								
B1	Insulation materials	Category Manager (global)	5	30				
B2	Scaffolding and machinery	Category Manager (global)	3,5	7,5				
B3	Surface protection and treatment	Category Manager (global)	5	9				
B4	Indirects (IT)	Category Manager (global)	3,5	10				
B5	N/A	Head of Corporate Supply Management	5	23				
B6	Indirects (Fleet; C-Parts)	Category Manager (global)	1,5	8				
B7	Multiple	Head of Category Management (Germany)	3	26				
Supplier representatives					Duration of (central) buyer–supplier relationship (in years)	Supplier number of employees	Supplier turnover 2018 (in bn EUR)	Supplier international scope
S1	Insulation materials	Commercial Director	3	20	12	> 30,000	> 9	> 250 locations in more than 90 countries
S2	Scaffolding and machinery	Business Unit Manager	10	24	10	> 1,000	not published	5 production sites; sales offices and engineers in > 15 countries
S3	Surface	Key Account	6	26	2	> 30,000	> 9	> 150

Interviewee	Category	Position	Tenure within position (in years)	Practical experience (in years)				
	protection and treatment	Manager						countries
S4	Surface protection and treatment	Global Sales Director	21	26	15	> 10,000	> 19	> 35 production facilities in > 20 countries; represented in > 100 countries
S5	Surface protection and treatment	Group Business Development Manager	5	20	5	> 5,000	> 1	> 80 countries
S6	Surface protection and treatment	Area Manager Nordics, Protective & Marine Coating	4	30	1,5	> 40,000	> 13	140 production facilities in > 60 countries

During the whole research process, we engaged in several procedures to enhance validity and reliability. These are summarized in Table 3 below.

For the time period 2016–2017, the analysis particularly focused on gaining an in-depth understanding of the TechInd procurement organizational structure as well as management of the global–local dimensions. As can be seen from Fig. 2, there were amendments to the management approach during 2017, which could be captured in the observations and the related material. The analysis process for both these materials as well as the interview data collected subsequently, focused on tabularizing the data, and the results were then discussed among the authors, contrasting them with existing literature to interpret the findings. This was done in multiple iterations to challenge the interpretations. While the data gathered via the observational approach yielded a comprehensive view on the current status of the organizational design at TechInd, which was later triangulated with the interview data, and for example later summarized in Fig. 2 in this paper, the organization structures and processes related to management of the buyer–supplier interface (Fig. 1) served as the basis for developing our research design and guided for data collection and analysis of the interview data. Following the logic of theory elaboration, we engaged in constant comparisons between data and theory (Ketokivi and Choi 2014). The ex-ante coding tree is shown in Appendix B. The ex-ante nodes are directly related to the constructs presented in and described in the sub sections preceding Fig. 1. This ex-ante coding tree facilitated coding of the interview data, by allocating quotes to nodes (as illustrated in the supplementary material) and then subsequently aggregating and interpreting the findings towards propositions. In the latter, the researchers engaged in cross-checking their analyses to ensure consistency and agreement among researchers analyzing the data.

Table 3 Addressing validity and reliability criteria (see e.g., Dubois and Gibbert 2010; Yin 2009)

Validity criterion	Means by which this was addressed in the case study
Objectivity: Establishing reasonable freedom from unacknowledged researcher biases and relative neutrality	• Transparent, detailed, and explicit data collection and analysis by developing and following a clear research design (details shown in Fig. 2)
Reliability: Demonstrating that the study process is consistent, reasonably stable over time and across researchers and methods	• Development of a case study database, facilitating data transparency and transparency of the analysis • Collection of data across a wide range of observations and carefully selected respondents • Development of an interview guide, shared among all interviewees • Cross-checking of analysis to ensure consistency and agreement among researchers analyzing the data
Construct validity: Establishing correct operational measures for the study concepts	• Use of a guiding theoretical framework as a basis to be elaborated by the empirical study (Fig. 1) • Multiple evidence and data sources through collection of all documentation prepared related to the organizational design (e.g., meeting minutes, workshop summaries, own observational notes) • Interview data summarized directly after each interview and sent to interviewees for cross-checking
Internal validity: Establishing causal relationships whereby certain conditions are shown to lead to other conditions, as distinguished from spurious relationships (of less concern in this study since causal inferences were not made from the data)	• Data collection in relation to the actual organizational aspects to avoid recall bias and enhance data accuracy • Both primary and archival data were analyzed to enable triangulation • Information and data accuracy were improved by motivated interviewees who were willing to participate in the study
External validity: Establishing a domain in which the study's findings can be generalized	• Clear description of case study company situation and context • Detailed descriptions of specific contextual considerations of case company studied

4 Empirical analysis

To illustrate how buyer–supplier interface is integrated for global sourcing, we analyzed the organization structures on both sides, as well as the processes for managing the BSR in line with the conceptual framework (Fig. 1).

4.1 Organization structures

We first present the procurement organization structure of TechInd, including global sourcing, and then the supplier sales organization structures (for details, please see Appendix C).

4.1.1 Buyer global sourcing organization structure

The area shaded in grey in Fig. 3 highlights how global sourcing is organized at TechInd. On the *global level*, the organization is split between category managers ('CAT', reporting directly to the CPO) and a procurement excellence department ('ACT', reporting directly to the CPO). On the *local level*, the country-based buying teams are organized into three process clusters: strategic sourcing, transactional purchasing, and the local process excellence department (i.e. performance management).Footnote2

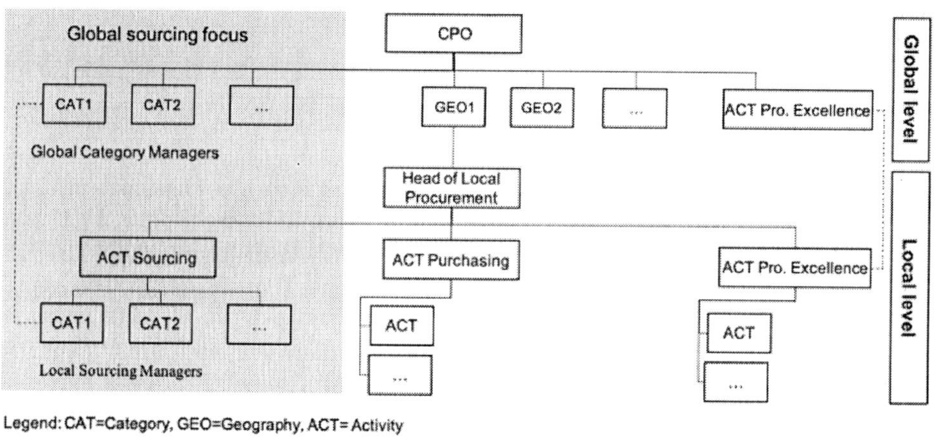

Fig. 3 Global sourcing organization of TechInd, adapted from company materials

Global sourcing at the company headquarters is organized mainly by category and carried out by global category managers. At the country level, there are local sourcing organizations based on the dimensions of activity and category. The global category managers are connected to the local country sourcing managers for each (major) global sourcing category with a dotted reporting line, facilitating alignment of actions and interests with the local sourcing counterparts for the respective category. Thus, the global category managers are the ones performing global sourcing activities and liaising with the local sourcing managers and other cross-functional stakeholders, as well as the management.

While the dotted reporting line between local sourcing managers and the global category managers facilitates their alignment of actions and interests throughout the categories, the local sourcing teams are represented by a *geography* in the overall procurement management team to further connect the country-based procurement organizations to the global level. This implies that the CPO would meet with the procurement heads of the three core countries, namely Germany, France, and the UK, on a quarterly basis during a management offsite event to jointly define priorities, targets, and development projects for both global and local procurement. This also facilitates alignment around global initiatives. The joint management team, consisting of the CPO and the country procurement heads, has become a forum for the global category managers to present proposals for global initiatives, as well as to ensure early buy-ins from the country procurement organizations for local stakeholder alignment, both in terms of internal stakeholders (e.g., local project managers) and external stakeholders (e.g., local suppliers).

4.1.2 Supplier sales organization structure

The supplier sales organizations are predominantly organized by geography referring to a country-based or regional organization structure, with decision making responsibility mainly at the country or regional level. This decentralized structure is combined with key account managers (KAM), thereby creating a hybrid structure. So, for example, buyer 2 (B2) described the structural orientation of supplier 2 (S2) like this: *"[Before nominating the global KAM] the maximum what they had was regional structure. So, they had a regional manager. Then then...our key account manager...he was the regional manager for Latin-America. And they have some regional manager for Asia Pacific [...]."*. And the Group Business Development Manager from supplier 5 (S5) explained: "*On the sales side it is based on geography. So, meaning that every country or region has its own commercial team and setup.*" In addition to the geography dimension, S3 and S6 have a slightly more elaborated structure with a business unit (BU)/customer dimension, complementing decentralization of decision making by geography (for full details, please see Appendix C).

4.2 **Integration of the buyer–supplier interface for global sourcing**

As the second aspect of organizational design, we analyzed integration of the BSRs in light of the conceptual framework (Fig. 1), i.e. the processes of coordination (alignment of actions) and cooperation (alignment of interests). A summary of illustrative quotes is presented in Appendix D. In addition to the analysis of how the buyer–supplier interfaces are integrated, we have also included quotes describing what the interviewees described as hindering management of the interface.

The findings illustrate that the three organizational dimensions of the degree of centralization and structural alternatives, at both global and local levels, facilitate understanding of the global sourcing organization structure. TechInd's category-based and activity-based hybrid organization structure makes the buyer–supplier interface fairly simple and clear: the suppliers have one point of contact globally, instead of multiple contacts in each country, providing a consolidated view on volume and requirements. This was associated with expectations regarding aggregated pricing for frame agreements and would be different if the buyer had a geography-based structure, for example, thereby implying that the supplier had to separately manage each country. For example, the Key

Account Manager from supplier 3 (S3) describes this as follows: *"Well, the relationship is now [managed] centrally. So, I'm running the frame agreements we have done. And yeah, that's only on the central level."*

4.2.1 Coordination: Alignment of actions

Our analysis points out that despite being a hybrid, suppliers perceived the TechInd organization structure as decentralized in some instances. The suppliers related this to the lack of empowerment of the global category managers; in particular, instances in which decisions made by the global category managers at headquarters are not effectively communicated to and/or supported by the local sourcing managers. As the Area Manager of Nordics, Protective and Marine Coating from supplier 6 (S6) explained: The empowerment is maybe not to deliver where they really want it to be... So, for that matter we sometimes sit and talk about the possibility to work together more globally. And we are able to handle that. [...]. But I mean it seems like there are some challenges on [TechInd'] side on making sure that the procurement manager [...has] the empowerment in their organization to do this."

In instances where empowerment and actually living the implemented category-oriented global sourcing structure works, management of the buyer–supplier interface is easier and more straightforward. As the Area Manager of Nordics, Protective and Marine Coating from S6 explained in relation to a different client: "I mean the ones that I know the best is a company like [global container logistics company] where we are coordinating everything [...] from this office here. And also, where there is clearly a communicated empowerment in their organization that when we talk to their procurement people then they also have the power to take decisions across their organization irrespective of where it is in the world. And there you actually have a...then you actually get these synergies also a benefit for both for our parties. Because when you have a central point of contact and that we have seen working pretty well to be quite honest." This indicates that the structure is associated with the ability to achieve coordination both internally and externally. Moreover, our analysis points out that suppliers consider that a high level of centralization, together with internal coordination in the buyer organization facilitates management of the interface. At the same time, it makes management of that relationship more important because if that one contact decides to buy from another, all business would be lost at once. As the Group Business Development Manager from S5 explained: "From a higher level point of view [to have one central contact] is very convenient because I have one contact and he decides. But commercially it also makes me very vulnerable. I mean if something goes wrong in the relationship or whatsoever and this person decides to go to competition you lose all the business globally. Yeah, so it is positive but also involves a very high risk when the relationship goes wrong. If you have one very dominant central organized purchase department for example."

Our analysis further indicates that geography-based, decentralized supplier sales organization structures pose challenges for the management of the buyer–supplier interface. This is because the buyer has a very different type of structure, implying that while the buyer has a single point of contact (SPOC) towards the supplier in each category, the suppliers tend to have multiple representatives for each category. This creates challenges in terms of information processing, for example, which was addressed by appointing key account managers (KAM). As buyer 1 (B1) accounted for S1: "*[At the beginning around 2014 it was about] I'm coming down to your country, negotiate with you and flying out and have some kind of global agreements, but only one or two because most of the suppliers didn't want to work with us on a global perspective. Because they are set-up also very regional. So, if we are looking into the [new] procurement organization on how it works then we have these countries where it is feasible to work on that because they are big enough for having the split in the [activity] pillars."*

Moreover, our analysis indicates that the decentralized geography-based supplier sales organization structure tried both to compensate decentralization and to achieve the benefits provided by a hybrid design (i.e. simultaneous management of global and local aspects) with KAMs. How the Commercial Director from S1 explained: "Well, we have several KAMs and they are doing the business with regional key accounts. For example, in the part of southern Germany, in the middle of Germany and in northern Germany. So, they are doing business together with the regional key accounts. Of course, we also have key accounts which are active Germany wide. And in that case the key account manager who has the headquarter in his area, he's responsible for that customer for the whole German business. That means that everyone has the same responsibility, the same structure regarding the area and number of customers. But they also have a very close link and information because everybody is involving the German business. And it's the same structure in other countries. If something is going abroad if we have for example contracting companies like [TechInd] or others who have a national business and also, international business everything which is international is on my desk. I'm involved. And because I'm leading the sales organizations I'm also involved in the local decisions." Or how the Area Manager of Nordics, Protective and Marine Coating from S6 described it: "There you need to take the next step in key account management and make a global or regional, but preferably global depending on the company of the customers of course. And then you have a global key account structure to manage that as I see it. But we have challenges in doing that as well because we are very geographically, and area based depending on our organizational structure. So [we face] exactly the same challenges just from the sales rather than a purchasing perspective that we have."

KAMs, as the central interface (SPOC) for the buyer in an otherwise decentralized sales organization, pose direct advantages; KAMs essentially represent a means to achieve coordination by simplifying the communication infrastructure between the two organizations.

4.2.2 Cooperation (alignment of interests)

Our analysis further points out the role of incentives in the management of the buyer-supplier interface, in particular, linking to cooperation and alignment of interests on the supplier side. For example, B1 explained it like this: *"[...] again it is about the incentives, right? [...]and he said yeah, but we have some trouble [...]. And I said [is it] because [of] who is getting the provision for that? He said 'yes, of course, because I'm doing all the work and my colleague will benefit.' He's doing the business, right. And I'm saying 'yeah, that's true. But that's not my problem.' [...] they find a new way of incentivizing."* And the Key Account Manager from S3 describes: *"Yeah, well theory meets practice. Yeah, sometimes we have a central deal, but the country manager [...] has a project locally for that same company. And he can take it but at more or less a price which is arranged central. And he will walk away from it. Why? Because it's below his target or in terms of margins. So, he says well it's very nice globally if we can take this project at that price but then I lose...then I don't hit my target and I lose bonus. And I cannot go on holiday for instance. So, yeah you cannot pay me obviously because it's his own pocket, his own wallet which is hurting. But overall, it's not good for [S3's company] bottom line, of course."*

Differing incentives seemed to especially hinder management of the interface; the analysis indicates a disconnect on the supplier side between the incentives of the geography-based organization structure (i.e. local sales managers have a certain sales target and bonus system) and the KAMs at the global level. For example, the local sales managers might want to drop a project, which is attractive from the company's perspective, but not from a local perspective, because of conflicting incentives (e.g., a country sales manager might lose his/her bonus if a sales offer becomes a 'global' contract).

4.3 The project-based operations context

As presented above, the findings illustrate that aligned structures between the buyer and the supplier organizations can facilitate management of the buyer–supplier interface, especially from the perspectives of alignment of actions and the related information processing. The findings further illustrate that the consequences of the lack of alignment of actions are aggravated by some of the underlying characteristics of the project-based operations context; for example, due to the nature of TechInd's projects, frame agreements cannot be enforced by a global category manager (e.g., in manufacturing operations, they would typically be implemented in a centralized ERP system and then remain relatively stable). Instead, as is typical for project-based operations, each and every project around the world that needs the negotiated material (e.g., blasting material) may or may not utilize the frame agreement. As the Key Account Manager from S3 mentions: "*Yeah, sometimes we have a central deal, but the country manager will...has a project locally for that same company. And he can take it but at more or less a price which is arranged central.*" This creates a need for coordination and alignment of actions between the buyer and the supplier, particularly if the organization structures do not support it by themselves.

Another issue is that projects come up locally and are only temporal in nature, making it critical to align early on, if possible. As the Key Account Manager from S3 explained: "*We have some clients that [jointly plan with us]. But unfortunately, they are not global. We have some suppliers in several countries [who] made a forecast with us. [...] They explained to us the projects they expect to have during the year. And then we can prepare ourselves. Unfortunately, with international companies this is very difficult because sometimes they don't know exactly the projects they are doing all around the world. So, sometimes you actually receive a phone call. I need for one week this material. So, with no planification this is difficult.*"

5 Discussion

5.1 Conclusions on the research question and research implications

Our research objective was to advance understanding of integration of the buyer–supplier interface for global sourcing by pursuing the research question: *How to integrate the buyer–supplier interface for global sourcing?* The study presents a conceptual framework on global sourcing organization design and integration of the buyer–supplier interface based on prior research (Giunipero and Monczka 1997; Gulati et al. 2005; Johnson and Leenders 2001; Narasimhan and Carter 1990; Yan and Dooley 2013) and empirically illustrates the framework. Our study provides further understanding of management of BSRs for global sourcing, especially in the project operations context as well as practical implications. In the following, we present 7 observations, discuss the findings as well as their implications to research.

> *Observation 1: Increased similarity of global sourcing and international sales organization structures (in terms of structural alternatives, degree of centralization, at both global and local levels) facilitates integration of the BSR.*

> *Observation 2: Alignment of the global sourcing organization structure and the supplier sales organization structure facilitates coordination and alignment of actions at the buyer-supplier interface.*

These observations can be linked to the law of requisite variety (Ashby 1956), which at the general level suggests that in order for the system to function well, the complexity of an organization should match the complexity of the environment and that matching organizational complexities on both sides of the interface facilitates functioning of the system. In the context of this study, we could interpret Ashby (1956) so that the organizational complexity on one side has implications for the organizational complexity on the other side. Similarly, but from the perspective of centralization only, research has proposed that management of BSRs is more successful if the supplier's customer-facing activities fit with the buyer's purchasing and supply activities (Toulan et al. 2006).

Furthermore, the information processing theory, suggesting that the buyer–supplier interface needs to be designed so that it facilitates the processing of inter-organizational information across the organizational interface (Galbraith 1973; Turkulainen et al. 2017), is also linked with these observations. On the other hand, information processing across organizational interfaces is hindered if there is asymmetry in the organizational setup; differences in organization structures across the interface imply that more managerial effort is needed in the processes of integration (Lawrence and Lorsch 1967; Turkulainen and Ketokivi 2012). This observation is in line with prior research suggesting that global sourcing increases the need for coordination between the buyer and suppler (Wieland et al. 2020) and that supplying firms are better able to serve their customers by having organization structures that mirror those of their customers (Gucsalaga et al. 2018; Homburg et al. 2000; Toulan et al. 2006).

> *Observation 3: When the global sourcing organization structure is based on categories at the global level and activity at the local level, the BSR can be managed key account management (KAM) in the supplier organization to facilitate coordination and alignment of actions.*

This observation is linked to prior research indicating that KAM as a practice aims at facilitating organizational alignment of actions (Storbacka 2012) and is designed to support fit between buyer and supplier organization structures (Homburg et al. 2000; Storbacka 2012; Toulan et al. 2006). Similarly, one of the reasons for why the activity-oriented design is suggested for facilitating coordination between the buyer and supplier in the case of outsourcing procurement is that the procurement providers are also often structured by activity (Bals and Turkulainen 2017). As such, KAM can facilitate information-processing between them and that organizational units or organizations arrive at mutually beneficial outcomes (Pagell 2004). This assignment of KAMs to manage the buyer–supplier interface is in line with research reporting that increasingly centralized approaches to purchasing are one of the reasons for introducing KAM to the supplier side (Capon and Senn 2010; Homburg et al. 2000; Swoboda et al. 2012). From a theoretical point of view, KAM thus facilitates coordination of activities, thereby enabling interaction and information processing across the organizational interface (Cousins and Menguc 2006; Foerstl et al. 2013).

> *Observation 4: Hybrid global sourcing organization structure can be managed with aligned incentives at global and local levels to facilitate cooperation and alignment of interests in the supplier organization.*

Our findings illustrate that global sourcing has direct implications for supplier sales incentives; there is a need for alignment of incentives and/or shared incentives at both the global level and local/regional level (local sales managers). From a theoretical point of view, alignment of incentives facilitates cooperation and alignment of interests (Gulati et al. 2005; Yan and Dooley 2013). This is needed in order to manage the buyer–supplier interface in the context of global sourcing.

By providing a detailed illustration of a contemporary global sourcing organization structure, we complement existing research on global sourcing (Faes et al. 2000; Quintens et al. 2006; Giunipero and Monczka 1997; Jia et al. 2014; Johnson and Leenders 2001; Schneider and Wallenburg 2013), highlighting how hybrid organizations require aligned incentives at the global and local level, and how an organization structure based on category at the global and activity at the local level increases the need for KAM at the supplier. Thus, we also complement prior research, which has mainly focused on the structural implications of global sourcing for the *buying* company (Bals et al. 2018; Bals and Turkulainen 2017; Trautmann et al. 2009b) by considering also the *sales* perspective. In addition, we empirically illustrate inter-organizational implications of global sourcing, going beyond existing studies on the role of social capital (Horn et al. 2014) and in line with the increasing scope of global sourcing to cover both internal and external coordination and integration (Wieland et al. 2020).

By taking an organizational design perspective, we provide illustrations of integration of the buyer–supplier interface for global sourcing. This complements research on BSRs, which has traditionally focused, for example, on different BSR types and integration in the buyer–supplier interface in a generic sourcing context (Gadde and Snehota 2000; Kaipia and Turkulainen 2017; Revilla and Knoppen 2015; Sheth and Sharma 1997; Vanpoucke et al. 2014). The case offered an illustration of how an increasingly complex global sourcing organization may require a more complex global sales organization from the supplier to facilitate management of the interface. This also gives support to the law of requisite variety (Ashby 1956); suppliers need to change their organizational complexity in order to react and adapt to the structure of the buyer, something prior research has only hinted at (Guesalaga et al. 2018; Homburg et al. 2000; Toulan et al. 2006). For example, while this notion of alignment between the buyer and supplier organization structures has been discussed in terms of the level of centralization (Toulan et al. 2006), our results imply that additional structural dimensions (i.e. the structural alternatives category, activity, geography and business unit) at the global and local level must be taken into account. Furthermore, the importance of the actual buyer organization structure for understanding the buyer–supplier interface has recently been highlighted in relation to the activity-oriented design, which was found to facilitate the focal buyer's work with external procurement providers (Bals and Turkulainen 2017). Therefore, we also respond to the calls for research on the interdependence between buyer–supplier organization structures (Bals and Turkulainen 2017; Guesalaga et al. 2018; Toulan et al. 2006). Moreover, we provide additional understanding on how coordination and alignment of actions, as well as cooperation and alignment of interests, are managed in the buyer–supplier interface (Gulati et al. 2005; Yan and Dooley 2013). Thereby the results illustrate how buyer–supplier interface is integrated for global sourcing as it is a particularly challenging setting for both buyers and suppliers.

The empirical findings also provide insight into global sourcing in the context of project-based operations.

> *Observation 5: The challenge of managing the buyer-supplier interface from the perspective of coordination and alignment of actions is associated with the uniqueness and temporality characterized by the project-based operations context.*

> *Observation 6: The challenge of managing the buyer-supplier interface from the perspective of cooperation and alignment of interests is associated with the uniqueness and temporality characterized by the project-based operations context.*

> *Observation 7: Managing the buyer-supplier interface can be managed with joint planning and early involvement between the buyer and the supplier to facilitate coordination and alignment of actions in the project-based operations context.*

These observations can be linked to the inherent uniqueness and temporality of the project-based operations context. Due to the projects being a vehicle to deliver outputs with at least some degree of uniqueness, and hence, being associated with at least partially changing needs for supplies and unique management processes, processing of information, coordination, and alignment of actions are typically needed on a project-by-project basis (Hayes and Wheelwright 1979; Ramasesh and Browning 2014). Even more, due to the temporality inherent in the project-based operations context, the organizational relationships are potentially changing and temporary in nature (Burke and Morley 2016; Lundin and Söderholm 1995; Turkulainen et al. 2013), implying that establishing information sharing and interaction, as well as aligning actions on a project-by-project basis, require significant emphasis.

The findings illustrate that incentives on the supplier sales side had a different scope than on the buyer side, which complicated the management of the buyer–supplier interface. This can be explained by the nature of the project-based operations context. Due to some degree of uniqueness always inherent in the project-based operations context, more emphasis is needed to establish common goals and to facilitate cooperation on a project-by-project basis. Moreover, due to the temporality inherent in the project-based operations context, the organizational relationships are potentially changing and temporary in nature (Burke and Morley 2016; Lundin and Söderholm 1995; Turkulainen et al. 2013), implying that additional emphasis is needed to establish commitment and alignment of interests between the buyer and supplier on a project-by-project basis (Yan and Dooley 2013).

The findings further illustrate the importance of joint planning by the buyer and the KAMs for management of the buyer–supplier interface. Joint planning facilitates sharing of information and interaction (Haartman and Bengtsson 2015), and early involvement of KAMs in projects implies that they have immediate access to information when a new project is on the horizon (Lahdenperä 2012), thus facilitating information processing, coordination, and alignment of actions between the buyer and supplier as the project kicks off. The project-based operations setting makes the anticipation of exact business in terms of their nature, volumes, and delivery times more difficult than compared to more stable operations (Hayes and Wheelwright 1979), increasing the need for joint planning to manage the interface. This provides further insight into management of project-based operations (Artto and Turkulainen 2018; Ramasesh and Browning 2014; Turkulainen et al. 2013), and also provides valuable practical insight, as the number and importance of project-based operations has continued to grow significantly (Maylor and Turkulainen 2019).

5.2 Managerial implications

This study provides practical insights for practitioners. For buyers, it illustrates different ways to design the global sourcing organization, which has shown to be highly challenging (Schiele et al. 2011). The presented framework can help to clearly differentiate decisions on structural alternatives and the degree of centralization, at both the global and local levels, as well as the implications for the buyer–supplier interface. Before the structural dimensions were clarified at TechInd, the discussions always came back to whether people could be transferred to new locations (i.e. physical location was understood as synonymous to centralization/decentralization). The physical location, however, is not necessarily dictated by the structural alternative; people can be governed with different degrees of centralization regardless of their physical location. The supplier statements on empowerment underline that even if buyers change their organization structures toward one that provides one central point of contact for global sourcing in order to facilitate *internal* integration and subsequently *external* integration, it may still take time for the external parties to truly see 'one face to the supplier'. For such a transition, suppliers could be seen as allies. By informing them about the envisioned future modes of integration, the suppliers could work on fostering intra-organizational alignment on their own side accordingly (e.g., by aligning national sales offers towards global frame agreements). For the project-based operations context, the results particularly highlight the importance of joint planning and early involvement.

For suppliers, the study provides a framework to facilitate the analysis of buyers' global sourcing organizations. As the findings indicate, different designs may warrant different responses from the supplier (e.g., KAM in response to a category-based and activity-based hybrid sourcing organization). A single customer's organizational redesign in procurement may, of course, not necessarily lead to a fundamental redesign of the supplier sales organization, but nevertheless, awareness of the organizational (re)designs on the buyer side and their implications can help suppliers to master a tailored response (e.g. by nominating a KAM for that customer within an otherwise country-organized sales organization). By also being conscious about design options, the supplier is able to monitor if there is a trend among the most important customers in how they (re)structure their procurement organizations and consider how to structure their own sales organization.

5.3 Limitations and suggestions for further research

The empirical part of this study was based on the single embedded unit case study of TechInd and six of its 1st tier suppliers. Although a single case study is well-suited for the illustrative purpose (Ketokivi and Choi 2014), it naturally poses limitations. These limitations, together with our findings, provide ideas for future research.

First, the various organizational design alternatives (Fig. 1) provide another interesting starting point for future research. Future research could build on this conceptualization to identify, for example, how contemporary companies engaging in global sourcing benefit from integration of the buyer–supplier interface. In practice, also studying which purchasing categories benefit most from such integration could be very enlightening.

Second, future research could further engage in studying the management of the buyer–supplier interface. This study offered illustrations of integration of the buyer–supplier interface for global sourcing, purposefully selecting certain kinds of suppliers based on the Kraljic (1983) matrix. Future research could address questions such as: How does the purchasing type further affect the BSR and its management (e.g. for strategic versus bottleneck categories)? How do different kinds of global sourcing organization structures (beyond the one illustrated here, e.g. Figure 3) affect management of the BSR? What are the implications of the buyer's global sourcing organization structure on the supplier side, in terms of, for example, the marketing and sales organizational design in different industries, and vice versa? Furthermore, research has indicated that organizational relationships have a fixed starting point and they evolve and develop over time (Ambrose et al. 2008; Vanpoucke et al. 2014) while depending on their history of interaction (van de Vijver et al. 2011). Future research could take a longitudinal perspective to see how the BSR and its management evolves over time. Research could also build on the contingency theory of organizations (Donaldson 2001), to assess global sourcing organizational structures and integration in BSRs in different operations contexts to identify potential contextual effects.

Appendix A: Full interview protocol

Buyer interviews

Interviewee background

1. What is your organizational position and role in this company?
2. What is your educational and professional background?
3. What is your tenure with the company and in this position?

Current PSO structure and its evolution

4. Where do you see your organization's Purchasing & Supply Management (PSM):
    a. Main strengths?
    b. Main weaknesses?
5. Please describe the organization structure of your PSM department
    a. What has been the development path to the current structure? I.e. what changes have recently been made in the PSM structure (pre and post 2016).
    b. What were the underlying reasons for the organizational changes?
6. How would you describe and classify your suppliers?
    a. How would you classify suppliers X, Y, Z in terms of dimensions of supplier risk and profit potential? (i.e. map examples on Kraljic's matrix)
7. How would you describe your overall approach to managing supplier relationships?
    a. Managing activities with suppliers and underlying reasons? What are the challenges? What works well? What would you do differently if you could? Could you give some examples?
    b. How has management of these supplier relationships changed over the past few years (pre and post 2016)? And why?
8. How would you describe your overall satisfaction with today's organizational set-up? And why?

Supplier interviews

Interviewee background

1. What is your organizational position and role in this company?
2. What is your educational and professional background?
3. What is your tenure with the company and in this position?
    a. Buyer relationships
4. What are you supplying to TechInd?
5. What is your company's history with this customer relationship?
6. How would you describe the relationship and how it is managed? Could you give some examples?

a. How has the buyer relationship and its management changed over the past few years (pre and post 2016)? And why?

7. How would you describe your overall satisfaction with the buyer relationship management? And why?

8. Did you notice particular changes in how the relationship is managed (during the last years)?

9. Are you aware of any changes in the organizational structure of your customer?

10. If yes, how has this affected how you manage the customer relationship and why? Has a change in customer organization (in procurement) ever led to any organizational adaptations on your company's side. If yes, could you describe that?

Appendix B: Ex-ante coding tree (based on conceptual framework)

	[Sub node level 1]	**[Sub node level 2]**	**Definition**
Organizational Structure			Structural alternatives as decisions on the structure along the dimensions of category, business unit/customer, geography, and activity, together with the decision on aspects, such as the degree of centralization and involvement (Bals et al. 2018)
	BUYER organizational structure	Macro-level geography	
		Macro-level business unit	
		Macro-level category	
		Macro-level activity	
		Micro-level (de)centralization	
	SUPPLIER sales organizational structure	Macro-level geography	
		Macro-level business unit	
		Macro-level	

	[Sub node level 1]	[Sub node level 2]	Definition
		category	
		Macro-level activity	
		Micro-level (de)centralization	
Coordination (alignment of actions)			Coordination refers to "the degree to which a manufacturer strategically collaborates with its supply chain partners and collaboratively manages intra- and inter-organization processes" (Flynn et al. 2010)
Cooperation (alignment of interests)			Cooperation refers to alignment of interests, which arise not just due to lack of information but also due to various behavioral aspects (Yan and Dooley 2013). This stream of research considers that behavior is motivated by personal interests and benefits and subsequent uncooperative behavior tends to divert shared resources from serving joint needs and benefits to satisfying individual firms' interests (Gulati et al. 2005)

Appendix C: The buyer–supplier interfaces and their management

Supplier	Supplier Organization Structure	Information on the sales organization	Information on the interface and its management
S1	Macro-level dimension(s): GEOGRAPHY Micro-level: hybrid	"[…] it depends very much on the project and the application of the project. In general, we can say we have got a very lean structure in our company so that we have a direct impact on product development and also on production. On the other side if [TechInd] is involving their project managers or their technical knowledge we can easily adapt their need to our development and vice versa we can find a very quick and easy solution which our competition and [TechInd's] competition cannot because their complexity in the organization is much, much higher." (S1) "Because most of the suppliers they	"[…] we are mostly talking about projects all over the world and whenever something is coming up I immediately get a request from [B1] or his colleagues to offer for the product." (S1) "So, we have two attempts working together with [TechInd]. One is working together nationally. Like in Germany or in other countries. And others are international projects where we are working together with the headquarter of [TechInd]." (S1) "[At the beginning around 2014 it was about] I'm coming down to your country, negotiate with you and flying out and have some kind of

Supplier	Supplier Organization Structure	Information on the sales organization	Information on the interface and its management
		are organized in regions or even in countries." (B1) "Yeah, I think [S1's company] for example. They only want production site, but they have sales managers for the regions. My first contact is the EMEA contact. But we are doing also some business, or we are planning to do some business with them for different regions in the world. And having some RFQs." (B1)	global agreements, but only one or two because most of the suppliers didn't want to work with us on a global perspective. Because they are set-up also very regional. So, if we are looking into the [new] procurement organization on how it works then we have these countries where it is feasible to work on that because they are big enough for having the split in the [activity] pillars. […] So, instead of having the split heads we are trying to really have experts in the different roles. Which is very, very interesting and good to see." (B1) "And [S1's company is] willing to do it by service which is a big part. We are not only focusing on price but like also the price is always competitive [compared] to his competitors." (B7) "In my opinion we not have any given strategy we have to represent. Of course, we have our company slogans and all that stuff. And then the relationship to the supplier should also have some kind of respect. Therefore, I'm the type of guy who's really looking for partnership and like a long-term relationship. […] If you try to fool somebody of course he will try to pay back sometimes. Or like if you really wear somebody out. That's my opinion to the last drop. And when he sees a chance to…if he has the chance for his turn then he will ask for a higher price for example. And you have to accept that because you have no choice." (B7)
S2	Macro-level dimension(s): GEOGRAPHY	"I am business unit manager for France, for Chile, Peru, Brazil and Spain where we have managing directors. […] I am a key account manager for two companies: [company X] and [TechInd], but globally. So, I receive some requests	"Well, we have some relationships locally. Each entity has the relationship with the managing director of [TechInd]. I think normally every month we have a meeting with the managing director of each company. In my case I used

Supplier	Supplier Organization Structure	Information on the sales organization	Information on the interface and its management
	Micro-level: hybrid	from Asia or from America or from Europe. Doesn´t matter. I am the key account that…I collect information and I distribute in my organization but I am let's say the official messenger between [S2's company] or [company X] in that case." (S2) "[TechInd] was very active with [S2's company] in Latin America especially. And I was area manager of Latin America when they told us we want to have a key account manager, [our] Holding […] decide[d] [I'm] the person because [I'm] the person that made [most] business in the world with [TechInd]. The same happened with [competitor y of TechInd]. And the same happened with this person in Germany. That is the managing director of Germany. He is the one who has made more business with [competitor y of TechInd]. So, he was appointed as key account manager for this company to try to get more business in all the countries." (S2) "And they are organized really all over the world. And we have other suppliers, competitors for them like [S2's company and] let's say none of the competitors has a really global footprint. They have region by regions, some are stronger some are weaker." (B2) "[Before nominating the global KAM] the maximum what they had was regional structure. So, they had a regional manager. Then then…our key account manager…he was the regional manager for Latin-America. And they have some regional manager for Asia Pacific […]." (B2)	to visit with all the [TechInd] companies in [Latin America] every quarter. […] And I have a close relationship with the holding with the procurement person [B2]. And we used to be in contact at least two or three times by skype every month. We have a very frequent contact between us. Because of these frame agreements we are trying to implement." (S2) "Yeah, [S2's company] was something where only local contacts were in the past. So, there was something in the past in South America already. Something in Spain. And I think it was my first supplier meeting year together with [B1]. We met [S2's company] and there we said clearly […] we want a key account. If you want to build up something with us…a business, then you need to have a counterpart. They have organized this. They have done this. They have done their homework. It was their Latin-American manager. We had at that time the biggest business with [S2's company] there. And the most contact. And he spoke English fluently." (B2) "We are discussing some payments that we want to postpone. Or stretch a bit the due dates. And with [S2's company] we have already now ninety days. And I could find an agreement quite quick with them to stretch even the ninety days a bit longer." (B2) "[To create competition by bringing S2's company in] helped against [competitor of S2]. And it will probably further help us to decrease the price level at the end. […] We have monopolists. [Sometimes] in our industry the customer puts the supplier name into the specification" (B5)

Supplier	Supplier Organization Structure	Information on the sales organization	Information on the interface and its management
S3	Macro-level dimensions: GEOGRAPHY, BUSINESS UNIT Micro-level: hybrid	"So, in protective coatings for instance, we also have key account manager power and energy which I did before. So, he will deal with [multinational energy technology and infrastructure company] and [multinational systems, services and equipment provider for the transport sector] and the likes like that." (S3) "Yeah, well the actual agreements sit in the commercial departments in head office. But I'm pretty much the only one who knows how to deal, where to deal, what's the latest status. I mean if I would not be there from one day to the other okay they could read through the things and read through my emails but yeah, they have to start… large deal to start again." (S3) "Yeah, you don't have the needs so, the personnel to cover every one of the key accounts with two persons. There is no budget for that. So, it is all slimmed down organizations and yeah, you have to deal with it alone. For handover and also within our company it's well…if you are lucky it should be almost a year with handover working side by side. But it's lucky if there is one month or one week even." (S3) "Yeah, sometimes we have a central deal, but the country manager will…has a project locally for that same company. And he can take it but at more or less a price which is arranged central." (S3)	"Well, the relationship is now centrally. So, I'm running the frame agreements we have done. And yeah, that´s only on the central level. So, I´m normally not involved in particular projects or countries. That is still dealt with between local [TechInd] and local [S3's company]. So, only at the end of the year then yeah… for the repay which is in the part of the agreement we sit together. And of course, there are many contacts where we are starting up because it takes some time to start up such a…So, basically in the form of regional meetings where I will attend, where [B3] will attend from the headquarter sides and our local colleagues from both sides. And yeah, then we discuss how to improve business essentially." (S3) "When it comes to passive fire protection [PFP] we have [S3]. Very successful. With placing a product […]. We are using just within one specific product that has been designed in Norway [and with them we have] by far the highest spend." (B3)
S4	Macro-level dimension(s): GEOGRAPHY Micro-level:	"So, we are…[S4's company] is a family company and we are believing very much in the matrix organization. We are supporting each other. […] So, being part of that specification is very much needed to be able to quote locally. Or in my position. Because we haven't had this position before. So, then in case of [multinational	"[TechInd] is of course the contractor. And the contractor is very often bound to fulfil their contract…Yeah, they have to follow a specification. If [S4's company] is part of this specification, then [TechInd] is free to buy from [us]. […] It's very rarely that you are kind of single specified. And then it is…

Supplier	Supplier Organization Structure	Information on the sales organization	Information on the interface and its management
	hybrid	energy technology and infrastructure company] has been building a power station in Vietnam it was not possible to give our Vietnamese colleagues quotation for this project in Vietnam. So therefore, we are…we know that this is kind of a glocal business. It's always one third or one fourth is above the water. You know if we are looking at the iceberg the rest remains under the water. Of course, you have to be in that specifications. And you have to be strong locally as well. So, that's how we do glocal business." (S4)	of course we provide our products and services. Meaning the technical sales support to make sure that these coatings are applied correct. And [TechInd has] the choice […]. Very often [TechInd] is then selecting the cheapest vendor as it is quite common in this industry." (S4)
S5	Macro-level dimension(s): GEOGRAPHY Micro-level: hybrid	"I would say for direct purchase it is organized geographically. So, local. On a local level. But that's really related to the concrete supply of products. More from a relationship point of view then we take our headquarters meeting at [TechInd headquarter location]." (S5) "On the sales side it is based on geography. So, meaning that every country or region has its own commercial team and setup." (S5) "I'm also commercially responsible for the group. Meaning I report to our headquarters […]. And we have a commercially coordinating role globally. Meaning that I coordinate international companies and projects together with my local organization on a need-to-need basis." (S5) "We have a team of […] twenty people at the moment. We are growing quite fast. The position itself is the same. We are all global key account managers. But for example, myself I come with the background oil and gas, at the moment I'm moving more towards wind customers. I have also customers dealing solely with engineering firms. Other colleagues are dealing with	"We don´t have a frame agreement in place. […] this is quite different for example Middle-East to South Europe etc. So, we struggle a little bit to cover that in a frame agreement." (S5) "And [S5] I also find very interesting because coming out of an area where they were just serving surface protection and now want to go into PFP maybe they look from the bottom up and say okay how can [TechInd] contribute. And I know they had some technical discussions with our experts in a way that they say 'okay, what's the crucial part in applying PFP"' […] And at least I think the guy from [S5] is really nice." (B3)

Supplier	Supplier Organization Structure	Information on the sales organization	Information on the interface and its management
		floating units for example. So, there is a segment difference. But the content of the positions is the same." (S5)	
S6	Macro-level dimension(s): GEOGRAPHY, BUSINESS UNIT Micro-level: hybrid	"[We are] a rather lean sales organization. We are part of a European sales organization where we have the sales office for the European marine and protective coatings sales organization so we are basically in [country] or in my region in each of the countries represented only with sales officers and a lot of our services like financial, customer service are in other parts of Europe. […] So, we are quite functionally organized as well." (S6) "Well we have a split on sales areas. We have a marine sales department and a protective coatings sales department." (S6)	"Well, I think […] on a technical level we […] have some very good discussions. Also, dialogues partly with the buyer and partly with [TechInd's] technical organization. And I think we have a good relationship with […] the central buyers in this area" (S6) "When it comes to passive fire protection we have again [S6's company]. Very successful. With placing a product." (B3) "We are pushing hard. We often even come to a stage with [S4's company] or [S6's company] that we might reach the frame agreement. I'm not yet sure if it is really satisfying then. I mean we go that way. And it's already a good step to have an agreement." (B7) "I just remember that we have closed a deal in Abu Dhabi with [S6's company] where their offer has been outstanding low. And I think they are offering it almost on cost level. That means you have a difference in price towards competitors…to the competition in a range of more than forty percent which is ridiculously high. And at the same time, we were preparing a quote for I think it was Kuwait. And there they have been out. Because they gave a quote. They have been on the list of suppliers to be addressed for a quote. And after the feedback […] that they have given at first they were far out of competition." (B3)

* mainly relevant dimension for sales counterparts when dealing with the global category managers.

Appendix D: Empirical analysis – Buyer–Supplier interface and its management

ORGANIZATIONAL STRUCTURE

BUYER Organization structure

Macro-level geography + micro-level (de)centralization

Positive examples

"For example in a very large wind customer which is based in south Europe, the purchase department is very centralized organized. Meaning that every decision is made in Spain. No matter where the project is executed globally. From an overview point of view that is very convenient because I have one contact and he decides. But commercially it also makes me very vulnerable. I mean if something goes wrong in the relationship or whatsoever and this person decides to go to competition you lose all the business globally. Yeah, so it is positive but also involves a very high risk when the relationship goes wrong. If you have one very dominant central organized purchase department for example." (S5, general statement)

"[…] if a country organization from a big group is more independent yeah, you are more free to maneuver around in terms of price and also guarantees or technically coating-wise. And yeah, but it also makes it difficult on the other side. Then you can agree something in the head office. And you arrive somewhere. You are very friendly welcome with coffee etc. But they say we are not interested. So, yeah that's…And everything in between." (S3, general statement)

Negative examples

"[F]or our material the main buyer is [B7] speaking for purchasing in whole Germany. And we are in contact regarding that. However, decision seems to be made on the regional level. And it seems that these regional buyers are not linked to [B7]. That's sometimes the feeling we get because the decisions are made in different regions. So, one thing we discuss with [B7 is that although] we have good discussions, good however on the local area in the region the decision is made in a total different way. And that is difficult to understand if you do not have the internal view." (S1, specific statement in relation to TechInd)

"[The national business] is very fragmented and also quite difficult because there are different buyers in different regions and we do not see a clear buying strategy. The only thing what we see is focused on price, but we do not see what else are the key buying factors like quality, like logistics. And also, we can´t see a purchasing strategy in Germany. Only thing is of course price which is a main driver in this business but there are also decisions made which are totally opposite in the north or in the south of Germany. So, it´s not easy to get a clear picture and also information […]." (S1, specific statement in relation to TechInd)

"I got told from the people working in the [TechInd] headquarter technically or commercial that they have hardly any influence on any local decision. This is something quite difficult because if it comes to areas like the middle east or what so ever then this…that's some other factors then logical sales argument and so on are playing into this you know. And then what we see we are losing quite sometimes some projects where factors coming into account which we cannot follow. And even the guys in the headquarter, [TechInd] headquarter cannot follow up. And sometimes this is a bit irritating I have to say." (S4, specific statement related to TechInd)

Macro-level category and geography + micro-level centralization

ORGANIZATIONAL STRUCTURE

Positive examples

"Yeah, well. The funny thing is on paper they are normally quite well organized centrally. So, the big groups like [TechInd], [and a multinational energy company]. But in practice you will find that not every country is on the same page in every different amount of freedom. Within [TechInd] they are more or less...yeah, more directive as the German company. It's marching orders." (S3, specific statement in relation to TechInd)

Negative examples

"But yeah, with [multinational energy company] it's a bit different. Yes, we deal with the central procurements director, global category managers. But there are still countries, refineries where they will say well, it's nice that you agree something with our head office, but [...] we don't recognize that. Or we take it as an indication or friendly advice...But not as an instruction." (S3, general statement)

"Yeah, well you have the risk of course. But on the other hand, then I see also with other accounts and my colleagues who have that situation where every [sales] decision is taken on a local level is that it's sometimes quite difficult to get all the knowledge to be on top of every situation, every opportunity. So, then you are very much depending on the effort of your local [sales] colleagues and your feedback." (S5, general statement)

SUPPLIER sales organization structure

Macro-level geography + micro-level decentralization + Key Account Role

Positive examples

"I mean if my customer is a key account that means I, no matter the question the key account has, regardless the type of products, I need to deal with the situation. Of course, we have departments and staff positions who are product specialists which I can rely on when I have a question or need assistance." (S5, general statement)

"So, the account management team will know what's going on [in R&D]. So, we try to align that. And also, have a...As I see they have a global alignment of what I say if a company like [TechInd] have subsidiaries all around the world then we need to make sure that we have a coordinated approach in each of those countries. So, we have let's say account managers saying sales people, service people whatever is necessary in each of those areas. So, in that way align to their organization. For again, if there is at the customer side within let's say [TechInd]... if they have a structure where all decisions on coatings are taken by a centralized procurement organization and maybe in the category management team then of course we need to reflect that as well. So, we have a... sort of a global account management system meaning the negotiations and the discussions on that level. So, that way I think you get the most benefit for both parties by doing that." (S6, specific statement in relation to TechInd)

Negative examples

"And every time I said okay who will place the order? The local entity. Okay then it would be my colleague from that region. Same to him. Yeah, that may be. But I'm located here. And I negotiate with you. So, whatever I would like to do is I would like to talk to you. Whatever you are doing internally it doesn't matter for me. But I would like to have a SPOC [Single Point of Contact]. So, my SPOC will be you. So, and he went back within his organization which is a smaller organization [...and] he came back and said okay we find a solution internally [despite differing incentives]." (B1, specific statement in relation to TechInd)

ORGANIZATIONAL STRUCTURE

"[Situation on the sales side is similar, as] at this moment the holdings of many companies want to centralize sales, want to centralize the contract. But it's different to find how to do it when you have subsidiaries all around the world. It's very similar in all the companies." (S2, general statement)

"Yeah, but also from our side there are sometimes resistances. There was…well we already have a good business with them locally why should we change something, or our pricing is very low. I don't have any space to pay a central rebate for a global turnover." (S3, general statement)

"Then he [the sales person] normally says, 'ah I mean pricing is a local issue. We shouldn't interfere. I think our guys can handle it.' So, where is the benefit for us? And that's actually something which we see very often." (B3)

"That is just as challenging for us on the sales side. That is challenging on the procurement side to make sure that this is aligned as well to make sure that let's say that [B3] needs to make sure that his purchasing organization is aligned with the contact he is making on a global level. We have the same challenges from our side to make sure that everybody are aligned in the way they do. So, I see we have exactly the same challenges. (S6, specific statement in relation to TechInd)

"But I mean as these organizations grow bigger and maybe also deal with global customers we need to be able to also show that you do the same service to for instance an oil major that is one of [TechInd] customers. We can service you around the world. Then they need to have that let's say alignment across their organization as well. And that is a sort of a…some of the challenges we see because then you actually…especially in that type of business because it's coming from a local orientation. Then it´s more difficult and more challenging to understand that you have to think about something is… now decisions which are taken on the other side of the globe. And that is some of the challenges I think. And again, I see exactly the same challenges both now on procurement and on sales perspective. Because this is basically the same as I see it." (S6, specific statement related to TechInd)

"The local [sales] organization had their own profit and loss model. Which of course then leads to the fact that they have to make also a local decision regarding pricing. When it comes to the supply of products…I mean we have a lot of products, but we also have [core products which] are globally available no matter where we operate. And I must say that many of the products that [TechInd] is using are a part of the global list. So, those products are globally available. But then of course [there needs to be global] agree[ment] on pricing terms." (S5, specific statement in relation to TechInd)

PROCESSES

Coordination (alignment of actions)

Intra-organizational alignment

Positive examples

"Yeah. So, companies like [multinational energy technology and infrastructure company] they have in their headquarter… they have a corporate buyer and they have of course technical guys, corporate technical persons. And I'm talking to those guys and they are very close to their project management. But they know exactly what's going on and they know exactly the benefits why they choose a different solution. And this is for their benefit at the end of the day. And for their clients' benefit." (S4, general statement)

ORGANIZATIONAL STRUCTURE

"I mean the ones that I know the best is a company like [global container logistics company] where we are coordinating everything [...] from this office here. And also, where there is clearly a communicated empowerment in their organization that when we talk to their procurement people then they also have the power to take decisions across their organization irrespective of where it is in the world. And there you actually have a...then you actually get these synergies also a benefit for both for our parties. Because when you have a central point of contact and that we have seen working pretty well to be quite honest." (S6, general statement)

Negative examples

"Absolutely. The other guys [i.e. the project managers] they are much, much more close to the project. And [TechInd] I feel they are far away at least in the headquarter. Very far away from the project and not knowing about the market situation, you know in this specific country where the project is going to be executed. They are too far away." (S4, specific statement related to TechInd)

"[...But] it seems to me that the empowerment of the global procurement manager or managers in [TechInd]... they are in [TechInd's] head office. The empowerment is maybe not to deliver where they really want it to be. If you know what I mean. So, for that matter we sometimes sit and talk about the possibility to work together more globally. And we are able to handle that. [...]. But I mean it seems like there are some challenges on [TechInd'] side on making sure that the procurement manager [...has] the empowerment in their organization to do this." (S6, specific statement related to TechInd)

"On regional level or in Germany I have to say it's difficult because you do not see the common mindset of all regional buyers. You can't really see a purchasing strategy. The only thing what we see when we look on the market if we compare experiences also listening to distributors. Only argument seems to be price." (S1, specific statement in relation to TechInd)

Inter-organizational alignment (Early Involvement and Commitment)

Positive examples

"Totally different is in the international business where we are talking directly with the project managers or with the category managers. There we get the information right from scratch when a project becomes obvious or known. We get involved about the timeline what kind of material specifications or needs [TechInd] or [TechInd's] customers have. And we can follow and support [TechInd] right from the beginning of there over to the customer until to the final end. That is a cooperation which I consider as very good. And we see especially over the last three years that we have continuously improved the business on both sides. For [TechInd] and as well for our company." (S1, specific statement in relation to TechInd)

"Yes. For strengths I just had... two weeks ago I came back with [multinational chemical company] with me and in Norway to visit our lab and research and development to apply coatings [...] Some weeks before [multinational energy technology and infrastructure company was] up there. And [TechInd] has been joining [our training program on paints]. So, we try really to build knowledge around that as well." (S4, general statement)

"We have some clients that [jointly plan with us]. But unfortunately, they are not global. We have some suppliers in several countries [who] made a forecast with us. [...] They explained to us the projects they expect to have during the year. And then we can prepare ourselves. Unfortunately, with international companies this is very difficult

ORGANIZATIONAL STRUCTURE

because sometimes they don't know exactly the projects they are doing all around the world. So, sometimes you actually receive a phone call. I need for one week this material. So, with no planification this is difficult." (S2, general statement)

"I have to say that normally the purchase organization of the international company are very professional. So, I don't think they need more tools to negotiate. What we always meet is what we talked about some minutes ago regarding some planification or forecast about what you are going to do. Because we are manufacturers." (S2, general statement)

Negative examples

"Yes, there is one point which really should considered more in general in our industry. It's category management because what I'm realizing is if I just look on the countries I'm responsible for I see that more than ninety percent of the category managers are just named category managers. However, they are just doing traditional purchasing jobs. And I was also experiencing contracting companies where the project managers where saying yes purchasing did a good job, but it did not get the right material. Because I would have needed a material which is a little bit more expensive which helps me with my installation. So, the branch is still too much focused on traditional purchasing and just only on price. And very often it seems that the price is the only driving factor and we see on the construction site that the workers have sometimes problems with the material because they are not involved in the buying process." (S1, general statement)

"I think it's quite similar the relationship in terms of communication. We try to have always a transparent and a clear communication. [...] So, it's difficult to match what the holding wants and what the operational companies want. At the same time, it's as well difficult to find agreements, global agreements because markets are different, prices are different. You have the transportation. And then it's not easy to find a global agreement. Because when you are talking about an agreement worldwide taxes are different. Export taxes are different. So, it's not difficult...sorry, it's a little bit difficult but it´s possible. [...] Our experience as well is that when we are trying to sign a frame agreement or a global agreement with some companies they want to have from us the better prices. They want to have from us the better conditions. They always reject to have any commitment with us. So, we ask for example we can sign an agreement with your company, but you have to guarantee to us [...] some millions of sales orders. And this is always reactive. So, they want to have very good prices, but any let´s say any commitment from his side. So, sometimes these papers or these documents can be only... what paper because finally to sign but they don't have any obligation to buy or to make business with us." (S2, general statement)

Cooperation (alignment of interests)

Incentives

Positive examples

"[...] again it is about the incentives, right? [...]and he said yeah, but we have some trouble [...]. And I said [is it] because [of] who is getting the provision for that? He said 'yes, of course, because I´m doing all the work and my colleague will benefit.' He's doing the business, right. And I'm saying 'yeah, that's true. But that's not my problem.' [...] they find a new way of incentivizing." (B1, specific statement in relation to TechInd)

"I mean that depends a little bit on the exact product category. For some product categories are commoditized, some are more specialized. And the more specialized or

ORGANIZATIONAL STRUCTURE

the more let's say technical oriented product, you need a more let's say involvement of the technical departments and technical people from both sides. And I would say that the…my experience with the… not only [global container logistics company] but also others globally more organized companies. Then you need to have both levels involved. I need to have both technical and you need to have a procurement purchasing but also if need the supply chain etc. involved in these things from both parties. So, I think it's a team from both sides. As ultimately these depends on both sides on the complexity of the customer. Or the… on the accounts. I think that here you need to have all involved, and my experience depending on the level of cooperation. The more people you need to have involved in that. And you need to have a specialist in different areas. You can't only have one account manager dealing with everything. Then you overlook people. If you understand what I mean." (S6, general statement)

Negative examples

"The sales people have quite a high share of the national business because their decision for the national key account and also in the area are affecting national business. For example, it can happen that a contractor in Munich is doing a project in Berlin area and vice versa. So, there is a high share regarding the whole German business. And on the other hand side, of course they are responsible for their local business. An it's more or less the same share. Of course, all the other effects are sales targets, margin targets and things like that." (S1, specific statement in relation to TechInd)

"Well, we have several key account managers and they are doing the business with regional key accounts. For example, in the part of southern Germany, in the middle of Germany and in northern Germany. So, they are doing business together with the regional key accounts. Of course, we also have key accounts which are active Germany wide. And in that case the key account manager who has the headquarter in his area, he's responsible for that customer for the whole German business. That means that everyone has the same responsibility, the same structure regarding the area and number of customers. But they also have a very close link and information because everybody is involving the German business. And it's the same structure in other countries. If something is going abroad if we have for example contracting companies like [TechInd] or others who have a national business and also, international business everything which is international is on my desk. I'm involved. And because I'm leading the sales organizations I'm also involved in the local decisions […]. Because sometimes distributors are offering for a project. We are offering for a project. And customers or competitors from other countries are also offering on the same project. So, you have to clarify that you do not make competition within your own organization. And also, that you are aware of the full scope of the orders and the project at the moment." (S1, specific statement in relation to TechInd)

"Because most of the suppliers they are organized in regions or even in countries. And they are also responsible for their profits, margins, etc. So, they don't like that somebody above them…they get the targets, but they take…their headquarter is taking away one of the opportunities to work on that target. Because saying whatever you are doing with [TechInd] this is the price. We negotiate it. Or the discount or whatever. If this is the case, then we need to reduce my target. But this is…for me honestly it is like everywhere else in the world. Incentives. It's all the time the question. So, if you are changing a process or an organization you need to change your way of incentives to the people." (B1, specific statement in relation to TechInd)

"Yeah, well theory meets practice. Yeah, sometimes we have a central deal, but the country manager […] has a project locally for that same company. And he can take it

ORGANIZATIONAL STRUCTURE
but at more or less a price which is arranged central. And he will walk away from it. Why? Because it´s below his target or in terms of margins. So, he says well it's very nice globally if we can take this project at that price but then I lose…then I don't hit my target and I lose bonus. And I cannot go on holiday for instance. So, yeah you cannot pay me obviously because it's his own pocket, his own wallet which is hurting. But overall it's not good for [S3's company] bottom line, of course. So, in such cases sometimes we make a separate deal that a certain project is not counted for the results on that country. Profits or loss, you can't. But yeah, you have some resistance also in that setup." (S3, specific statement in relation to TechInd) "And what you say about bonuses that's let's say spot on some of the challenges we have to deal with. And that is from…if you look at it from a traditionally geographically organized structure it's typically a challenge. There you need to take the next step in key account management and make a global or regional, but preferably global depending on the company of the customers of course. And then you have a global key account structure to manage that as I see it. But we have challenges in doing that as well because we are very geographically, and area based depending on our organizational structure. So [we face] exactly the same challenges just from the sales rather than a purchasing perspective that we have." (S6, specific statement in relation to TechInd)

Notes

1. 'Global sourcing' refers to the worldwide integration of engineering, operations, and procurement centers, looking for common items, processes, design, technologies, knowledge, and suppliers across functions and locations (Kotabe and Murray 2004; Trent and Monczka 2003a, 2005). Prior research has used terms such as 'global purchasing' (Trent and Monczka 2003b) and 'international purchasing' (Quintens et al. 2006) as synonymous for the same concept.
2. The purpose of this study is to illustrate a design and by no means to suggest that the organization structure at TechInd is ideal and should be followed by other firms.

References

Ambrose E, Marshall D, Fynes B, Lynch D (2008) Communication media selection in buyer-supplier relationships. Int J Oper Prod Manag 28:360–379

Ambrose E, Marshall D, Lynch D (2010) Buyer supplier perspectives on supply chain relationships. Int J Oper Prod Manag 30:1269–1290

Araujo L, Dubois A, Gadde LE (1998) Managing interfaces with suppliers. Ind Mark Manage 28:497–508

Arnold U (1999) Organization of Global Sourcing: Ways toward an optimal degree of centralization. Euro J Purchas Supp Manag 5:167–174

Artto K, Turkulainen V (2018) It takes two to tango: Product-organization interdependence in managing major projects. Int J Oper Prod Manag 38:1312–1339

Ashby WR (1956) Introduction to Cybernetics. Chapman & Hall, London

Ates MA, van Raaij E, Wynstra F (2017) The impact of purchasing strategy-structure (mis)fit on purchasing cost and innovation performance. J Purch Supply Manag 24:68–82

Bals L, Turkulainen V (2017) Achieving efficiency and effectiveness in purchasing and supply management: organization design and outsourcing. J Purch Supply Manag 23:256–267

Bals L, Hartmann E, Ritter T (2009) Barriers of purchasing departments' involvement in marketing service procurement. Ind Mark Manage 38:892–902

Bals L, Laine J, Mugurusi G (2018) Evolving purchasing and supply organizations: a contingency model for structural alternatives. J Purch Supply Manag 24:41–58

Bensaou M, Venkatraman N (1995) Configurations of interorganizational relationships: A comparison between US and Japanese automakers. Manage Sci 41:1471–1492

Burke CM, Morley MJ (2016) On temporary organizations: A review, synthesis and research agenda. Human Relations 69:1235–1258

Burton RM, DeSanctis G, Obel B (2006) Organizational design – a step-by-step approach. Cambridge University Press, New York, NY

Caldwell N, Roehrich JK, Davies AC (2009) Procuring complex performance in construction: London Heathrow Terminal 5 and a Private Finance Initiative hospital. J Purch Supply Manag 15:178–186

Capon N, Senn C (2010) Global customer management programs: how to make them really work. Calif Manage Rev 52:32–55

Cavinato JL (1991) Evolving procurement organizations: logistics implications. J Bus Logist 13:27–45

Chae S, Lawson B, Kull TJ, Choi T (2019) To insource or outsource the sourcing? A behavioral investigation of the multi-tier sourcing decision. Int J Oper Prod Manag 39:385–405

Cousins PD, Menguc B (2006) The implications of socialization and integration in supply chain management. J Oper Manag 24:604–620

Cousins PD, Lawson B, Squire B (2006) An empirical taxonomy of purchasing functions. Int J Oper Prod Manag 26:775–794

Cousins PD, Lawson B, Squire B (2008) Performance measurement in strategic buyer–supplier relationships: The mediating role of socialization mechanisms. Int J Oper Prod Manag 28:238–258

Das AJ, Narasimhan R, Talluri S (2006) Supplier integration – finding an optimal configuration. J Oper Manag 24:563–582

Donaldson L (2001) The contingency theory of organizations. Sage, Thousand Oaks

Dubois A, Gibbert M (2010) From complexity to transparency: Managing the interplay between theory, method and empirical phenomena in IMM case studies. Ind Mark Manage 39:129–136

Faes W, Matthyssens P, Vandenbempt K (2000) The pursuit of global purchasing synergy. Ind Mark Manage 29:539–553

Flynn BB, Huo B, Zhao X (2010) The impact of supply chain integration on performance: A contingency and configuration approach. J Oper Manag 28:58–71

Foerstl K, Hartmann E, Wynstra F, Moser R (2013) Cross-functional integration and functional coordination in purchasing and supply management: Antecedents and effects on purchasing and firm performance. Int J Oper Prod Manag 33:689–721

Gadde LE, Snehota I (2000) Making the most of supplier relationships. Ind Mark Manage 29:305–316

Galbraith JR (1973) Designing complex organizations. addison-wesley, Reading, MA

Giunipero LC, Monczka RM (1997) Organizational approaches to managing international sourcing. Int J Phys Distrib Logist Manag 27:321–336

Gonzalez-Zapatero C, Gonzalez-Benito J, Lannelongue G (2016) Antecedents of functional integration during new product development: The purchasing–marketing link. Ind Mark Manage 52:47–59

Guesalaga R, Gabrielsson M, Rogers B, Ryals L, Cuevas JM (2018) Which resources and capabilities underpin strategic key account management? Ind Mark Manage 75:160–172

Gulati R, Lawrence PR, Puranam P (2005) Adaptation in vertical relationships: Beyond incentive conflict. Strateg Manag J 26:415–440

von Haartman R, Bengtsson L (2015) The impact of global purchasing and supplier integration on product innovation. Int J Oper Prod Manag 35:1295–1311

Hayes RH, Wheelwright SC (1979) Link manufacturing process and product life cycles. Harv Bus Rev 57:133–140

Homburg C, Workman JP Jr, Jensen O (2000) Fundamental changes in marketing organization: The movement toward a customer-focused organizational structure. J Acad Market Sci 28:459–478

Horn P, Scheffler P, Schiele H (2014) Internal integration as a pre-condition for external integration in global sourcing: a social capital perspective. Int J Prod Econ 153:54–65

Hwang S, Kim H, Hur D, Schoenherr T (2019) Interorganizational information processing and the contingency effects of buyer-incurred uncertainty in a supplier's component development project. Int J Prod Econ 210:169–183

Jia F, Lamming R, Sartor M, Orzes G, Nassimbeni G (2014) Global purchasing strategy and international purchasing offices: Evidence from case studies. Int J Prod Econ 154:284–298

Jia F, Orzes G, Sartor M, Nassimbeni G (2017) Global sourcing strategy and structure: Toward and integrated conceptual framework. Int J Oper Prod Manag 37:840–864

Johnson PF, Leenders MR (2001) The supply organizational structure dilemma. J Supply Chain Manag 37:4–11

Kaipia R, Turkulainen V (2017) Managing integration in outsourcing relationships – the influence of cost and quality priorities. Ind Mark Manage 61:114–129

Karjalainen K (2011) Estimating the cost effects of purchasing centralization—Empirical evidence from framework agreements in the public sector. J Purch Supply Manag 17:87–97

Ketokivi M, Choi T (2014) The renaissance of case research as a scientific method. J Oper Manag 32:232–240

Kotabe M, Murray JY (2004) Global sourcing strategy and sustainable competitive advantage. Ind Mark Manage 33:7–14

Kraljic P (1983) Purchasing must become supply management. Havard Business Review 61:109–117

Kulangara NP, Jackson SA, Prater E (2016) Examining the impact of socialization and information sharing and the mediating effect of trust on innovation capability. Int J Oper Prod Manag 36:1601–1624

Lahdenperä P (2012) Making sense of the multi-party contractual arrangements of project partnering, project alliancing and integrated project delivery. Constr Manag Econ 30:57–79

Lawrence PR, Lorsch JW (1967) Differentiation and integration in complex organizations. Adm Sci Q 12:1–47

Lundin RA, Söderholm A (1995) A theory of temporary organization. Scand J Manag 11:437–455

Luzzini D, Caniato F, Ronchi S, Spina G (2012) A transaction costs approach to purchasing portfolio management. Int J Oper Prod Manag 32:1015–1042

Luzzini D, Longoni A, Moretto A, Caniato F, Brun A (2014) Organizing IT purchases: Evidence from a global study. J Purch Supply Manag 20:134–155

March JG, Simon HA (1958) Organizations. Blackwell, Cambridge, MA

Matthyssens P, Faes W (1997) Coordinating Purchasing: Strategic and Organizational Issues: Relationships and Networks in International Markets. Elsevier, London, UK

Maylor H, Turkulainen V (2019) The concept of organizational projectification: past, present and beyond? International Journal of Managing Projects in Business forthcoming

Mintzberg H (1983) Structure in fives: Designing effective organizations. Prentice Hall, Englewood Cliffs, NJ

Monczka RM, Trent RJ (1991) Global sourcing: a development approach. Iinternational Journal of Purchasing and Materials Management 27:2–8

Nadler DA, Tushman ML (1997) Competing by design – the power of organizational architecture. Oxford University Press, New York

Narasimhan R, Carter JR (1990) Organization, communication and co-ordination of international sourcing. Int Mark Rev 7:6–20

Pagell M (2004) Understanding the factors that enable and inhibit the integration of operations, purchasing and logistics. J Oper Manag 22:459–487

Piekkari R, Plakoyiannaki E, Welch K (2010) 'Good' case research in industrial marketing: Insights from research practice. Ind Mark Manage 40:109–117

Procurement Strategy Council (ed) (2013) Procurement Organizational Structure: Aggregate Trends

Quintens L, Pauwels P, Matthyssens P (2006) Global purchasing strategy: Conceptualization and measurement. Ind Mark Manage 35:881–891

Ramasesh RV, Browning TR (2014) A conceptual framework for tackling knowable unknown unknowns in project management. J Oper Manag 32:190–204

Revilla E, Knoppen D (2015) Building knowledge integration in buyer-supplier relationships – The critical role of strategic supply management and trust. Int J Oper Prod Manag 35:1408–1436

Roehrich J, Lewis M (2014) Procuring complex performance: implications for exchange governance complexity. Int J Oper Prod Manag 34:221–241

Rozemeijer F, van Weele A, Weggeman M (2003) Creating corporate advantage through purchasing: Toward a contingency model. J Supply Chain Manag 39:4–13

Schiele H, Horn P, Vos B (2011) Estimating cost-saving potential from international sourcing and other sourcing levers: Relative importance and trade-offs. Int J Phys Distrib Logist Manag 41:315–336

Schleper MC, Blome C, Stanczyk A (2020) Archetypes of sourcing decision-making The influence of contextual factors on consensus, argumentation and cabal. Int J Oper Prod Manag 40:117–143

Schneider L, Wallenburg CM (2013) 50 Years of research on organizing the purchasing function: Do we need any more? J Purch Supply Manag 19:144–164

Sheth JN, Sharma A (1997) Supplier relationships – Emerging issues and challenges. Ind Mark Manage 26:91–100

Stanczyk A, Foerstl K, Busse C, Blome C (2015) Global sourcing decision-making processes: Politics, intuition, and procedural rationality. J Bus Logist 36:160–181

Storbacka K (2012) Strategic account management programs: Alignment of design elements and management practices. J Bus Indust Market 27:259–274

Swoboda B, Schlüter A, Olejnik E, Morschett D (2012) Does centralising global account management activities in response to international retailers pay off? Manag Int Rev 52:727–756

Terpend R, Tyler BB, Krause DR, Handfield RB (2008) Buyer-supplier relationships: Derived value over two decades. J Supply Chain Manag 44:28–55

Toulan O, Birkinshaw J, Arnold D (2006) The role of interorganizational fit in global account management. Int Stud Manag Organ 36:61–81

Trautmann G, Bals L, Hartmann E (2009a) Global sourcing in integrated network structures: the case of hybrid purchasing organizations. J Int Manag 15:194–208

Trautmann G, Turkulainen V, Hartmann E, Bals L (2009b) Integration in the global sourcing organization – an information processing perspective. J Supply Chain Manag 45:57–74

Trent RJ, Monczka RM (2003a) International purchasing and global sourcing-what are the differences? J Supply Chain Manag 39:26–36

Trent RJ, Monczka RM (2003b) Understanding integrated global sourcing. Int J Phys Distrib Logist Manag 33:607–662

Trent RJ, Monczka RM (2005) Achieving excellence in global sourcing. MIT Sloan Manag Rev 47:24

Turkulainen V, Ketokivi M (2012) Cross-functional integration and performance - what are the real benefits? Int J Oper Prod Manag 32:447–467

Turkulainen V, Swink ML (2017) Supply chain personnel as knowledge resources for innovation ––a contingency view. J Supply Chain Manag 53:41–59

Turkulainen V, Kujala J, Artto K, Levitt R (2013) Organizing in the context of global project-based firm – the case of sales-operations interface. Ind Mark Manage 42:223–233

Turkulainen V, Kauppi K, Nermes E (2017) Institutional Explanations – Missing link in operations management? Insights on supplier integration. Int J Oper Prod Manag 37:1117–1140

van de Vijver M, Vos B, Akkermans H (2011) A tale of two partnerships: Socialization in the development of buyer-supplier relationships. J Supply Chain Manag 47:23–43

Vanpoucke E, Vereecke A, Boyer KK (2014) Triggers and patterns of integration initiatives in successful buyer–supplier relationships. J Oper Manag 32:15–33

Vesalainen J, Kohtamaki M (2015) Toward a typological view of buyer–supplier relationships: Challenging the unidimensional relationship continuum. Ind Mark Manage 49:105–115

Villena VH, Revilla E, Choi TY (2011) The dark side of buyer–supplier relationships: A social capital perspective. J Oper Manag 29:561–576

Wieland A, Bals L, Mol MJ, Handfield RB (2020) Overcoming blind spots in global sourcing research: Exploiting the cross-sections between supply chain management and international business. J Intern Manag 26:100709

Yan T, Dooley KJ (2013) Communication intensity, goal congruence, and uncertainty in buyer–supplier new product development. J Oper Manag 31:523–542

Yan T, Dooley KJ (2014) Buyer-supplier collaboration quality in new product development projects. J Supply Chain Manag 50:59–83

Yin RK (2009) Case Study Research – Design and Methods, Revised. Sage, Thousand Oaks, CA

7

Uncovering Dimensions of the Impact of Blockchain Technology in Supply Chain Management

Ulpan Tokkozhina, Ana Lucia Martins & Joao C. Ferreira

Business Research Unit (BRU-IUL), Lisbon, Portugal
Instituto Universitário de Lisboa (ISCTE-IUL), 1649-026, Lisbon, Portugal
Inov Inesc Inovação—Instituto de Novas Tecnologias, 1000-029, Lisbon, Portugal

Abstract

Supply chains around the globe are faced with difficulties and disruptions due to the worldwide pandemic situation and digital solutions are needed. There is significant research interest in the implementation of blockchain technology (BCT) for supply chain management (SCM). A challenge that remains is analyzing the interactions of BCT in different areas of SCM. This study aims to identify the influential dimensions of the impact of BCT adoption in SCM and to discuss the synergetic and counter-synergetic effects between these dimensions. Advantages, disadvantages, and constraints of adopting BCT in the SCM context are explored through a systematic literature review, which provides the foundation for identifying the dimensions of impact. The interactions between these dimensions are conceptually discussed. This study introduces three dimensions of the impact of implementing BCT in SCM: 'operations and processes', 'supply chain relationships', and 'innovation and data access'. These dimensions are interrelated and have overlapping areas within them, which leads to synergetic and counter-synergetic effects. The overlaps and synergies of the three dimensions of impact are illustrated, and the virtuous and vicious cycles of BCT adoption in SCM cases are highlighted. This study assists scholars and practitioners by clarifying the synergetic relationships within the dimensions of the impact of BCT in SCM and by providing considerations to prevent undesirable effects and expand desired ones.

Keywords: *Blockchain technology · Supply chain management · Dimensions of impact · Advantages · Disadvantages · Constraints*

1 Introduction

Supply chains (SCs) face unprecedented challenges. The tendency to lengthen them (Chopra et al. 2021) increases their vulnerability in terms of information sharing, and trust poses difficulties in their management. To overcome this problem, SC managers actively seek disruptive solutions that bring innovativeness, efficiency, and effectiveness to their operations (Behnke and Janssen 2020). The global state of emergency due to the Covid-19 pandemic in 2020 highlighted the need for SC digitalization. The digitalization phenomenon is already shaping new realities and relationship models throughout the entire SC network (Queiroz and Fosso Wamba 2019). One of the most recognizable disruptive technologies for SC adoption is blockchain technology (BCT) (Queiroz et al. 2020).

Blockchain is defined as a 'cryptographically guaranteed non-tamperable and unforgeable distributed decentralized ledger' (Liu and Li 2020, p.2). BCT makes it possible for supply chain management (SCM) activities and operations to occur in a highly secure and transparent way, without the need for a central organization (Gonczol et al. 2020). Thus, it is a potential game-changer for supply chains (SCs) in terms of information exchange and verified transactions (Hackius and Petersen 2020). However, the adaptation blueprint of BCT still requires a more focused and comprehensive evaluation (Wong et al. 2020a), as well as an understanding of the critical requirements, issues, and challenges across the SC (Ghode et al. 2020b; Wang et al. 2020b) for successful BCT deployment.

Endeavours to systematize BCT in the SCM context have been undertaken by numerous scholars, with a focus on, i.e. application areas (Queiroz et al. 2019; Chang and Chen 2020; Duan et al. 2020), industrial contexts (Wang et al. 2019a; Idrees et al. 2021), concept definition (Fosso Wamba et al. 2020a, b), bibliometric analysis (Fosso Wamba et al. 2020a; Müßigmann et al. 2020), and article coding (Lim et al. 2021). Systematization has also been explored in the transport and logistics sector (Kummer et al. 2020; Pournader et al. 2020), food SC (Kayikci et al. 2020; Stranieri et al. 2021), and from information-sharing perspectives (Wan et al. 2020). The potential benefits, challenges, drivers, and barriers to BCT adoption in SCM have also been studied using empirical data (van Hoek 2019; Wang et al. 2019b; Stranieri et al. 2021) as well as in specific fields such as agriculture (Kamilaris et al. 2019), the textile and clothing industry (Agrawal et al. 2021) and modern military solutions (Saadiah and Rahayu 2021). A common feature of these wide-ranging attempts to study BCT in SC is a case-specific perspective.

There are as well more generalized reviews that were found in prior literature, that were not attaching findings to a specific area of application. Such studies were building comprehensive maps of separate BCT application topics and themes for supply chain performance (Mahyuni et al. 2020), indicating the most influential authors and publications in the area (Moosavi et al. 2021), separately summarizing enablers, benefits, and risks of BCT adoption (Karakas et al. 2021), conceptualizing stages and factors behind the adoption (Vu et al. 2021).

Extant literature reviews offer many contributions in specific sectors, e.g. food and agriculture SCs (Galvez et al. 2018; Lezoche et al. 2020; Sharma et al. 2021), or reviews of a mix of different technologies under the scope of Industry 4.0 (Bodkhe et al. 2020; Mistry et al. 2020). There as well were studies that grouped themes into clusters (Klerkx et al. 2019) and structured topics and trends into mind maps (Casino et al. 2019). Recently scholars were conducting bibliometric analysis of literature in the field (Moosavi et al. 2021; Tandon et al. 2021), in the context of operations management, mechanisms of a traceability feature of BCT were explored (Feng et al. 2020). Thematic analysis, identifying the orders of benefits and challenges domains of BCT adoption in food SC was as well performed (Chen et al. 2021). However, there is still a lack of a more holistic understanding of the ways in which BCT implementation impacts SCM and operations, outside of a specific application area or context, based on systematized data.

Among open issues of BCT exploration in SC context, such research gaps as suitability of BCT for specific projects, and a mechanism to choose a proper blockchain network that would suite the actual needs of the application was highlighted (Casino et al. 2019). The need of leading through emerging technologies adoption was mentioned (Klerkx et al. 2019), in order to enhance the benefits and alleviate potential negative effects. Research is needed to guide through decision-making process of the adoption of BCT for businesses (Frizzo-Barker et al. 2020). It is also necessary to investigate the societal, organizational, and environmental factors that affect BCT implementation in SCM (Tandon et al. 2021).

Therefore, the contribution of the present research goes beyond prior studies to provide a broader vision and holistic understanding of the existing features of BCT in the SCM context, grouping them into unified general dimensions, without limiting it further to a specific industry or area of application. Like this, it would contribute to gaps identified by previous scholars in the field. Against this backdrop, this research aims to create a systematized understanding of BCT in the SCM context. The goals of this study are threefold: (1) to explore the dimensions of the impact of BCT implementation in SCM; (2) to explore the synergies of these dimensions; and (3) to explore the virtuous and vicious cycles of the adoption of BCT use in SCM.

To achieve these goals, a systematization of the existing literature is pursued. Specifically, BCT features found in the literature are systematized, the operations management dimensions of the impact of BCT implementation in SCM are exposed, and the synergetic and counter-synergetic effects of these dimensions in terms of the advantages, disadvantages, and constraints of BCT implementation are discussed.

The remainder of this paper is organized as follows. Section 2 provides a literature review of the BCT phenomenon in the SC context, as well as current SCM challenges. Section 3 details the methodology adopted in this study. Section 4 provides a systematized understanding of BCT features in the SCM context, which are conveniently displayed in tables and clarifies the logic process underpinning the dimensions and their synergies. Section 5 discusses the theoretical and managerial contributions of this study and suggests areas to be addressed in future studies. Finally, Sect. 6 provides the conclusions of the study and critically identifies its limitations.

2 Literature review

Today, supply chains are beginning to lose the necessary visibility across networks due to their length (Mubarik et al. 2021). SC visibility is the transparency to identify product transit status throughout and outside the supply chain (Roy 2021). It plays a crucial role in strengthening trust and collaboration among different stakeholders (Baah et al. 2021). Thus, to gain visibility for SCs, organizations must establish a way to share timely and reliable information across networks (Tapscott and Tapscott 2020).

Another major SCM focus of organizations is a long-term stability perspective: building confidence and reliance among SC participants (i.e., building trust) (Paluri and Mishal 2020). The long and complex nature of SC networks requires interactions between multiple entities, resulting in challenges in establishing trust among them (Doroudi et al. 2020). An increasing level of trust in the SC scale leads to risk reduction (Collier and Sarkis 2021) and more stable end-consumer behavior (Doroudi et al. 2020).

2.1 Blockchain technology

Blockchain is a fully distributed and decentralized system that can capture and store cryptographically encoded data and transactions in a block manner, similar to a distributed ledger (Queiroz et al. 2019). The mechanism behind BCT then connects each block—which is identified with a unique hash code (a cryptographic algorithm that transforms a data input into a fixed-length irreversible output)—to a previous block, thus connecting all blocks into a chain (Queiroz et al. 2020; Wang et al. 2020c). This chain structure is the fundamental feature that ensures immutable and reliable data in the ledger, as each block holds details (the unique hash code) of the previous blocks' content (Gonczol et al. 2020). Thus, BCT allows safe data exchange within the SC in a distributed manner (Wang et al. 2019b).

BCT brings traceability to SCs, allowing assets to be tracked and providing stakeholders with the visibility required to do so (Choi 2020; Wang et al. 2020b). Through BCT adoption, it is possible to reduce the incidence of unfair practices and counterfeits (Juma et al. 2019; Stranieri et al. 2021) and boost the overall efficiency of SC operations (Leng et al. 2018). Another important innovation that BCT entails is smart contracts, which are, essentially, 'digital contracts that flow across enterprises' (Kamble et al. 2019, p.2011), enabling the automation of processes (Nandi et al. 2020) because smart contracts are self-executable (Min 2019). Overall, BCT has the potential to manage resources efficiently and reduce inventory levels (Kamble et al. 2019), reduce SC risks through traceability features (Kshetri 2018; Montecchi et al. 2019), and optimize planning and forecasting decisions (Perboli et al. 2018).

2.2 Blockchain benefits and challenges in the context of supply chain management

BCT also has attractive capabilities for SC participants; it can improve collaboration between entities (Mao et al. 2018), especially in untrusted environments (Liu and Li 2020), and reduce the bullwhip effect (Perboli et al. 2018). Increasing SC performance and data visibility (Hald and Kinra 2019) results in product quality compliance and improves trust among consumers (Ghode et al. 2020b; Nandi et al. 2020). To improve practitioners' experience, BCT can, for example, be used together with other artificial intelligence technologies (Kayikci et al. 2020) and combined with Internet of Things (IoT) devices (Rejeb et al. 2019).

However, BCT has several disadvantages. Although BCT can provide traceability through digital records, it cannot ensure the real condition of physical products in transit (Yadav and Singh 2020) and is not always a suitable solution, depending on the cost of the product. For example, for lower-cost products, there is less need to thoroughly trace products (van Hoek 2019). Smart contracts are also considered difficult to implement if the coding of the contract is of poor quality, which usually leads to a series of problems throughout the SC (Cole et al. 2019). The lack of central authority within the SC is sometimes considered a disadvantage, especially when resolving disputes among SC entities (Wang et al. 2019a, b). Another major concern is an environmental one: BCT consumes excessive amounts of energy to conduct transaction-related activities (Öztürk and Yildizbaşi 2020; Yadav et al. 2020).

Some challenges still exist in modern SCM, including, e.g. relationship and trust issues between participants in complex SCs, considerations regarding firms' social responsibilities, concerns over the visibility of operations that reveal the dynamics of supply processes, and issues related to exploiting SCM to influence consumers' buying decisions and gain a competitive advantage (Cole et al. 2019; van Hoek 2020a, b; Rogerson and Parry 2020). BCT is considered a possible solution to these limitations of modern SCs; however, a rigorous academic investigation is still required to understand the extent to which BCT may create value for firms (Treiblmaier 2018).

Additionally, there are some practical constraints in the adoption of BCT in the SCM context. For example, a lack of a relevant legal framework (Sheel and Nath 2019) can lead to difficulties in convincing all stakeholders to adopt BCT (Duan et al. 2020). A lack of trust among SC network participants, national circumstances, and cultural differences can also result in different decisions during the adoption process (Kopyto et al. 2020; Queiroz et al. 2020; Wong et al. 2020a). Currently, most SCs are not yet ready for BCT adoption due to either the lack of an organized ecosystem (Kamble et al. 2019) or the novelty of the technology (Min 2019), as adoption of this technology is a complex process. Not only it requires appropriate infrastructure, but it also needs to overcome challenges related to existing regulatory and legal governance systems (Kamble et al. 2021).

BCT adoption poses constraints for supply chain participants in terms of coping with the innovative decentralized structure (Omar et al. 2020). Dimensions of BCT characteristics were introduced in the context of supply chain collaboration (Rejeb et al. 2021), manufacturing industry (Karamchandani et al. 2021), healthcare supply chains (Aich et al. 2021), and categorized key enablers of BCT accordingly to its aims and opportunities (Ali et al. 2021). However, to the best of our knowledge, a more holistic approach on BCT dimensions of impact and their intersections exploration in terms of supply chain implementation was not yet performed. A perceptible knowledge gap between managers of various organizations and their comprehension of BCT was revealed (Walsh et al. 2021), thus an intelligible representation of potential dimensions of impact and their interconnection would assist practitioners in terms of novel technology understanding and applications.

3 Methodology

To comprehensively address this study's aims, a systematic literature review (SLR) was chosen as the most suitable methodology, as it enables following a pre-planned route to enable the most relevant existing literature to be chosen, evaluated, and analyzed to generate the study's findings (Denyer and Tranfield 2009). For the SLR, this study followed the Preferred Reporting Items for Systematic Reviews and Meta-Analysis (PRISMA) checklist (Moher et al. 2009). Adherence to the PRISMA checklist ensures clarity in the review process for others and maintains a structured process, as it requires a transparent motion in the study selection and analysis processes (Saunders et al. 2012). As implied by the PRISMA checklist, for convenience, the literature selection process needs to be schematically presented in a flow diagram; Fig. 1 introduces the selection process conducted for this study.

Three academic databases were selected for this study: Web of Knowledge (WoS), ABI/Inform, and Scopus. These databases were chosen as trusted global platforms for academic searches and for their ability to provide top multidisciplinary journal and article results. The keywords for the search were 'blockchain' and 'supply chain'; an advanced search function was used to collect articles with both keywords found in the title and abstract. The search was also limited to peer-reviewed articles written in English. All publications available up to January 2022 were included, without any limitations per year.

As can be seen in Fig. 1, the number of studies identified in each database was as follows: WoS (356), ABI/Inform (212), and Scopus (383). Thus, a total of 951 articles were identified. The first step was to exclude the duplicates, which resulted in 466 unique articles. The next stage was a prior screening of articles based on the titles and abstracts, to include articles focused on operations management, logistics, specific supply chain applications, and to avoid more technical articles that go beyond the scope of the following research. Examples of topics that did not meet the prior screening criteria include, but are not limited to: humanitarian SCs, supply chain finance, detailed technical descriptions of smart contracts and protocols, cryptoasset applications, energy delivery

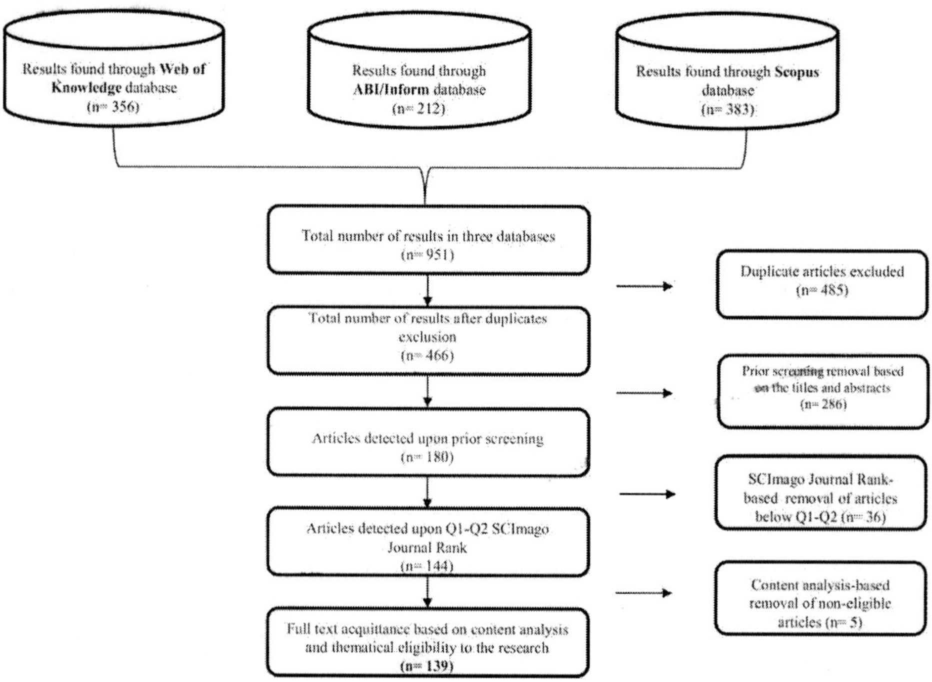

***Fig. 1** Literature selection process*

systems etc. It is important to note, that the research objects were not limited to any specific article types, due to the novelty of the topic, thus all studies, that were compliant with the screening criteria mentioned above, were included. The prior screening step resulted in 180 selected articles. Next, to increase the level of screening and classification, only articles from Q1 and Q2 academic journals (based on SCImago Journal Rank) were included, which resulted in a total of 144 articles. The full texts of these 144 articles were screened, and based on content analysis and eligibility to the study, 139 articles were selected for inclusion in this SLR.

Table 1 shows the exemplary list of journals and the number of publications that were found among the final selected set of 139 articles, to identify the most frequent journals in which the articles were published. The three leading journals are (1) the International Journal of Production Research, (2) IEEE Access and (3) the International Journal of Information Management. This sequence once again highlighted the multidisciplinary nature of the topic, given that academic articles were found in both SCM and production/logistics journals, as well as IT-focused journals. The types of articles also varied from more theoretical to technological applications. These 139 articles were then thoroughly and carefully analyzed to identify the advantages, disadvantages, and constraints (features) of BCT application to SCM, highlighted by the authors. These features were further classified based on meaning and content to ensure the integrity of the findings.

Table 1 Journals with the top number of published articles in the field of blockchain technology in supply chain management

JOURNALS	NUMBER OF ARTICLES
International Journal of Production Research	15
IEEE access	11
International Journal of Information Management	10
Supply Chain Management – An International Journal	8
International Journal of Production Economics	7
Sustainability (Switzerland)	7
Journal of Business Logistics	6
Future Internet	4
Computers and Industrial Engineering	4
Operations Management Research	3
Production Planning & Control	3
Resources Conservation and Recycling	3
Technological Forecasting and Social Change	3

Table 2 Advantages of blockchain technology in supply chain management context

Advantages of BCT in SCM context	Authors	Explanation
Transparency and traceability	Treiblmaier 2018; Leng et al. 2018; Mao et al. 2018; Min 2019; Fu and Zhu 2019; Juma et al. 2019; Kamble et al. 2019; Saberi et al. 2019; Montecchi et al. 2019; Wang et al. 2019a; Queiroz and Fosso Wamba 2019; Cole et al. 2019; Hald and Kinra 2019; Chang et al. 2019; Rejeb et al. 2019; O'Leary 2019; Azzi et al. 2019; Cui et al. 2019; Gurtu and Johny 2019; Wang et al. 2019b; Kamilaris et al. 2019; Schmidt and Wagner 2019; van Hoek 2019; Chang et al. 2020; Gonczol et al. 2020; Cha et al. 2020; Bai and Sarkis 2020; van Hoek 2020a; van Hoek 2020b; Durach et al. 2020; Öztürk and Yildizbaşi 2020; Sternberg et al. 2020; Choi 2020; Howson 2020; Rogerson and Parry 2020; Behnke and Janssen 2020; Di Vaio and Varriale 2020; Kamble et al. 2020; Liu and Li 2020; Tönnissen and Teuteberg 2020; Ghode et al. 2020b; Nandi et al. 2020; Casino et al. 2020; Kayikci et al. 2020; Wang et al. 2020a, b, c; Köhler and Pizzol 2020; De Giovanni 2020; Duan et al. 2020; Fosso Wamba et al. 2020a; Kopyto et al. 2020; Fosso Wamba et al. 2020b; Dutta et al. 2020; Wan et al. 2020; Shoaib et al. 2020; Xue et al. 2020; Sunny et al. 2020; Stranieri et al. 2021; Musamih et al. 2021; Lim et al. 2021; Ahmad et al. 2021; Kayikci et al. 2021; Menon and Jain 2021; Li et al. 2021a; Li et al. 2021b; Centobelli et al. 2021; Reddy et al. 2021; Yang et al. 2021	BCT transparency is increasing the visibility (Min 2019), thus enabling actions like tracing, recording and tracking (Kamble et al. 2019)
Cost reduction	Perboli et al. 2018; Kshetri 2018; Min 2019; Fu and Zhu 2019; Cui et al. 2019; Gurtu and Johny 2019; Montecchi et al. 2019; Queiroz et al. 2019; Fosso Wamba et al. 2020a; Wang et al. 2019b; Cole et al. 2019; Chang et al. 2019; Azzi et al. 2019; van Hoek 2019; Schmidt and Wagner 2019;	Performance outcomes result in cost reduction (Nandi et al. 2020), as well as smart contracts, which reduce costs due to their ability to execute themselves (Min 2019)

Advantages of BCT in SCM context	**Authors**	**Explanation**
	Chang et al. 2020; Yadav and Singh 2020; Gonczol et al. 2020; Öztürk and Yildizbaşi 2020; Sternberg et al.2020; Ghode et al. 2020a; Kamble et al. 2020; Nandi et al. 2020; Wang et al. 2020a, b, c; Yadav et al. 2020; De Giovanni 2020; Lohmer et al. 2020; Esmaeilian et al. 2020; Kopyto et al. 2020; Qian and Papadonikolaki 2020; Valle and Oliver 2020; Ada et al. 2021; Li et al. 2021a; Centobelli et al. 2021	
Supply chain actors' trust improvement	Min 2019; Cole et al. 2019; Hald and Kinra 2019; Rejeb et al. 2019; Schmidt and Wagner 2019; Sheel and Nath 2019; Wang et al. 2019a; Gonczol et al. 2020; Bai and Sarkis 2020; Durach et al. 2020; Ghode et al. 2020a; Di Vaio and Varriale 2020; Liu and Li 2020; Tönnissen and Teuteberg 2020; Casino et al. 2020; Kayikci et al. 2020; Wang et al. 2020a, b, c; Köhler and Pizzol 2020; De Giovanni 2020; Lohmer et al. 2020; Duan et al. 2020; Fosso Wamba et al. 2020a; Shoaib et al. 2020; Xue et al. 2020; Agrawal et al. 2021; Liu et al. 2021; Rejeb et al. 2021; Qian and Papadonikolaki 2020; Ada et al. 2021; Al-Rakhami and Al-Mashari 2021; Centobelli et al. 2021; Rana et al. 2021; Sivula et al. 2021	BCT improves trust among networked partners in supply chain (Rejeb et al. 2019) and creates an environment that does not require personal trust between the involved parties (Schmidt and Wagner 2019)
Data security	Kim and Laskowski 2018; Treiblmaier 2018; Mao et al. 2018; Leng et al. 2018; Juma et al. 2019; Wang et al. 2019a, b; Hald and Kinra 2019; Rejeb et al. 2019; Queiroz et al. 2019; Gurtu and Johny 2019; Cui et al. 2019; Bai and Sarkis 2020; Durach et al. 2020; Li et al. 2020; Howson 2020; Kamble et al. 2020; Nandi et al. 2020; Casino et al. 2020; Kayikci et al. 2020; Pournader et al. 2020; Fosso Wamba et al. 2020a; Kopyto et al. 2020; Dutta et al. 2020; Wan et al. 2020; Shoaib et al. 2020; Sunny et al. 2020; Li et al. 2021a; Musamih et al. 2021; Mukherjee et al. 2021; Wang et al. 2021	BCT provides a security guarantee mechanism (Leng et al. 2018) and data security for information sharing purposes (Wang et al. 2019a)

Advantages of BCT in SCM context	Authors	Explanation
Data visibility	Perboli et al. 2018; Mao et al. 2018; Min 2019; Kamble et al. 2019; Montecchi et al. 2019; Wang et al. 2019a, b; Cole et al. 2019; Queiroz et al. 2019; Hald and Kinra 2019; Azzi et al. 2019; van Hoek 2019; van Hoek 2020a; Chang et al.2020; Hackius and Petersen 2020; Durach et al. 2020; Rogerson and Parry 2020; Di Vaio and Varriale 2020; Tönnissen and Teuteberg 2020; Kayikci et al. 2020; Wang et al. 2020a, b, c; Yadav et al. 2020; Lohmer et al. 2020; Esmaeilian et al. 2020; Duan et al. 2020; Wan et al. 2020; Xue et al. 2020; Stranieri et al. 2021; Agrawal et al. 2021; Reddy et al. 2021	Data in BCT-based supply chain is visible to all stakeholders (Yadav et al. 2020), visibility increases because of real-time sharing data access in the network (Lohmer et al. 2020)
Product safety assurance	Perboli et al. 2018; Kshetri 2018; Juma et al. 2019; Kamble et al. 2019; Saberi et al. 2019; Montecchi et al. 2019; Cole et al. 2019; Azzi et al. 2019; Kamilaris et al. 2019; Mattke et al. 2019; Chang et al. 2020; Bai and Sarkis 2020; van Hoek 2020b; Durach et al. 2020; Rogerson and Parry 2020; Behnke and Janssen 2020; Kamble et al. 2020; Liu and Li 2020; Ghode et al. 2020b; Nandi et al. 2020; Casino et al. 2020; Fan et al. 2020; Kayikci et al. 2020; Köhler and Pizzol 2020; Duan et al. 2020; Kouhizadeh et al. 2021; Kramer et al. 2021; Agrawal et al. 2021; Li et al. 2021a; Yang et al. 2021	BCT enhances product safety by providing records of safety conditions (Cole et al. 2019), strengthens food safety assurance (Azzi et al. 2019), and helps to control more efficiently food-caused contaminations (Köhler and Pizzol 2020)
Efficiency improvement	Leng et al. 2018; Cole et al. 2019; Chang et al. 2019; Rejeb et al. 2019; van Hoek 2019; Cui et al. 2019; Gonczol et al. 2020; Durach et al. 2020; Sternberg et al. 2020; Choi 2020; Di Vaio and Varriale 2020; Tönnissen and Teuteberg 2020; Nandi et al. 2020; Köhler and Pizzol 2020; Esmaeilian et al. 2020; Duan et al. 2020; Fosso Wamba et al. 2020a; Kopyto et al. 2020; Dutta et al. 2020; Hastig and Sodhi 2020; Wan et al. 2020; Shoaib et al. 2020; Ada et al. 2021; Chen et al. 2021; Kayikci et	BCT boosts operational efficiency (Sternberg et al. 2020), as well as the overall efficiency of the system (Leng et al. 2018)

Advantages of BCT in SCM context	Authors	Explanation
	al. 2021; Li et al. 2021a; Lim et al. 2021; Centobelli et al. 2021; Park and Li 2021; Rana et al. 2021	
Information authenticity	Perboli et al. 2018; Mao et al. 2018; Leng et al. 2018; Juma et al. 2019; Saberi et al. 2019; Montecchi et al. 2019; Cole et al. 2019; O'Leary 2019; Azzi et al. 2019; Schmidt and Wagner 2019; Mattke et al. 2019; Cui et al. 2019; Cha et al. 2020; Durach et al. 2020; Li et al. 2020; Wong et al. 2020a; Choi 2020; Rogerson and Parry 2020; Di Vaio and Varriale 2020; Liu and Li 2020; Wong et al. 2020b; Ghode et al. 2020b; Nandi et al. 2020; Köhler and Pizzol 2020; Duan et al. 2020; Shoaib et al. 2020; Ahmad et al. 2021; Li et al. 2021a; Stranieri et al. 2021	BCT improves the information flow (Ghode et al. 2020b) and provides access to verified information and data (Perboli et al. 2018)
Intermediary elimination	Perboli et al. 2018; Montecchi et al. 2019; Wang et al. 2019b; Queiroz and Fosso Wamba 2019; Cole et al. 2019; Gurtu and Johny 2019; Hald and Kinra 2019; Gonczol et al. 2020; Durach et al. 2020; Öztürk and Yildizbaşi 2020; Li et al. 2020; Choi 2020; Howson 2020; Behnke and Janssen 2020; Casino et al. 2020; Yadav et al. 2020; De Giovanni 2020; Esmaeilian et al. 2020; Duan et al. 2020; Pournader et al. 2020; Dutta et al. 2020; Li et al. 2021b; Centobelli et al. 2021; Rana et al. 2021; Saurabh and Dey 2021	There is no need of a trusted authority when using BCT (Dutta et al. 2020) who would verify transaction attributes (Esmaeilian et al. 2020)
End consumers' trust improvement	Perboli et al. 2018; Fu and Zhu 2019; Kamble et al. 2019; Montecchiet al. 2019; Queiroz and Fosso Wamba 2019; Azzi et al. 2019; Kamilaris et al. 2019; van Hoek 2019; Gonczol et al. 2020; Bai and Sarkis 2020; Fan et al. 2020; Sternberg et al. 2020; Ghode et al. 2020a; Rogerson and Parry 2020; Casino et al. 2020; Köhler and Pizzol 2020; Fosso Wamba et al. 2020a; Shoaib et al. 2020; Xue et al.2020; Stranieri et al. 2021; Agrawal et al. 2021; Cao et al. 2021;	BCT adoption in SC processes can boost the trust of a customer (Ghode et al. 2020a), consequently this results in extra sales and helps to find the best customer (Shoaib et al. 2020)

Advantages of BCT in SCM context	Authors	Explanation
	Kayikci et al. 2021	
Transactions automation (smart contracts)	Cole et al. 2019; Hald and Kinra 2019; Chang et al. 2020; Kamilaris et al. 2019; Schmidt and Wagner 2019; Queiroz et al. 2019; Bai and Sarkis 2020; Durach et al. 2020; Li et al. 2020; Kamble et al. 2020; Tönnissen and Teuteberg 2020; Nandi et al. 2020; Wang et al. 2020a, b, c; Pournader et al. 2020; Kopyto et al. 2020; Shoaib et al. 2020;Bekrar et al. 2021;Büyüközkan et al. 2021; Li et al. 2021a; Lim et al. 2021; Lou et al. 2021; Rana et al. 2021	Smart contracts automatically execute payments once the contract terms and conditions are met (Wang et al. 2020a, b, c), enabling thus automatic trading of data between different SC network participants (Li et al. 2020)
"Single version of truth" access	Fu and Zhu 2019; Kamble et al. 2019; Cole et al. 2019; Rejeb et al. 2019; Chang et al. 2020; Azzi et al. 2019; Gurtu and Johny 2019; Yadav and Singh 2020; Hackius and Petersen 2020; van Hoek 2020b; Öztürk and Yildizbaşi 2020; Di Vaio and Varriale 2020; Ghode et al. 2020b; Nandi et al. 2020; Köhler and Pizzol 2020; Lohmer et al. 2020; Pournader et al. 2020; Fosso Wamba et al. 2020a, b; Kopyto et al. 2020; Wong et al. 2020b; Mukherjee et al. 2021	BCT retains permanent and tamperproof records of data and transactions (Schmidt and Wagner 2019), which guarantees a single truth access to various SC participants (Gonczol et al. 2020)
Supply chain speed improvement	Fu and Zhu 2019; Kamble et al. 2019; Cole et al. 2019; Rejeb et al. 2019; Chang et al. 2020; Azzi et al. 2019; Gurtu and Johny 2019; Yadav and Singh 2020; Hackius and Petersen 2020; van Hoek 2020b; Öztürk and Yildizbaşi 2020; Di Vaio and Varriale 2020; Ghode et al. 2020b; Nandi et al. 2020; Köhler and Pizzol 2020; Lohmer et al. 2020; Pournader et al. 2020; Fosso Wamba et al. 2020a; Kopyto et al. 2020; Ada et al. 2021; Li et al. 2021a	BCT use speeds up international shipment and documentation processing (van Hoek 2020b), as well as enables to respond to SC anomalies more rapidly (Rejeb et al. 2019)
Data immutability	Perboli et al. 2018; Kim and Laskowski 2018; Treiblmaier 2018; Min 2019; Juma et al. 2019; Queiroz and Fosso Wamba 2019; Hald and	The nature of BCT transactional data is immutable (Behnke and Janssen 2020), meaning that data is resistant to any modification

Advantages of BCT in SCM context	Authors	Explanation
	Kinra 2019; Chang et al. 2020; Kamilaris et al. 2019; Schmidt and Wagner 2019; Yadav and Singh 2020; Cha et al. 2020; Bai and Sarkis 2020; Behnke and Janssen 2020; Kamble et al. 2020; Fosso Wamba et al. 2020a; Dutta et al. 2020; Shoaib et al. 2020; Lou et al. 2021; Menon and Jain 2021; Rana et al. 2021	(Casino et al. 2019)
New value propositions	Perboli et al. 2018; Cole et al. 2019; Hald and Kinra 2019; Sheel and Nath 2019; Hackius and Petersen 2020; Sternberg et al. 2020; Ghode et al. 2020a; Howson 2020; Di Vaio and Varriale 2020; Ghode et al. 2020b; Queiroz et al. 2020; De Giovanni 2020; Esmaeilian et al. 2020; Fosso Wamba et al. 2020a; Dutta et al. 2020; Xue et al. 2020; Wang et al. 2020a, b, c; Karuppiah et al. 2021; Hong and Hales 2021; Stranieri et al. 2021; Sivula et al. 2021	BCT brings opportunities for new value propositions to the market (Hald and Kinra 2019) for instance in terms of facilitating conditions and social influence (Queiroz et al. 2020), including competitive advantage and better firm performance (Sheel and Nath 2019)
Transaction reliability	Mao et al. 2018; Leng et al. 2018; Saberi et al. 2019; Queiroz and Fosso Wamba 2019; Cole et al. 2019; Rejeb et al. 2019; Queiroz et al. 2019; Kamilaris et al. 2019; Schmidt and Wagner 2019; Mattke et al. 2019; Gonczol et al. 2020; Durach et al. 2020; Li et al. 2020; Wong et al. 2020a; Ghode et al. 2020b; Casino et al. 2020; Wang et al. 2020a, b, c; Duan et al. 2020; Fosso Wamba et al. 2020a	BCT is a reliable platform to collect data about transactions (Mao et al. 2018), which ensures fast and secure transactions without traditional authorities services (Casino et al. 2020)
Sustainability verification	Kshetri 2018; Saberi et al. 2019; Kamilaris et al. 2019; van Hoek 2019; Gurtu and Johny 2019; Gonczol et al. 2020; Bai and Sarkis 2020; Öztürk and Yildizbaşi 2020; Howson 2020; Rogerson and Parry 2020; Köhler and Pizzol 2020; Esmaeilian et al. 2020; Hastig and Sodhi 2020; Shoaib et al. 2020; Venkatesh et al. 2020; Wang et al. 2020a; Kouhizadeh et al. 2021; Centobelli et al. 2021	BCT links energy and water consumption information, which final consumer can then scan through barcode and see the environmental impact (van Hoek 2019), thus enabling a positive impact on environmentally and socially sustainable SCs (Rogerson and Parry 2020)
Fraud detection	Min 2019; Saberi et al. 2019; Azzi et	BCT adoption reduces fraudulent

Advantages of BCT in SCM context	Authors	Explanation
	al. 2019; Gurtu and Johny 2019; Gonczol et al. 2020; Öztürk and Yildizbaşi 2020; Rogerson and Parry 2020; Kamble et al. 2020; Wong et al. 2020a; Ghode et al. 2020b; Nandi et al. 2020; Köhler and Pizzol 2020; Fosso Wamba et al. 2020a; Wan et al. 2020; Balamurugan et al. 2021; Calvão and Archer 2021; Chen et al. 2021; Tezel et al. 2021	activities (Kamble et al. 2020), because any malicious attempt to change the information will be visible (Wan et al. 2020)
Risk reduction	Kshetri 2018; Min 2019; Fu and Zhu 2019; Montecchi et al. 2019; Hald and Kinra 2019; Gurtu and Johny 2019; Hackius and Petersen 2020; Choi 2020; Kamble et al. 2020; Kayikci et al. 2020; De Giovanni 2020; Duan et al. 2020; Dutta et al. 2020; Ada et al. 2021	BCT fully removes the risk in purchasing, services and transactions (De Giovanni 2020) and overall lowers the level of operational risk (Choi 2020)
Provenance assurance	Kim and Laskowski 2018; Montecchi et al. 2019; Gurtu and Johny 2019; Sternberg et al. 2020; Rogerson and Parry 2020; Kamble et al. 2020; Wang et al. 2020a, b, c; Dutta et al. 2020; Menon and Jain 2021; Musamih et al. 2021; Yiu 2021a; Kramer et al. 2021; Yiu 2021b	BCT's provenance feature allows SCs to make products more transparent (Gurtu and Johny 2019), enabling interorganizational provenance (Sternberg et al. 2020)
Counterfeit reduction	Perboli et al. 2018; Min 2019; Juma et al. 2019; Cole et al. 2019; Mattke et al. 2019; Cui et al. 2019; Gonczol et al. 2020; Rogerson and Parry 2020; Liu and Li 2020; Musamih et al. 2021; Yiu 2021a, b	BCT prevents the trade of fake or counterfeit assets (Min 2019) and protects SC from counterfeit products (Cui et al. 2019)
Supply chain collaboration improvement	Mao et al. 2018; Sternberg et al. 2020; Ghode et al. 2020b; Kayikci et al. 2020; Lohmer et al. 2020; Xue et al. 2020; Wang et al. 2020a, b, c; Hastig and Sodhi 2020; Musamih et al. 2021; Liu et al. 2021; Rejeb et al. 2021; Stranieri et al. 2021	BCT-based supply chains facilitate better collaboration among stakeholders (Mao et al. 2018), enhance trustful relationships and develop deeper cooperation (Xue et al. 2020)
Decentralized structure	Kshetri 2018; Leng et al. 2018; O'Leary 2019; Di Vaio and Varriale 2020; Kamble et al. 2020; Yadav et al. 2020; Duan et al. 2020; Fosso Wamba et al. 2020a; Kopyto et al. 2020; Wan et al. 2020; Falcone et	BCT's decentralized structure (Kshetri 2018) can help eliminating information inequality (Duan et al. 2020)

Advantages of BCT in SCM context	Authors	Explanation
	al. 2021	
Supply chain performance improvement	Hald and Kinra 2019; Chang et al. 2019; Sheel and Nath 2019; Ghode et al. 2020a; Choi 2020; Kayikci et al. 2020; Aslam et al. 2021; Kayikci et al. 2021; Li et al. 2021a; Centobelli et al. 2021	BCT distibuted system is expected to result in better performance throughout SC (Chang et al. 2019), getting rid off service fees can also potentially improve SC performance (Choi 2020)
Real-time auditing	Cole et al. 2019; Rejeb et al. 2019; Chang et al. 2020; Di Vaio and Varriale 2020; Kamble et al. 2020; Liu and Li 2020; Köhler and Pizzol 2020; Menon and Jain 2021; Rejeb et al. 2021	BCT-based supply chains enables audit of the transaction processes in time (Liu and Li 2020) and provides real time auditing via time-stamping (Cole et al. 2019)
Human error reduction	Perboli et al. 2018; Min 2019; Saberi et al. 2019; Wang et al. 2019b; Azzi et al. 2019; Bai and Sarkis 2020; Öztürk and Yildizbaşi 2020; Hastig and Sodhi 2020; Liu et al. 2021	BCT reduces the chances of human-caused errors (Perboli et al. 2018) that are hindering current operations (Öztürk and Yildizbaşi 2020)
Possible integration with other technologies	Rejeb et al. 2019; Gonczol et al. 2020; van Hoek 2020b; Kayikci et al. 2020; Duan et al. 2020; Pournader et al. 2020; Ada et al. 2021;Varriale et al. 2021	BCT pilot can be based on data feeds from other technologies (van Hoek 2020b), for instance combined with IoT devices (Duan et al. 2020)
Cyber security measures	Min 2019; Wang et al. 2019b; Gurtu and Johny 2019; Yadav and Singh 2020; Cha et al. 2020; Duan et al. 2020; Alkahtani et al. 2021	BCT-provided data security feature could protect SCs from cybercrimes and attacks (Wang et al. 2019b), such SCs are not feasible for data change or hacking (Yadav and Singh 2020)
Processes automation	Chang et al. 2019; Gurtu and Johny 2019; Öztürk and Yildizbaşi 2020; Tönnissen and Teuteberg 2020; Nandi et al. 2020; Kayikci et al. 2020; Tezel et al. 2021	Automated controls of processes are expected to disrupt existing SC ecosystem (Gurtu and Johny 2019) and increase the scope for SC process automation using smart contracts (Nandi et al. 2020)
Inventory reduction	Kamble et al. 2019; Cole et al. 2019; van Hoek 2019; Sternberg et al. 2020; Ada et al. 2021; Balamurugan et al. 2021; Kayikci et al. 2021	BCT adoption in SC is able to improve inventory management (Cole et al. 2019) and reduce inventory levels (Sternberg et al. 2020)
Paperwork	Wang et al. 2019b; Azzi et al. 2019;	BCT reduces paperwork and

Advantages of BCT in SCM context	Authors	Explanation
reduction	Gonczol et al. 2020; van Hoek 2020b; Centobelli et al. 2021; Sundarakani et al. 2021	administrative costs throughout SC (Azzi et al. 2019), as well as speeds up custom documentation for the shipment (van Hoek 2020b)
Bullwhip effect reduction	Perboli et al. 2018; Fu and Zhu 2019; Ghode et al. 2020a; Chen et al. 2021	The bullwhip effect can be minimized in BCT-based supply chains (Fu and Zhu 2019; Ghode et al. 2020a)
Planning optimization	Perboli et al. 2018; van Hoek 2020b; Esmaeilian et al. 2020; Büyüközkan et al. 2021	BCT-adopted supply chains support efficient operations planning (Esmaeilian et al. 2020), like shipment planning for instance, could begin earlier (van Hoek 2020b)
Vulnerabilities detection	Azzi et al. 2019; Köhler and Pizzol 2020; Stranieri et al. 2021	BCT gives insights into all the system's vulnerabilities (Azzi et al. 2019) and discover firm weaknesses (Stranieri et al. 2021)
Forecast improvement	Perboli et al. 2018; Kamble et al. 2019	BCT helps the organizations to build and improve accurate demand forecasts (Perboli et al. 2018; Kamble et al. 2019)

Table 3 Disadvantages of blockchain technology in supply chain management context

Disadvantages of BCT in SCM context	Authors	Explanation
Information privacy concerns	Perboli et al. 2018; Kamble et al. 2019; Montecchi et al. 2019; Wang et al. 2019a; Hald and Kinra 2019; Chang et al. 2019; Schmidt and Wagner 2019; van Hoek 2019; Wang et al. 2019b; Gonczol et al. 2020; Öztürk and Yildizbaşi 2020; Sternberg et al. 2020; Ghode et al. 2020a; Rogerson and Parry 2020; Behnke and Janssen 2020; Liu and Li 2020; Ghode et al. 2020b; Yadav et al. 2020; Esmaeilian et al. 2020;	On the interorganizational level, some organisations may assume open-access information as a competitive advantage, that is unwilling to be shared across SC (Kouhizadeh et al. 2021), thus information security is considered by practitioners as a potentil barrier for the BCT implementation in SC (Kopyto et al. 2020)

Disadvantages of BCT in SCM context	Authors	Explanation
	Kopyto et al. 2020; Fosso Wamba et al. 2020b; Dutta et al. 2020; Wan et al.2020; Kouhizadeh et al. 2021; Agrawal et al. 2021; Li et al. 2021a; Centobelli et al. 2021; Xu et al. 2021; Yiu 2021a	
Scalability	Perboli et al. 2018; Mao et al. 2018; Min 2019; Juma et al. 2019; Chang et al. 2020; Azzi et al. 2019; Schmidt and Wagner 2019; van Hoek 2019; Gonczol et al. 2020; Cha et al. 2020; Öztürk and Yildizbaşi 2020; Li et al. 2020; Rogerson and Parry 2020; Behnke and Janssen 2020; Casino et al. 2020; Köhler and Pizzol 2020; Yadav et al. 2020; De Giovanni 2020; Esmaeilian et al. 2020; Duan et al. 2020; Pournader et al. 2020; Dutta et al. 2020; Chen et al. 2021; Musamih et al. 2021; Reddy et al. 2021; Yiu 2021a	Each node on the BCT network needs to store the entire history of transactions, so the growing size then becomes an issue (Mao et al. 2018), and there is a limited capacity in handling a large amount of data (Azzi et al. 2019)
Low awareness and knowledge of technology	Treiblmaier 2018; Min 2019; Kamble et al. 2019; Wang et al. 2019a; van Hoek 2019; Montecchi et al. 2019; van Hoek 2020a; Chang et al. 2020; Gonczol et al. 2020; Hackius and Petersen 2020; Bai and Sarkis 2020; Fan et al. 2020; Öztürk and Yildizbaşi 2020; Wong et al. 2020b; Rogerson and Parry 2020; Köhler and Pizzol 2020; Duan et al. 2020; Fosso Wamba et al. 2020a; Wan et al. 2020; Büyüközkan et al. 2021; Chen et al. 2021; Stranieri et al. 2021; Katsikouli et al. 2021; Karuppiah et al. 2021; Li et al. 2021b; Reddy et al. 2021	BCT still does not represent a single monolithic artifact and is constantly being developed (Treiblmaier 2018), so there is still skepticism among practitioners due to low awareness about technology (Wong et al. 2020b)
High implementation cost	Perboli et al. 2018; Kamble et al. 2019; Cole et al. 2019; Schmidt and Wagner 2019; Wang et al. 2019a; Öztürk and Yildizbaşi 2020; Sternberg et al. 2020; Ghode et al. 2020a; Choi 2020; Howson 2020; Rogerson	BCT platforms is expensive, especially for small-scale companies (Howson 2020) so the adoption of it may not pay off (Cole et al. 2019)

Disadvantages of BCT in SCM context	Authors	Explanation
	and Parry 2020; Wong et al. 2020a; Kayikci et al. 2020; De Giovanni 2020; Dutta et al. 2020; Wan et al. 2020; Chen et al. 2021; Musamih et al. 2021; Kshetri 2021; Li et al. 2021a; Lim et al. 2021; Stranieri et al. 2021	
Low quality data input	Wang et al. 2019b; Chang et al. 2019; Rejeb et al. 2019; Azzi et al. 2019; Schmidt and Wagner 2019; Cha et al. 2020; Sternberg et al. 2020; Ghode et al. 2020a; Howson 2020; Rogerson and Parry 2020; Behnke and Janssen 2020; Ghode et al. 2020b; Köhler and Pizzol 2020; Esmaeilian et al. 2020; Duan et al. 2020; Pournader et al. 2020; Kopyto et al. 2020; Dutta et al. 2020; Fosso Wamba et al. 2020b; Chen et al. 2021; Stranieri et al. 2021	Information stored in BCT network is only as accurate as the incoming raw data (Wang et al. 2019b), since data cannot be further changed after it entered, there is a chance of a poor quality data (Köhler and Pizzol 2020)
Data manipulation / security concerns	Kamilaris et al. 2019; Cui et al. 2019; Behnke and Janssen 2020; Liu and Li 2020; Ghode et al. 2020b; Yadav et al. 2020; Esmaeilian et al. 2020; Wang et al. 2019a; Kopyto et al. 2020; Musamih et al. 2021; Yiu 2021a; Agrawal et al. 2021; Karuppiah et al. 2021; Yiu 2021b	Security problem is emergent for open access BCT networks (Liu and Li 2020), even though it offers advanced security, there are still high risks of funds losses (Kamilaris et al. 2019)
Lack of physical traceability	Kamilaris et al. 2019; Chang et al. 2020; Yadav and Singh 2020; Howson 2020; Köhler and Pizzol 2020; Esmaeilian et al. 2020; Kopyto et al. 2020; Rao et al. 2021; Stranieri et al. 2021; Yiu 2021b	There is no certainty if the link between digital records and physical goods is verdically established (Esmaeilian et al. 2020), thus it makes confusion about real quality conditions of physical products (Stranieri et al. 2021)
High energy consumption	Öztürk and Yildizbaşi 2020; Kamble et al. 2020; Yadav et al. 2020; Esmaeilian et al. 2020; Kopyto et al. 2020; Musamih et al. 2021; Lim et al. 2021; Kramer et al. 2021	BCT consumes excessive energy (Öztürk and Yildizbaşi 2020) due to high number of network participants (Kopyto et al. 2020)
Lack of Blockchain	van Hoek 2020a; van Hoek 2020b; Ghode et al. 2020b; De	Low cost products may not have a need in traceability if value of it is

Disadvantages of BCT in SCM context	Authors	Explanation
suitability in some product/context	Giovanni 2020; Shoaib et al. 2020; Kshetri 2021; Menon and Jain 2021	not justified for such high-cost technology (van Hoek 2020a), so it might not be a right technology for any SC context (van Hoek 2020b)
Lack of central authority / coordination – 6	Wang et al. 2019b; Kamilaris et al. 2019; Cha et al. 2020; Fan et al. 2020; Wang et al. 2020a, b, c; Karuppiah et al. 2021	Lack of central authority might be missing for resolving potential disputes (Wang et al. 2019b), especially for private chains (Cha et al. 2020)
Difficulties in smart contract adoption	Cole et al. 2019; Hald and Kinra 2019; Esmaeilian et al. 2020; Kopyto et al. 2020; Menon and Jain 2021	Poor smart contact coding may lead to problems (Cole et al. 2019) and difficulties in their further modification (Hald and Kinra 2019)
ROI concerns	Wang et al. 2019b; Cole et al. 2019; van Hoek 2019; van Hoek 2020a	The progress of such a disruptive technology as BCT might be slow due to low level of knowledge, thus resulting in a lack of visible financial benefits (Wang et al. 2019b). The costs and the ROI of BCT implementation to SC are still obscure (van Hoek 2019)

Table 4 Constraints of blockchain technology in supply chain management context

Constraints of BCT in SCM context	Authors	Explanation
Early stage of Blockchain adoption in practice	Fu and Zhu 2019; Saberi et al. 2019; Wang et al. 2019b; van Hoek 2020a; Schmidt and Wagner 2019; Gonczol et al. 2020; Hackius and Petersen 2020; Bai and Sarkis 2020; van Hoek 2020b; Öztürk and Yildizbaşi 2020; Ghode et al. 2020a; Wong et al. 2020b; Kamble et al. 2020; Fosso Wamba and Queiroz 2020b; Kayikci et al. 2020; Köhler and Pizzol 2020; Fosso Wamba et al. 2020b; Xue et al. 2020; Büyüközkan et al. 2021; Chen et al. 2021; Collart and Canales 2021; Liu et al. 2021; Reddy	BCT is still at the stage of testing and analysis, and does not yet have examples of large-scale application in practice (Fu and Zhu 2019), therefore implemention in such an early stage brings potential risks for organizations (Schmidt and Wagner 2019)

Constraints of BCT in SCM context	Authors	Explanation
	et al. 2021; Teodorescu and Korchagina 2021	
Lack of organizational policies/legal regulations	Min 2019; Saberi et al. 2019; Chang et al. 2019; Chang et al. 2020; Gonczol et al. 2020; Hackius and Petersen 2020; Howson 2020; Rogerson and Parry 2020; Kamble et al. 2020; Ghode et al. 2020b; Fosso Wamba and Queiroz 2020b; Kayikci et al. 2020; Yadav et al. 2020; Esmaeilian et al. 2020; Wang et al. 2019a; Duan et al. 2020; Fosso Wamba et al. 2020a; Dutta et al. 2020; Musamih et al. 2021; Katsikouli et al. 2021; Wang et al. 2020a, b, c; Chen et al. 2021; Karuppiah et al. 2021; Li et al. 2021a	Lack of standards, legal issues and protocols (Chang et al. 2019) poses a problem in BCT recognition and its features in laws and regulations (Hackius and Petersen 2020)
Technology complexity	Min 2019; Kamble et al. 2019; Wang et al. 2019a; Wang et al. 2019b; Azzi et al. 2019; Hoek 2019; Gonczol et al. 2020; Öztürk and Yildizbaşi 2020; Sternberg et al. 2020; Wong et al. 2020a; Behnke and Janssen 2020; Kamble et al. 2020; Fosso Wamba and Queiroz 2020a; Wan et al. 2020; Tönnissen and Teuteberg 2020; Köhler and Pizzol 2020; Esmaeilian et al. 2020; Fosso Wamba et al. 2020a; Sunny et al. 2020; Wong et al. 2020b; Li et al. 2021a; Mathivathanan et al. 2021; Stranieri et al. 2021	Practitioners have a need in developing greater understanding of how to integrate BC into their SC processes (Hoek 2019), so this challenge is technical and native by its nature due to the current state of the BCT (Gonczol et al. 2020)
Supply chain participants' inertia	Perboli et al. 2018; Kshetri 2018; Juma et al. 2019; Montecchi et al. 2019; van Hoek 2019; Gonczol et al. 2020; Sternberg et al. 2020; Rogerson and Parry 2020; Behnke and Janssen 2020; Di Vaio and Varriale 2020; Liu and Li 2020; Köhler and Pizzol 2020; Wang et al. 2019a; Duan et al. 2020; Fosso Wamba et al. 2020a; Wan et	There could potentially arise an unwillingness to share valueable information across SC (Wang et al. 2019a) and without all SC entities participation the disclosure of BCT's fullpotential in SCM will not be possible (Kshetri 2018)

Constraints of BCT in SCM context	Authors	Explanation
	al. 2020; Kouhizadeh et al. 2021; Caldarelli et al. 2021; Kayikci et al. 2021; Sharma et al. 2021;Valle and Oliver 2020; Yang et al. 2021; Yiu 2021a	
Interoperability	Min 2019; Rejeb et al. 2019; O'Leary 2019; van Hoek 2020b; Öztürk and Yildizbaşi 2020; Howson 2020; Liu and Li 2020; Wong et al. 2020a; Kayikci et al. 2020; Wang et al. 2020a, b, c; Yadav et al. 2020; De Giovanni 2020; Dutta et al. 2020; Menon and Jain 2021; Musamih et al. 2021	It is still unclear how BCT and its systems will interoperate and integrate with other technologies (Rejeb et al. 2019), so the interface between BCT and existing enterprise systems is a very important issue (Liu and Li 2020)
Information reliability assurance	Montecchi et al. 2019; Chang et al. 2019; Azzi et al. 2019; Cui et al. 2019; Cha et al. 2020; Sternberg et al. 2020; Ghode et al. 2020a; Rogerson and Parry 2020; Kayikci et al. 2020; Esmaeilian et al. 2020; Duan et al. 2020; Kopytoet al. 2020; Fosso Wamba et al. 2020b	SC network participants need to make sure that data input is safe and reliable before storing it in an immutable ledger (Azzi et al. 2019), because historical data needs to be reliable, non-tempered, but also balancing between transparency and confidentiality issues (Ghode et al. 2020a)
Lack of infrastructure for Blockchain adoption	Kamble et al. 2019; Öztürk and Yildizbaşi 2020; Wong et al. 2020a; Behnke and Janssen 2020; Di Vaio and Varriale 2020; Wong et al. 2020b; Yadav et al. 2020; Queiroz et al. 2019; Kouhizadeh et al. 2021, Sivula et al. 2021	BCT sill lacks an organized ecosystem for starting its application to SC (Kamble et al. 2019), including the inadequacy of current existing technological infrastructure (Öztürk and Yildizbaşi 2020)
Lack of trust between supply chain actors	Chang et al. 2020; Sternberg et al. 2020; Wong et al. 2020b; Behnke and Janssen 2020; Liu and Li 2020; Ghode et al. 2020b; Yadav et al. 2020; Kopyto et al. 2020	The fact that actors may have different relationships with each other in different situations is complicating BCT adoption to SCs, e.g. the same entities can be competitors in the one market segment and customer–supplier in other (Behnke and Janssen 2020). Thus, trust issues among SC participants become a crucial issue to overcome in order

Constraints of BCT in SCM context	Authors	Explanation
		to implement the system (Liu and Li 2020)
Cultural differences of supply chain participants	Kshetri 2018; Öztürk and Yildizbaşi 2020; Liu and Li 2020; Wong et al. 2020a; Ghode et al. 2020b; Queiroz et al. 2020; Fosso Wamba et al. 2020a; Kayikci et al. 2021	Some SC participants may be located in developing or least developed countries, which obstructs their participation in BCT adoption (Kshetri 2018). Moreover, organizational culture may result in a different decision-making process when adopting BCT to SC (Wong et al. 2020a)
Standardization of processes	van Hoek 2019; Gonczol et al. 2020; Behnke and Janssen 2020; Hastig and Sodhi 2020; Sunny et al. 2020; Chen et al. 2021	The key boundary conditions is the standardization of traceability processes, quality compliance etc. among all SC parties involved within a given network (Gonczol et al. 2020), so standardization towards BCT platform adoption is required (Behnke and Janssen 2020)
Limited technology access	Saberi et al. 2019; Kamilaris et al. 2019; Howson 2020; Sunny et al. 2020; Wu et al. 2021; Vivaldini and de Sousa 2021	While BCT is able to connect complex global SCs, the information infrastructure required to operate might prevent access to markets for new users (Kamilaris et al. 2019), so technology access limitation is also an important issue to overcome in future (Saberi et al. 2019)

The three most reported advantages of BCT use in the SCM context (Table 2) are (1) transparency and traceability, (2) cost reduction, and (3) supply chain actors' trust improvement. This can be explained by the nature of the decentralized distributed ledger, that creates a trusted environment among SC players (Büyüközkan et al. 2021) and has beneficial outcomes in terms of enhancing the efficiency of SCs. The transparency afforded by BCT spreads to processes and products, thereby ensuring information authenticity (Bai and Sarkis 2020).

The three most mentioned disadvantages of BCT use in the SCM context (Table 3) are (1) information privacy concerns, (2) scalability, and (3) low awareness and knowledge of technology. Overall, these three disadvantages can be explained by the fact that this technology is still novel, and thus doubts and concerns remain regarding its application in the SCM context (Fosso Wamba et al. 2020b). Moreover, low awareness may arise not only from the side of SC partners, but also from the side of final consumers' low acquaintance with BCT features; consequently, this might be a critical factor of adoption renouncement (Fan et al. 2020).

Further, the three most mentioned constraints of BCT use in the SCM context (Table 4) are (1) the early stage of blockchain adoption in SCM practices, (2) lack of organizational policies/legal regulations, and (3) technology complexity. Overall, these constraints highlight the novelty of BCT and practical considerations in its application. Early-stage creating barriers in terms of implementation indicates that future research must be conducted to overcome them (Saberi et al. 2019).

Thus, there is a wide range of features reported in the literature related to the implementation of BCT in SCM. Their nature and areas of impact vary, and systematization is required to perceive the full extent of their interrelations. Consequently, these areas of impact are further analyzed to highlight the interrelated influence of the perceived advantages, disadvantages, and constraints.

The features of BCT can be considered from different perspectives, and as shown in Tables 2, 3 and 4, they are extremely varied and somewhat contradictory. Inspired by a study found in the extant literature, where BCT adoption was explored from the point of view of Malaysian small-medium enterprises (SMEs) under three dimensions: technological, organizational, and environmental (Wong et al. 2020a), we wanted to bring a general view on the adoption process and which benefits and challenges BCT can cause to SCs. Thus, we propose an attempt to group and systematize BCT features into the comprehensive dimensions of the impact of technology adoption under general SCM context, not attached to a specific context/sample group, in order to see in which areas and in what ways it can influence SC improvements and performances.

Novel digital technologies play a major role in managing information flow and processes for operations and SCs (Wong et al. 2020a), both scholars and practitioners are aiming to improve operations and processes of business practices with capabilities that disruptive technologies bring (Boutkhoum et al. 2021). When examining BCT from the SC perspective, its application in large-scale production is justified (Fu and Zhu 2019); it acts as a unified ledger for manufacturing and processes (Cole et al. 2019). Thus, it improves SC processes because there is no need for an intermediary (Öztürk and Yildizbaşi 2020). As a result, it optimizes and enhances operations and inbound efficiency (Perboli et al. 2018). Hence, the first dimension of impact is characterized as organic SCM activities; because it mostly relates to process efficiency and operations in the SCM context, the first dimension of impact is labeled as 'operations and processes'.

The main component of any SC is its entities/participants. BCT connects multiple stakeholders (Mao et al. 2018), reducing trust issues (Kamble et al. 2019) and potentially removing third-party actors with more power over prices and processes who can become manipulative (Wang et al. 2019a, b). Thus, BCT plays a role in collaborative behavior among stakeholders (Chang et al. 2019), improves the information flow between partners (Hackius and Petersen 2020), and provides authenticity and knowledge provenance to end consumers (Montecchi et al. 2019). As a disruptive technology, implementation of BCT requires commitment from upper management as well, to encourage team spirit in the adoption process and to help overcome related challenges (Zhou et al. 2020). It was recently revealed that social influence, or in the SC context a partnership experience, plays a substantial role when introducing novel systems (Alazab et al. 2021). Consequently, the second dimension of impact is aimed to shed light on those BCT features that impact relationships among organizations' representatives, and is called 'supply chain relationships'.

Considered as the 'latest transformative innovation' (Schmidt and Wagner 2019), characterized by innate features such as its immutability and distributed nature (Gonczol et al. 2020), BCT requires SC participants to be open-minded to innovative ideas (Min 2019). The inherent characteristics of BCT can enhance and optimize SC potential (Juma et al. 2019) while building an authentic and trustworthy ecosystem (Azzi et al. 2019) with a novel view on data access. One of the success factors for a blockchain-based SC is 'system strength', which encompasses the representative capabilities of BCT, including a trustless environment and network resistance to attacks (Shoaib et al. 2020). The need to examine innovation trends of BCT-based solutions for business networks was highlighted (Dehghani et al. 2020), expected to bring innovation in both aspects: technological and managerial (Dehghani et al. 2021). Overall, this highlights the need in the third dimension of impact, that would represent impact of the distinctive features of BCT itself: named as 'innovation and data access' dimension.

Above-mentioned dimensions are rather emerging naturally when addressing the impact of BCT in SCM practices, thus further translated into the dimensions, it brings clarity for the classification of specific BCT features. The logic behind defining these dimensions of impact is to represent them graphically as clusters and classify the characteristics from Tables 2, 3 and 4 within the formulated dimensions to determine the existence of interrelationships and the overlapping areas that arise between dimensions.

4.1 Advantages of blockchain technology when implemented in supply chains

Figure 2 represents the advantages classified within each of the three impact dimensions. For graphical representation purposes, a Venn diagram highlights the coexistence and overlap within these dimensions. It is relevant to understand, that overlapping areas represent features intrinsic to a mix of different dimensions; the overlapping areas are from now on going to be called "synergies".

Synergy #1, between 'operations and processes' and 'supply chain relationships', indicates advantages such as the reduction of human error, which is enabled by smart contracts features, that are characterized by self-verification and self-integrity, allowing elimination of previously trusted third parties (Deebak and Fadi 2021). It therefore potentially results in reduced errors in order fulfilment (Min 2019), process deployment (Saberi et al. 2019), and reduced paperwork errors (Wang et al. 2019a, b). Decentralized BCT-based networks also reduce risk in operations (Öztürk and Yildizbaşi 2020) in data manipulation coming from the administrative side in current centralized systems (Hewa et al. 2021). Cost reduction stems as well from the automation of transactions (Cole et al. 2019): automation simplifies SCs because intermediaries are no longer needed (Montecchi et al. 2019), which substantially reduces transaction costs (Yadav et al. 2020).

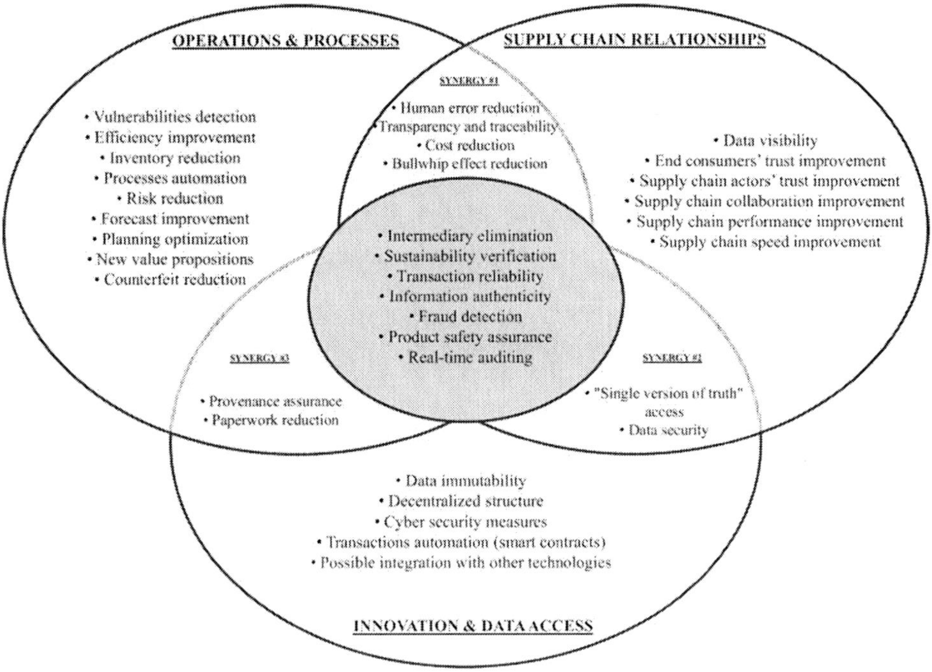

Fig. 2 *Venn diagram for advantages of blockchain technology implementation in supply chain management*

Synergy #2 relates to features that bring advantages from the perspectives of 'supply chain relationships' and 'innovation and data access' of BCT. The advantages are clearly discernible; BCT, as a digital transaction ledger (Kamilaris et al. 2019), can store everything within the SC's memory, and any actor can access it at any time (Hald and Kinra 2019), thus enabling 'timely information acquisition and sharing'(Wong et al. 2020b, p.2102). BCT also provides highly secure access to data (Kim and Laskowski 2018); thus, its immutable nature combined with cryptographic security leads to a new level of trust between actors (Treiblmaier 2018).

Synergy #3, which lies between 'operations and processes' and 'innovation and data access', is extremely interesting. The BCT-based flow of information reduces physical risks to individuals, preventing potential health harm to consumers, therefore protecting entities from failures through the availability of transparent records; it increases the knowledge provenance of a product (Montecchi et al. 2019), both to SC actors and end customers (Rogerson and Parry 2020). For instance, shipping processes reduce trade documentation (Wang et al. 2019a, b), enable customs documentation processing to commence earlier (van Hoek 2020b), and decrease paperwork in general (Gonczol et al. 2020).

This classification allows us to identify the key advantages of all three dimensions of impact. This centre area in the diagram cannot be considered to represent the 'main' advantages, but it does reveal the characteristics that are common to all three dimensions:

1. *Intermediary elimination:* There is no need to verify transactions through a third party (Pournader et al. 2020) or a trusted authority (Dutta et al. 2020).

2. *Sustainability verification:* BCT enables the visibility of water and energy consumption throughout the SC processes (van Hoek 2019), as, when applied to a fast-fashion industry (Wang et al. 2020a), thus helping achieve emergent sustainability goals (Bai and Sarkis 2020). BCT can also shed more light on social sustainability: it can bring transparency into working safety and conditions, preventing working exploitation practices and inequality (Venkatesh et al. 2020).

3. *Transaction reliability:* BCT assures transaction authenticity (Leng et al. 2018); being fully traceable, organisations can see the origins of transactions (Queiroz and Fosso Wamba 2019).

4. *Information authenticity:* This implies both the availability of verified information accessible to any entity part of the network (Nandi et al. 2020) and backward monitoring available to the end consumer (Casino et al. 2019).

5. *Fraud detection:* This refers to entity verification, given that the authenticity of each device is verified (Cui et al. 2019), which guarantees that each user is authorised (Duan et al. 2020) and enables the detection of potentially fraudulent activities within the network (Kshetri 2018).

6. *Product safety assurance:* This mainly emerged among food SCs, where the characteristics of food, its storage conditions, etc., can improve safety and avoid contamination (Kamilaris et al. 2019) by enabling the on time recall of products (Azzi et al. 2019). Safety assurance is also applicable for other types of SCs; BCT ensures the safety and quality of products for end consumers (Montecchi et al. 2019);

7. *Real-time auditing:* Owing to its decentralised nature (O'Leary 2019) and the automation of processes, BCT enables real-time auditing through time-stamping (Cole et al. 2019).

4.2 **Disadvantages of blockchain technology when implemented in supply chains**

Interestingly, the three dimensions of impact have some overlap in terms of advantages, disadvantages, and constraints. Figure 3 provides an illustrative example of how the same feature can be read an advantage or disadvantage, depending on the context.

At Synergy #1, between 'operations and processes' and 'supply chain relationships', security concerns and the data manipulation are noted as disadvantages. Data manipulation is mainly a characteristic of open access blockchain networks (Liu and Li 2020). It is demonstrated by examples of hacking attack incidents with some cryptocurrencies (Wang et al. 2019a), where a data miner could invade at one point of a BCT network to compromise original nodes to get a fraudulent high revenue (Karuppiah et al. 2021). Even in private blockchain networks, this is a potential issue in cases where, for example, the account owner accidentally loses the pair of private keys, thus losing access to the network and authorisation (Kamilaris et al. 2019), and in the case of such security breach, documents can potentially be tampered, resulting in disturbance of SC operations. However, the order placed in the network cannot be tampered (Ada et al. 2021); thus, even if BCT leaves opportunities for data manipulation or infringement, when compared with a centralized network, peer-to-peer BCT architecture it is still a more secure system (Büyüközkan et al. 2021).

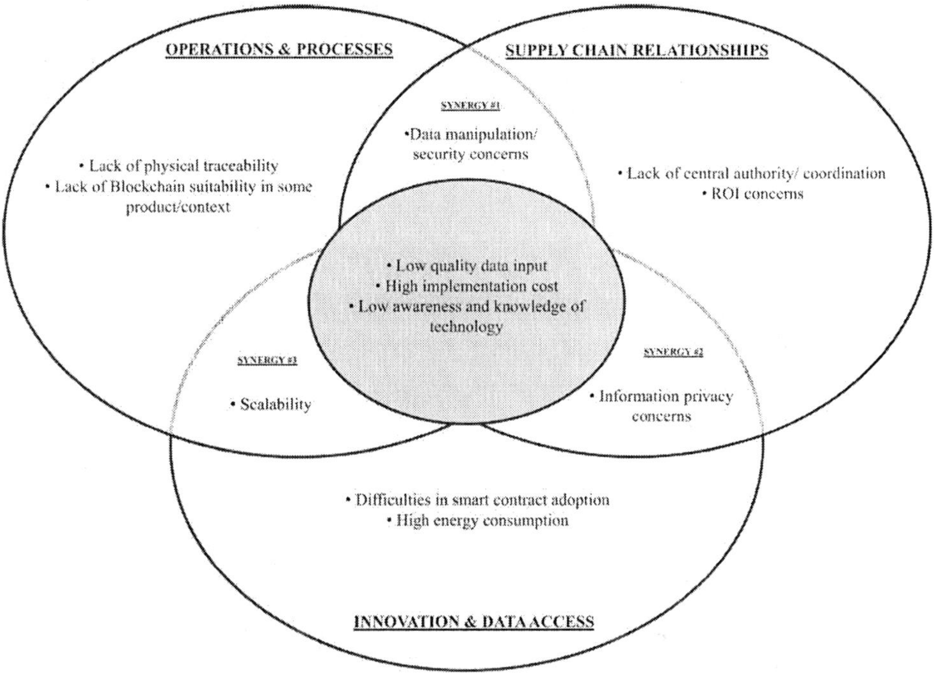

Fig. 3 *Venn diagram for disadvantages of blockchain technology implementation in supply chain management*

Synergy #2, between 'supply chain relationships' and 'innovation and data access', is a similar, albeit slightly different, disadvantage: information privacy concerns. Such concern is mainly explained by the unwillingness of stakeholders to share full information along the complex multi-tier SCs (Perboli et al. 2018). The perspective on BCT-enabled transparency is controversial upon different tiers of players, e.g. upper tiers have more motivation to keep its information confidential from lower tiers of SC (Öztürk and Yildizbaşi 2020). Thus, it is crucial for SC players to jointly define to what extent of detailed information network should go, in order to keep information transparency at justifiable level, and to prevent misuse of information (Behnke and Janssen 2020). This issue may as well occur when a stakeholder considers valuable information a competitive advantage and is unwilling to share it with other participants in the SC (Kouhizadeh et al. 2021).

Finally, Synergy #3, between 'innovation and data access' and 'operations and processes', relates to scalability issues, which depend on the novelty of the technology itself and the efficiency of operations. The scalability issue is explained by the fact that each blockchain node needs to contain the network's entire history (Mao et al. 2018), which limits the capacity to deal with big data and limits data storage (Cha et al. 2020).

One of the disadvantages in the centre, overlapping area relates to the high cost of implementing this technology, which seems to contradict a feature shown in Fig. 2: that BCT can reduce costs due to its innate qualities. Both of these arguments arise when an organisation considers implementing BCT- it has a high investment cost (Öztürk and Yildizbaşi 2020), and such platforms can be too expensive for small-scale stakeholders within the chain (Howson 2020). The other two central issues can be seen as a continuation of each other: low-quality data input means possible errors related to the incoming data to the platform (Stranieri et al. 2021), due to a lack of sufficient knowledge about technology and the concepts behind it (Öztürk and Yildizbaşi 2020), which are constantly being developed (Treiblmaier 2018).

4.3 Constraints of blockchain technology when implemented in supply chains

When assessing the constraints of BCT in the SC context, most constraints turned out to be organisation- and technology-related issues in terms of practice, which are shown in Fig. 4.

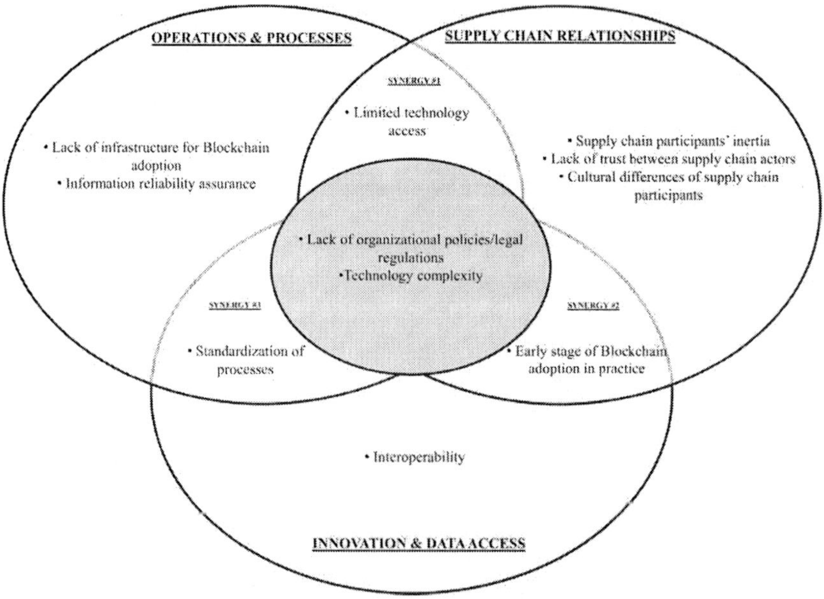

Fig. 4 Venn diagram for constraints of blockchain technology implementation in supply chain management

For example, Synergy #1 reveals limitations in accessing the technology (Saberi et al. 2019). Although BCT can connect complex international SCs, it can hinder or prevent new players and stakeholders from joining the system (Kamilaris et al. 2019).

Synergy #2 reveals another typical constraint for practitioners in the early stages of BCT adoption. While still in the testing and analysis stages (Fu and Zhu 2019), there is a limited understanding of how to adopt and roll it out effectively (van Hoek 2019), which creates uncertainty in the decision-making process (Ghode et al. 2020b), thereby creating organisational risk (Schmidt and Wagner 2019).

The standardisation of processes in Synergy#3 is also related to the early stages of technology adoption. It primarily concerns uncertainty regarding BCT integration into SC processes (van Hoek 2019), encompassing traceability, compliance, and quality requirements (Gonczol et al. 2020).

The constraint issues in the centre area regarding BCT implementation in the SC context may require considerable time to overcome because they are common to all three dimensions. There is still a lack of government regulatory processes (Min 2019), as well as a lack of legal standards and protocols (Chang et al. 2019), highlighting the need to develop new BCT-related governing policies (Ghode et al. 2020a). Another common difficulty is the complexity of the BCT. Non-technical experts lack sufficient knowledge (Gonczol et al. 2020) regarding the numerous new concepts that practitioners need to be aware of, such as smart contracts, cryptography, programming languages, and much more (Köhler and Pizzol 2020). Technical knowledge, therefore, needs to be addressed in the future (Kamble et al. 2019).

5 Discussion

There were three aims of this study: (1) to explore the dimensions of the impact of BCT implementation in SCM; (2) to explore the synergies of these dimensions; and (3) to explore the virtuous and vicious cycles of the adoption of BCT use in SCM. The study's findings reveal the most emergent and distinctive features of BCT in the SCM context, enabling us to visualise overlaps and interrelationships between the dimensions of impact schematically. The remainder of this section identifies the theoretical contributions, managerial implications, and areas for future research.

5.1 Theoretical contribution

The theoretical contribution of this study is twofold. First, our study proposes a systematisation of BCT features in the SCM context that have been analysed, formulated, and classified in a unified manner, in contrast to the wide dispersion of classifications in prior literature. One of the reviewed articles adopted a similar approach: an SLR where potential benefits and challenges related to BCT were identified and later generalised and grouped into 'high-value benefits/challenges' (Fosso Wamba et al. 2020a, b). The proposed systematisation in the present study contributes to an understanding of the features of BCT in the SCM context that is up-to-date and summarised in Tables 2, 3 and 4. This is important to fully comprehend the breadth of BCT features and their meaning in the SCM context.

In addition to the aforementioned study, other prior studies have adopted a similar approach, including listing the critical success factors for BCT adoption in SCs (Yadav and Singh 2020), categorising performance-measure features (Bai and Sarkis 2020), focusing on benefits and barriers (Kamilaris et al. 2019), and summarising the advantages and challenges of BCT adoption (Schmidt and Wagner 2019; Gonczol et al. 2020).

However, the contribution of the present study goes beyond prior studies to provide a generalised vision and holistic understanding of the existing features of BCT in the SCM context, without limitation to a specific industry or area of application.

The second theoretical contribution of this research is the identification of the three dimensions of the impact of BCT adoption in SCM. The ability to distinguish BCT features between the three dimensions and their intersections (Figs. 2, 3 and 4) alone brings a fresh perspective to this area of study. Thus, it improves our understanding of considerations under the detected dimensions of impact and their synergies, systematises knowledge of BCT in the SCM context, and broadens the perspective to a more holistic approach. To the best of our knowledge, these operations management dimensions have not yet been considered in the context of BCT features in SCM. Similar contributions have been made, but only in grouping the success factors of BCT-based SCs (Shoaib et al. 2020). Therefore, the present study advances the literature on BCT adoption in SCM, revealing new perspectives on BCT features' consideration and grouping.

5.2 **Managerial implications**

The findings of this research clarify the BCT features for SCM practitioners. Firms intending to begin a pilot for BCT adoption in their SC processes are now able to, by examining the proposed diagrams (Figs. 2, 3 and 4), critically assess, for instance, whether the advantages of BCT adoption outweigh the disadvantages and constraints in their specific SC context. Thus, SC managers will also be able to assess the consequences of their investment in one of the dimensions of impact, noting the existence of an impact on the other two dimensions, given that all three dimensions are interrelated and overlapping. Practitioners can position their SCs to benefit from the positive synergetic effect from BCT advantages while decreasing the counter-synergetic effect. Another implication is that practitioners should consider the constraints, which would allow them to, for example, apply the 'Solution Canvas' for BCT adoption based on their unique SCs, as done in previous research (Perboli et al. 2018).

Prior literature has highlighted the benefits and challenges of BCT adoption only in the context of specific SCs (Dutta et al. 2020), which suggests another opportunity for practitioners. The identified features in Tables II–IV could also be used and applied to a specific industrial area of interest in order to build a practical understanding of the features in different areas of application. One of the reviewed articles coded performance categories, identifying the impact of BCT on them (Stranieri et al. 2021), which represents another opportunity for practitioners. The features identified in this study could be applied to specific performance categories to evaluate the need for BCT adoption. BCT is being discussed actively and 'promises a revolutionary approach to data storage which could give rise to new business models' (Wong et al. 2020b, p.2115). In this context, the present study provides a veridical picture of not only the virtuous but also the vicious cycles of adopting BCT in SCM, which is relevant for practitioners in terms of improving their understanding before beginning a pilot.

5.3 **Future research opportunities**

The identification of dimensions of the impact of BCT in operations area and SCs in specific opens many doors for future research. One of the most interesting and valuable future paths would be to apply the identified BCT dimensions of impact to a specific

SCM area. For instance, it could be applied to cross-border logistics (Chang et al. 2020), e-commerce SCs (Liu and Li 2020), construction industry (Tezel et al. 2021), automobile SCs (Ada et al. 2021) and other industries, to determine whether there are differences in dimensions between specific areas. It would be interesting to examine differences between the SCM areas themselves, and differences between industries to reveal the key motivation factors and constraints of BCT adoption in various industries.

Moreover, the interaction between dimensions and synergies can vary in the same industry for different types of products. As one of the most common areas of BCT applications are food SCs, it would be valuable to examine dimensions separately for different types of food, e.g. marine conservations (Howson 2020), perishable food products (Kayikci et al. 2021), agri-food (Menon and Jain 2021) and see if the type of product plays a role in the perception of dimensions and features of BCT. It would be as well important to see the perspectives on the dimensions and synergies from the view of multiple tier SC players (Khan et al. 2021), as depending on the SC tier, the motivation and reasons for BCT adoption may vary.

Also, future studies could examine whether dimensions of impact and various cycles for manufacturing cases are different from those for service providers. Another research avenue is measuring differences in the large-scale adoption of BCT to SCM between for-profit and non-profit organisations, such as governmental pilots and business pilots. Further, inspired by existing research (Nandi et al. 2020), a framework for implementing BCT in SCM could be built based on the detected features and dimensions of impact to develop an understanding of their outcomes concerning SCM. We also suggest verifying this study's proposed dimensions of impact through empirical research, including, for example, separate groups of various SC players, grouped based on their supply chain position (e.g. upper tiers separately from the lower tiers SC) to gather unbiased empirical data based on the views of a particular SC position. Such comparison of views on BCT adoption from different SC players would enrich the area of research with an understanding of the motivation for potential BCT pilots from different perspectives. It would bring value to both scholars and practitioners.

6 Conclusions and limitations

To the best of our knowledge, this study is the first attempt of defining and exploring the dimensions of the impact of BCT implementation in SCM context. Not only we classify features of BCT under the proposed dimensions, but the vicious and virtuous cycles of dimensions' synergies were also explored and discussed. This study provides room for future researchers to empirically investigate the proposed dimensions and their impacts on real use-cases/ pilots of BCT in the SCM area.

Although this study reveals valuable findings, it has limitations. Our study is an SLR, relying on prior studies to extract our findings, and due to the novelty of the research area, it is only based on 139 chosen studies. For example, BCT features have been identified in case studies (van Hoek 2019), and the benefits and challenges of BCT application have been identified based on interviews with SC experts (Wang et al. 2019a, b). Our findings are thus limited by the prior studies reviewed, including the methodologies used in prior studies. Therefore, it is crucial to further explore the field based on empirically collected data, using various data collection techniques, not limiting the study to be quantitative or qualitative.

We hope that this study will help create a fresh perspective on the dimensions of BCT adoption in the SC context and reveal new opportunities for managers and firms to understand the interrelations among dimensions and the probable advantages, disadvantages, and constraints of adopting such novel and disruptive technology.

Acknowledgements

This work was supported by EEA Grants Blue Growth Programme (Call #5), Project PT-INNOVATION-0069 – Fish2Fork, Logistics Department of Molde University College and Fundacao para a Ciencia e a Tecnologia, grant UIDB/00315/2020.

References

Ada N, Ethirajan M, Kumar A, KEk V, Nadeem SP, Kazancoglu Y, Kandasamy J (2021) Blockchain technology for enhancing traceability and efficiency in automobile supply chain–A case study. Sustainability 13(24):136–167. https://doi.org/10.3390/su132413667

Agrawal TK, Kumar V, Pal R, Wang L, Chen Y (2021) Blockchain-based framework for supply chain traceability: A case example of textile and clothing industry. Comp Ind Eng 154:107130. https://doi.org/10.1016/j.cie.2021.107130

Ahmad RW, Salah K, Jayaraman R, Yaqoob I, Omar M, Ellahham S (2021) Blockchain-based forward supply chain and waste management for COVID-19 medical equipment and supplies. IEEE Access 9:44905–44927. https://doi.org/10.1109/ACCESS.2021.3066503

Aich S, Tripathy S, Joo MI, Kim HC (2021) Critical dimensions of blockchain technology implementation in the healthcare industry: an integrated systems management approach. Sust 13(9):5269. https://doi.org/10.3390/su13095269

Alazab M, Alhyari S, Awajan A, Abdallah AB (2021) Blockchain technology in supply chain management: an empirical study of the factors affecting user adoption/acceptance. Cl Comp 24(1):83–101. https://doi.org/10.1007/s10586-020-03200-4

Alkahtani M, Khalid QS, Jalees M, Omair M, Hussain G, Pruncu CI (2021) E-agricultural supply chain management coupled with blockchain effect and cooperative strategies. Sust 13(2):816. https://doi.org/10.3390/su13020816

Al-Rakhami MS, Al-Mashari M (2021) A blockchain-based trust model for the internet of things supply chain management. Sensors 21(5):1759. https://doi.org/10.3390/s21051759

Ali MH, Chung L, Kumar A, Zailani S, Tan KH (2021) A sustainable blockchain framework for the halal food supply chain: Lessons from Malaysia. Tech for Soc Ch 170:120870. https://doi.org/10.1016/j.techfore.2021.120870

Aslam J, Saleem A, Khan NT, Kim YB (2021) Factors influencing blockchain adoption in supply chain management practices: A study based on the oil industry. J Innov Know 6(2):124–134. https://doi.org/10.1016/j.jik.2021.01.002

Azzi R, Chamoun RK, Sokhn M (2019) The power of a blockchain-based supply chain. Comp Ind Eng 135:582–592. https://doi.org/10.1016/j.cie.2019.06.042

Baah C, Agyeman DO, Acquah ISK, Agyabeng-Mensah Y, Afum E, Issau K, Faibil D (2021) Effect of information sharing in supply chains: understanding the roles of supply chain visibility, agility, collaboration on supply chain performance. Benchm Int J. https://doi.org/10.11 08/BIJ-08-2020-0453

Bai C, Sarkis J (2020) A supply chain transparency and sustainability technology appraisal model for blockchain technology. Int J Prod Res 58(7):2142–2162. https://doi.org/10.1080/ 00207543.20 19 .1708989

Balamurugan S, Ayyasamy A, Joseph KS (2021) IoT-Blockchain driven traceability techniques for improved safety measures in food supply chain. Int J Inf Tech. https://doi.org/10. 1007/ s41870-020-00581-y

Behnke K, Janssen MFWHA (2020) Boundary conditions for traceability in food supply chains using blockchain technology. Int J Inf Manag 52:101969. https://doi.org/10.1016/ j.ijinfomgt. 2019.05.025

Bekrar A, El Cadi AA, Todosijevic R, Sarkis J (2021) Digitalizing the closing-of-the-loop for supply chains: a transportation and blockchain perspective. Sust 13(5):2895. https://doi.org /10. 3390/su13052895

Bodkhe U, Tanwar S, Parekh K, Khanpara P, Tyagi S, Kumar N, Alazab M (2020) Blockchain for industry 4.0: A comprehensive review. IEEE Access 8:79764–79800. https://doi.org/ 10.1109/ ACCESS. 2020.2988579

Boutkhoum O, Hanine M, Nabil M, El Barakaz F, Lee E, Rustam F, Ashraf I (2021) Analysis and evaluation of barriers influencing blockchain implementation in moroccan sustainable supply chain management: An Integrated IFAHP-DEMATEL Framework. Math 9(14):1601. https://doi.org/10. 3390/math9141601

Büyüközkan G, Tüfekçi G, Uztürk D (2021) Evaluating blockchain requirements for effective digital supply chain management. Int J Prod Econ 242:108309. https://doi.org/10.1 016/j.ijpe.2021. 108309

Caldarelli G, Zardini A, Rossignoli C (2021) Blockchain adoption in the fashion sustainable supply chain: Pragmatically addressing barriers. J Org Ch Manag 34(2):507–524. https://doi .org/10. 1108/JOCM-09-2020-0299

Calvão F, Archer M (2021) Digital extraction: Blockchain traceability in mineral supply chains. Polit Geo 87:102381. https://doi.org/10.1016/j.polgeo.2021.102381

Cao S, Powell W, Foth M, Natanelov V, Miller T, Dulleck U (2021) Strengthening consumer trust in beef supply chain traceability with a blockchain-based human-machine reconcile mechanism. Comp Electr Agr 180:105886. https://doi.org/10.1016/j.compag.2020.105886

Casino F, Dasaklis TK, Patsakis C (2019) A systematic literature review of blockchain-based applications: Current status, classification and open issues. Tel Inf 36:55–81. https://doi.org/ 10.101 6/j. tele.2018.11.006

Casino F, Kanakaris V, Dasaklis TK, Moschuris S, Stachtiaris S, Pagoni M, Rachaniotis NP (2020) Blockchain-based food supply chain traceability: a case study in the dairy sector. Int J Prod Res. https://doi.org/10.1080/00207543.2020.1789238

Centobelli P, Cerchione R, Del Vecchio P, Oropallo E, Secundo G (2021) Blockchain technology for bridging trust, traceability and transparency in circular supply chain. Inf Manag 103508 (Article in Press). https://doi.org/10.1016/j.im.2021.103508

Cha S, Baek S, Kim S (2020) Blockchain based sensitive data management by using key escrow encryption system from the perspective of supply chain. IEEE Access 8:154269–154280. https://doi.org/10.1109/ACCESS.2020.3017871

Chang SE, Chen YC, Lu MF (2019) Supply chain re-engineering using blockchain technology: A case of smart contract based tracking process. Tech for Soc Ch 144:1–11. https://doi.org/10.1016/j.techfore.2019.03.015

Chang SE, Chen Y (2020) When blockchain meets supply chain: A systematic literature review on current development and potential applications. IEEE Access 8:62478–62494. https://doi.org/10.1109/ACCESS.2020.2983601

Chang Y, Iakovou E, Shi W (2020) Blockchain in global supply chains and cross border trade: A critical synthesis of the state-of-the-art, challenges and opportunities. Int J Prod Res 58(7):2082–2099. https://doi.org/10.1080/00207543.2019.1651946

Chen S, Liu X, Yan J, Hu G, Shi Y (2021) Processes, benefits, and challenges for adoption of blockchain technologies in food supply chains: A thematic analysis. Inf Syst e-Bus Manag 19:909–935. https://doi.org/10.1007/s10257-020-00467-3

Choi TM (2020) Supply chain financing using blockchain: impacts on supply chains selling fashionable products. An Op Res. https://doi.org/10.1007/s10479-020-03615-7

Chopra S, Sodhi M, Lücker F (2021) Achieving supply chain efficiency and resilience by using multi-level commons. Dec Scien. https://doi.org/10.1111/deci.12526

Cole R, Stevenson M, Aitken J (2019) Blockchain technology : implications for operations and supply chain management. Sup Ch Man: Int J 24(4):469–483. https://doi.org/10.1108/SCM-09-2018-0309/full/html

Collart AJ, Canales E (2021) How might broad adoption of blockchain-based traceability impact the US fresh produce supply chain?. App Econ Persp Pol. https://doi.org/ 10.1002/ aepp.13134

Collier ZA, Sarkis J (2021) The zero trust supply chain: Managing supply chain risk in the absence of trust. Int J Prod Res. https://doi.org/10.1080/00207543.2021.1884311

Cui P, Dixon J, Guin U, Dimase D (2019) A blockchain-based framework for supply chain provenance. IEEE Access 7:157113–157125. https://doi.org/10.1109/ACCESS.2019.2949951

De Giovanni P (2020) Blockchain and smart contracts in supply chain management : A game theoretic model. Int J Prod Econ 228:107855. https://doi.org/10.1016/j.ijpe.2020.107855

Deebak BD, Fadi AT (2021) Privacy-preserving in smart contracts using blockchain and artificial intelligence for cyber risk measurements. J Inf Sec App 58.102749. https://doi.org/ 10.1016/j.jisa.2021.102749

Dehghani M, Mashatan A, Kennedy RW (2020) Innovation within networks–patent strategies for blockchain technology. J Bus Ind Market 36(12):2113–2125. https://doi.org/10.1108/ JBIM-05-2019-0236

Dehghani M, Popova A, Gheitanchi S (2021) Factors impacting digital transformations of the food industry by adoption of blockchain technology. J Bus Ind Market. https://doi.org/10. 1108/ JBIM-12-2020-0540

Denyer D, Tranfield D (2009) Producing a systematic review In: D. A. Buchanan & A. Bryman (ed) The Sage handbook of organizational research methods. Sage Publications Ltd, pp 671–689

Di Vaio A, Varriale L (2020) Blockchain technology in supply chain management for sustainable performance: Evidence from the airport industry. Int J Inf Man 52:102014. https://doi.org/10.1 016/j. ijinfomgt.2019.09.010

Doroudi R, Sequeira P, Marsella S, Ergun O, Azghandi R, Kaeli D, Griffin J (2020) Effects of trust-based decision making in disrupted supply chains. PLoS ONE 15(2):e0224761. https://doi. org/ 10.1371/journal.pone.0224761

Duan J, Zhang C, Gong Y, Brown S, Li Z (2020) A content-analysis based literature review in blockchain adoption within food supply chain. Int J Env Res Pub Health 17(5):1784. https://doi. org/10.3390/ijerph17051784

Durach CF, Blesik T, Maximilian von During M, Bick M (2020) Blockchain applications in supply chain transactions. J Bus Log 42(1):7–24. https://doi.org/10.1111/jbl.12238

Dutta P, Choi TM, Somanic S, Butala R (2020) Blockchain technology in supply chain operations: Applications, challenges and research opportunities. Transp Res Part E 142:102067. https://doi. org/10.1016/j.tre.2020.102067

Esmaeilian B, Sarkis J, Lewis K, Behdad S (2020) Blockchain for the future of sustainable supply chain management in Industry 4.0. Res Cons Recycl 163:105064. https://doi.org/ 10.1016/j. resconrec.2020.105064

Falcone EC, Steelman ZR, Aloysius JA (2021) Understanding managers' reactions to blockchain technologies in the supply chain: The reliable and unbiased software agent. J Bus Log 42(1):25–45. https://doi.org/10.1111/jbl.12263

Fan ZP, Wu XY, Cao BB (2020) Considering the traceability awareness of consumers: should the supply chain adopt the blockchain technology?. Ann Oper Res. https://doi.org/10.1007/ s10479-020-03729-y

Feng H, Wang X, Duan Y, Zhang J, Zhang X (2020) Applying blockchain technology to improve agri-food traceability: A review of development methods, benefits and challenges. J Clean Prod 260:121031. https://doi.org/10.1016/j.jclepro.2020.121031

Fosso Wamba S, Kamdjoug JRK, Bawack RE, Keogh JG (2020a) Bitcoin, Blockchain and Fintech: a systematic review and case studies in the supply chain. Prod Plan Cont 31(2–3):115–142. https://doi.org/10.1080/09537287.2019.1631460

Fosso Wamba S, Queiroz MM, Trinchera L (2020b) Food supply chain in the era of Industry 4.0 and supply chain performance: An empirical investigation. Int J Prod Econ 229:107791. https://doi. org/10.1016/j.ijpe.2020b.107791

Fosso Wamba S, Queiroz MM (2020a) Blockchain in the operations and supply chain management: Benefits, challenges and future research opportunities. Int J Inf Manag. https://doi.org/10.1016/j. ijinfomgt.2019.102064

Fosso Wamba S, Queiroz MM (2020b) Industry 4.0 and the supply chain digitalisation: a blockchain diffusion perspective. Prod Plan Cont 33(2–3):193–210. https://doi.org/ 10.1080/ 09537 287. 2020.1810756

Frizzo-Barker J, Chow-White PA, Adams PR, Mentanko J, Ha D, Green S (2020) Blockchain as a disruptive technology for business: A systematic review. Int J Inf Manag 51:102029. https://doi. org/10.1016/j.ijinfomgt.2019.10.014

Fu Y, Zhu J (2019) Big production enterprise supply chain endogenous risk management based on blockchain. IEEE Access 7:15310–15319. https://doi.org/10.1109/ACCESS. 2019.2895327

Galvez JF, Mejuto JC, Simal-Gandara J (2018) Future challenges on the use of blockchain for food traceability analysis. Tr An Chem 107:222–232. https://doi.org/10.1016/j.trac. 2018.08.011

Ghode D, Yadav V, Jain R, Soni G (2020a) Adoption of blockchain in supply chain: an analysis of influencing factors. J Ent Inf Manag 33(3):437–456. https://doi.org/10.1108/JEIM-07-2019-0186

Ghode DJ, Yadav V, Jain R, Soni G (2020b) Blockchain adoption in the supply chain: an appraisal on challenges. J ManTech Manag 32(1):42–62. https://doi.org/10.1108/JMTM-11-2019-0395

Gonczol P, Katsikouli P, Herskind L, Dragoni N (2020) Blockchain implementations and use cases for supply chains-a survey. IEEE Access 8:11856–11871. https://doi.org/ 10.1109/ACCESS. 2020. 2964880

Gurtu A, Johny J (2019) Potential of blockchain technology in supply chain management : A literature review. Int J Phys Distr Log Manag 49(9):881–900. https://doi.org/10. 1108/IJPDLM-11-2018-0371

Hackius N, Petersen M (2020) Translating high hopes into tangible benefits: How incumbents in supply chain and logistics approach blockchain. IEEE Access 8:34993–35003. https://doi. org/ 10.1 109/ ACCESS.2020.2974622

Hald KS, Kinra A (2019) How the blockchain enables and constrains supply chain performance. Int J Phys Distr Log Man 49(4):376–397. https://doi.org/10.1108/IJPDLM-02-2019-0063

Hastig GM, Sodhi MS (2020) Blockchain for supply chain traceability: Business requirements and critical success factors. Prod Oper Manag 29(4):935–954. https://doi.org/10. 1111/ poms.13147

Hewa T, Ylianttila M, Liyanage M (2021) Survey on blockchain based smart contracts: Applications, opportunities and challenges. J Net Comp App 177:102857. https://doi.org/ 10.1016/ j.jnca. 2020.102857

Hong L, Hales DN (2021) Blockchain performance in supply chain management: application in blockchain integration companies. Ind Manag Data Sys. https://doi.org/10.1108/IMDS-10-2020-0598

Howson P (2020) Building trust and equity in marine conservation and fisheries supply chain management with blockchain. Mar Pol. https://doi.org/10.1016/j.marpol.2020.103873

Idrees SM, Nowostawski M, Jameel R, Mourya AK (2021) Security aspects of blockchain technology intended for industrial applications. Elec 10(8):951. https://doi.org/10.3390/ electronics 10080951

Juma H, Shaalan K, Kamel I (2019) A survey on using blockchain in trade supply chain solutions. IEEE Access 7:184115–184132. https://doi.org/10.1109/ACCESS.2019.2960542

Kamble S, Gunasekaran A, Arha H (2019) Understanding the Blockchain technology adoption in supply chains-Indian context. Int J Prod Res 57(7):2009–2033. https://doi.org/10.1080/ 00207543. 2018.1518610

Kamble SS, Gunasekaran A, Sharma R (2020) Modeling the blockchain enabled traceability in agriculture supply chain. Int J Inform Manag. https://doi.org/10.1016/j.ijinfomgt. 2019.05 .023

Kamble SS, Gunasekaran A, Kumar V, Belhadi A, Foropon C (2021) A machine learning based approach for predicting blockchain adoption in supply Chain. Tech for Soc Ch 163:120465. https://doi. org/10.1016/j.techfore.2020.120465

Kamilaris A, Fonts A, Prenafeta-Boldú FX (2019) The rise of blockchain technology in agriculture and food supply chains. Tren Food Sc Tech 91:640–652. https://doi.org/10.1016/ j.tifs.2019.07.034

Karakas S, Acar AZ, Kucukaltan B (2021) Blockchain adoption in logistics and supply chain: A literature review and research agenda. Int J Prod Res. https://doi.org/10.1080/ 00207543 .2021.2012613

Karamchandani A, Srivastava SK, Kumar S, Srivastava A (2021) Analysing perceived role of blockchain technology in SCM context for the manufacturing industry. Int J Prod Res. https://doi. org/10.1080/00207543.2021.1883761

Karuppiah K, Sankaranarayanan B, Ali SM (2021) A decision-aid model for evaluating challenges to blockchain adoption in supply chains. Int J Log Res App. https://doi.org/ 10.1080/13675567. 2021.1947999

Katsikouli P, Wilde AS, Dragoni N, Høgh-Jensen H (2021) On the benefits and challenges of blockchains for managing food supply chains. J Sc Food Agr 101(6):2175–2181. https://doi. org/10. 1002/jsfa.10883

Kayikci Y, Subramanian N, Dora M, Bhatia MS (2020) Food supply chain in the era of Industry 4.0: Blockchain technology implementation opportunities and impediments from the perspective of people, process, performance, and technology. Prod Plan Cont 33(2–3):301–321. https://doi.org/ 10.1080/09537287.2020.1810757

Kayikci Y, Usar DD, Aylak BL (2021) Using blockchain technology to drive operational excellence in perishable food supply chains during outbreaks. Int J Log Manag. https://doi. org/10.1108/IJLM-01-2021-0027

Khan SAR, Zkik K, Belhadi A, Kamble SS (2021) Evaluating barriers and solutions for social sustainability adoption in multi-tier supply chains. Int J Prod Res 59(11):3378–3397. https://doi. org/10.1080/00207543.2021.1876271

Kim HM, Laskowski M (2018) Toward an ontology-driven blockchain design for supply-chain provenance. Int Sys Acc Fin Manag 25(1):18–27. https://doi.org/10.1002/isaf.1424

Klerkx L, Jakku E, Labarthe P (2019) A review of social science on digital agriculture, smart farming and agriculture 4.0: New contributions and a future research agenda. NJAS-Wag J L Sc 90:100315. https://doi.org/10.1016/j.njas.2019.100315

Köhler S, Pizzol M (2020) Technology assessment of blockchain-based technologies in the food supply chain. J Clean Prod. https://doi.org/10.1016/j.jclepro.2020.122193

Kopyto M, Lechler S, von der Gracht HA, Hartmann E (2020) Potentials of blockchain technology in supply chain management: Long-term judgments of an international expert panel. Tech for Soc Ch. https://doi.org/10.1016/j.techfore.2020.120330

Kouhizadeh M, Saberi S, Sarkis J (2021) Blockchain technology and the sustainable supply chain: Theoretically exploring adoption barriers. Int J Prod Econ 231:107831. https://doi. org/ 10.1016/j. ijpe. 2020.107831

Kramer MP, Bitsch L, Hanf J (2021) Blockchain and its impacts on agri-food supply chain network management. Sustainability 13(4):2168. https://doi.org/10.3390/su13042168

Kshetri N (2018) 1 Blockchain's roles in meeting key supply chain management objectives. Int J Inf Manag 39:80–89. https://doi.org/10.1016/j.ijinfomgt.2017.12.005

Kshetri N (2021) Blockchain and sustainable supply chain management in developing countries. Int J Inf Manag 60:102376. https://doi.org/10.1016/j.ijinfomgt.2021.102376

Kummer S, Herold DM, Dobrovnik M, Mikl J, Schäfer N (2020) A systematic review of blockchain literature in logistics and supply chain management: identifying research questions and future directions. Fut Int 12(3):60. https://doi.org/10.3390/fi12030060

Leng K, Bi Y, Jing L, Fu HC, Van Nieuwenhuyse I (2018) Research on agricultural supply chain system with double chain architecture based on blockchain technology. Fut Gen Comp Sys 86:641–649. https://doi.org/10.1016/j.future.2018.04.061

Lezoche M, Hernandez JE, Díaz MD, Panetto H, Kacprzyk J (2020) Agri-food 4.0: A survey of the supply chains and technologies for the future agriculture. Comp Ind 117:103187. https://doi.org/10.1016/j.compind.2020.103187

Li K, Lee JY, Gharehgozli A (2021a) Blockchain in food supply chains: a literature review and synthesis analysis of platforms, benefits and challenges. Int J Prod Res. https://doi.org/10. 1080/00207543.2021.1970849

Li ZP, Ceong HT, Lee SJ (2021b) The Effect of Blockchain Operation Capabilities on Competitive Performance in Supply Chain Management. Sustainability 13(21):12078. https://doi.org/ 10.3390 /su132112078

Li Z, Guo H, Barenji AV, Wang WM, Guan Y, Huang GQ (2020) A sustainable production capability evaluation mechanism based on blockchain, LSTM, analytic hierarchy process for supply chain network. International J Prod Res 58(24):7399–7419. https://doi.org/10. 1080/00207543.2020.1740342

Lim MK, Li Y, Wang C, Tseng ML (2021) A literature review of blockchain technology applications in supply chains: A comprehensive analysis of themes, methodologies and industries. Comp Ind Eng 154:107133. https://doi.org/10.1016/j.cie.2021.107133

Liu Z, Li Z (2020) A blockchain-based framework of cross-border e-commerce supply chain. Int J Inf Manag. https://doi.org/10.1016/j.ijinfomgt.2019.102059

Liu J, Zhang H, Zhen L (2021) Blockchain technology in maritime supply chains: applications, architecture and challenges. Int J Prod Res. https://doi.org/10.1080/ 00207543. 2021.19 30239

Lohmer J, Bugert N, Lasch R (2020) Analysis of resilience strategies and ripple effect in blockchain-coordinated supply chains: An agent-based simulation study. Int J Prod Econ 228:107882. https://doi.org/10.1016/j.ijpe.2020.107882

Lou M, Dong X, Cao Z, Shen J (2021) SESCF: a secure and efficient supply chain framework via blockchain-based smart contracts. Sec Com Net. https://doi.org/10.1155/2021/8884478

Mahyuni LP, Adrian R, Darma GS, Krisnawijaya NNK, Dewi IGAAP, Permana GPL (2020) Mapping the potentials of blockchain in improving supply chain performance. Cog Bus Manag 7(1):1788329. https://doi.org/10.1080/23311975.2020.1788329

Mao D, Wang F, Hao Z, Li H (2018) Credit evaluation system based on blockchain for multiple stakeholders in the food supply chain. Int J Env Res Pub Health 15(8):1627. https://doi.org/10.3390/ijerph15081627

Mathivathanan D, Mathiyazhagan K, Rana NP, Khorana S, Dwivedi YK (2021) Barriers to the adoption of blockchain technology in business supply chains: a total interpretive structural modelling (TISM) approach. Int J Prod Res 59(11):3338–3359. https://doi.org/10. 1080/ 00207543 .2020.1868597

Mattke j, Hund A, Maier C, Weitzel T (2019) How an enterprise blockchain application in the US pharmaceuticals supply chain is saving lives. MIS Quart Exec 18(4):246–261. https://doi. org/ 10.17705/2msqe.00019

Menon S, Jain K (2021) Blockchain technology for transparency in agri-food supply chain: Use cases, limitations, and future directions. IEEE Trans Eng Manag. https://doi.org/ 10.1109/ TEM.2021.3110903

Min H (2019) Blockchain technology for enhancing supply chain resilience. Bus Hor 62(1):35–45. https://doi.org/10.1016/j.bushor.2018.08.012

Mistry I, Tanwar S, Tyagi S, Kumar N (2020) Blockchain for 5G-enabled IoT for industrial automation: A systematic review, solutions, and challenges. Mech Sys Sig Proc 135:106382. https://doi.org/10.1016/j.ymssp.2019.106382

Moher D, Liberati A, Tetzlaff J, Altman DG, PRISMA Group (2009) Preferred reporting items for systematic reviews and meta-analyses: the PRISMA statement. Ann Int Med 151(4):264–269. https://doi.org/10.7326/0003-4819-151-4-200908180-00135

Montecchi M, Plangger K, Etter M (2019) It's real, trust me! Establishing supply chain provenance using blockchain. Bus Hor 62(3):283–293. https://doi.org/ 10.1016/ j.bushor. 2019.01.008

Moosavi J, Naeni LM, Fathollahi-Fard AM, Fiore U (2021) Blockchain in supply chain management: A review, bibliometric, and network analysis. Env Sc Pol Res. https://doi.org /10. 1007/s11356-021-13094-3

Mubarik MS, Naghavi N, Mubarik M, Kusi-Sarpong S, Khan SA, Zaman SI, Kazmi SHA (2021) Resilience and cleaner production in industry 4.0: Role of supply chain mapping and visibility. J Clean Prod 292:126058. https://doi.org/10.1016/j.jclepro.2021.126058

Mukherjee AA, Singh RK, Mishra R, Bag S (2021) Application of blockchain technology for sustainability development in agricultural supply chain: Justification framework. Oper Manag Res. https://doi.org/10.1007/s12063-021-00180-5

Musamih A, Salah K, Jayaraman R, Arshad J, Debe M, Al-Hammadi Y, Ellahham S (2021) A Blockchain-based approach for drug traceability in healthcare supply chain. IEEE Access 9:9728–9743. https://doi.org/10.1109/ACCESS.2021.3049920

Müßigmann B, Von Der GH, Hartmann E (2020) Blockchain technology in logistics and supply chain management – A bibliometric literature review from 2016 to January 2020. IEEE Tran Eng Manag 67(4):988–1007. https://doi.org/10.1109/TEM.2020.2980733

Nandi ML, Nandi S, Moya H, Kaynak H (2020) Blockchain technology-enabled supply chain systems and supply chain performance: a resource-based view. Sup Ch Manag: an Int J 25(6):841–862. https://doi.org/10.1108/SCM-12-2019-0444

O'Leary DE (2019) Some issues in blockchain for accounting and the supply chain, with an application of distributed databases to virtual organizations. Int Sys Acc Fin Manag 26(3):137–149. https://doi.org/10.1002/isaf.1457

Omar IA, Jayaraman R, Salah K, Debe M, Omar M (2020) Enhancing vendor managed inventory supply chain operations using blockchain smart contracts. IEEE Access 8:182704–182719. https://doi.org/10.1109/ACCESS.2020.3028031

Öztürk C, Yildizbaşi A (2020) Barriers to implementation of blockchain into supply chain management using an integrated multi-criteria decision-making method: a numerical example. Soft Comp 24(19):14771–14789. https://doi.org/10.1007/s00500-020-04831-w

Paluri RA, Mishal A (2020) Trust and commitment in supply chain management: a systematic review of literature. Benchmarking an Int J 27(10):2831–2862. https://doi.org/10.1108/BIJ-11-2019-0517

Park A, Li H (2021) The effect of Blockchain technology on supply chain sustainability performances. Sust 13(4):1726. https://doi.org/10.3390/su13041726

Perboli G, Musso S, Rosano M (2018) Blockchain in logistics and supply chain: A lean approach for designing real-world use cases. IEEE Access 6:62018–62028. https://doi. org/10. 1109/ACCE SS.2018.2875782

Pournader M, Shi Y, Seuring S, Koh L (2020) Blockchain applications in supply chains, transport and logistics: A systematic review of the literature. Int J Prod Res 58(7):2063–2081. https://doi.org/10.1080/00207543.2019.1650976

Queiroz MM, Fosso Wamba S (2019) Blockchain adoption challenges in supply chain: An empirical investigation of the main drivers in India and the USA. Int J Inf Manag 46:70–82. https://doi.org/10.1016/j.ijinfomgt.2018.11.021

Queiroz MM, Fosso Wamba S, De Bourmont M, Telles R (2020) Blockchain adoption in operations and supply chain management: Empirical evidence from an emerging economy. Int J Prod Res. https://doi.org/10.1080/00207543.2020.1803511

Queiroz MM, Telles R, Bonilla SH (2019) Blockchain and supply chain management integration: A systematic review of the literature. Sup Ch Manag: an Int J 25(2):241–254. https://doi.org/10.1108/SCM-03-2018-0143

Qian XA, Papadonikolaki E (2020) Shifting trust in construction supply chains through blockchain technology. Eng Constr Architect Manag 28(2):584–602. https://doi.org/10.1108/ ECAM-12-2019-0676

Rana SK, Kim HC, Pani SK, Rana SK, Joo MI, Rana AK, Aich S (2021) Blockchain-based model to improve the performance of the next-generation digital supply chain. Sustainability 13(18): 10008. https://doi.org/10.3390/su131810008

Rao S, Gulley A, Russell M, Patton J (2021) On the quest for supply chain transparency through blockchain: Lessons learned from two serialized data projects. J Bus Log 42(1):88–100. https://doi.org/10.1111/jbl.12272

Reddy KRK, Gunasekaran A, Kalpana P, Sreedharan VR, Kumar SA (2021) Developing a blockchain framework for the automotive supply chain: A systematic review. Comp Ind Eng 157:107334. https://doi.org/10.1016/j.cie.2021.107334

Rejeb A, Keogh JG, Treiblmaier H (2019) Leveraging the internet of things and blockchain technology in supply chain management. Fut Int 11(7):161. https://doi.org/10.3390/ fi11070161

Rejeb A, Keogh JG, Simske SJ, Stafford T, Treiblmaier H (2021) Potentials of blockchain technologies for supply chain collaboration: A conceptual framework. The Int J Log Manag 32(3):973–994. https://doi.org/10.1108/IJLM-02-2020-0098

Rogerson M, Parry GC (2020) Blockchain: Case studies in food supply chain visibility. Sup Ch Manag: an Int J 25(5):601–614. https://doi.org/10.1108/SCM-08-2019-0300

Roy V (2021) Contrasting supply chain traceability and supply chain visibility: are they interchangeable?. The Int J Log Manag 32(3):942–972. https://doi.org/10.1108/IJLM-05-2020-0214

Saadiah S, Rahayu SB (2021) Consortium blockchain for military supply chain. Turk J Comp Math Ed (TURCOMAT) 12(3):1825–1831. https://doi.org/10.17762/turcomat.v12i3.1011

Saberi S, Kouhizadeh M, Sarkis J, Shen L (2019) Blockchain technology and its relationships to sustainable supply chain management. Int J Prod Res 57(7):2117–2135. https://doi.org/10. 1080/00207543.2018.1533261

Saurabh S, Dey K (2021) Blockchain technology adoption, architecture, and sustainable agri-food supply chains. J Clean Prod 284:124731. https://doi.org/10.1016/j.jclepro.2020.124731

Saunders M, Lewis P, Thornhill A (2012) Research methods for business students, 6th edn. Essex, Pearson Education Limited

Schmidt CG, Wagner SM (2019) Blockchain and supply chain relations: A transaction cost theory perspective. J Purch Sup Manag 25(4):100552. https://doi.org/10.1016/j.pursup. 2019.100552

Sharma M, Joshi S, Luthra S, Kumar A (2021) Managing disruptions and risks amidst COVID-19 outbreaks: role of blockchain technology in developing resilient food supply chains. Oper Manag Res. https://doi.org/10.1007/s12063-021-00198-9

Sheel A, Nath V (2019) Effect of blockchain technology adoption on supply chain adaptability, agility, alignment and performance. Manag Res Rev 42(12):1353–1374. https://doi.org/10. 1108/M RR-12-2018-0490

Shoaib M, Lim MK, Wang C (2020) An integrated framework to prioritize blockchain-based supply chain success factors. Ind Manag Data Sys 120(11):2103–2131. https://doi.org/10. 1108/IMDS-04-2020-0194

Sivula A, Shamsuzzoha A, Helo P (2021) Requirements for blockchain technology in supply chain management: An exploratory case study. Oper Sup Ch Manag 14(1):39-50. https://doi.org/ 10.3138 7/ oscm0440284

Sternberg HS, Hofmann E, Roeck D (2020) The struggle is real: Insights from a supply chain blockchain case. J Bus Log. https://doi.org/10.1111/jbl.12240

Stranieri S, Riccardi F, Meuwissen MPM, Soregaroli C (2021) Exploring the impact of blockchain on the performance of agri-food supply chains. Food Contr 119:107495. https://doi.org/1 0.1016/j.foodcont.2020.107495

Sundarakani B, Ajaykumar A, Gunasekaran A (2021) Big data driven supply chain design and applications for blockchain: An action research using case study approach. Omega 102:102452. https://doi.org/10.1016/j.omega.2021.102452

Sunny J, Undralla N, Pillai VM (2020) Supply chain transparency through blockchain-based traceability: An overview with demonstration. Comp Ind Eng 150:106895. https://doi.org/ 10. 1016/j. cie.2020.106895

Tandon A, Kaur P, Mäntymäki M, Dhir A (2021) Blockchain applications in management: A bibliometric analysis and literature review. Tech For Soc Ch 166:120649. https://doi.org/10. 1016/j.techfore.2021.120649

Tapscott D, Tapscott A (2020) Blockchain solutions in pandemics: A call for innovation and transformation in public health. Block Res Inst. https://app.hubspot.com/documents /5052729/ view/72133013?accessId=54ef98

Teodorescu M, Korchagina E (2021) Applying blockchain in the modern supply chain management: Its implication on open innovation. J Op Innov: Tech, Mar Complex 7(1):80. https://doi.org/10.3390/joitmc7010080

Tezel A, Febrero P, Papadonikolaki E, Yitmen I (2021) Insights into blockchain implementation in construction: models for supply chain management. J Manag Eng 37(4):04021038. https://doi. org/10.1061/(ASCE)ME.1943-5479.0000939

Tönnissen S, Teuteberg F (2020) Analysing the impact of blockchain-technology for operations and supply chain management: An explanatory model drawn from multiple case studies. Int J Inf Manag 52:101953. https://doi.org/10.1016/j.ijinfomgt.2019.05.009

Treiblmaier H (2018) The impact of the blockchain on the supply chain: A theory-based research framework and a call for action. Sup Ch Manag 23(6):545–559. https://doi.org/10. 1108/ SCM-01-2018-0029/full/html

Valle DF, Oliver M (2020) Blockchain enablers for supply chains: How to boost implementation in industry. IEEE Access 8:209699–209716. https://doi.org/10.1109 /ACCESS.2020.3038463

van Hoek R (2019) Exploring blockchain implementation in the supply chain - Learning from pioneers and RFID research. Int J Oper Prod Manag 39(6/7/8):829–859. https://doi.org/10. 1108/IJOPM-01-2019-0022

van Hoek R (2020a) Unblocking the chain – findings from an executive workshop on blockchain in the supply chain. Sup Ch Manag: an Int J 25(2):255–261. https://doi.org/10. 1108/SCM-11-2018-0383

van Hoek R (2020b) Developing a framework for considering blockchain pilots in the supply chain – lessons from early industry adopters. Sup Ch Manag Int J 25(1):115–121. https://doi.org/10.11 08/SCM-05-2019-0206

Varriale V, Cammarano A, Michelino F, Caputo M (2021) New organizational changes with blockchain: a focus on the supply chain. J Org Ch Manag 34(2):420–438. https://doi.org /10.1108/ JO CM-08-2020-0249

Venkatesh VG, Kang K, Wang B, Zhong RY, Zhang A (2020) System architecture for blockchain based transparency of supply chain social sustainability. Rob Comp Int Man 63:101896. https://doi.org/10.1016/j.rcim.2019.101896

Vivaldini M, de Sousa PR (2021) Blockchain connectivity inhibitors: weaknesses affecting supply chain interaction and resilience. Bench An Int J 28(10):3102–3136. https://doi. org/10.1108/BIJ-10-2020-0510

Vu N, Ghadge A, Bourlakis M (2021) Blockchain adoption in food supply chains: A review and implementation framework. Prod Plan Cont. https://doi.org/10.1080/ 09537287. 2021. 1939902

Walsh C, O'Reilly P, Gleasure R, McAvoy J, O'Leary K (2021) Understanding manager resistance to blockchain systems. Eur Manag J 39(3):353–365. https://doi.org/10.1016/j.emj. 2020.10.001

Wan PK, Huang L, Holtskog H (2020) Blockchain-enabled information sharing within a supply chain: A systematic literature review. IEEE Access 8:49645–49656. https://doi.org/10.1109/ ACCESS. 2020.2980142

Wang Y, Han JH, Beynon-Davies P (2019a) Understanding blockchain technology for future supply chains: a systematic literature review and research agenda. Sup Ch Manag Int J 24(1):62–84. https://doi.org/10.1108/SCM-03-2018-0148

Wang Y, Singgih M, Wang J, Rit M (2019b) Making sense of blockchain technology: How will it transform supply chains? Int J Prod Econ 211:221–236. https://doi.org/ 10.1016/ j.ijpe.2019. 02.002

Wang B, Luo W, Zhang A, Tian Z, Li Z (2020a) Blockchain-enabled circular supply chain management: A system architecture for fast fashion. Comp Ind 123:103324. https://doi.org/ 10.10 16/j. compind.2020.103324

Wang M, Wu Y, Chen B, Evans M (2020b) Blockchain and supply chain management: A new paradigm for supply chain integration and collaboration. Oper Sup Ch Manag An Int J 14(1):111–122. https://doi.org/10.31387/oscm0440290

Wang Y, Chen CH, Zghari-Sales A (2020c) Designing a blockchain enabled supply chain. Int J Prod Res 59(5):1450–1475. https://doi.org/10.1080/00207543.2020.1824086

Wang Z, Zheng Z, Jiang W, Tang S (2021) Blockchain-enabled data sharing in supply chains: Model, operationalization, and tutorial. Prod Oper Manag. https://doi.org/10. 1111/ poms.13356

Wong LW, Leong LY, Hew JJ, Tan GWH, Ooi KB (2020a) Time to seize the digital evolution: Adoption of blockchain in operations and supply chain management among Malaysian SMEs. Int J Inf Manag 52:101997. https://doi.org/10.1016/j.ijinfomgt.2019.08.005

Wong LW, Tan GWH, Lee VH, Ooi KB, Sohal A (2020b) Unearthing the determinants of Blockchain adoption in supply chain management. Int J Prod Res 58(7):2100–2123. https://doi. org/10. 1080/00207543.2020.1730463

Wu XY, Fan ZP, Cao BB (2021) An analysis of strategies for adopting blockchain technology in the fresh product supply chain. Int J Prod Res. https://doi.org/10.1080/0020 7543.2021.1894497

Xu P, Lee J, Barth JR, Richey RG (2021) Blockchain as supply chain technology: Considering transparency and security. Int J Phys Distr Log Manag 51(3):305–324. https://doi.org/10. 1108/IJPDLM-08-2019-0234

Xue X, Dou J, Shang Y (2020) Blockchain-driven supply chain decentralized operations – information sharing perspective. Bus pro Manag J 27(1):184–203. https://doi.org/10. 1108/BPMJ-12-2019-0518

Yadav S, Singh SP (2020) Blockchain critical success factors for sustainable supply chain. Res Cons Rec 152:104505. https://doi.org/10.1016/j.resconrec.2019.104505

Yadav VS, Singh AR, Raut RD, Govindarajan UH (2020) Blockchain technology adoption barriers in the Indian agricultural supply chain: An integrated approach. Res Cons Rec 161:104877. https: //doi. org/10.1016/j.resconrec.2020.104877

Yang L, Zhang J, Shi X (2021) Can blockchain help food supply chains with platform operations during the COVID-19 outbreak?. Elec Com Res App 49:101093. https://doi.org/ 10.1016/j.elerap.2021.101093

Yiu NC (2021a) Toward blockchain-enabled supply chain anti-counterfeiting and traceability. Fut Int 13(4):86. https://doi.org/10.3390/fi13040086

Yiu NC (2021b) Decentralizing supply chain anti-counterfeiting and traceability systems using blockchain technology. Fut Int 13(4):84. https://doi.org/10.3390/fi13040084

Zhou Y, Soh YS, Loh HS, Yuen KF (2020) The key challenges and critical success factors of blockchain implementation: Policy implications for Singapore's maritime industry. Mar Pol 122:104265. https://doi.org/10.1016/j.marpol.2020.104265

INDEX